A PRACTICAL GUIDE TO
TRADE MARK LAW

AUSTRALIA
LBC Information Services
Sydney

CANADA AND USA
Carswell
Toronto

NEW ZEALAND
Brooker's
Auckland

SINGAPORE AND MALAYSIA
Thomson Information (S.E. Asia)
Singapore

INTELLECTUAL PROPERTY GUIDES

A Practical Guide to Trade Mark Law

Amanda Michaels
B.A. (Dunelm), M.A. (Bruges)
Barrister of Gray's Inn

LONDON • SWEET & MAXWELL • 1996

First Edition 1982 *A Practical Guide to Trade Marks*

Published in 1996 by
Sweet & Maxwell Limited of
100 Avenue Road, Swiss Cottage, London NW3 3PF
Typeset by York House Typographic Ltd, London
Printed in England by Clays Ltd, St Ives plc

No natural forests were destroyed
to make this product; only farmed timber was used and replanted.
A CIP catalogue record for this book is available
from the British Library.

ISBN 0 421 45200 5

Printed and bound in Great Britain by
Butler & Tanner Ltd, Frome and London

For Dennis, Paul and Toby, with love

FOREWORD

Amanda Michaels set herself a formidable task: writing an intelligible book about trade marks. She wrote a very good book for the old law — a book which avoided the arcane, was readable and which was replete with practical examples — and she has done it again. This time her task was much harder because the new law, although set out in an Act based on a Directive, is in truth only the bare bones of a new system. How it will work out remains to be seen. But Miss Michaels has faced up to the practical problems. She has tried to envisage practical problems and give practical examples of how they are likely to be treated.

Actually I think she has gone rather further than this. She discusses, in a wholly refreshing and pragmatic way, some points of difficulty. See, for instance, how she deals with the theoretically important (but perhaps less important in practice) question of "association" in Chapter 2. It is all there, but she makes it seem simple.

Furthermore she is bang up-to-date. I do not know how she did it, but I think she has included all the more recent cases. Two of these, *Wagamama* and *British Sugar* must have required her to re-write whole chunks of text at the very last moment, but it does not show.

I commend this work to anyone who has to deal with trade marks. I shall have a copy ready to hand.

Hon. Sir Robin Jacob
July 1996

PREFACE TO THE SECOND EDITION

The Trade Marks Act 1994 came into force on October 31, 1994. The new edition of this book is designed to deal with the substantial changes in trade mark law effected by the Act in the light of the relevant case-law to date.

The book incorporates a full discussion of the new rules on the registrability of marks and the practice and procedure in the Registry, both for registration, and for revocation, etc., of registered marks. There is also discussion of the Community Trade Mark Regulation and the Madrid Protocol. Separate chapters then deal with infringement, the related tort of passing off and the remedies available for each, with particular reference to interlocutory injunctions. Lastly, there is a discussion of assignment and licensing.

Throughout the book, I have attempted to give a comprehensive explanation of the law, in accessible terms, in the hope that this book will be of use to the non-specialist, and even to the non-lawyer! Wherever necessary, I have incorporated references to the old law, and the E.C. law position.

I have attempted to state the law as at September 1, 1996. However, there are some recent developments which it has not been possible to incorporate into the text. First, there have been some recent cases on parallel imports from the European Court of Justice, which have yet to be reported; these are Joined Cases 427/94, 429/94 and 436/94, *Paranova*, Joined Cases 71, 72 and 73/94, *Eurim-Pharm*, and Case 232/94, *MPA Pharma*, all decided July 11, 1996. Secondly, the WIPO Trade Mark Law Treaty has now been ratified by the U.K. The Treaty aims to harmonise national trade mark formalities, and it is anticipated that it will cause changes abroad, but not in the U.K.

I would like to express my thanks to all those who have helped me to produce this second edition. Almost all the members of my chambers have been kind enough to help on one point or another, and my special thanks must go to Gregory Banner, Edward Bragiel, Nicholas Caddick, Julia Clark, Gwylim Harbottle, Jonathan Rayner James and Tony Martino (in strictly alphabetical order!). My grateful thanks also to Caroline Shea for her help whilst a pupil in chambers.

I would also like to thank my clerks and my husband, Dennis Sharpe, for their help and support.

Amanda Michaels
5 New Square
Lincoln's Inn
October 1996

CONTENTS

TABLE OF CASES

TABLE OF STATUTES

TABLE OF STATUTORY INSTRUMENTS

TABLE OF EUROPEAN LEGISLATION

INTRODUCTION

(1) CHANGES IN U.K. TRADE MARK LAW

1.1 On October 31, 1994 trade mark law in the United Kingdom was substantially changed by the entry into force of the Trade Marks Act 1994. The new Act had two main aims: first, to put Directive 89/104, harmonising national trade mark laws, into direct force here, and secondly, to pave the way to the United Kingdom's ratification of the "Madrid Protocol" on the International Registration of Marks.

1.2 Since the first U.K. Trade Marks Act of 1875, this country had protected trade marks by a dual system under which registered and unregistered marks co-existed and were largely complementary. The registered mark system depended upon the interventionist approach of the Trade Marks Registry. Applications were carefully screened both for objective suitability for registration, according to occasionally vigorous criteria, and for conflicts with similar prior rights. The difficulties of attaining registration were, however, (theoretically at least) worthwhile in view of the strength of the registrations eventually attained. Such marks were not merely valid in principle, by virtue of a paper title, but were genuinely likely to be found to be valid and safe from attack. A registration was, therefore, of real benefit in protecting the mark and its proprietor's goodwill.

1.3 However, such were the demands of the registration process that many marks or other distinguishing "indicia" used by traders to distinguish their goods or services from those of their competitors were incapable of registration, were simply never sought to be registered, or were required to be relied upon before completion of the (lengthy) registration process. In all such cases the proprietor of the unregistered mark was forced to rely upon the amorphous tort of passing off to protect his business and goodwill. Passing off is in many ways a usefully adaptable and flexible remedy, applicable in many situations falling outside the scope of the protection offered by the Trade Marks Act 1938 and, indeed, some situations outside the scope of the 1994 Act too, as we shall see. However, it has the drawback of requiring substantial evidence to be available of the strength and extent of the unregistered mark's goodwill. Passing off actions therefore lack some of the simplicity of trade mark infringement actions, with consequential costs burdens.

1.4   Nonetheless the two systems were complementary, the strength or simplicity of the one being contrasted with the breadth of the other.[1]

1.5   Under the new regime, the two systems will continue to co-exist, but it remains to be seen how they will complement each other in the future. The changes effected by the 1994 Act all relate to the registered trade mark system; the law of passing off is not directly affected at all by the 1994 Act (for passing off generally see Chapter 5). However, the changes to the registered trade mark system are intended to be (and in many respects certainly are) substantial and may be extended in the future.

Reasons for the changes

1.6   The protection offered to trade marks by national trade mark laws and the differences between the national trade mark systems of the member states of the European Union have for many years been considered as inconsistent with the overall objectives of the E.U., in creating barriers to inter-state trade which impede the aim of creating a single, unified market. The dilemma was this: the functions of trade marks required that they be accorded protection in the form of a monopoly right, which protection could endure indefinitely, as long as the trade mark proprietor took care to maintain the right. Such rights, granted under the separate national trade mark systems of the member states of the E.U., were apt to divide the market and create precisely the sort of barriers to free trade which the E.U. Treaty objectives aimed to dismantle. How could those objectives be reconciled with the Treaty's obligation to respect national property laws, such as trade mark laws?[2]

1.7   As a result of this dilemma, and in the light of the voluminous case-law of the European Court of Justice ("the ECJ") relating to trade marks (and, indeed, similar cases relating to other intellectual property rights), the E.U. institutions have for many years been considering ways of dealing with these problems. Since at least the mid-1970s it has been proposed that there should be harmonisation of national trade mark systems alongside the provision of a new supra-national E.U. trade mark system. Eventually, these plans culminated in the adoption on December 21, 1988 of Directive 89/104 and on December 20, 1993 of Regulation 40/94.[3] The Directive provided for the harmonisation of the national trade mark laws of the member states,[4] whilst the Regulation provides for a Community trade mark, that is to say, for a supra-national trade mark law, granting a proprietor a unitary trade mark right valid throughout the E.U. The Regulation has its own direct effect and the Community trade mark has now come into being (see Chapter 3(11), below) but the Directive had to be implemented by national legislation which, in the United Kingdom, took the form of the Trade Marks Act 1994.

---

[1]   The merits of registered trade marks over rights in unregistered marks were recently summarised by Laddie J. in *Mercury Communications Limited v. Mercury Interactive (U.K.) Limited* [1995] F.S.R. 850 at 863–4.
[2]   See further paras. 1.9–1.13 and Chap. 7(13), below.
[3]   Throughout this book, these are referred to simply as "the Directive" and "the Regulation."
[4]   Including the pre-existing tripartite "Benelux" Uniform Trade Mark Law.

Background to the Directive and Regulation

1.8 Before going on to discuss the scope of the changes effected by the Trade Marks Act 1994, it may be useful to examine in rather more detail the background to the Directive and Regulation.

1.9 The Treaty of Rome has little immediate application to trade marks. Nonetheless, Article 222 protects national laws governing the ownership of property and "industrial and commercial property" may be protected from the full rigours of the Articles on the free movement of goods (Article 30 *et seq*) by the provisions of Article 36. All the same, the major Treaty objectives of the free movement of goods and services, as well as freedom of competition, were from the outset seen to be difficult to reconcile with the inherent monopolies created by national industrial or intellectual property rights such as trade marks. Whatever the differences in detail between the trade mark laws of the member states, the essence of trade mark protection in each case lay in the exclusive right granted to the proprietor to use the mark within the national territory, which, as a general rule, included a right to exclude from that territory the same or similar goods bearing identical or confusingly similar marks, even where those marks had been legitimately applied to the goods by the proprietor of the mark in another member state. Such a position was not simply anathema to the Treaty aim of free movement of goods, but was also open to abuse by trade mark proprietors who could divide up the common market by separating the ownership of national trade mark rights.

1.10 The solution adopted in a long series of cases before the ECJ was to distinguish those elements of trade mark protection vital to the "existence" of the trade mark, which were accepted as necessary to the economy as guarantors of fair competition, and without which incentives to trade might be destroyed, from those elements of the "exercise" of trade mark rights, which were deemed unjustifiably to restrict competition. It was in this context that the ECJ developed its theory of trade mark functions, which is discussed in Chapter 7(13), below. In general terms, the elements of national laws on trade mark infringement which were maintained, respected and protected by the ECJ have been those vital to the protection of the essential function of trade marks, or as the ECJ put it, their "specific subject-matter".

1.11 The lengthy history of the development of the ECJ's theory of trade mark functions is described in Chapter 7(13) below. At this stage, it is only necessary to refer to the current position, as seen in the most recent cases. Firstly, in *Hag II*[5] the Court held:

> " ... the essential function of the mark ... is to give the consumer or final user a guarantee of the identity of the origin of the marked product by enabling him to distinguish, without any possible confusion, that product from others of a different provenance ... the essential function of the mark would be compromised if the owner of the right could not exercise his option under national law to prevent the importation of the similar product under a name likely to be confused with his own

---

[5] Case C–10/89 *SA CNL-Sucal NV v. HAG GF AG*: [1990] I E.C.R. 3711; [1990] 3 C.M.L.R. 571; see further in Chap. 7 at para. 7.60.

mark because, in this situation, consumers would no longer be able to identify with certainty the origin of the marked product and the bad quality of a product for which he is in no way responsible could be attributed to the owner of the right."

1.12 Then, in *Deutsche Renault*[6] the German subsidiary of Renault wished to expunge the registration of Audi's mark "Quattro", so as to be free to use its own confusingly similar[7] mark "Quadra". In confirming the applicability of the relevant national rules, the Court stated:

" .... that the specific subject-matter of trade mark rights consists in protecting the proprietor of the mark against a risk of confusion such as to allow third persons to take unlawful advantage of the reputation of the proprietor's goods."

1.13 Lastly, in *Ideal Standard*[8], after analysing the repercussions of the territorial restrictions of national trade marks, the ECJ reaffirmed its decision in *Hag II* that it is the possibility of central control of quality which must be protected. Thus, where there had in the past been a genuine assignment, dividing the ownership *and* control of national marks, national trade mark laws could legitimately be exercised to prevent parallel imports.[9] On the other hand, where such divisions of ownership of a mark are made with the illegitimate purpose of dividing the market, or where a proprietor deliberately chooses different marks for the same goods or services in different member states, again so as to divide the market,[10] national trade mark rights will not be enforced.

1.14 The ECJ's view of the function of a trade mark is reflected in the wording of the recitals to both the Directive and the Regulation, as being "in particular to guarantee the trade mark as an indication of origin". It will be seen that the recognition of this function of the trade mark is reflected both in the requirements imposed in respect of registrability of marks and in the protection offered to marks by the Community and national systems, including the new regime introduced in the United Kingdom by the 1994 Act.[11]

1.15 The limitations of judicial control of national trade mark laws as a means of alleviating the natural propensity of trade mark rights to divide the single market along national frontiers were recognised at an early stage in the development of the E.U. The ideal solution, in theory, would have been the substitution of national trade mark rights by a unitary community right, incapable of being divided in such a way as to create artificial barriers to inter-state trade. However, it was recognised that in many cases the registration of a community-wide mark would have been either impossible or unjustified.[12] The

---

[6] Case C–317/91 *Deutsche Renault AG v. Audi AG*: [1993] I E.C.R. 6277; [1995] 1 C.M.L.R. 461 at 476; [1995] F.S.R. 738 at 748.
[7] Confusingly similar in Germany, if not in the U.K.
[8] Case C–9/93, *IHT Internationale Heiztechnik GmbH v. Ideal Standard GmbH* [1994] I E.C.R. 2789; [1994] 3 C.M.L.R. 857.
[9] See further Chap. 7, paras. 7.61–64.
[10] See *e.g.* Case 3/78, *Centrafarm BV v. American Home Products Corp*: [1978] E.C.R. 1823; [1979] 1 C.M.L.R. 326.
[11] See Chap. 2, para. 2.8, and Laddie J. in *Wagamama Limited v. City Centre Restaurants Plc* [1995] F.S.R. 713.
[12] See recital 5 of the Regulation, cited at para. 3.87 of Chap. 3, below.

eventual solution was, therefore, the dual approach – the Regulation to provide the unitary, community-wide mark, and the Directive to harmonise as far as possible national trade mark laws. The Directive, therefore, covers the type of signs which may be registered, the resolution of conflicts between existing rights and trade mark applications, the rights conferred by a registration, and grounds for invalidity or revocation of a registration, that is to say, all of the elements of registered trade mark law, in the hope that this "approximation" of national laws will remove certain of the barriers to inter-state trade.

The effect of the Directive

1.16   Under E.U. law, whilst Directives may have some immediate and direct effects in national law, they essentially require national implementing legislation in each member state. The 1994 Act achieves that aim for the Directive and it is clear from the reports of Parliamentary debates on the Trade Mark Bill that it was intended that the Act should implement the Directive as closely and accurately as possible[13]. The Act, therefore, implements all of the "compulsory" parts of the Directive as well as many of its "optional" provisions. The Parliamentary draftsmen also made strenuous efforts to maintain as closely as possible the precise wording of the Directive, thus ensuring that a number of new concepts will enter United Kingdom trade mark law and doubtless provide work for the courts for some time to come.

The general scope of changes in the law

1.17   The 1994 Act reduces the regulatory role previously given to the U.K. Trade Marks Registry, bringing the United Kingdom further into line with less interventionist member states of the E.U. This is largely a function of the important changes effected in the range of signs which may now be registered as trade marks, and in the manner in which such marks may now be licensed or transferred. There is scope for the Registry's examination of applications to be further reduced in the future.[14] Once this happens, and possibly even now, the strength of registrations granted under the new Act will be reduced, and successful challenges to the validity of registrations may become more common.

1.18   The Act also alters very significantly the scope of actions for infringement of registered trade marks. Section 4 of the 1938 Act, defining infringement, may have been obscure in many ways, but it was at least clear that an infringement action could be brought only where the acts complained of were carried out in relation to goods or services for which the plaintiff's mark was registered. Under the 1994 Act, the action for infringement is broadened to prevent use of the same or a similar mark to the proprietor's upon goods or services other than those for which his mark is registered.[15] In this respect, as in the need for the proprietor to prove more than the simple registration of his mark,

---

[13] Although there are a number of sections of the Act which it has been suggested do not implement it accurately!
[14] See discussion of s. 8 in Chap. 2.157-2.159, below.
[15] See discussion of subss. 10(2) and (3) in Chap. 4.58 *et seq*.

the action for infringement of a registered mark is brought much closer to a passing off action.[16]

(2) APPLICATION OF THE NEW ACT

1.19   At the time of writing, there is still relatively little guidance as to how the new Act will work, either in terms of the registration of marks or of their protection in use. Clearly, the unfamiliar language used in the Directive and repeated in the Act will require careful construction by the Registry and by the court.[17] They will be guided in this task by the principle that our courts will seek to interpret statutes based on E.U. legislation in conformity with the latter.[18]

1.20   The system by which national courts can refer cases to the ECJ for guidance[19] will lead, in time (such references generally are slow), to a body of case-law emanating from the ECJ construing the Directive, the Regulation and national laws based on the Directive[20]. Such decisions will be applied by the English courts[21] and should help in construing the 1994 Act, given the aim of giving effect here to the Directive and the latter's overriding aim of harmonising the national trade mark laws of the member states.

1.21   On the other hand, although certain parts of the Directive, and thus the new Act, have been said to be based on the Benelux Uniform Trade Mark Law (or decisions made under that law), it seems that there are good reasons to doubt whether this is the case,[22] or at any rate whether an English court could be persuaded to look behind the Directive other than to the limited extent already known to E.U. law.[23] The English courts have always been reluctant to construe legislation by reference to Parliamentary intentions, save to the extent that they might look to a White Paper to identify the "mischief" intended to be remedied by the new Act, so as to give a "purposive" construction to the statute, and it is suggested that there must be doubts as to how far back down the supposed line of "heredity" of any part of the 1994 Act our courts might be willing to look. The House of Lords' decision in *Pepper v. Hart*[24] has altered the previous rules, so that where a provision is unquestionably ambiguous or leads to absurdity, regard may now be given to Parliament's intentions (as expressed by the Minister or other promoter of the bill) by looking at Hansard. However, the case defines the occasions when recourse to Hansard may be made quite narrowly, and does not suggest that one may look further "back" than

---

[16] See Chap. 5.
[17] s. 75 of the 1994 Act provides that references to the court mean the High Court, where trade mark matters are assigned to the Chancery Division. Passing off actions should also be brought there.
[18] See, *e.g. Duke v. GEC Reliance Limited* [1988] A.C. 618 at 639–40; *Webb v. EMO Air Cargo (U.K.) Limited* [1993] 1 W.L.R. 49.
[19] Namely, Article 177 of the Treaty which allows national courts to seek rulings from the ECJ on the interpretation of treaties or of statutes of E.U. bodies, where such a ruling is necessary to enable it to decide the case, or where such an issue is raised before a court whose decision will be final. Generally, see Vol. 51 of Halsbury's Laws (4th ed).
[20] Such as *Deutsche Renault*; see n. 6, above.
[21] Indeed, *Deutsche Renault* was relied upon by Laddie J. in *Wagamama*; see n. 11, above.
[22] *ibid.*, at 723–8.
[23] This seems particularly unlikely given the *Wagamama* decision. Generally on the materials available in the interpretation of Directives see paras. 2.265–2.283 of Vol. 51 of Halsbury's Laws (4th ed). As to the effect of Benelux law see the useful article by Professor Gielen in [1992] E.I.P.R. 262.
[24] [1993] A.C. 593.

to Hansard. Moreover, the view has already been expressed[25] that the *Pepper v. Hart* doctrine cannot apply where the Act in question, as here, was to enact an E.U. Directive, for in such a case the court should instead look to the terms of the Directive itself.

1.22 As a matter of "comity", the courts here may think it right to look at how equivalent provisions to those of the 1994 Act have been interpreted by courts in the other member states of the E.U. However, it seems that the courts here will not be overly keen to apply a construction of the 1994 Act which is consistent with a decision reached by a tribunal in another member state unless persuaded that such construction is right in any event, and certainly no such decision will be followed where the English court thinks that it may be wrong.[26] It is suggested that many English judges would be reluctant to give much weight to judgments of foreign tribunals, on the effects of a law which may not be identically worded to the 1994 Act, especially without knowing how fully the case may have been argued or supported by the evidence. Such case law is likely to be only of academic interest here, at least until relied upon or supported by a relevant decision of the ECJ itself.

1.23 As for the use of the reports of the debates on the Trade Marks Bill itself, clearly there is more scope to rely on these in proceedings here. However, whilst these debates are of interest to trade mark practitioners, again it is suggested that they will probably be of little use in practice in construing the Act. The Parliamentary debates upon the least clearly comprehensible parts of the Bill tend to offer little help beyond suggesting that it would be for the courts to put a sensible construction on the new phraseology employed by the draftsmen! The more obscure provisions also tend to be those most closely derived from the Directive, and it would seem likely that reference to decisions of the ECJ, or indeed a reference *to* the ECJ might be a more appropriate course to adopt than to look to the promoter's view of what a particular provision of the Act was to mean.

1.24 At the time of writing, we also wait to see the effects of the implementation of the Madrid Protocol and the opening of the Community Trade Mark Office.

1.25 All in all there is much more new law and practice to come in the near future.

A general note to the reader: marks for services

1.26 For many years, trade mark registration was available only for goods marks. However, marks for services have been registrable for some years now, and this is reflected in the Classes annexed to the Trade Marks Rules 1994. Generally, in this book, where reference is made just to goods or marks for goods such references should not be taken as excluding marks for services, which are treated by the 1994 Act as wholly equivalent to goods marks (in contrast to the complicated position under the 1938 Act, as amended). In particular, marks for goods and services may conflict with each other for the purposes of registration and infringement.

---

[25] By Jacob J. in *British Sugar Plc v. James Robertson and Sons* [1996] R.P.C. 281 at 292.
[26] Again see *Wagamama* at 728, above where Laddie J., in putting forward this point, said "The scope of European legislation is too important to be decided on a first past the post basis."

Chapter 2

REGISTRABILITY UNDER THE 1994 ACT

(1) TRADE MARK FUNCTIONS

2.1 Before looking at the practical legal aspects of acquiring trade marks, it may be helpful to examine briefly their functions and to consider how the choice of a new mark should be made. The criteria rendering a sign worthy of protection as a mark, as well as the circumstances in which protection will be offered, depend upon the trade mark functions protected by the law.

2.2 The economic functions of trade marks in the modern economy are dictated by the sheer size of the market; they have become indispensable in a market dominated by mass-production and the proliferation of comparable, competing products sold, in many instances, through self-service outlets. Producers are increasingly forced to rely upon trade marks to identify their products, as they have lost any direct contact with the consumer. For the same reasons, consumers rely increasingly upon personal experience, recommendation or advertising, to identify a product or to repeat purchases. The vital characteristic of the mark necessary to permit it to carry out this "origin" or "product identification" function is thus its distinctiveness.

2.3 The corollary of the identificatory role of the mark is the implied assurance of quality which it carries; whether the consumer makes a purchase because of personal experience of the product, through word-of-mouth recommendation or because of the image of the marked product projected by advertising, he will expect it to live up to the standards found in the earlier product, or implied by its presentation on the market.[1]

2.4 The essential criterion for the qualification of a trade mark for protection is, therefore, that it should be distinctive, whether the protection depends upon a trade mark registration or upon the common law protection of passing off. Equally, a trade mark will in general be protected only against acts which could lead to its confusion with other marks and products, or where other types of confusion may cause damage to the goodwill attached to the mark.[2]

2.5 In the Trade Marks Act 1938 (as amended) the definition of a trade mark given in section 68(1) demonstrated this adoption of the origin theory, as a sign used "for the purpose of indicating ... a connection in the course of trade between the goods and some person having the right either as proprietor or as registered user to use the mark, whether with or without any indication of the identity of that person ... "[3]

2.6 This definition also showed acceptance of the economic reality of licensing, acknowlededging that multiple sources for a marked product would not automatically destroy the vital distinctive character of the mark. It was established that licences need not even be registered, if there were sufficient quality controls by the proprietor.[4] The result was that the trade mark indicated " ... merely that the goods in connection with which [the mark] is used emanate from the same – possibly anonymous – source or have reached the consumer through the same channels as certain other goods that have already given the consumer satisfaction, and that bore the same trademark."[5]

2.7 Such an indication of origin in the broad sense would not necessarily be accurate, of course, where the goods in question might emanate from any one of a variety of legitimate producers, who might be producing goods with differing tastes, composition or qualities, for sale under the mark in different territories. This lead to the development of the "exhaustion theory", which could lead to parallel sales of such differing goods under the one mark.[6]

---

[1] Minor variations in the product will usually be acceptable, as improvements, but the essential qualities and composition of the product will be expected to remain stable. Generally, on trade mark function, see the famous article written in 1927 by Frank Schechter in (1927) 40 Harvard L.R. 813.

[2] Thus "the trade mark was not viewed as a property right in the symbol *per se*, but rather a right that derived from the association of the mark with certain goods, and the goodwill that was created as a result of the association." *per* Wilkof, *Trade mark Licensing* (1995) at p. 23 and see generally Chap. 1 of this work as to trade mark functions.

[3] See, *e.g.* the leading case of *Aristoc v. Rysta* [1945] A.C. 68.

[4] Contrast the pre-1938 case of *Bowden Wire Limited v. Bowden Brake Co.* (1914) 31 R.P.C. 385 (H.L.) with *"Bostitch" Trade Mark* [1963] R.P.C. 183; and *Aktiebolaget Manus v. Fullwood & Bland* (1949) 66 R.P.C. 71; [1949] Ch. 208.

[5] See Schechter, n. 1, above at 816.

[6] See Chaps. 4.24 *et seq.*, and 7.51 *et seq.*, on the exhaustion theory. For a variety of cases demonstrating the difficulties which may occur where there are "parallel imports" see, *e.g.* *Champagne Heidsieck et Cie Monopole SA v. Buxton* [1930] 1 Ch. 330; (1929) 47 R.P.C. 28; *Revlon v. Cripps & Lee* [1980] F.S.R. 85; *Castrol Limited v. Automotive Oil Supplies Limited* [1983] R.P.C. 315; and *Colgate-Palmolive Limited v. Markwell Finance Limited* [1989] R.P.C. 497. On s. 12, see paras. 4.109–4.111, below.

Functions under the 1994 Act

2.8 The 1994 Act continues to protect the origin function of trade marks. Section 1(1) provides: "A 'trade mark' means any sign ... which is capable of distinguishing goods or services of one undertaking from those of other undertakings". The reason for this continued adoption of the origin theory can be found in the antecedents of the 1994 Act itself, that is to say, in the Directive,[7] and, before that, in the acceptance by the European Court of Justice of the origin theory.[8] In one of the few decisions on the 1994 Act at the time of writing, *Wagamama*, Laddie J. confirmed that the origin function alone was protected by English law and construed section 10(2) accordingly.[9]

(2) CHOICE OF A NEW TRADE MARK

2.9 The choice of a new mark to suit a product or service requires considerable care and will usually entail both commercial and legal research. The elements which add up to a commercially viable and desirable mark depend upon the functions which the mark will be fulfilling in the market-place. The most important quality, for the reasons set out above, is the distinctiveness of the mark.

2.10 The mark will also need to pass a double legal test of objective suitability for registration and compatibility with existing or prior marks.[10] Both requirements will usually be met only after the state of the market has been examined, looking particularly at existing marks in the same or related fields, and after the existing entries have been checked on all of the relevant national trade mark registers and (in time) the Community Trade Mark Register.

2.11 Moreover, the mark should be easily memorable so that the consumer will recall it when repurchasing or when making the initial purchase stimulated by advertising or recommendation. The mark must be readily distinguishable from marks being used on competing products, both in its pronunciation and presentation.

2.12 Ideally, however, the mark should also suit the marked product's image and properties, to the extent that it is possible to do so without the mark becoming descriptive of the product – this of itself will reinforce its memorability. A mark which consists of an everyday word can, without being actually descriptive of the product, evoke strong subjective images which suggest the product's qualities, *e.g.* "Vim" for the strength of scouring powder, "Flash" for the speed and effects of a household cleaner, "Country Life" for the goodness of butter, even "Opium" for the intoxicating effects of a perfume!

2.13 A word mark must also be easily pronounceable, especially if a foreign word is intended to add a certain "chic" to the product.[11] Similarly, where goods are intended to

---

[7] See recital 10.
[8] See paras. 7.52 *et seq.*
[9] See *Wagamama Limited v. City Centre Restaurants plc* [1995] F.S.R. 713 at 730–731.
[10] See parts (6) to (8) of this Chap.
[11] See, *e.g.* in *Parfums Givenchy SA v. Designer Alternatives Limited* [1994] R.P.C. 243, the difficulties in pronouncing "Xeryus" and "Xereux".

be exported, or where it is hoped to use the mark in several countries whether by exportation or local production, care should be taken to choose a mark suitable in all the languages concerned.[12]

An example

2.14   For the purposes of illustrating various points later in this book, it is hoped that it may be helpful to use a consistent example of a group of marks. Let us assume, therefore, that the perhaps somewhat unlikely choice is made of the mark "Sea-lion" to be used on a range of hypo-allergenic soaps and other toiletries, aimed at children – or, at least, at their parents! "Sea-lion" has been chosen for this purpose in the belief that there is no registered mark consisting either of that word or of any device featuring a sea-lion; certainly, the example is not intended to have any reference to any such existing registered or unregistered mark.

Let us suppose that apart from the word mark, the proprietor would like to register a device of a sea-lion wearing a hat and blowing bubbles, and the shapes of a box and of a bottle shaped like a sea-lion.

2.15   The initial choice would have to be checked against the Register for potential clashes with prior registered marks in Class 3 (covering the toiletries), Class 16 (covering the packaging) and other related classes. Personal searches may be carried out at the Registry by members of the public, with the help of Registry staff. Searches of trade literature might also disclose clashes with prior unregistered marks. Any possible clashes might be capable of resolution by consent and such avenues should be pursued before the decision is made whether to proceed with an application to register or to choose again.

(3) CHARACTERISTICS OF A REGISTRABLE MARK UNDER THE 1994 ACT

s.1(1)   "In this Act a 'trade mark' means any sign capable of being represented graphically which is capable of distinguishing goods or services of one undertaking from those of other undertakings. A trade mark may, in particular, consist of words (including personal names), designs, letters, numerals or the shape of goods, or their packaging"

2.16   It is interesting to compare the definition of a mark given in section 68(1) of the 1938 Act as further qualified by section 9 of the 1938 Act, with sections 1(1) and 3(1) of the 1994 Act. The Courts gave an essentially restrictive interpretation to the ambit of the 1938 Act, despite the apparently broad effect of the definition of a mark in section 68(1) as *including* a device, brand, etc. (*e.g.* in the general refusal to permit the registration of shapes as marks[13]).

---

[12] The adoption of separate trade marks in each territory, whilst necessary at times when the mark originally envisaged is either already in use in another market or is not registrable for another reason, may otherwise fall foul of E.C. competition rules if it is seen as designed to partition markets. See, *e.g.* Case 3/78, *Centrafarm BV v. American Home Products Corporation* [1978] E.C.R. 1823; [1979] 1 C.M.L.R. 326.

[13] See, *e.g.* the notorious decision to refuse registration of the Coca Cola bottle shape as a mark at [1986] R.P.C. 421.

2.17   There can be no doubt but that the new Act is not intended (or expected) to be construed in a similarly restrictive fashion. The manner in which section 1(1) is worded is clearly meant to limit prima facie registrability by reference to two criteria only; first, can the sign be represented "graphically", and secondly, is it "capable of distinguishing" the goods or services of the proprietor:

(4) "CAPABLE OF BEING REPRESENTED GRAPHICALLY"

2.18   "Graphically" in this sense means, it seems, capable of being represented or described, in some way, on paper. It would seem that this requirement is a practical and administrative one. If there were no insistence upon the mark being capable of being represented graphically (and being so presented to the Registry for registration) it is hard to see how the Registry could categorise and examine applications, nor how searches could realistically be carried out by the Registry or by proprietors (or intended proprietors) of marks or their agents, save by visual examination either on paper or on screen. How could sound marks be stored so as to be aurally searched, for instance, and how could they be indexed or categorised for this purpose? Comparison of non-verbal or two-dimensional marks may be difficult enough, without the added burden of having to examine shape marks in three-dimensional form, listen to sounds or sniff smells.

2.19   The requirement also reflects the reality that the vast majority of registered marks has hitherto, and doubtless will in the future, consisted of verbal or other two-dimensional marks which are, and are intended to be, *used* graphically, as well as in other ways such as orally, in the form of labels, tickets, stamps, etc., applied to goods and upon packaging generally, in the form of advertisements, and upon invoices, receipts and other business paperwork. The exciting new concepts in registrable marks, shapes, sounds and smells, etc., however fascinating legally and technically, will surely always be of minority interest only. Were it not so, then the law of passing off would doubtless have played a much greater role than it has done to date in protecting these categories of marks, since mere lack of registrability would not have prevented proprietors from seeking to protect them.

2.20   Marks which may be represented graphically will obviously include marks consisting of or combining words (real or invented), names, surnames, signatures, phrases and slogans, devices, initials, numerals and colours (in combination or even singly).

2.21   Moreover, clearly the manner in which section 1(1) is phrased deliberately leaves open the possibility of registering marks consisting of shapes, sounds or even smells or tastes. These possibilities led to a good deal of discussion in Parliament (and outside it) as to *how* precisely one would represent such marks graphically. Shapes are obviously relatively easy; one needs only produce a sufficiently clear and detailed sketch, plan or perhaps photograph of the item concerned. Strangely, given the unregistrability of shapes as marks under the 1938 Act, rule 27 of the Trade Marks and Service Marks Rules 1938 provided: "Where a representation [of the mark applied for] cannot be filed .... .a specimen or copy of the mark either of full size or on a reduced scale may, subject to the consent of the Registrar, be filed in any convenient form." There is no equivalent provision in the 1994 Rules, so the sole way to represent a shape mark will have to be graphically. The notes on the back of Form TM3 (Application to register a trade mark) are interesting in this respect, since note (h) provides:

> "A representation of the mark should be provided in section 2. A trade mark must be capable of being represented graphically if it is not a word or a picture. This means you may need to give us a clear description of the mark in section 2.
>
> We can accept applications if the mark is larger than 8cm by 8cm, but no larger than A4. If you want to make a subsequent application for an International registration, under the Madrid Protocol for example, then the application [sic] must be no larger than 8cm by 8cm."

For the limitations on the registrability of certain shapes imposed by section 3(2) of the 1994 Act see paragraphs 2.48 *et seq.*, below.

2.22 Sounds, too, may be easy to represent graphically, depending somewhat upon the type of sound concerned. For instance, a musical jingle could be represented graphically by musical notation, if necessary with added reference in musical or layman's terms to any specified style and/or tempo of performance, instrumentation or vocalisation. As for other sounds, it may suffice to describe the sound sufficiently clearly in words. An example much quoted from the discussion of the Trade Marks Bill in Committee in the House of Lords was that a sound mark consisting of the roar of a lion would be represented graphically by writing down 'the roar of a lion''.[14] But would such a description really be sufficient to distinguish the mark from other animal noises? Does not a tiger roar? If so, how likely is it that the tiger's roar would be mistaken by the averagely ignorant member of the public (such as the writer) for a lion's roar? ... answers on a postcard, please .... As for less intrinsically distinctive sounds, apart from the difficulty of describing them sufficiently clearly and precisely for the purpose of registration, there would be problems of showing that they were distinctive, so as to be entitled to registration, and then probable problems in showing that similar, but not identical, sounds infringed the mark.

2.23 Smells are bound to be even more problematic.[15] Apparently, in the United States, registration has proceeded upon the basis of a verbal description of the smell. Again, one wonders how accurate such a description could be, or would need to be, to be acceptable to the Registrar. Parfumiers and wine masters, of course, have methods of describing smells, these may be capable of being adapted for trade marks. Another suggestion is to register a description in the form of a chart based on gas- or high-performance liquid-chromatography,[16] although the author does not know how easily such charts could be used, particularly for the purpose of comparison in searching the Register. In this respect, it is important to note that the Registry's Draft Work Manual emphasises that the manner in which smells are represented graphically must be such as to enable an ordinary member of the public to understand it when searching the Register. In any event, applications have already been made to register a smell and it seems that these take the route of simply describing the smell. It remains to be seen how these will fare as applications and then as marks.

---

[14] H.L. Committee Stage 18/1/94, col. 35.
[15] See the excellent article by Helen Burton in [1995] E.I.P.R. 378.
[16] See article by Debrett Lyons, [1994] E.I.P.R. 540.

(5) "Capable of distinguishing goods or services"

2.24   The second, vital overall requirement for registrability set out in section 1(1) of the 1994 Act is that the sign to be registered must be "capable of distinguishing" the goods or services of the applicant from those of his competitors.

2.25   The wording of this provision is again taken verbatim from Article 2 of the Directive. It is also the same as the wording of section 10 of the 1938 Act, which set out the criteria for registration in Part B of the Register. The requirement that the registered mark be capable of distinguishing the proprietor's goods in the market place is, as discussed above, to require the mark to be capable of fulfilling its essential function as a trade mark. If the mark has no such capacity, it clearly should not be registrable as a *trade* mark.[17] The need for a mark to be distinctive in use is reflected by the proviso to section 3(1), which permits the registration of marks which are prima facie "devoid" of distinctive character, or which otherwise appear to be overly descriptive, if they can be shown to have acquired "a distinctive character" through use.[18]

2.26   It is not yet known how strict a test of capacity to distinguish may be applied under the 1994 Act, in comparison to the occasional peculiarities of the previous law.[19] However, two points may be made. First, it would seem to be implicit in the new Act, however wide its definition of a mark is intended to be, that there is some "absolute" standard of distinctiveness by reference to which the Registry is to act, since section 3(1)(b) refers to marks "which are devoid of any distinctive character". This must mean marks which are wholly descriptive of the goods or services concerned, *e.g.* "Carpet Shampoo" for carpet shampoo or "Car Insurance Services" for car insurance. Such marks seem on the face of it quite incapable of indicating a trade source, or otherwise distinguishing particular goods or services from others, however much the marks might be used and promoted in the market place. Secondly, however, unlike the position under the 1938 Act, the Registry will not be able to refuse to register even such apparently non-distinctive marks if it can be shown that prior to the application being made for registration they have acquired the necessary distinctive qualities of a trade mark by user in the market place. This change is effected by the proviso to section 3(1) and should prevent the repetition of decisions such as that in the *York Trailers* case,[20] where the finding that the mark was inherently incapable of distinguishing the goods of its proprietor prevented its registration, despite its factual capacity to carry out its functions, by reason of acquired distinctiveness.

2.27   In *Re Dee Corporation Plc*,[21] registration under the 1938 Act was refused of applications by a number of supermarket chains to register their marks for "retail services". These consisted of various services offered gratuitously to customers, such as car parking, credit facilities, a creche, etc. The Court of Appeal held that such services were merely ancillary to the applicants' true businesses of selling a variety of goods and

---

[17] See, *e.g.* comments of Jacob J. as to the use of the term "Toffee Treat" in *British Sugar Plc v. James Robertson and Sons* [1996] R.P.C. 281 at 305–306.
[18] On the test for such distinctiveness see *British Sugar* ibid., and paras. 2.71–2.72, below.
[19] See App. A, para. 6.
[20] [1984] R.P.C. 231.
[21] [1990] R.P.C. 159.

were not provided for money or money's worth. As such, the applications were refused. The statutory requirement that services be provided for money or money's worth has been dropped in the 1994 Act, but certainly in the Parliamentary debates on the Bill it was made plain that the Government did not intend the 1994 Act to cover the registration of such retail marks (and see the current Classes of service marks in Schedule 4 to the Trade Marks Rules 1994). Such services may well, therefore, not fall within the definition in section 1(1) of marks distinguishing the *services* of one undertaking from those of other undertakings. During the passage of the Bill various amendments were proposed, seeking to extend section 1(1), but these were rejected, and it seems unlikely that an argument that such services are now comprised within the breadth of the definition in section 1(1) would succeed.[22]

(6) Signs registrable under the 1994 Act

s.1(1)   "A trade mark may ... consist of words (including personal names), designs, letters, numerals or the shape of goods, or their packaging"

2.28   The manner in which section 1(1) is worded is intended to be non-exhaustive, so that the list of registrable signs included within it should not be construed *ejusdem generis*, as was the case to some extent under the 1938 Act. Instead it was intended that any sort of sign which could overcome the dual hurdles described above should be capable of registration under the 1994 Act.

(a) Word marks

2.29   Section 1(1) specifically refers to word marks, which will, for the reasons mentioned above, continue to represent *a* most important if not *the* most important category of marks. Such marks may consist of names, whether real names, nicknames or fictional names, signatures, real or invented single words, or combinations of words, as well as slogans.[23] In this respect apart from points on distinctiveness/deceptiveness any change from the position under the 1938 Act seems unlikely.

Word marks registrable under the 1938 Act

Names and signatures

2.30   Section 9(1)(a) of the 1938 Act provided that a trade mark might consist of, or contain, "the name of a company, individual or firm, represented in a special or particular manner". This was generally a real, rather than an invented name, although it need not be that of the trader. This was clearly useful where the name might be chosen so as to suggest the product's quality, source or composition; for instance, a whisky firm might register a

---

[22] However, see the view expressed at para. 2.6 of Morcom, *A Guide to the Trade Marks Act 1994* that the possibility of registering such a mark remains open under the new Act.

[23] See, *e.g.* "*I Can't Believe it's Yogurt*" [1992] R.P.C. 533 compared to *Have a Break trade mark* [1993] R.P.C. 217; and see para. 17 of App. A.

Scottish name as a mark. Additionally, the name of a fictional person was registrable, *e.g.* "Robin Hood".[24]

2.31 Under section 9(1)(b) a signature could be a distinctive sign where it consisted of a device rather than merely a name in script form. Under the 1994 Act there is, of course, no specific restriction upon signatures being represented in some distinctive manner; the mark simply needs to be sufficiently distinctive to be registered. However, there are potential drawbacks in the use of a signature as a mark when the original applicant may sever his connection with the business and then wish to trade separately under his own name. Just such an unfortunate situation lay at the root of the *Barry Artist* case[25]: Mr Artist was a dress designer whose work had been the mainstay of the fashions sold by Barry Artist Limited. The company's trade mark consisted of a facsimile of Mr Artist's signature. After leaving the company's employment, he applied to register his signature as a mark for his own designs. The application failed because of the likelihood that his mark would be confused with the company's mark.

Invented words

2.32 These were registrable under section 9(1)(c) and were often highly valuable distinctive marks, *e.g.* "Kodak". The major problem in finding an acceptable invented word was in determining the level of inventiveness required, for two proper words run together or mis-spelt did not qualify as invented words. In a similar way, the use of ordinary foreign words was generally unacceptable, although at times a word which appeared "invented" but was actually an obscure foreign word might be registrable.[26] In the leading case, *Solio*,[27] the House of Lords decided that to qualify as an invented word, the word need not be "wholly meaningless"; consequently "Solio" was permitted to be registered for photographic paper. The aim of the control over such registrations was to ensure that no other trader would be unfairly deprived of the right to use ordinary existing vocabulary, or a proper description of his goods.

2.33 Words which were held not to be invented might even include words once clearly invented which had passed into the language and had acquired a reputation as having a direct reference to the character or quality of the goods. Such was the case of "Tarzan", which was refused registration as a mark for films and toys.[28]

Words having no direct reference to the character of the goods

2.34 Section 9(1)(d) permitted the registration of everyday English words which did not directly describe the goods on which they were to be used. It is relatively easy to give

---

[24] *Standard Cameras Limited's Application* (1952) 69 R.P.C. 125. However, this case was perhaps influenced by the mark's full compliance with the second, more important, element of s. 9(1)(a), that is the requirement that the name be presented in "a special or particular manner". Here, the "R" of "Robin Hood" was represented containing an archer and the final "D", a target.

[25] "*Barry Artist*" [1978] R.P.C. 703.

[26] *e.g.* "Kiku" (for perfume) is the Japanese word for chrysanthemum, so no direct reference to the nature of the goods was found in "*Kiku*" [1978] F.S.R. 246 (Eire Supreme Court); contrast to "*Rijn Staal*" (meaning "Rhine steel") refused registration for chemicals connected to steel-making processes [1991] R.P.C. 400.

[27] *Eastman Photographic Materials Co.'s Application* [1898] A.C. 571.

[28] "*Tarzan*" *trade mark* [1970] R.P.C. 450.

examples of word marks which would fail this test in referring much too directly to the nature of the goods upon which they were to be used, for instance "sleeping tablets", "tranquillisers",[29] "carpet shampoo", and "chocolate drops". On this basis, "Apple Pie" would be unregistrable for apple pies, but registrable for beds. For examples of marks consisting of everyday words which are not overtly descriptive, see paragraph 2.12 above. For the reasons discussed above, this category of marks was also most important commercially because of its suitability for encapsulating the image of the marked goods or services.

2.35   One peculiarity of the 1938 Act was that words which could be shown to be fully distinctive in practice could not be registered under this sub-section if they made direct reference to the character or quality of the goods.[30] There were many borderline cases – compare, for example, the refusal to register "Nectar" for tea, coffee and cocoa[31] with the registration of "Dustic" for glue.[32]

Geographical name and surname exceptions

2.36   There were two further qualifications to section 9(1)(d) preventing the registration of any word which, ordinarily, was either a geographical name or a surname.[33] Under the 1938 Act, the non-registrability of geographical names generally would not prevent registration as a mark of a word which had an everyday meaning as well as being by chance a place name, *e.g.* "Magnolia" could be registered although also being the name of a small American town.[34] More surprisingly, perhaps, "St. Raphael" was registered for an aperitif without any geographical connection being implied.[35] However, where the word was predominantly geographical, and so could be taken as denoting origin by area rather than by source, registration would generally be refused under the 1938 Act, and might only be allowed if the registration was restricted to goods produced in the geographical area concerned.[36] Extraordinarily, registration could be refused even where the "geographical" mark could be shown to be wholly distinctive in practice: see *"York"*.[37]

2.37   The second restriction on section 9(1)(d) prevented the registration of marks too commonly known as a surname. Under the 1938 Act, the Registry's practice on this point was quite strict, with reference being made to telephone directories; a name appearing

---

[29] Examples given in *Daiquiri Rum* [1969] R.P.C. 600.
[30] See, *e.g. "Multilight" trade mark* [1978] R.P.C. 601 – refusal to register a mark used since 1939. See also the refusal to register "Budget" as being referable to the quality of car hire services, despite evidence of distinctiveness; [1991] R.P.C. 9.
[31] (1901) 18 R.P.C. 34.
[32] (1955) 72 R.P.C. 151 and see *Kerly's Law of Trade Marks and Trade Names* (12th ed., 1986), Chap. 8–31 for further examples.
[33] See now s. 3(1)(c) of the 1994 Act.
[34] *Magnolia trade mark* [1897] 2 Ch. 371; see also the similar case of *"Farah" trade mark* [1978] F.S.R. 234 in Eire where the mark was found to be registrable as not having the normal meaning of either a surname or a geographical name to the Irish consumer.
[35] *"St. Raphael" trade mark* [1900] 1 Ch. 114, although "Kent" could not be registered for cigarettes not made in Kent [1985] R.P.C. 117.
[36] See, *e.g. Domgarden trade mark* [1982] R.P.C. 155, in which registration was allowed if used only on wines of German origin; contrast *Jagerschoppen trade mark* [1980] R.P.C. 11 in which registration was allowed without any such limitation.
[37] [1984] R.P.C. 231.

more than twice in an English telephone directory would not be registered under section 9(1)(d); more than five entries would prevent registration in Part B.[38]

Laudatory epithets

2.38 The other sorts of words which were unlikely to qualify as distinctive, even in use, were "laudatory epithets".[39] The classic case on this resulted in an application being refused to register "Perfection" for soap, despite its distinctiveness in use.[40]

Name of the goods

2.39 A mark was not distinctive within the meaning of section 9 if it consisted of the name of the goods. This was the danger for the proprietors of marks which became the generic name of innovatory goods; examples of such "lost" trade marks are "aspirin", "cellophane", "escalator", "lanolin", "linoleum", "shredded wheat" and "gramophone". The loss of validity of the trade mark depended upon whether the proprietor himself had used the mark as a descriptive term, or on whether the trade in general so used the mark.[41]

2.40 Perhaps the true justification of this rule was not so much that the mark would be descriptive, but that it would enable proprietors to extend the monopoly rights enjoyed under a patent, which by the use of renewed trade mark registrations could last indefinitely. Such was the case of "Shredded Wheat" which was struck off the Register as being descriptive because it did not distinguish the product by reference to origin but identified the sort of product made under the patent.[42]

Word marks under the 1994 Act

2.41 Under the 1994 Act, the test for sufficiency of distinctiveness will undoubtedly be different to that under the 1938 Act. Certainly, many words which are not purely distinctive of the goods or services to which they are to be applied may be deemed to have some capacity to distinguish in use, whilst the proviso to section 3(1) (discussed at paras. 2.71–2.72, below) will permit the registration of some marks which might previously have been deemed too inherently descriptive.

2.42 However, as discussed above, the problem for the proprietor of an intrinsically descriptive or otherwise non-distinctive mark is that it requires a much greater effort to ensure that the mark acquires a distinctive (and therefore functional) character in the market place, than would be the case with an intrinsically distinctive mark. Furthermore, a descriptive mark is likely to be harder to protect against infringement than a more distinctive mark. For these reasons, the liberalisation of the regime for registration, whilst welcome in bringing the Register into line with more modern trade practices, will not, in

[38] *Ciba trade mark* [1983] R.P.C. 75.
[39] Again s. 8 was relevant as a description of the quality of goods by others must be permitted.
[40] [1910] 1 Ch. 130, compare this to *Coats Limited's Application* (1936) 53 R.P.C. 355 in which the wide use of the mark "Sheen" was deemed to have overcome its initial lack of distinctiveness.
[41] See also s. 15 of the 1938 Act, and note the similarity to s. 3(1) and 46(1)(c) of the 1994 Act.
[42] (1940) 57 R.P.C. 137.

the author's opinion, be wholly beneficial, if it encourages proprietors to seek to register less functional marks.

(b) Designs

2.43 Under this general heading will fall another group of important marks, namely device marks or logos. These may or may not be capable of distinguishing goods or services, depending upon the simplicity and/or descriptiveness of the device. Under the 1938 Act, such marks were registrable, but only upon sufficient evidence of distinctiveness being provided, so the only difference in the new Act may be in the level of distinctiveness which may be required. Nonetheless, such marks will have to be considered, like all other marks, in relation to the tests of absolute and relative registrability (see below).

(c) Letters and numerals

2.44 Such marks were again registrable under the 1938 Act on proof of sufficient distinctiveness. This seems likely to be the case under the 1994 Act also, albeit with the less stringent test to be applied of capacity to distinguish, and the aid of the proviso to section 3(1) in certain cases.

2.45 Under the 1938 Act, initials were considered to be inherently ill-adapted to distinguish goods. Registry practice was to allow registration in Part B of the Register of two letter marks if they were presented as words and were clearly pronounceable. Otherwise, the success of an application to register initials depended upon the distinctiveness of their presentation. At times, the use of a distinctive device would lead to registration, but with disclaimer of exclusive rights to the initials.[43] Initials again seem likely to be registrable under the 1994 Act where they appear to be sufficiently distinctive to perform their necessary function, as reflected in section 1(1), or where they have achieved distinctiveness in use, by virtue of the proviso to section 3(1). The Draft Work Manual suggests that only marks consisting of five or more digits will be registered without evidence of distinctiveness.

(d) Shapes

2.46 Shapes are specifically mentioned in section 1(1) as being capable of being registered as trade marks, representing a change from the position under the 1938 Act.[44] The obvious limitations upon such registrations are those mentioned above, of the potential difficulty of representing a shape graphically, and the distinctiveness of the shape so as to function as a mark. Again, here it is likely that the proprietor's desire to acquire a valuable and functional trade mark will ensure that the number of such applications remains relatively small and that applications to register banal shapes are rare. Where, however, there might be doubts as to the intrinsic registrability of a shape mark, the section 3(1) proviso may again come into play.

---

[43] See, *e.g. General Electric Co. v. The General Electric Co.* [1973] R.P.C. 297; *BP v. EP* [1968] R.P.C. 54; and more recently *IQ trade mark* [1993] R.P.C. 379.
[44] See, *e.g.* comments in *Smith Kline & French v. Sterling-Winthrop Group* [1976] R.P.C. 511 at 535 contrasted to the decisions refusing the registration of shapes, such as *Sobrefina* [1974] R.P.C. 672, *Coca–Cola* [1986] R.P.C. 421 and *John Wyeth* [1988] R.P.C. 233.

2.47 A further general, but somewhat obvious, point to be made in relation to shape marks is that although the Act and Rules require the registration of the mark to be effected in the form of a two-dimensional representation of the mark, use of the shape in any manner, including three-dimensions, will be taken into account for all the purposes of the Act (whether one is considering legitimate use by the proprietor or by a third party, or use by way of an infringement) courtesy of section 103(2).

The illustrations on the Trade Mark Register for the 3-dimensional shape of the Coca-Cola contour bottle (with and without the wording Coca-Cola).

'Coca-Cola' and the design of the contour bottle are registered trade marks of The Coca-Cola Company. These images are reproduced with the kind permission from The Coca-Cola Company.

Section 3(2): Exceptions to the registrability of shapes

2.48 The registrability of shapes is, however, restricted by the provisions of section 3(2), preventing shapes from being registered when they are essentially functional rather than fanciful adjuncts to the goods. Moreover, the provisions of section 3(2) are absolute in that they cannot be overcome by evidence of distinctiveness in use.

2.49 Sub-section 3(2)(a) excludes from registration as marks shapes which consist *exclusively* of the shape "*which results from the nature of the goods*" in respect of which the "*mark*" is sought to be registered. Save in the rare cases where a proprietor is indirectly seeking to extend the protection which he has acquired for an innovatory product under patent, design or registered design law, by the acquisition of the infinitely renewable protection of a trade mark, it is hard to conceive of examples in which a proprietor might realistically wish to choose a mark consisting of a shape which was *exclusively* the result of the shape of the goods, as such a "mark" would seem to be unlikely to be very distinctive, in order to perform its function properly. It is also hard to think of examples of shapes which are wholly the result of the function of the goods; could this be said of the shape of a light bulb for instance, or could one say (and convince the Registry) that some of the elements of the shape of the bulb were prompted by aesthetic considerations? Similarly, what of the shape of a "plug" night-light; obviously some parts of the night-light would be the result of the function which it was to perform, but might it not also be said that other parts of its design — the shape of the illuminated bulb cover, for instance — were purely matters of design, such that the overall shape was registrable?

2.50 It is thought that fancy-shaped containers which owe nothing to the goods which they contain, such as the Coca–Cola bottle, the "Dimple" whisky bottle or the Jif lemon, should not, in any event, be deemed to fall within section 3(2)(a).

2.51 Sub-section 3(2)(b) similarly excludes from registration as a mark a shape consisting *exclusively* of the shape "*which is necessary to obtain a technical result*". This would exclude any parts of the light-bulb or night-light which are necessary to fit the bulb into a light-fitting, or plug the night-light into the socket, or even perhaps which were intended to make the night-light especially easy to push into or pull out of the socket. On the other hand, it would not seem to exclude any shape being registered which *also* included fanciful elements of design, such as a night-light designed in the shape of a teddy bear or Humpty-Dumpty.

2.52 Lastly, sub-section 3(2)(c) excludes from registration as a mark a shape which consists *exclusively* of the shape "*which gives substantial value to the goods*". Would this exclude from registration as a mark the shape of a night-light in the form of Humpty-Dumpty? It may do so if the shape is *exclusively* that which gives substantial value to the product. In this example, the attractiveness of such a night-light might well lie in the adoption of the Humpty-Dumpty shape, so perhaps the night-light would fall foul of sub-section(2)(c). But if the night-light were not so cute, and was not shaped like Humpty but was simply of an elegant but simple shape, would it be precluded from registration by this sub-section? It is thought not, since the *substantial* value of the product would be in the function performed by the light, with the design of the goods as an additional, but insubstantial, benefit. This seems in some ways illogical, since the more attractive shape might be seen as the more memorable mark, providing a better indication of its source, but, on the other hand, it is likely that the Humpty-Dumpty light might be more easily registrable than a simpler bulb cover as a Registered Design or simply protected by design right. And what of the Coca–Cola or Dimple bottle, or Jif lemon-shaped juice container? Again, it is thought that these should not fall within sub-section 3(2)(c), as the contents of the container must also give substantial value to the goods. But can the same be said for an unusual and distinctively shaped bottle containing perfume? Is it solely the fragrance which gives it the value, or does the bottle shape also give substantial value?

(e) Packaging, get-up and trade dress

2.53   Section 1(1) specifically provides that packaging may be registered as a mark. It also seems clear that the section would apply to other distinctive features of trade-dress or get-up. Again, however, there may be real problems of distinctiveness with such marks, especially where some of the elements of the packaging or get-up might be said to consist of signs "common to the trade".

2.54   With such marks, though, the real difficulty may lie in the inevitable time-lag between making a trade mark application and being able to rely upon it for the purposes of bringing infringement actions. Moreover, by the time one particular version of the get-up will have been registered, the proprietor may well wish to update it.[45] The further difficulty with registering get-up in such a way as to be of practical value to the proprietor is that often get-up consists of a number of features applied to the packaging or presentation of the product. Assuming that it would be necessary to register all such features as *together* constituting "the mark", there would doubtless be serious concerns as to how many such features would have to have been adopted or copied by an alleged infringer before an infringement action might succeed.

2.55   In terms of a passing off action, it is certainly not inconceivable that a combination of features of get-up or trade dress could be protectable.[46] However, such cases are not easy to sustain, and the difficulties of protecting distinctive get-up consisting of a combination of different features or signs have been well publicised over recent years (and especially prior to the passing of the Act in 1993/94) in relation to supermarket chains' own-brand "look-alikes" of leading brand products. Complaints were manifold in this field, as the brand leaders considered that the supermarkets were deliberately setting out either to confuse the public into thinking that the "own-label" product was the brand leader, or to give the public the (usually) erroneous impression that the own-label product was so similar to the brand leader as to have been manufactured by the maker of the brand leader for the supermarket,[47] or at least that it was an equivalent product to the brand leader. To date these complaints have been dealt with (if at all) by the law of passing off, and there was much discussion of the issue in Parliament during the passage of the Trade Marks Bill. Again, proposed amendments designed to ensure that own-label look-alike products would be caught by the provisions of the Act were rejected. As a result, it seems that such problems may be dealt with under the 1994 Act (as opposed to the law of passing off) only by registration of the details of the brand-leading products' get-up, etc., as marks, and by their proprietors subsequently being able to show sufficient similarity between the registered mark and the "own-label" get-up to show infringement, despite (in most cases) clear labelling showing the source of the latter.

2.56   Simple elements of get-up consisting of one or maybe two distinctive elements (such as the Jif yellow plastic lemon[48]) may well prove to be both registrable and useful

---

[45]   But note the difficulty in amending a registered mark under s. 44, see para. 3.34 below.
[46]   See Chap. 5(4), below.
[47]   Heinz *is* now to manufacture baked beans for sale as "own-brand" products – will this confuse consumers further?
[48]   *Jif* [1990] 1 W.L.R. 491; [1990] R.P.C. 341.

How the Sunlight soap trade mark has developed and changed over the years.

1894

1963

1950

1981

1958

1996

Illustrations courtesy of Unilever plc, the proprietor of the trade mark.

marks. However, it seems likely that the potential for registering complicated combinations of specific signs, each of which might, or might not, be separately registrable, may be of limited practical use.

(f) Other marks

2.57 Under this heading will fall all manner of other marks which may, or may not, have been registrable under the 1938 Act.

Colours

2.58 Colours will be registrable, if sufficiently distinctive. Here, it seems probable that the Registry will, at least to begin with, be guided by prior decisions as to the registrability of colours, so that unusual or eye-catching colour combinations may be registrable, but single colours or simple combinations of colours will be harder to register.[49] It is worth noting that, in any event, for the reasons mentioned above, a very simple colour mark might not be a particularly attractive property.

Examples of the problems of counterfeiting, reproduced by kind permission of International Distillers & Vinters Ltd. The genuine product is on the right

---

[49] See *Smith Kline & French Labs' "Cimetidine"* [1991] R.P.C. 17 and *Parke Davis & Co's Application* [1976] F.S.R. 195 (Eire).

Colours under the 1938 Act

2.59   Under the 1938 Act, colours could be registered as marks if sufficiently "adapted to distinguish". Alternatively, a mark could be limited to one or several colours by section 16, although this could be an impediment to the proprietor, hampering both his own potential use of the mark and any action for infringement. In *Reddaway's Application*[50] registration was permitted of a mark which consisted of coloured lines running along the length of hosepipes. In a more recent case, *Smith Kline & French*,[51] the registration of a half-coloured, half-transparent drug capsule was permitted because the transparent half contained a number of tiny multi-coloured granules. The House of Lords found that the coloured capsules had become distinctive through use and allowed the registration despite the fact that this in effect gave an extension of the previous patent protection. It was held that nothing in section 68(1) excluded a mark covering the whole of the visible surface of the goods from registration as a trade mark. Nonetheless, registrability depended upon being able to show distinctiveness in fact.[52]

Colours under the 1994 Act

2.60   The previous case-law seems likely to be of general application under the new Act, as in both cases the question is one of potential distinctiveness. However, again, the proviso to section 3(1) may well be significant in attempts to register colour marks, since it seems likely that colour marks which might be deemed to lack "any distinctive character" in theory, may be capable of being shown to be distinctive in practice so as to be registrable.[53]

Smells and Sounds

2.61   There has been much discussion of the registrability of such marks, more perhaps than their importance in practice will probably justify. The major problem with each, apart from that of deciding how to represent them graphically (discussed above) is that it may well be hard to persuade the Registry that such marks are capable of distinguishing goods or services, and the Draft Work Manual states that such marks will be accepted only upon evidence of distinctiveness. In particular, the Registry will resist attempts to register as marks, smells which are inherent to the goods or which are added to goods to make them more pleasant to use, rather than as a true trade mark. It may be significant that apparently no smell mark was registered in the United States until 1990, although the legislation had made this a possibility since 1946.[54] There might also be significant problems in relying upon such a mark for the purposes of an infringement action, and, all in all, there must be some doubt as to the real value of such marks. However, it is understood that some applications have already been made for scent marks at the time of writing, and it remains to be seen how they fare in the Registry and beyond.

---

[50] *Reddaway & Co (No. 1)* [1914] 1 Ch. 856.
[51] [1976] R.P.C. 511; see also *Parke Davis & Co's Application* [1976] F.S.R. 195 (Eire).
[52] Thus in *Smith Kline & French Labs' ("Cimetidine")* [1991] R.P.C. 17, the registration of a single colour for a tablet was refused, see too *John Wyeth* n.44, above.
[53] This was essentially the distinction between the two *SK & F* cases cited in n.49, above.
[54] See Burton [1995] E.I.P.R. 378.

(7) ABSOLUTE GROUNDS FOR REFUSAL OF REGISTRATION

2.62 Section 3 of the 1994 Act requires marks to satisfy certain "absolute" standards before they may be registered. Certain of these absolute grounds for refusal are reminiscent of parts of section 9 and section 11 of the 1938 Act, in excluding from registration overly descriptive marks or marks having a direct reference to the character or quality of the goods. On the other hand, it may be said that one significant difference between the Acts lies in the general approach taken by each, with the 1938 Act defining registrable marks, and the 1994 Act defining unregistrable ones.

2.63 The standards are absolute only in terms of not being dependant upon a comparison with any particular prior trade mark or other earlier right (see discussion of section 5 below for such "relative" grounds of refusal); even so, the question of "absolute" acceptability for registration may depend upon other signs which are in use in the relevant trade (see sub-paragraph (d)) or upon the effect of user on otherwise "absolutely" unregistrable marks.

2.64 Again, the significant difference in approach between sections 9 and 11 of the 1938 Act and section 3 of the 1994 Act lies in the proviso to the latter, permitting marks which would otherwise fail the absolute tests to be registered, if they can be shown to have acquired a distinctive character in use. It is this proviso which will permit the registration of a number of marks which would have been refused registration under the 1938 Act.

Sub-section 3(1)(a): signs not satisfying the requirements of s.1(1)

2.65 This sub-section is self-explanatory and the reader should refer back to the sections above on registrability to see which signs may not fall within section 1(1). It is almost axiomatic that the proviso to the sub-section does not apply to this sub-paragraph.

Sub-section 3(1)(b): signs "devoid of any distinctive character"

2.66 This prevents the registration of marks which are "devoid of any distinctive character". Again, this sub-paragraph refers back in effect to the requirement in section 1(1) that a mark must be capable of distinguishing its proprietor's goods or services from those of others. Oddly enough, the proviso to sub-section 3(1) *does* apply to this sub-paragraph, so that in the case of a sign which is on the face of it wholly undistinctive or wholly descriptive, but which has acquired a "distinctive character" by use, registration may follow. This will probably just mean that a mark which would be refused registration when unused, as seemingly too descriptive or unmemorable to be capable of being distinctive (*e.g.* possibly two-letter initial marks like "BP"[55]), will be registered when the application is accompanied by sufficiently cogent evidence of a reputation acquired by use.[56]

---

[55] [1968] R.P.C. 54 and see 2.44–2.45, above.
[56] As to the level of distinctiveness required, see paras. 2.71–2.72, below.

Sub-section 3(1)(c): descriptive marks

2.67 This sub-paragraph prevents the registration of descriptive marks, at least until they show themselves capable of acquiring distinctiveness in use, so as to merit the application of the proviso. The purpose of this sub-paragraph, and of the next one, is to prevent traders from registering as marks for their exclusive use, words which another trader might *legitimately* wish to use in the course of his business.[57]

2.68 This sub-paragraph obviously largely echoes, but in more specific terms and in regard to all types of marks, the requirement in section 9 of the 1938 Act that a word mark should not make a direct reference to the character or quality of the goods.[58] Again, however, the use of the word *exclusively* may limit the scope of application of this sub-paragraph, in particular in relation to combination or non-word marks, where extraneous, distinctive matter may be added to words found to fall within one of the "forbidden" categories, or where fanciful presentation prevents the mark from being *exclusively* descriptive. On the other hand, the provisions of this sub-paragraph may be used in combination with those in sub-paragraph 3(1)(d) to prevent the registration of marks which consist of a combination of a descriptive term and a term common to the trade.[59] Equally, sub-paragraph (c) might be used in combination with sub-section 3(3) to prevent the registration of a term which could be descriptive if used in relation to certain goods, but would be deceptive if used in relation to other sorts of goods.[60]

2.69 Marks are to be refused registration where they consist exclusively of "signs or indications which may serve ..... to designate ... " one or more of the following:

> *Kind*: An example of such a mark might be the word "Glasscan" for a glass beverage container[61]; or a photograph of a pile of coffee beans on a jar of coffee; or a picture of a squeeze of toothpaste on a toothbrush to be registered in relation to toothpaste.[62]
>
> *Quality*: An example of such a mark might be "5 star" whether for hotel services or brandy (and for either, such a mark would also be likely to fall under sub-paragraph 3(1)(d) as common to the trade); it might also catch the nicely named "Le XV du President" for wine having 15 per cent of alcohol; this classification would catch "Standard"[63], and "Perfection".[64]
>
> *Quantity*: It is hard to think of any simple and exclusive indication of quantity which a sane trade mark proprietor might wish to register and which would be caught by

---

[57] See, *e.g.* comments of Whitford J. in *"Have a Break" trade mark*, reported 10 years after judgment in [1993] R.P.C. 217 at 230: the test of registrability was "whether these are words that others might, perfectly fairly, want to use", and *Budget trade mark* [1991] R.P.C. 9.

[58] See para. 2.34 above.

[59] See, *e.g. Superwound trade mark* [1988] R.P.C. 272; a combination of "super" and "wound", the latter being common to the trade in guitar strings.

[60] Here, the classic example is "Orlwoola", deemed descriptive if used for all-wool garments, but deceptive if used on wool-mix or non-wool fabrics: *"Orlwoola" trade mark* [1910] 1 Ch. 130.

[61] See *"Glasscan" trade mark* [1994] R.P.C. 23.

[62] *Unilever* [1984] R.P.C. 155.

[63] (1910) 27 R.P.C. 789.

[64] [1910] 1 Ch. 130; 26 R.P.C. 837.

this provision. However, clearly, any direct and exclusive reference to weight, length, etc., would fall under this heading.

Intended purpose: This will catch most purely descriptive marks, such as the examples of "sleeping tablets" or "carpet shampoo" given above.

Value: This may be hard to distinguish from "quality" above, but would probably catch marks like "Budget"[65] or "Kwiksave".

Geographical origin: This provision in particular is designed to ensure that traders remain free to indicate the geographical origin of their goods, which may in some cases be of value to them. Marks such as "York" would still be caught by the provision, although obviously a different result would follow an application to register such a mark now, if it benefited from strong enough distinctiveness in fact, by reason of the proviso to section 3(1).

The time of production of goods or rendering of services: Such designations again seem unlikely to be chosen as marks, but might catch something like "Dawn Fresh" for milk.

Other characteristics: This general heading catches all other descriptive marks, perhaps "Motor Lodge"[66] for food, "Soflens"[67] for contact lenses and accessories, "Profitmaker"[68] for software for financial and energy trading risk management (this was also rejected on the grounds that it was laudatory).

Sub-section 3(1)(d): signs customary in the trade

2.70 This sub-section prevents the registration of signs which are customarily used in the relevant trade. Again, this was a reason for rejection of a mark under the 1938 Act and there would seem to be no reason why this provision should be applied differently. Such unregistrable signs may consist not just of common trade descriptions in words or phrases, but also commonly used devices or logos, or any commonly used shapes. For instance, as mentioned above, the use of a number of stars in relation to different grades or types of brandy or hotel services would clearly be caught by this section.

The proviso to section 3(1)

" ... a trade mark shall not be refused registration by virtue of paragraph (b), (c), or (d) ... if, before the date of application for registration, it has in fact acquired a distinctive character as a result of the use made of it."

2.71 Enough has been said above in relation to the use of this proviso to show that any mark which falls into one or more of the categories of sub-paragraphs (b) to (d) may yet be registered if sufficient evidence can be adduced to satisfy the Registry of the mark's distinctiveness in practice. The question then will be, what level of distinctiveness will suffice for this purpose? This was one of the issues considered by Jacob J. in *British Sugar*

---

[65] [1991] R.P.C. 9.
[66] [1965] R.P.C. 35; (an example of a business trying to protect services (motels) by a registration for goods (food) before service marks were registrable).
[67] [1976] R.P.C. 694.
[68] [1994] R.P.C. 613.

Plc v. James Robertson and Sons.[69] He found, first, that the onus of showing that the mark had become distinctive through use fell on the proprietor. The plaintiff sought to rely on survey evidence as to the reputation of the mark, which the judge found to be flawed.[70] Nonetheless, he did find that a proportion of members of the public recognised the word "Treat" as a trade mark. The plaintiff had estimated the proportion as 60 per cent, but Jacob J. held that even if that were the right figure (which he doubted) that would not suffice to show that the mark had the necessary distinctive character. He held that " ... it must be shown in a case of this sort that the mark has really become accepted by a substantial majority of persons as a trade mark – is or is almost a household word."

2.72   Jacob J.'s judgment in *British Sugar* will clearly much restrict the extent to which reliance could be placed on the provisos to section 3(1) and section 47(1), if it is of general application. It remains to be seen how the judgment may be applied. In view of his reference to "a case of this sort", it may be that the requirement to show so strong a reputation will apply only where the mark consists of a laudatory word (which "Treat" was deemed to be) or of a very ordinary descriptive term.

Sub-section 3(2): exceptions to the registrability of shapes

2.73   For a discussion of this sub-section please see paragraphs 2.48–2.52, above on registration of shapes.

Sub-section 3(3): marks contrary to public policy or of such a nature as to deceive the public

2.74   This sub-section largely reflects section 11 of the 1938 Act and it may well be that case-law on that section will be of application under the 1994 Act, despite the more specific wording of the latter.

Section 11 of the 1938 Act

2.75   Sections 11 and 12 of the 1938 Act both added restrictions to the registrability of marks by establishing a general rule precluding the registration of marks likely to cause confusion or deception. Very often, the two sections were used together by the proprietor of an existing mark in opposition to the registration by another trader of a mark which might be confused with his own mark, or which might interfere with the distinctiveness of his products. In both cases the burden of proof fell upon the applicant to demonstrate that confusion or deception was not likely to occur.

2.76   Section 11 contained "absolute" standards of mandatory application, which is to say, standards applied on an absolute basis, without consideration of the other marks on the market, as well as comparative or subjective elements, which took into consideration

---

[69] [1996] R.P.C. 281 esp. at 305–306; note that the case related to an alleged infringement of the registration "Treat" for dessert sauces and syrups. The defendant counterclaimed for a declaration of invalidity under s. 47 under various heads of s. 3 and one issue was whether the mark had acquired sufficient distinctiveness to fall within the proviso to s. 3 or the similar proviso to s. 47.

[70] As to the unreliability of survey evidence generally, see Chap. 4.64.

such other marks and other factors. These "absolute" grounds for refusal were first, the prohibition of registration of marks which were contrary to morality[71] or "scandalous designs", and secondly, the prohibition on marks which were deceptive as to the quality or composition of the goods. Marks refused registration on these grounds included "Orl-woola" for non-woollen textiles,[72] "Portalto" for wine which was not a genuine port,[73] and "China-Therm" for plastic cups and containers.[74]

2.77 The section was also used to prevent the registration of names falsely implying a geographical connection so that, for instance, "Royal Worcester"[75] was held to be misleading for an American product. Even less direct references which were misleading as to origin could be enough to preclude registration, such as the use of a shamrock device and name for goods not of Irish origin.[76]

2.78 Section 11 was also used to prevent the registration of marks which because of their similarity to other marks might, even where the goods were dissimilar, lead to dangerous confusion, as for instance where disinfectant and meat extract carried confusing marks.[77]

Application of sub-section 3(3)

2.79 In the light of the practice under section 11 and the wording of section 3(3) itself, it seems probable that the sub-section will be used to deny registration to otherwise distinctive marks which offend against good taste or decency in all sorts of ways: obscenity, racism, sexism, affronts to religious beliefs or to common decency of any kind. Doubtless such absolute standards will move with (or, perhaps, a little behind) the times. The "*Hallelujah*"example given above might, for instance, be decided differently today.

2.80 Marks will also be rejected under sub-section 3(3) if they are liable to lead to confusion or deception, and the sub-section itself gives the examples of such confusion being as to the "nature, quality or geographical origin of the goods or service". So, not only could one not register "Kenyan" for Kenyan coffee, under sub-section 3(1)(c) (subject to the proviso), but one could not register it for use on Jamaican coffee either, as this would be deceptive as to origin.[78]And note that the proviso applies *only* to sub-paragraphs (b) to (d) of sub-section 3(1) and does not apply to save a deceptive mark liable to be rejected under sub-section 3(3).

---

[71] These cases were rarely reported as they were rejected at so early a stage but see *"Hallelujah" trade mark* [1976] R.P.C. 605, where the mark was refused registration for women's clothing as being contrary to morality.

[72] *"Orwoola" trade mark* [1910] 1 Ch. 130; (1909) 26 R.P.C. 683.

[73] *"Portalto" trade mark* [1967] R.P.C. 617; this case resembled the later *Champagne* and *Advocaat* cases requiring marks associated with a particular area or recipe only to be used on goods from that area/recipe.

[74] *"China-Therm" trade mark* [1980] F.S.R. 21.

[75] [1909] 1 Ch. 459; (1909) 26 R.P.C. 185.

[76] *McGlennon's Application* (1908) 25 R.P.C. 797; alternatively, the mark might be accepted but only for use upon goods coming from the place suggested by the name, see para. 2.36 and n.36, above.

[77] *Edwards' Application* (1945) 63 R.P.C. 19.

[78] See discussion in para. 2.36, above.

Sub-section 3(4): marks prohibited by law

2.81 No trade mark is to be registered if this would be contrary to any rule of United Kingdom or European law. This covers certain older rules, precluding the registration of certain words or emblems, such as "Red Cross", and would, more importantly, cover the case of a registration which offends against any European law rule. See Chapter 7(13).

2.82 These are grounds which may well not be raised against a mark upon application being made to register it, but which might be raised against it subsequently as grounds for showing that the mark ought never to have been registered for the purposes of rectification of the Register.

Sub-section 3(5) and section 4: specially protected emblems

2.83 Sub-section 3(5) just refers to the grounds for refusal to register a mark which are set out in section 4. This lists a number of national flags, emblems, royal arms, etc., which are not to be registrable as trade marks, as well as marks which would tend to lead to the belief that the applicant has some royal patronage.[79] Some of these provisions emanate from prior United Kingdom law (indeed from section 11 of the 1938 Act), some from the Directive, and some from the Paris Convention. The section is self-explanatory. Section 99 goes further, and makes it an offence to use a copy of the Royal Arms in connection with any business or so as to imply a Royal clientele. See, similarly, section 57.

2.84 A further sub-section 4(5) was added by the Olympic Symbol, etc., (Protection) Act 1995, preventing the unauthorised registration of marks consisting of or containing the Olympic symbol or motto.[80] Section 3(2) of the 1995 Act also restricts the use of the symbol and motto generally in connection with a trade or business. Infringing use gives rise to a right to all the usual remedies for infringements of a property right, and also constitutes a criminal offence in certain circumstances.

Sub-section 3(6): marks registered in bad faith

2.85 This prevents the registration of any mark where the application is made in bad faith. This concept is not defined, but will doubtless cover a number of different scenarios.

2.86 First, it would clearly cover a case where the application has been made, not with a view to the proprietor himself trading under the mark, but with an intention either of stopping someone else with a better claim to the mark from using it, or forcing that other person to negotiate with the registered proprietor in order to gain control of the mark. Such cases occurred under the previous Act where someone registered his employer's or

---

[79] See, *e.g. Queen Diana trade mark* [1989] R.P.C. 557 (for Scotch whisky!) allowed on appeal at [1991] R.P.C. 395.

[80] The symbol is the five interlocking rings; the motto is "Citius, altius, fortius".

principal's mark.[81] The application might also be deemed to be made in bad faith if the applicant was seeking to register a mark well-known abroad but not yet used or registered here, for example, if someone here, who was not linked in any way to the makers of the Teenage Ninja Turtles series, had sought to register the phrase and the names of each of the turtles for toys, stationery, etc.[82]

2.87   Secondly, it would occur where the applicant had no genuine intention to use or licence[83] the use of the mark as a trade mark in relation to the goods or services for which the application was made.[84] Such might be the case in relation to all the goods or services to be covered by the registration, in which case the whole registration would be bad, or might merely mean that the specification of goods and/or services in respect of which the application was made was so wide as to be deemed to have been made in bad faith, rather than simply out of acceptable caution. In the latter case, presumably only the excessive parts of the registration would be liable to be deemed invalid. An example of the former type of case may still be found in the *"Nerit"* case,[85] in which the plaintiff tobacco company had wished to use the mark "Merit" for cigarettes but thought that it would be unregistrable (as a laudatory epithet). It had, therefore, registered "Nerit" as a "ghost mark", making some desultory use of it in 1976 and 1977. In 1976 a competitor introduced cigarettes onto the market under the mark "Merit" and the plaintiff brought an infringement action against it. The defendant admitted that the two marks were similar enough to be confused, but counterclaimed that the plaintiff's registration was invalid because it had lacked a bona fide intention to use "Nerit" as a mark. The counterclaim succeeded as there had never been any bona fide use of "Nerit" as a true commercial venture, but only as a cosmetic exercise.[86]

2.88   Thirdly, there might be bad faith where an application is made in some other way in misleading terms, such as by misrepresenting the extent of the user upon which it is sought to justify registration of a descriptive mark.

2.89   The fact that the reference to bad faith appears in this sub-section does not, of course, necessarily mean that an application made in bad faith will be able to be identified, and therefore rejected, prior to registration. On the contrary, this seems unlikely to be the

---

[81]   *e.g. Zoppas trade mark* [1965] R.P.C. 381; but note that under the 1938 Act, s. 17 required an application to be made by someone claiming to be the proprietor of the mark and see the recent case of *Al Bassam trade mark* [1995] R.P.C. 511, in which Courtaulds was held entitled to register a mark used on goods which it manufactured for sale in the Middle East, although its Middle Eastern clients were the proprietors of the mark abroad. See also *Radiation Limited's Application* (1930) 47 R.P.C. 37.

[82]   To some extent this was the position in *Rawhide trade mark* [1962] R.P.C. 133, where the application was (ostensibly, at least) refused because it was considered that the applicant had no bona fide intention to use the mark, rather than because of distaste at his business methods. See by analogy also *Glaxo Plc v. Glaxowellcome Limited* ([1996] F.S.R. 388) where an injunction was granted to stop the use of the registered company name "Glaxowellcome", registered just after announcement of the intended Glaxo bid for Wellcome, on the basis of passing off.

[83]   Under the 1938 Act, it sufficed that use was to be made of the mark by a licensee: *Bostitch* [1963] R.P.C. 183.

[84]   The specific requirement under ss. 68(1), 9 and 10 of the 1938 Act, that the mark applied for had to be used, or proposed to be used, by the applicant or his registered user, is not repeated in the 1994 Act.

[85]   *Imperial Group Limited v. Philip Morris & Co. Limited* [1982] F.S.R. 72.

[86]   *ibid.,* and see *Palm trade mark* [1992] R.P.C. 258.

case very often. Instead, it is more likely that the complaint will be raised in the context of invalidity proceedings under section 47(1) (see Chapter 3(7) below).

The Sea-lion mark example

2.90   Let us return to the example given above of the mark "sea-lion" chosen for soaps, etc., in Class 3. In examining the various "sea-lion" signs upon the basis of their *absolute* suitability for registration, that is to say without considering any clash with prior rights, the position would seem to be:

> *Word*: Under the 1938 Act, one could have registered the word "sea-lion" for such goods, upon the basis that it was an ordinary English word, but one having no direct reference to the character, quality, etc., of the goods. The word would equally be registrable under the new Act.
>
> *Device*: Under the 1938 Act, the sea-lion device described in Chapter 1 could also have been registered, and again there would seem to be no change under the new Act.
>
> *Packaging*: Under the 1938 Act, it would not have been possible to register any of the details of the get-up or packaging described in Chapter 1. Under the 1994 Act, all such distinctive features of trade dress or packaging may be registered, including for example a fancy sea-lion-shaped box for toilet soap and a sea-lion-shaped plastic bottle for liquid soap, perhaps with a fancy lid in the shape of a ball balanced on his head.
>
> *Shape*: Under the 1938 Act, it would not have been possible to register a sea-lion-shaped soap itself as a trade mark. Under the 1994 Act, this might also be problematic, not because the shape might not be capable of distinguishing the products of the proprietor, but because this shape might well amount to a shape "which gives substantial value" to the goods. The question would be whether it could be shown that the public would purchase the soap because of its value as a pleasantly perfumed, good quality, hypo-allergenic product, suitable for the children who might wish to buy (if not use) it, or whether it was the sea-lion shape of the goods *exclusively* which gave it its substantial value. It may be seen that sub-section 3(2)(c) will at times be very hard to apply.
>
> *Goods specification*: There may be a difficult choice to be made as to precisely which goods to cover in the specification, with the need to weigh breadth of specification for safety from harmful infringement, against the intrinsic insecurity of having a registration part of which might be invalid as having been applied for in bad faith, or which might become invalid if not used. A broad specification might cover: cosmetics, dermatological preparations and substances, moisturisers, hand, face and body washing preparations, shower gels, shampoos, soaps, hair lotions, essential oils, toilet preparations, dentifrices, all included in Class 3. However, let us assume that the proprietor either seeks or achieves his registration solely for "hand, face and body washing preparations, shower gels, shampoos, and soaps".

(8) RELATIVE GROUNDS FOR REFUSAL OF REGISTRATION: THE COMPARISON OF TRADE MARK APPLICATIONS WITH OTHER MARKS AND RIGHTS

2.91   The relative grounds for refusal of registration are set out in section 5 of the Act. These provisions prevent the registration of marks which may clash with previous registered or unregistered marks, and various other categories of unregistered or non-trade mark rights. The section replaces sections 11 and 12 of the 1938 Act, and many of the considerations raised in cases under those sections will probably be of help in applying the new law. For instance, the manner of comparing marks for potentially confusing or deceptive similarity will be the same, and the test of similarity of goods seems likely to be based on the previous concept of "goods of the same description".[87]

Relative grounds for refusal under the 1938 Act

2.92   Sections 11 and 12 provided for the comparison of the mark applied for and prior marks or other prior rights. There were differences in the scope of the two sections.[88] Section 12(1) applied to registered marks only and gave protection against a confusing mark used on the same or similar goods; it was subject to the exceptions of s.12(2) and (3). Section 11, on the other hand, could be used to protect unregistered marks, as well as registered marks, and was not restricted to protection from the use of confusing marks on the same or same description of goods. Indeed, section 11 could be used to protect a trader from damage even to non-trade mark interests such as copyright.[89]

Section 11

2.93   Section 11 was also used by proprietors of registered or unregistered marks, or other prior rights likely to be affected by the registration sought, to protect their marks against the registration or continued presence on the Register of marks likely to cause confusion or deception. The advantage of section 11 lay in its flexible wording, which, unlike the more restrictive section 12(1), allowed it to be used to protect goods, even of different descriptions from those on which the contested mark would be used,[90] as well as unregistered trade marks which might not have established a sufficiently good reputation or have shown a sufficient likelihood of confusion to succeed in a passing off action.[91] There was no requirement in section 11 that the contested mark should be identical to or nearly resemble another *mark*, so that it could be perhaps a trade name or get-up that would be confused with the contested mark.

Confusing or deceptive similarity

2.94   The tests of confusing or deceptive similarity to be applied under sections 11 and 12 were essentially the same as those used to test a likelihood of confusion for infringement. Under the 1938 Act, section 68 (2B) provided that references in the Act "to a near resemblance of marks are references to a resemblance so near as to be likely to deceive or cause confusion." The criteria by which the likelihood of confusion were judged were

---

[87]   See *British Sugar*, n.69 above and para. 2.116, below.
[88]   The leading case on the differences between sections 11 and 12 was *Smith Hayden & Co's Application* (1946) 63 R.P.C. 97, updated by *GE* [1973] R.P.C. 297.
[89]   See *Karo Step trade mark* [1977] R.P.C. 255; *Oscar trade mark* [1979] R.P.C. 173; and *Re Europasian Equipment Limited's trade mark application The Times*, May 15, 1980, in which Graham J. held that where there was a copyright infringement, s. 11 must be applied to refuse registration.
[90]   See, *e.g. Player's Trade Mark* [1965] R.P.C. 363 in which the registration of "Players" for chocolate cigarettes was prevented.
[91]   See *Bali* [1969] R.P.C. 472.

"essentially practical"[92] and the court approached the issue of confusing similarity from the purchaser's point of view. "The judge must consider the evidence adduced and use his own common sense and his own opinion as to the likelihood of deception",[93] but his opinion would, of course, be affected by any evidence of actual confusion adduced before him. It was a "jury" assessment, where the judge was substituted for the jury.

2.95 Goods bearing competing marks might well not be sold side by side, whilst competing services would be even less likely to be offered concurrently, so that the consumer could see for himself any differences between the marks. It was, therefore, held that the comparison which had to be made was between the *essential features* of the marks.[94] This rule applied equally to the phonetics or the sense of word or name marks and the essential features or ideas of logos or other device marks. Where the marks consisted of invented or meaningless words, "the court gives as much weight to phonetic as to visual resemblance".[95]

2.96 In making such comparisons, a useful guideline also was to look at the marks in the light of a notion of "imperfect recollection", that is whether a customer, having seen or purchased goods marked with the first mark, might confuse it with the second mark, when his recollection of the first was imperfect. This rule reflects the realistic consideration that the average customer has only "an ordinary memory"[96] and the test is whether the customer, rather than an expert, would be confused.[97] This would allow for slightly different standards to be applied to cases where the goods or services might be recommended by word of mouth,[98] and others where the purchase would follow careful thought.[99]

2.97 Frequently, marks were and are recognised by consumers not by the producer's name (indeed they are often ignorant of the origin of the product in this sense) but by the salient features of a device. Two rules flowed from the recognition of this fact. First, as a result, registration might be refused of a device, the central feature or idea of which was the same as that of an earlier mark, even where there were quite substantial differences of style or presentation.[1] This rule, though old, seems particularly appropriate in these days of regular modernisation of marks and packaging, when consumers may be likely to assume that differences in the look of a product's packaging or the mark itself do not denote any change in the product or its source, but merely a change of get-up. Secondly, registration might be refused of a mark with confusingly similar essential features, even

---

[92] *per* Laddie J. in *Wagamama Limited v. City Centre Restaurants Plc* [1995] F.S.R. 713 at 720.
[93] *per* Jacob J. in *Neutrogena Corp v. Golden Limited* [1996] R.P.C. 473 at 482 referring to *GE* [1973] R.P.C. 297 at 321.
[94] See Lord Radcliffe in *de Cordova v. Vick Chemical Co* (1951) 68 R.P.C. 103 at 106.
[95] *per* Nourse L.J. in *Parfums Givenchy SA v. Designer Alternatives Limited* [1994] R.P.C. 243.
[96] See *"Kleenoff"* (1934) 51 R.P.C. 129.
[97] See *Unilever Plc v. Johnson Wax* [1989] F.S.R. 145.
[98] Word of mouth recommendation was, for instance, a relevant factor in the decision of Jacob J. in *Neutrogena*, n.93 above.
[99] See cases at n.4, below.
[1] See, *e.g. Danish Bacon's Application* (1934) 51 R.P.C. 148; two devices featuring pigs.

Further examples of the problems of counterfeiting, reproduced by kind permission of United Distillers plc.

The genuine article is in the middle

The genuine products are on the right and second from the left

where the name of the competing proprietor was clearly shown on the product or there was some disclaimer of any connection with the proprietor of the earlier mark.[2]

2.98   Phonetics could be important, especially where the first syllables of the two marks were the same, but the Registrar or court would look at the general impression given by the mark. For instance, "Ping" and "Zing" were found to be confusingly similar, especially given the onomatopoeic nature of each of them, but "Fif" was not found to be too close to "Jif", partly as the former lacked the meaning of the latter.[3]

2.99   Deception was not considered "likely" to occur where, despite a similarity of name, the differences between the products' get-up, contents and/or price were such that someone using ordinary care and of ordinary intelligence would not be misled.[4]

Section 12

2.100   Under section 12(1) the registration could be prevented of a mark which was similar to a mark previously registered for the same goods, or goods "of the same description", where the use of the later mark would be likely to deceive or cause confusion.

2.101   Similarity between marks for this purpose was to be judged by imagining the marks in "notional" use in a "normal and fair manner", to see whether the use of the mark for which application was sought alongside the prior owner's mark might be likely to cause deception and confusion among a substantial number of people.[5] On the other hand, if the marks were already in use, they would be looked at in the light of that use. Otherwise, the major guideline in assessing the similarity of the marks was again to see whether the central "idea" of each mark was the same (see paragraph 2.95, above).

Goods of the same description

2.102   The first important limitation of section 12(1) was that it applied only to registered marks; the second was the limitation to confusion or deception between the same or similar goods. There was a fair amount of case law defining the concept of "goods of the same description" and it is important to appreciate that this term was not restricted to goods in the same class, for one class may contain goods of different descriptions, and goods of the same description may fall into separate classes. The ability to describe the goods in general terms by reference to a single trade description would not suffice either, since a definition consisting of the "lowest common denominator" might well be unfair.

2.103   Instead, the proprietor had to satisfy a test, described over the years as a business and practical test, defined in the 12th edition of *Kerly* as the following:

---

[2] See Dankwerts J. in *Tavener Rutledge Limited v. Specters Limited* [1959] R.P.C. 83 at 88–89, and C.A. at 355.
[3] See *Zing trade mark* [1978] R.P.C. 47 and *Fif trade mark* [1979] R.P.C. 355.
[4] Taking due account of the market for which the goods were intended, *e.g.* if the difference would be apparent only to literate English speakers, but the goods were intended for export: *White Hudson v. Asian Organisation* [1965] R.P.C. 45. Account would also be taken of the nature of the goods; see *Lancer trade mark* [1987] R.P.C. 303; care would be taken when buying an expensive car.
[5] See *Smith Hayden* (1946) 63 R.P.C. 97 at 101.

"Are the two sets [of goods] so commonly dealt in by the same trader that his customers, knowing his mark in connection with one set and seeing it used in relation to the other, would be likely to suppose that it was so used also to indicate that they were his?"[6]

2.104 Recently, the overall test was defined by Robin Jacob Q.C. (as he then was) in the case of *Invicta trade mark*[7] as "are these goods too alike to have the same trade mark?" having due regard to all technical and commercial factors concerned.

2.105 The traditional test was set out in *Jellinek's application*[8] and was subsequently approved by the House of Lords in *Daiquiri Rum*.[9] It was a threefold test, namely (a) the nature and composition of the goods, (b) the respective uses of the articles and (c) the trade channels through which each would be sold. It seems that it was not necessary for all three of the limbs of the test to be satisfied before the goods could be found to be of the same description, since the test depended upon the facts of each case. In *Invicta*,[10] the Registry had rejected the application where it had found two of the elements of the test present, but on appeal to the Board of Trade, it was found that only one of the three tests was satisfied, and the mark was able to proceed to registration. In *Jellinek*, shoes and shoe polish were found not to be goods of the same description, failing all three aspects of the test. In *Daiquiri Rum*, rum and rum cocktails were found to be of the same description. Slightly by contrast, in *Floradix*[11] dietetic herbal elixirs were found to be of the same description as medicated mouthwashes.

2.106 The cases under the 1938 Act demonstrate how difficult it may be to be categorical about which goods may be found to be of the same description. The line was sometimes a fine one. For instance, in *Invicta*,[12] which concerned marks for pharmaceutical fungicides for humans on the one hand, and animals on the other, the goods were not found to be of the same description, but in *Univer*,[13] which concerned marks for cardiovascular medicines for humans on the one hand (available through a doctor only), and similar medicines for veterinary use, they were found to be of the same description. The former decision is considered more persuasive.

2.107 A similar comparative exercise would obviously also have to be carried out in relation to potential conflicts between a mark for services and a goods mark.[14]

---

[6] See *Kerly's Law of Trade Marks and Trade Names*, (12th ed., 1986) at Chap. 10–12.
[7] [1992] R.P.C. 541 at 547.
[8] (1946) 63 R.P.C. 59.
[9] [1969] R.P.C. 600.
[10] See n.7, above.
[11] [1974] R.P.C. 583.
[12] See n.7, above.
[13] [1993] R.P.C. 239.
[14] See *Fingals trade mark* [1993] R.P.C. 21; under the 1938 Act marks for goods and services could conflict where they were "associated" with each other by s. 12(1) (as amended), and s. 68(2A): " ... goods and services are associated ... if it is likely that those goods might be sold or otherwise traded in and those services might be provided by the same business, and so with descriptions of goods and descriptions of services."

2.108   The Registry adopted a similar test to that approved in *Jellinek*[15] in relation to services/services conflicts, which involved a consideration of the nature of the services and their purposes, the users of the services and the businesses in which the services were normally provided.

2.109   The conflicting marks (whether for goods or services) were compared and their similarity evaluated according to their "notional" use. They were presumed to be used according to the particulars of their registration and the effects of particular get-up, colouring, etc., were incidental; the test was of "normal and fair use". Nevertheless, if evidence could be brought of the actual manner of use, it would not be ignored and could help the opponents to establish potential or existing confusion or deception.

Section 5: relative grounds for refusal under the 1994 Act

2.110   Section 5 contains the rules for the comparison of marks applied for with earlier rights. These are not restricted to existing registered marks. Sub-sections 5 (1) to (3) refer to "earlier trade marks" and this phrase is defined in section 6 of the Act. Such marks include registered United Kingdom trade marks, international trade marks or Community trade marks, which benefit from earlier priority dates than the mark applied for (section 6(1) (a) and (b)). They also include pending applications for such marks, which would benefit from such an earlier priority date if accepted onto the relevant Register (section 6 (2)), and marks whose registrations have lapsed up to one year earlier, unless there was no use of such marks for the two years before expiry of the registration (section 6(3)).

2.111   Lastly, "earlier trade marks" also comprise unregistered trade marks which are well-known within the meaning of the Paris Convention and which are further defined in section 56 of the Act (on which see discussion in Chapter 4(6)). Briefly, such trade marks may be wholly unregistered in any relevant jurisdiction (otherwise, indeed, it is unlikely that reliance would have to be placed upon the fact of their being well-known) but can be protected here if their reputation extends to the United Kingdom, even if no goodwill as such exists here.

Section 5(1): identical marks/identical goods

2.112   This sub-section is quite straightforward, since it prevents the registration of a trade mark which is identical to an earlier trade mark on goods or services which are also identical to the specification of goods or services for which the earlier mark is "pro-tected".

2.113   Two potential areas for difficulty nevertheless arise, in theory at least. First, there may be some room for argument as to what is meant by "identical" in this context, where the marks do not consist simply of a word or, say, some initials. Where the marks in question consist of devices, for instance, it may not always be easy to say with certainty when the two are so close as to be identical, *for practical purposes*, which is presumably what the term means in this context. It seems probable that wholly minimal differences

---

[15] See n.8, above.

between two marks ought to be ignored, so as to avoid having to go on to bring in concepts of likelihood of confusion under sub-section(2).

2.114 Secondly, the use of the word "protected", whilst obviously necessary where some of the earlier marks in question might not be registered, leaves open the question of whether, in relation to registered marks at least, the phrase really means "the goods or services for which the earlier mark is registered" or whether it may mean that a wider specification of goods could be relied upon, for instance, if the mark had been used on some goods for which it was not registered. It is suggested that the latter construction of the sub-section may be unnecessary, since it would usually spill into a consideration of the same factors as under sub-section 5(2)(a). Moreover, in *British Sugar*[16], Jacob J. made it plain that the specification of goods for which registration has been made must be construed strictly, bearing in mind not simply the description of the goods, but also the Class in which they are registered, which indicates that a strict construction of the meaning of "identical" goods will be adopted.

Sub-section 5(2)(a): identical or similar marks/identical or similar goods

2.115 Under this sub-section, a mark will be refused registration if it is either:

(a) identical to an earlier trade mark and is to be used on similar or identical goods or services, or

(b) similar to the earlier trade mark and to be used on identical or similar goods or services,

as long as such identity/similarity results in there being a likelihood of confusion on the part of the public.

2.116 The sub-section therefore requires that there be a similarity between the marks *or* the goods. There is, however, no guidance in the Act as to what sort of similarity is required, save presumably, that it is to be such similarity as may lead to confusion on the part of the public. However, in *British Sugar*[17], in relation to the substantially similar wording of section 10(2)(a), Jacob J. held that the question of the similarity of the goods/services must be answered in the affirmative before the court would go on to consider whether there was *also* a likelihood of confusion. As for the criteria by which both similarity and confusion are to be judged, it seems that these will follow those under the equivalent sections of the 1938 Act[18], which applied in cases on conflicts between marks in the context of the registrability of marks as much as to cases of infringement.

2.117 Certainly, in *Wagamama*,[19] Laddie J. applied a number of old authorities in deciding whether there was such similarity between the marks as to lead to a possibility of

---

[16] [1996] R.P.C. 281 at 289.
[17] *ibid.* at 294.
[18] The similarity of approach was accepted in *Wagamama Limited v. City Centre Restaurants Plc* [1995] F.S.R. 713; *Origins Natural Resources Limited v. Origin Clothing Limited* [1995] F.S.R. 280, a decision under both the 1938 and the 1994 Acts, in which Jacob J. held that for the purposes of s. 10 of the 1994 Act the comparison of the marks would be, as under the old law, in notional fair use; and *British Sugar*. For the test of similarity between marks, see paragraphs 2.94–101 above, for the test for similarity of goods, see 2.102–109.
[19] *ibid.*, at 721.

confusion so as to amount to infringement. He held that under the 1938 Act "the confusion which was looked for was confusion as to source or origin of the goods" but added that:

> "It was enough that the similarity of the marks would make a customer believe that the alleged infringer's goods were associated with the proprietor's goods or services, for example that they were an extension of the range of goods made by the proprietor".

It was accepted by the parties in that case that such "classic" infringement would also be infringement within the meaning of section 10.

2.118   The facts were that the plaintiff owned the mark "Wagamama", registered in several Classes for a variety of goods and services connected with its restaurant business, and that the defendants had opened a restaurant initially under the name "Rajamama's" and later under the amended name "Raja Mama's". Laddie J. held (at trial) that there was an infringement due to confusion between the two:

> "That confusion is likely to take the form that some members of the public as a result of imperfect recollection will think the marks are the same while others will think that they are associated in the sense that one is an extension of the other ... or otherwise derived from the same source."[20]

2.119   These criteria apply to the consideration of confusing similarity under section 5 as much as to the same question in relation to infringement. Equally they apply to the question of what is confusing similarity between the marks and to the question of what are similar goods or services. With regard to the latter question it seems likely that the rules on "goods of the same description" applied under the 1938 Act will be applied now.[21] This approach was taken by Jacob J. in *British Sugar*,[22] who held that the courts should have in mind similar considerations to those used to define "goods of the same description", as each section was intended to offer a similar protection. He held that the factors to take into account were an elaboration of the old judicial test, namely:

> "(a) The respective uses of the respective goods or services;
> (b) The respective users of the respective goods or services;
> (c) The physical nature of the goods or acts of service;
> (d) The respective trade channels through which the goods or services reach the market;
> (e) In the case of self-serve consumer items, where in practice they are respectively found or likely to be found in supermarkets and in particular .... on the same or different shelves;
> (f) The extent to which the respective goods or services are competitive. This inquiry may take into account how those in the trade classify goods ...."

---

[20] *ibid.* at 733.
[21] Again, see paras. 2.102–2.109, above.
[22] See n.16, above at pp. 296–297.

Similarity causing confusion

2.120 Even if the necessary similarity of marks and/or goods or services is found to exist, registration will only be refused if it is considered that such similarity will cause confusion. In many cases, there will be no room for doubt that such would be the case. Indeed, although a similarity of marks may well not cause confusion if there is no similarity of goods ("Swan" for matches hardly clashing with "Swan" for soap, for example), it would seem very likely that the necessary similarity of *both* marks and goods would be likely to lead to confusion in many cases, and the exceptions would tend to depend upon special circumstances, such as honest concurrent use, itself provided for in section 7.

Likelihood of association

2.121 The likelihood of confusion referred to in sub-section 5(2) is described as *including* "the likelihood of association" with the mark. This is a concept about which there has been much discussion and which, it has been fairly generally accepted, stems from the Benelux Uniform trade mark law.[23] There it seems to encompass cases where the mark complained of merely "brings to mind" the more famous, established mark, but does *not* necessarily lead to the type of confusion usually recognised here, that is to say, the belief that the two marks are linked in some way, or have some common owner or source, or that the goods marked with the two marks are the same. Professor Gielen put the test thus:

> "there is a similarity between a mark and a sign when, taking into account the particular circumstances of the case, such as the distinctive power of the mark, the mark and the sign, ... show such a resemblance auditively, visually or conceptually that by this resemblance alone associations between the sign and the mark are evoked."[24]

His example was that there would be "association" if Nissan adopted the name "Tercel" for a new model of car, given that Toyota already has the model name "Tercel" as a mark. Oddly, of course, the goods in this example are the same, so that classical confusion would seem quite likely.

2.122 Yet it seems that under the Benelux law "association" has been found in cases of quite different goods, *e.g.* "Apple" for computers and advertising services, "Davidoff" for tobacco products and a bar.

2.123 Thus, it seems, under the Benelux law, merely conjuring up a recollection of the earlier mark would suffice for "association", as this, whilst not injuring the trade mark proprietor in the usual way, could lead to an injurious loss of exclusivity and dilution.[25]

2.124 However, in the *Wagamama* case,[26] Laddie J. carefully reviewed the question of whether the phrase "likelihood of association" in the 1994 Act was derived from Benelux

---

[23] See, *e.g.* the "Introduction" to the *Current Law Statutes* annotated version of the Act, Annand & Norman, *Blackstone's Guide to the Trade Marks Act 1994*, and Morcom's *A Guide to the Trade Marks Act 1994*.
[24] See the article by Professor Gielen [1992] E.I.P.R. 262 at 266.
[25] See the discussion of "dilution" or "erosion" of trade mark rights in paras. 5.42 *et seq.*
[26] *Wagamama Limited v. City Centre Restaurants Plc* [1995] F.S.R. 713 at 723–728.

law. It seems that the question was fully argued in the course of the trial, and that the learned judge had the benefit of seeing Professor Gielen in the witness box to give evidence as to the provisions of the Benelux law and to seek to justify his view that the draftsmen of the Directive did indeed intend to incorporate into it the wide protection offered by the Benelux law. The learned judge gave apparently comprehensive reasons for his decision and found that there was no compelling reason to think that the Directive *was* intended to ensure that the Benelux concept of "association" should be applied throughout the Community, but that on the contrary there were good reasons to doubt that this was the case. Nor did he feel compelled for reasons of "comity" to abide by decisions of the Benelux courts, which had apparently already applied the new Benelux law (amended so as to implement the Directive) as they would have applied the earlier law, when it seemed that they had simply assumed that their old rules still applied.[27]

2.125   In any event, it would seem that the wording of sub-section 5(2) clearly requires the words "the likelihood of association" to be construed as a sub-species of "confusion" (not the other way around, as was suggested in argument in *Wagamama*).[28]

2.126   It also seems that the German law implementing the Directive recognises two forms of confusion – direct (classical) confusion and indirect confusion " ... when the mistaken assumption relates to the existence of an organisational or economic link between the undertaking concerned, such as a licensing agreement ... .".[29] The author assumes that the latter is the German version of likelihood of association, which would, of course, be consistent with the construction put upon it in *Wagamama*.

2.127   It therefore seems that the "likelihood of association" is but a particular form of confusion, meaning that the public would be misled into thinking that the two marks, or the relevant goods or services, were in some way associated. This was precisely how Laddie J. construed it in *Wagamama*.[30] This type of "association" has frequently been the basis of the complaint made in passing off actions – the allegation is not that it would be thought that the goods or services were those of the plaintiff, but that the public would think that the plaintiff had licensed the use of his mark on the defendant's goods. In such cases, it is usually said that the overall similarity of the goods or services (and, of course, sub-section 5(2) only applies where there is such similarity) would lead to a belief that the plaintiff had expanded in some way, that is that he had branched out into the defendant's "field of activity" or had licensed the use of his mark upon similar but not identical goods.

2.128   It is submitted that such a form of "association" is indeed a sort of confusion and so would be covered by this sub-section, and *Wagamama* supports this view. Indeed, in *Wagamama* the case was also based upon passing off, and Laddie J. held that there was indeed the necessary misrepresentation as the evidence showed that members of the

---

[27] *ibid.*, at 728. See Professor Gielen's riposte on one of the points (relating to the use of statements in Council meeting minutes) rejected by Laddie J. in [1996] 1 E.I.P.R. 82.

[28] Indeed, Professor Gielen accepts this also in his original article [1992] E.I.P.R. 262 at 267.

[29] See ECJ judgment in Case C-317/91, *Deutsche Renault AG v. Audi AG*: [1993] I E.C.R. 6227; [1995] 1 C.M.L.R. 461, para. 36.

[30] [1995] F.S.R. 713 at 730.

public had been confused into thinking that the parties' restaurants were connected or associated in some way.

2.129 Taking the facts of two reported passing off cases may help further to illustrate the problem of infringement by association. First, in the *"Miss Alternative World"*[31] case, the proprietors of the "Miss World" contest failed in a passing off action against the makers of a transvestite burlesque film entitled "Miss Alternative World", as it was found that no-one seeing the film would think that it had anything to do with the plaintiff's business, or would even buy tickets to see it on that basis. There was, in other words, no confusion of the type necessary to amount to an actionable misrepresentation. However, probably the implicit reference would have amounted to "association" in terms simply of causing the public to think of the plaintiff's business when seeing the film or reference to it. In the light of *Wagamama*, this sort of use of a mark would still not be problematic under sub-section 5(2) or actionable under sub-section 10(2), as there was found to be no likelihood of confusion on the part of the public.

2.130 The *"Miss Alternative World"* case can be contrasted to the case of *Insert Media*[32], in which the proprietors of various newspapers complained about the insertion by newsagents of the defendant's advertising material into their newspapers. Mummery J. considered that the first question that he had to answer in order to decide if these acts constituted passing off was:

> "Do the proposed activities of the ... Defendant involve the making of a mis-representation, either express or implied? e.g. that the advertising material of his clients inserted into the publications of the plaintiffs without their consent is connected or associated with the plaintiffs."[33]

The learned judge found such a misrepresentation. The confusion or association arose from the representation that "the insert was made as a result of some arrangement or collaboration with the plaintiffs".[34] In the Court of Appeal, the matter was again put in terms of "association" between the defendant's products and the plaintiffs': " ... it is of the essence of the Defendant's business plan *to associate the insert* made into the newspapers *with the paper* into which it is inserted, so as to give it the seal of approval ... of appearing in a national publication of high standard" [emphasis added],[35] which association would amount to a misrepresentation of a connection between the parties. It is submitted that were such facts to form the basis of infringement proceedings under sub-section 10(2), the action would probably succeed, since the court would find the particular type of confusion being caused to be a likelihood of association.

2.131 However, if Laddie J. was wrong in *Wagamama* and the analysis above is wrong, so that there can be "association" without "confusion", then this would extend the previous

---

[31] *Miss World (Jersey) Limited v. James St Productions Limited* [1981] F.S.R. 309.
[32] *Associated Newspapers Plc v. Insert Media Limited* [1990] 1 W.L.R. 900 (Mummery J.) and [1991] F.S.R. 380, C.A.
[33] *ibid.* at 908D.
[34] *ibid.*, at 912A.
[35] *ibid.*, *per* Sir Nicholas Browne-Wilkinson V.-C. [1991] F.S.R. 380 at 387.

law of passing off as well as the law on infringement of registered marks, and cases such as those in the Benelux courts may succeed here. This may be a matter which will be decided in the future by further decisions of the English courts or the European Court of Justice, until then it is suggested that the approach adopted in *Wagamama* is very persuasive and should be followed here. So far as the author is aware, *Wagamama* is not the subject of an appeal.

Sub-section 5(3): dissimilar goods, but damage to the mark

2.132   This is a new form of protection, which covers cases of identical or similar marks, where despite a *lack* of identity or similarity of the goods/services, there may (without due cause) be some unfair advantage taken of the earlier trade mark, or some damage done to its "distinctive character or repute". The earlier mark can only be so protected to the extent that it has a reputation in the United Kingdom. The sub-section is based upon Articles 4(3) and 4(4)(a) of the Directive and is, again, apparently in turn based upon the Benelux Uniform Trade Mark Law, with its protection for marks from harmful "association".[36]

2.133   This sub-section brings in a rather new form of protection for registered marks, which previously could have been offered (if at all) only under section 11 or by a passing off action.[37] The proprietor of the earlier mark can, if he has a reputation in the mark in the United Kingdom (or in the E.U., if it is a Community mark) object to the use of the mark on dissimilar goods. Such cases were occasionally found under section 11 of the 1938 Act, where there was some potential for dangerous confusion.[38]

2.134   The protection offered by sub-section 5(3) at first glance seems to be somewhat wider than the previous application of section 11 of the 1938 Act. It is noticeable that the sub-section does not specify that there must be confusion, of any kind, before it will apply. Instead, what seems to be relevant is whether the use of the later mark would take an unfair advantage of, or be detrimental to, the distinctive character or repute of the earlier trade mark. The sub-section may thus appear to put into statutory form the kind of protection against dilution of a trade mark which has been recognised, relatively recently only in the United Kingdom, in cases such as *Taittinger v. Allbev*.[39] However, even that case depended upon an element of confusion being present, and in *BASF Plc v. CEP (UK) Plc*,[40] Knox J., when dealing with the parallel terms of section 10(3),[41] found that " ... neither the distinctive character nor the repute of the mark is adversely affected when there is no risk of relevant confusion." He based that decision upon the view that, were it otherwise, it would in effect be possible to claim that any use of the earlier mark in relation

---

[36] See discussion at paras. 2.121–2.128, above.
[37] Or possibly by the special regime offered by "defensive registration" under s. 27 of the 1938 Act. See App. A, para. A35.
[38] See, *e.g. Player's Trade Mark* [1965] R.P.C. 363 where the registration of "Players" for chocolate cigarettes was prevented and "*Jardex*" (1946) 63 R.P.C. 19 a conflict between disinfectant and meat extract of similar names, facts which are somewhat reminiscent of the Benelux case of *Claeryn/Klarein* (mark for gin infringed by mark for detergent which sounded the same).
[39] [1993] F.S.R. 641, C.A. and see Chap. 5(9), below.
[40] October 26, 1995, (1996) I.P.D. 19030.
[41] On which see Chap. 4, para. 4.65.

to any class of goods at all, when sold to consumers of the goods sold under the earlier mark, would necessarily be detrimental to that mark, so that "much of the effect of having classes of goods in relation to the registration of trade marks would disappear." It therefore seems that despite the lack of reference to confusion in the sub-section, it will be necessary to find some kind of confusion in order to make sense of the rest of its terms. Knox J.'s judgment seems likely to restrict the scope of section 5(3) considerably.

2.135 The sub-section applies only where the proprietor of the earlier mark has a reputation in the United Kingdom. The Act does not define what is meant by a reputation in this context, and in particular it is not clear whether the proprietor of the earlier mark would have to show that he would have been in a position (in terms of having the necessary goodwill) to bring a passing off action against the mark applied for. On the whole, the use of the word "reputation", rather than "goodwill", would seem to indicate that a lower standard will be required than in the case of a passing off action, and it may well be that the proprietor of the earlier mark will not even need to have traded in the United Kingdom under the earlier mark, if he is able to show that the earlier mark nonetheless has some sort of reputation here. On the other hand, the wording of the sub-section should perhaps be contrasted with that of section 56 (which protects "well-known" trade marks),[42] which specifically provides that goodwill is *not* a prerequisite to protection.

2.136 The extent of the reputation required to base such a claim upon a Community trade mark is even less clear, since the requirement is that the Community trade mark should have a reputation in the European Community. It is not made clear whether this means the whole of the European Community (which certainly seems doubtful) or just some part of it, and if it is only in a part of the Community, it is not clear whether that part must include the United Kingdom. Taking this analysis to its logical conclusion, registration of a mark might be denied here by reason of the reputation of a Community trade mark which has never been used in the United Kingdom and which has no reputation here. It will be interesting to see if the courts do indeed interpret this part of this sub-section in this way. It seems unlikely.

2.137 It is also a matter of conjecture at present as to what is meant by the provision in the sub-section that objection can be raised only when the use of the later mark would take the unfair advantage, etc., "without due cause". This phrase is not explained and it is perhaps a little difficult to know what kind of circumstances would be seen as giving "due cause" to use a mark which could take *unfair* advantage of or be detrimental to an earlier trade mark. One situation in which "due cause" might be successfully raised by the applicant might be that he had made prior use of his mark which had not caused confusion, but this would seem to be covered already by the provisions of section 7 as to honest concurrent use. The only example which occurs to the author and which is not directly covered by any other provision in the Act, is that "due cause" might be shown by the mark applied for being the name of the applicant, thus providing some equivalence to section 11(2), that is the defence to infringement actions based on honest use of one's own name.[43]

---

[42] See Chap. 4, para. 4.87 *et seq.*
[43] See Chap. 4 paras., 4.102–4.106, below.

Here, the proprietor of the later mark might well not be using the name "without due cause", but on the other hand, it is hard to see how genuinely honest use of one's own name could be deemed to be taking *unfair* advantage of the earlier mark in any event.

Sub-section 5(4): protection of non-trade mark rights

2.138   This sub-section is like section 11 of the 1938 Act in protecting non-trade mark rights against the registration of new trade marks which may cause them difficulties. However, the provision is not of identical effect to section 11.[44] First, reference is made to the protection of unregistered trade marks or signs provided by any rule of law, and in particular the law of passing off. This reflects Article 4(4)(b) of the Directive. It would seem to require a rather higher standard of proof of the reputation, etc., of the earlier unregistered mark or sign than would have been required under section 11 of the 1938 Act, since under section 11 it was *not* necessary to show that the opponent's mark could have been successfully protected by a passing off action.[45]

2.139   Sub-section 5(4)(b) protects rights which pre-date the trade mark for which application is sought and which are not in themselves rights in the nature of a trade mark, such as the rights conferred by copyright, design right or registered designs.[46] Section 5(4)(b) seems most likely to apply to device marks or other pictorial marks which infringe copyright, or marks consisting of shapes or packaging which may infringe copyright, and/ or design right or a registered design. However, conceivably the sub-section could also apply to a mark consisting of music, as long as the piece of music concerned was protected by copyright as an original musical work.

2.140   There was no directly equivalent provision to section 5(4)(b) under the 1938 Act but it was possible to object the registration of trade marks which were alleged to infringe copyright under section 11 of the 1938 Act. See for example *Oscar trade mark*.[47]

2.141   Alternatively, under section 17 of the 1938 Act, an objection might have been made to the registration of a trade mark which infringed another earlier right upon the basis that the applicant was not the true proprietor of the mark.[48] There is no direct equivalent of section 17 of the 1938 in the 1994 Act, the nearest provision probably being section 3(6): registrations made in bad faith.[49]

---

[44] On which see above.

[45] See *Bali Trade Mark* [1969] R.P.C. 472, H.L., where it was held that in order to establish that a mark offended against section 11 it was necessary only to show a likelihood of deception or confusion, and not necessary to show a real and substantial likelihood of success in a passing off action. The reason behind this was that section 11 was intended to protect the public rather than just the proprietor of the unregistered mark: see Lord Upjohn at 495.

[46] On each of these subjects see *Copinger & Skone James on Copyright*, (13th ed. 1991).

[47] [1979] R.P.C. 173 and see para. 2.92, above.

[48] This provided that an application for a trade mark could only be made by "any person claiming to be the proprietor of a trade mark used or proposed to be used by him . . . " on which see *Al Bassam trade mark* [1995] R.P.C. 511.

[49] See paras. 2.85–2.89, above.

Section 5(5): consent of the proprietor of an earlier mark

2.142 This provision simply permits the proprietor of any earlier trade mark or earlier right (that is to say the rights protected by sub-section 5(4)), to consent to the registration of a mark which would otherwise offend against any of the other sub-sections of section 5.

2.143 This is another instance of the difference in the approach taken by the old and the new law, in that this Act looks to the proprietor of earlier rights to make the commercial judgments as to the necessity of protecting his rights against later registered trade marks, whereas under the old law such a decision would have lain in the hands of the Registrar, regardless of the view taken by the proprietor of the earlier right.

Section 7: honest concurrent use

2.144 Section 7 of the 1994 Act brings into play the concept of honest concurrent use developed in relation to section 12(2) of the 1938 Act. The provision was introduced into the 1994 Act at a late stage during the Bill's passage through Parliament, and there are arguments that its provisions are not consistent with the Directive or the Community Trade Mark Regulation.[50] Section 7 applies to cases where an applicant satisfies the Registrar that there has been honest concurrent use of the trade mark for which he seeks registration, despite conflict with an earlier trade mark or earlier right which would otherwise disentitle him to registration pursuant to sub-sections 5(1) to (4) inclusive. Sub-section 7(3) makes it plain that such "honest concurrent use" is indeed such honest concurrent use as would have satisfied the requirements of section 12(2) of the 1938 Act.

Honest concurrent use under the 1938 Act

2.145 Section 12(2) gave a power to the Registrar or court to register confusingly similar marks for the same goods or same description of goods where justified by special circumstances. The most important of these special circumstances was "honest concurrent use". This doctrine had its roots in the common law of trade marks developed before Trade Marks Registration Act 1875. The expansion of trade and improvements in communications in the nineteenth century meant that goods produced independently under similar marks, which once had been sold in separate areas without coming into conflict, could be offered for sale side by side, with potential for confusion adverse to one or both traders. Adjustments necessarily had to be made to accommodate both the proprietors' interests and the public interest.

2.146 The doctrine of honest concurrent use entitled each proprietor to register and to continue to use his respective mark, as long as each had been properly acquired and the deception which subsequently had arisen was not the result of any blameworthy act on the part of the proprietors. The application of the doctrine resulted in parallel use of the

---

[50] See the interesting arguments in Annand and Norman, *Blackstone's Guide to the Trade Marks Act 1994*, pp. 110–111.

confusing marks being possible, neither proprietor being able to restrain the other's use, although both were entitled to prevent infringements by a third party.

2.147 There was some suggestion in the older case-law that honest concurrent use could only be successfully demonstrated where the registered mark had actually been in use alongside the concurrent mark for some time,[51] this meant, quite illogically, that the proprietor of a trade mark which had never actually been used had a better chance of resisting the registration of another mark whose proprietor wished to rely upon honest concurrent use than one whose mark had been used. This approach was disapproved, quite rightly it is suggested, by Jacob J. in *Origins Natural Resources Limited v. Origin Clothing Limited*.[52]

2.148 Under section 12(2) the Registrar was required to examine not only the parties' own interests but also the public interest. Where undue confusion was likely to occur, special circumstances might be needed to justify parallel registration.[53] The applicant, not the opponent, had to justify his reliance upon section 12(2) by giving evidence of the honesty of his concurrent use and the substantiality of that use. The Registrar or, on appeal, the court had an unfettered discretion whether or not to permit registration.

2.149 The most important qualification for the use of section 12(2) was that the use of the mark should have been honest, even where there was a likelihood of confusion. In *Buler*[54] it was held that the honesty of the applicant for registration outweighed the question of the likelihood of confusion, so that, given the other circumstances, it would be just to register the mark. This did not preclude registration where the opposing mark was known to exist when the second mark was chosen, but did prevent dishonest, piratical or speculative use of a mark.[55] Generally, the mark had to have been used for some period of time before honest concurrent user would be accepted, partly perhaps so that the true effects of the concurrent use could be properly assessed; the Registry normally required several years concurrent use but special circumstances might justify a shorter period. It was a question of fact in each case, and modern marketing and advertising techniques may have rendered some of the older authorities unreliable.[56]

2.150 As for the relationship between sections 11 and 12(2), it was confirmed by the House of Lords in *GE*[57] that a mark could be allowed to remain on the Register where it was initially validly registered and where a confusing or deceptive situation had arisen through no fault of the proprietor. These elements are comparable with the criteria found in the application of section 12(2) in cases of honest concurrent user.

---

[51] See *L'Amy trade mark* [1983] R.P.C. 137.
[52] [1995] F.S.R. 280.
[53] It seems that the existence or registration of two other marks of a similar kind did not amount to such special circumstances: see *e.g. "Terbuline"* [1990] R.P.C. 21.
[54] *Buler trade mark* [1975] R.P.C. 275.
[55] *Pirie's Application* (1933) 50 R.P.C. 147; see also *J.R. Parkinson & Co's Application ("Carmen")* (1946) 63 R.P.C. 171.
[56] In *Buler* above, three and a half years use was sufficient; in *Granada* [1979] R.P.C. 303 only two years 10 months sufficed.
[57] [1973] R.P.C. 297.

Honest concurrent use under the 1994 Act

2.151 However, it is a little difficult to see quite how the principles developed under section 12(2) of the 1938 Act will be capable of being directly applied to all of the relative grounds of refusal in sub-sections 5(1) to (4) of the 1994 Act, since, for instance, section 12(2) *only* applied where the goods concerned were identical or of the same description, whilst sub-section 5(3) applies where the parties' respective goods are not similar. Equally, it is hard to see how the 1938 Act doctrine of honest concurrent user, which applied only to registered trade marks, could be deemed to apply to the other types of earlier right which are described in sub-section 5(4) of the 1994 Act.

2.152 It may, therefore, sometimes be a difficult matter to satisfy the Registrar that the old doctrine of honest concurrent use applies in the context of an application under the 1994 Act, where the relative grounds of refusal are not grounds which would have arisen under section 12 of the 1938 Act. Apart from this difficulty, however, there is at least a helpful body of case law as to the meaning and extent of honest concurrent use.

2.153 A further uncertainty may arise, as it is not clear quite how the honest concurrent use doctrine will be brought into effect in relation to the 1994 Act. The first stage at which it may be applied is clear enough, since sub-section 7(2) provides that where the Registrar is satisfied that honest concurrent use has been made of the mark for which registration is sought, he shall not refuse the application by reason of the earlier conflicting trade mark or other right. This would seem to mean, as a matter of practice, that the Registrar would accept the application for advertisement. However, such acceptance would be (as always) liable to be the subject of opposition proceedings by the owner of the earlier trade mark or other right. Presumably, therefore, the matter would go off to a hearing in the normal way before the Registrar, when he would re-consider the question of whether to allow the registration to go ahead, in the light of the evidence lodged on the opposition proceedings.[58]

2.154 Unfortunately, section 7 does not specify what is to occur in the event of such an opposition proceeding. In other words, it is not clear from section 7 itself whether the Registrar must seek to follow the usual rules set out in section 5, or whether he has some greater discretion because of the provisions of section 7. To this extent, it may be right to say that sub-section 7(2) is indeed ambiguous, such that it may be right to look to the explanation given of the section in Parliament. Just such an explanation was given by Lord Strathclyde, the promoter of the Bill in the House of Lords, when he indicated that if on such an opposition it seemed to the Registrar that the marks and the goods were identical, then the registration would have to be refused under section 5(1), but where the marks or the goods were only similar, the Registrar would have to assess the likelihood of confusion in the light of the honest concurrent use which had been made.[59] This explanation seems to indicate that the criteria to be applied by the Registrar in hearing such opposition proceedings would be no different from those where there was no plea of honest concurrent use. If this is the proper construction of section 7, then it would seem to be

---

[58] See Chap. 3(4), below.
[59] See *Hansard*, H.L., vol. 553, col. 71 (March 14, 1994) *per* Lord Strathclyde.

consistent, at least, with Article 4(1)(a) of the Directive and it may well be that, for this reason alone, this is the proper construction of the section.

2.155 Sub-section 7(4) makes it plain that section 7 does not affect the absolute grounds for refusal of registration mentioned in section 3 of the Act. Nor does it affect the rights of any person to apply for a declaration of invalidity of a trade mark registration. Presumably, on such an application under section 47(2), similar considerations would apply to those mentioned by Lord Strathclyde (see above).

2.156 Section 7 will cease to have effect at all when and if an Order is made by the Secretary of State under section 8 of the 1994 Act (see below).

Section 8: future changes: objections to be raised by opponents, not by the Registry

2.157 This provision looks to the future. It permits the Secretary of State to make an Order which would have the effect of removing the Trade Mark Registrar's powers to object to the registration of trade marks upon the relative grounds for refusal set out in section 5. In other words, the Registry's job in relation to the assessment of applications would only be to satisfy itself that the trade mark for which registration was sought met the absolute grounds of section 3. Relative grounds of refusal would be matters to be raised by the proprietors of the relevant earlier rights.

2.158 This important potential change in English law would bring the United Kingdom into line with other European trade mark systems, in which Trade Mark Registries have a much reduced role, and in which the control over conflicting marks is left very much in the hands of the proprietors of earlier marks. However, there are certainly grounds for believing that it is the vigilance of the Registry in relation to earlier rights which gives the current United Kingdom system so much strength and the marks registered under it much of their value.

2.159 In any event, section 8 may not be brought into effect until 10 years after the day upon which applications for Community trade marks may first be filed under the Regulation.

Transitional provisions

2.160 Paragraphs 10 and 11 of Schedule 3 of the 1994 Act deal with the position of applications for registration made prior to the entry into force of the Act but not completed before October 31, 1994. Such applications fall into two groups. Those which were advertised under section 18 of the 1938 Act before the commencement of the 1994 Act are, according to paragraph 10(1) of Schedule 3, to be dealt with under the old law. They would then be dealt with as if they were existing registrations under the 1938 Act, and would thereafter be treated as trade marks registered under the 1994 Act, pursuant to paragraph 2 of Schedule 3. Trade mark applications made under the old Act which had not been advertised prior to October 31, 1994 were given the option of continuing with the application under the 1938 Act or changing it to a 1994 Act application, but such option had to be exercised within six months of October 31, 1994 under paragraph 11(2) of Schedule 3.

CHAPTER 3

PRACTICE AND PROCEDURE IN THE TRADE MARKS REGISTRY

(1) APPLYING TO REGISTER A TRADE MARK

3.1 Under section 66 of the 1994 Act, the Registrar may require the use of such forms as he may decide in relation to all proceedings in the Registry. Rule 3 of the Trade Marks Rules 1994 provides first, that such forms shall be published in the Trade Marks Journal and secondly, that it is sufficient either to use a replica of any such form or a form which is otherwise acceptable to the Registrar containing the information required by the form as published.

3.2   Section 79 of the Act similarly provides that rules may be made as to the payment of fees for trade mark registration procedures; the current scale of fees is set out in the Trade Marks (Fees) Rules 1994.[1] Rule 4(2) of the Trade Marks Rules 1994 provides that the appropriate fee must be paid at the time of filing any form if the filing is to be effective.

3.3   Otherwise, Rules 60 to 64 of the Trade Marks Rules 1994 make general provisions for correction of irregularities of procedure, calculation of times, alteration of time limits and filing of documents. Rule 65 provides for the publication of the Trade Marks Journal, pursuant to section 81 of the Act, in which all changes to the Register are to be published.

3.4   Officials at the Registry are generally extremely helpful to those making personal inquiries or seeking to apply for a mark. In particular, it is possible on payment of a modest fee to make a personal search of the Register with their expert help, which may be helpful in choosing a mark or establishing what prior rights may be likely to pose a problem. However, there is much to be said, when pursuing an application, for utilising the services of a trade mark agent, whose practical experiences of the daily workings of the Registry are unparalleled.

(2) THE APPLICATION

3.5   Section 32 of the Act controls applications for registration of a mark. The application is to be made to the Registrar and must be accompanied by the appropriate application fee. Rule 5 provides that the application must be filed on Form TM3, which is a self-explanatory document in many respects, leaving space for the details required by section 32(2), such as the name and address of the applicant, the goods or services in relation to which the registration is sought and a representation of the trade mark. On this last point, please see the comments made in Chapter 2 above as to the necessity of being able to represent the mark graphically. Note (h) on Form TM3 provides "a representation of the mark should be provided in section 2. A trade mark must be capable of being represented graphically if it is not a word or a picture. This means you may need to give a clear description of the mark in section 2." The note goes on to explain that the representation of the mark must be no larger than 8 cm square. The form can be used for a multiplicity of marks (that is to say, a series of marks) or for registration of the same mark for a variety of different goods and services, even if they are in different Classes.

3.6   The form simply requires that the Classes (see below) be listed in consecutive numerical order, with a description of the relevant goods or services appropriate to each such Class alongside its number.

3.7   Towards the end of the Form is a sort of certificate to be signed by the applicant stating "the Trade Mark is being used by the applicant or with his or her consent, in

---

[1] S.I. 1994 No. 2584.

relation to the goods or services stated, or there is a bona fide intention that it will be so used." This statement repeats the wording of section 32(3) which requires this bona fide intention to use. Presumably, for such an intention to be bona fide, it must be a genuine intention to make commercial use of the mark, rather than an intention of using the mark in some defensive manner.[2] It is thought that if it can be shown that the application was not made with this bona fide intention, the application might be deemed to have been made in bad faith, contrary to section 3(6) of the Act.

3.8   An application may be made by a sole proprietor or by a number of co-proprietors.[3] Alternatively, a registration made in the name of one person may subsequently be transferred into multiple names.[4] Where there is co-ownership of a registered mark, each co-proprietor may exploit the mark and do all acts which would otherwise be infringements, without the consent of his co-proprietor(s).[5] Eventually, this could clearly lead to confusion (see comments on section 46, below). However, by sub-section 23(4), all co-proprietors must act together to licence or assign or mortgage the mark. By sub-section 23(5), one co-proprietor may issue infringement proceedings by himself, but must join his co-proprietor(s) to proceed with the action beyond an interlocutory stage.

A series of trade marks

3.9   Under section 14(1) there is provision for the registration of a series of trade marks. A series is defined in sub-section 41(2) as meaning "a number of trade marks which resemble each other as to their material particulars and differ only as to matters of a non-distinctive character not substantially affecting the identity of the trade mark". The advantage of this form of application is to avoid the expense of making a number of individual applications.

Classification of goods

3.10   For many years, the Register has been divided into a number of different Classes of goods. This requirement is now contained in section 34 of the Act. The current Classification is to be found in Schedule 4 to the 1994 Rules. At the time of writing, there are 34 Classes of goods and eight for services, and the Classes are periodically revised following the international classification agreed by WIPO.[6] Section 65 of the Act makes provision for the rules to empower the Registrar to do whatever is necessary to implement any amended classification of goods or services and, in particular to amend existing entries on the Register. That section is echoed in Rule 40, which, together with Rule 41, provides a sort of opposition procedure in relation to proposed re-classification.

---

[2] Thus, for example, the registration of the "Nerit" mark would be refused on this basis, as under the 1938 Act: see [1982] F.S.R. 72 and para. 2.87
[3] See ss. 23 and 27.
[4] This would simply come within the usual rules on assignments, see discussion of s. 24, in Chap. 7, below.
[5] s. 23(3).
[6] A revision of the classes for service marks is now being undertaken, so that the "Miscellaneous" Class 42 may be expanded into a number of more specific classes. See [1995] E.I.P.R. D/268.

3.11 Rule 8 provides that one application may cover a number of different Classes, which should be set out in consecutive numerical order, and list under each Class the relevant goods or services. If the applicant makes a mistake as to the classification of his goods or services, he may by Rule 8(3) request that the application be amended by filing Form TM3A. The decision as to whether or not any particular goods or services fall into a particular Class is a decision to be taken by the Registrar and by sub-section 34(2) his decision on this is final.

3.12 A quick glance at the classification will show that goods or services which are not "of the same description" may well fall within the same Class, whilst goods or services which could be "of the same description" may well come within more than one Class. This imposes a necessity of vigilance in the choice of Class and specification of goods or services and, indeed, in preliminary searches carried out before making one's application to ensure that all relevant Classes are researched. The choice of Class in which to register, or indeed the decision whether to register in a number of Classes may well eventually affect the value of the mark, since it is easier to prove infringement if the goods upon which the alleged infringing mark is being used are identical to the goods covered by the registration, and a registration which is limited to one Class is not deemed to cover goods which are listed separately in another Class.[7]

Date of filing

3.13 A number of different sections in the Act refer to the "date of application for registration". Sub-section 33(2) defines that date as the date of filing of the application, and sub-section 33(1) makes it plain that if the application is not wholly satisfactory at the outset, and further documents are required to be furnished by the applicant to the Registry, the date of filing will be the date upon which the last of the necessary documents is delivered. By Rule 11, the Registrar is to send notice to the applicant if the application does not fulfil the formal requirements of sections 32(2), (3) or (4) or Rules 5 or 8(2), so that any deficiencies can be put right, failing which the application is to be treated as abandoned. It is obviously sensible to attempt to get the application right in the first place, where a conflict with other marks may make the date of filing of importance.

3.14 The Act also makes provision for applications by proprietors of foreign trade marks to gain priority, for the purposes of registering the same trade mark for some or all of the same goods or services in the United Kingdom, for a period of six months from the date of filing of the first application abroad in a Convention country or other countries to which the same rights may be extended by Order in Council pursuant to section 36 of the Act. Rule 6 of the 1994 Rules provides that where priority is claimed under sections 35 or 36, particulars of the claim must be included in the application, and there is an appropriate space to be filled in Form TM3 to this effect. A certificate from the country from which priority is claimed verifying the foreign application is required to be filed within three months of the filing of the United Kingdom application under Rule 6(2).

---

[7] See Jacob J. in *British Sugar* [1996] R.P.C. 281 and his reference to *GE trade mark* [1969] R.P.C. 418.

(3) OFFICIAL EXAMINATION OF THE APPLICATION

3.15   Under section 37 of the Act the Registrar is to examine whether the application for registration of a mark satisfies the requirements of the Act and the Rules. In other words, he is to examine it with a view to ensuring that it complies with section 1(1), with the absolute grounds for refusal of section 3 and he is to carry out a search of earlier trade marks to ensure that there are no relative grounds for refusal pursuant to section 5.[8]

3.16   If the Registrar is concerned that the requirements for registration are not met, he is to inform the applicant of his concerns and give him an opportunity either to make representations or to amend the application. Presumably, such representations might concern the extent to which the mark had acquired distinctiveness in use or as to the effect of any consents to registration obtained from a proprietor of any earlier trade mark. It is worthy of note that Form TM3 does not provide space for details to be given of any use relied upon nor of any such consents.

3.17   If the objections of the Registrar cannot be dealt with in this way, the applicant may have no choice but to amend the application. Unfortunately, the extent of any amendment which may be allowed is limited by section 39. This provides, on the one hand, that the applicant may at any time restrict the goods or services to be covered by the application but, on the other, provides that in other respects the application may only be amended by correcting the name or address of the applicant, errors of wording or of copying, or obvious mistakes and then subject to the proviso that such amendments may be allowed "only where the correction does not substantially affect the identity of the trade mark or extend the goods or services covered by the application." It seems that the deliberate intention behind this section is that applications which are unacceptable for any reason other than having too wide a specification of goods or services should be rejected, rather than amended, with the applicant having to start over again and suffer the potential disadvantages of a later filing date.[9] Amendments to be made pursuant to sub-section 39(2) must be made on Form TM21 by Rule 17.

3.18   Sub-sections 37(4) and (5) indicate the restriction intended to be placed upon the discretionary powers of the Registrar under the new Act. Under sub-section 37(4) the Registrar *shall* refuse to accept an application which he considers does not meet the requirements of the Act, and under sub-section 37(5) he *shall* accept an application which does meet those requirements. Obviously, some residual discretion is left to the Registrar in deciding whether the requirements of the Act are met, but subject to that power, his discretion is somewhat limited by these sub-sections.

(4) PUBLICATION, OPPOSITION PROCEEDINGS AND OBSERVATIONS

3.19   When the Registrar has decided to accept an application he will publish it in the Trade Marks Journal.[10]

---

[8] On each of these sections please see Chap. 2, above.
[9] See the comments at para. 4.09 of the White Paper on the reform of trade mark law Cm. 2103.
[10] s. 38(1) and Rule 12.

3.20   Anyone who objects to the proposed registration of the mark can make his objections known to the Registrar in one of two ways.

Opposition

3.21   First, as was the case under the 1938 Act, an objector may give notice to the Registrar of opposition to the registration, see sub-section 38(2). Rule 13 provides the procedure for the opposition, which is essentially a hearing in the Registry (in the first instance) in which the Registrar weighs up evidence filed by the opponent and by the applicant in order to decide whether the application may proceed to registration. As was the case under the 1938 Act, doubtless the largest number of oppositions will be brought by the proprietors of earlier trade marks, registered or unregistered, or of other prior rights, who might be entitled to raise objections under section 5 of the Act, but whose rights may not have been apparent to the Registrar upon his examination of the application. This is not to say that opposition proceedings may not be brought by the proprietors of earlier registered marks whose registrations would have been taken into consideration by the Registrar, but who may feel more threatened by the mark applied for than the Registrar would have anticipated, perhaps because of the manner in which their mark is actually being used. However, opponents are not limited to owners of such earlier rights, and any person who feels sufficiently interested could theoretically oppose the application. Realistically, however, only those who have a vested interest to protect are likely to wish to go through the lengthy procedure set out in Rule 13.

3.22   First of all, the opponent must send in Form TM7 within three months of the date of publication of the application, including within that Form a statement of grounds of opposition. That is sent to the applicant who then has three months to file a counter-statement on Form TM8. The counter-statement is then sent to the opponent, who must then within a further three month period file evidence by way of statutory declaration or affidavit, if his opposition is not to be deemed to have been abandoned.[11] If the opponent files evidence, the applicant has three months in which to file his own evidence. Finally, the opponent has a further three months to file evidence in reply.

3.23   Once the evidence is, finally, complete, the matter proceeds to a hearing in front of the Registrar or, in effect, one of his hearing officers. Rules 48 to 56 deal with proceedings, evidence, etc., in hearings before the Registrar. Those proceedings are of a judicial nature. By Rule 52, the Registrar has all the powers in relation to the examination of witnesses on oath and to require discovery and production of documents of an Official Referee of the Supreme Court. He may also make an award of costs as well as make an order for security for costs to be provided by any party.[12]

3.24   The Registrar is to give his decision in writing. Rule 56 deals with this requirement in relation to all proceedings, and Rule 14(1) makes the specific requirement that the result of the opposition proceedings be given in writing.

---

[11] See the wording of Rule 13(4) which gives the Registrar a discretion to decide that the opposition shall not be deemed abandoned, although no indication is given as to the circumstances in which such a direction might be given.

[12] See Rules 52, 54, 55 and ss. 68 and 69 of the Act.

3.25 Such decisions of the Registrar are subject to appeal to the High Court or to the "appointed person".[13]

3.26 It may be seen from the lengthy procedure contemplated by Rule 13, that opposition proceedings are really only viable for a party who has a commercial interest in opposing the registration of a conflicting mark.

Observations

3.27 Section 38(3) provides a new procedure whereby interested parties who would like to oppose a proposed registration, but who, for one reason or another, do not wish to or are not in a position to pursue opposition proceedings, can "make observations in writing to the Registrar as to whether the trade mark should be registered".

3.28 It is not known how the Registrar will deal with such observations, other than to comply with his obligation under sub-section 38(3) to inform the applicant of those observations. However, it would seem reasonable to presume that where those observations raise matters which are new to the Registrar, and which lead him to think that the trade mark is not registrable, perhaps because of the existence of an earlier right of which he was unaware, then he may refuse to register the trade mark, pursuant to the caveat to sub-section 40(1). Otherwise, where no notice of opposition is received within the three month period from publication of the application, or the opposition proceedings are withdrawn or decided in favour of the applicant, the Registrar shall register the trade mark.

(5) REGISTRATION, DURATION, RENEWAL AND RESTORATION

3.29 When the application is accepted, the Registrar will publish the registration in the Trade Marks Journal and the registration will be complete, subject only to the payment of the appropriate fee. Sub-section 40(3) provides that the registration shall be "as of" the date of the complete filing of the application for registration.

3.30 The initial period of registration is for 10 years from the date of registration and the registration may be renewed indefinitely for further 10 year periods. (Equivalent periods under the 1938 Act were seven years, followed by subsequent periods of 14 years. There are transitional provisions in paragraph 15 of Schedule 3 of the Act in relation to the renewal of existing trade marks.) Under Rule 27, the Registrar is obliged to send the proprietor of the mark notice of an approaching expiry date not earlier than six months nor later than one month before the expiry of the 10 year period. The proprietor then must make a request for renewal of the registration and pay the renewal fee before the registration expires.[14] By Rule 28, if the fee is duly paid, the renewal runs with immediate effect from the expiry of the previous registration.

3.31 However, if the renewal fee is not paid by the date of the expiry of the registration, the Registrar is to publish that fact. If within six months from the expiry date he receives

[13] See para. 3.74, below.
[14] By subs. 43(3).

a request for renewal and payment of the appropriate fees, he will renew the registration. If no request for renewal is filed, however, the Registrar will remove the mark from the Register (see Rule 29(1) and (2)).

3.32   If a mark is removed from the Register pursuant to these Rules for non-payment of renewal fees, it is not necessarily lost forever. On the contrary, under section 43(5) and Rule 30, if the Registrar receives a request for restoration filed on Form TM13 within six months of the date of removal of the mark, and the appropriate fees, he may restore the mark to the Register and renew the registration, if he is satisfied that it is just to do so in the light of the circumstances of the case. The Rule does not specify how the proprietor is to satisfy the Registrar that the circumstances are such that the restoration should be permitted. Strangely, perhaps, Form TM13 does not make provision for a statement as to the circumstances in which the registration was allowed to lapse, nor is there any indication in the Rule itself as to how this is to be done. This will no doubt be a matter for the internal practice of the Registry.

(6) DISCLAIMERS, ALTERATION OR SURRENDER OF REGISTRATION

3.33   Under the 1938 Act the Registrar was able to impose, as a condition of registration, a requirement that a registration be made subject to a disclaimer. Such disclaimers may now only be made voluntarily under section 13 of the 1994 Act, where the applicant considers that this will aid him in achieving registration of his application. Rule 24 applies for such disclaimers and also for similar disclaimers or limitations, geographical or otherwise, to be voluntarily placed upon a mark by its proprietor. Any such disclaimer or limitation is to be published.

3.34   Once a mark has been registered, the opportunity to alter it is absolutely minimal. Under section 44 of the Act, the only alteration permitted is as to the name and address of the proprietor, if this is part of the mark itself. Rule 25 provides the procedure for such alterations, including publication of the proposal and an opposition procedure for interested parties.

Correction of the Register

3.35   Under section 64 anyone who has a sufficient interest in a mark may apply for the rectification of an error or omission in the Register. Rectification in terms of this section does not mean what it meant under the 1938 Act, where the term was used in relation to the complete revocation of an entry of an invalid mark. Here, sub-section 64(1) makes it plain that this type of application for rectification "may not be made in respect of a matter affecting the validity of the registration of a trade mark". Those sorts of applications are dealt with by sections 46 and 47, discussed below. Section 64, therefore, probably has a somewhat limited ambit and is designed really to keep the Register up to date and accurate.

3.36   The wording of Rule 38, which provides for changes pursuant to section 64(4) provides for changes in names or addresses. Sub-section 64(5) also permits the Registrar to remove any out-dated material from the Register. Rule 39 makes it plain that this is a discretionary power, and that the Registrar has a further discretion, where appropriate, to publish his intention to remove that material from the Register and to send notice of his intention to any one who he thinks might be affected by the removal. Rule 39(2) provides a form of opposition procedure to such amendments to the Register.

Surrender

3.37 The proprietor of a registered mark may surrender the registered trade mark by sending the appropriate notice to the Registrar; if he surrenders the mark in relation to all the goods and services for which it is registered, he uses Form TM22; if he surrenders it only in relation to certain goods and services, he uses Form TM23. No surrender will be effective unless the proprietor has given the name and address of anyone having "a registered interest in the mark" and certifies that that person has been given three months notice of the proposed surrender. Persons having such a registered interest presumably include licensees or mortgagees of the mark.[15]

(7) REVOCATION AND INVALIDITY

3.38 All of the previous parts of this Chapter have dealt with applications by the proprietor of a mark to register a mark, whether opposed or not, and with the maintenance of that mark on the Register by the proprietor. The Act also provides procedures for third parties to seek to remove marks from the Register on a variety of grounds. Obviously, these sections are of great importance to a person who wishes to make use of a mark which is identical or similar to a registered mark so that the marks might conflict. These sections may be used by the proprietors of earlier rights, who had failed to oppose the registration of the mark in the first place, or proprietors of later marks who wish to clear a conflicting earlier mark from the Register, with a view to use and/or register the mark themselves. It was not uncommon, whilst the 1938 Act was in force, for defendants to infringement proceedings to counterclaim for rectification (that is to say, in the terms of the 1994 Act, to seek revocation) of the plaintiff's mark. No doubt, defendants to infringement proceedings under the 1994 Act will also seek to counterclaim for revocation of the plaintiff's registration or for a declaration of the invalidity of that registration.[16]

Section 46: revocation of registration

3.39 Sub-section 46(1) gives a variety of grounds upon which the registration of a trade mark may be revoked. These grounds will be applicable to all trade marks, including "existing registered marks", that is to say, marks registered pursuant to the 1938 Act.[17]

3.40 Section 46 is intended to give effect to Articles 10 and 12 of the Directive. However, it may be said that sub-section 46(1) gives a discretion to revoke a registration, rather than imposes an obligation to revoke the registration, on any of the grounds set out in the sub-section, thus reflecting the position under the 1938 Act rather than the exact wording used

---

[15] See the definition of "registrable transaction" in s. 25 of the Act.
[16] See paras. 4.87–4.89 in Chap. 4, below and see *Second Sight Limited v. Novell U.K. Limited* [1995] R.P.C. 423.
[17] See para. 17 of Sched. 3.

in the Directive. On the other hand, where there is a clear case made out for revocation, for example for non-use, then the discretion would probably only relate in reality to weighing up the reasons given for the non-use, and if these were not found to be "proper reasons" within the meaning of the section, revocation would almost undoubtedly follow.

Non-use

3.41   Sub-sections 46(1)(a) and (b) make provision for revocation of a registration which has not been used for five years. Sub-section 46(1)(a) covers the position where the mark has not been used in the five year period following registration, and 46(1)(b) covers situations where use of the mark has been "suspended" for an uninterrupted period of five years at any later stage. To some extent, these sub-sections reflect the position under section 26 of the 1938 Act. However, under that section, it was possible to attack a mark for non-use at any time, upon the basis that it had been registered without a bona fide intention to use it. This meant that it was possible to attack a registration which had been on the Register for under five years. This is clearly not possible under the provisions of section 46(1)(a). The alternative route would appear to be to seek a declaration of invalidity of such a mark pursuant to section 47 of the 1994 Act on the grounds that, if the proprietor lacked the bona fide intention to use the mark on the goods or services concerned at the time of registration, his application to register had been made in bad faith in breach of sub-section 3(6). Realistically, an opponent of a registration may well find himself in considerable difficulty in making such an allegation in the usual run of cases. There are of course exceptional circumstances in which such an allegation might be made and might succeed, for instance, where the registered mark was registered with a view to stopping somebody else from using it, or with a view to protecting another, unregistrable mark.[18]

3.42   The relevant period of five years for sub-section 46(1)(a) is five years from the date of completion of the registration procedure, rather than from the date of filing of the application for registration. The question then arises as to whether genuine use has been made of the mark in that period. Under the 1938 Act, the phrase used was "bona fide use" but it may be that there is no change in meaning in the 1994 Act, so that what will need to be established is that some genuine commercial use has been made of the mark. Bona fide use under the 1938 Act did not need to be very extensive, as long as it was genuine, and could even consist of acts which could only be described as preparatory to launching goods under the mark onto the market. Thus in *Hermes trade mark*[19] mere preparatory acts were sufficient to prevent the application of section 26, as the respondents were found to have been taking positive steps to acquire goods to be marketed under the mark and in *Bon Matin trade mark*,[20] similarly, very slight use of the mark, which was found to be of a genuine and commercial nature, sufficed to protect it from rectification.

---

[18] See cases discussed in reference to subs. 3(6) at paras. 2.85–2.89 of Chap. 2, above.
[19] [1982] R.P.C. 425.
[20] [1989] R.P.C. 537.

3.43   Sub-section 46(2) provides that the use made of the trade mark need not be use of the mark exactly as registered, as long as the use is "in a form differing in elements which do not alter the distinctive character of the mark".

3.44   In any event, it is for the proprietor to show what use, if any, has been made of the mark, pursuant to section 100.

3.45   Sub-section 46(3) deals with the position where a period of five years non-use has elapsed, but use of the mark recommences prior to the application for revocation being made. Essentially, the resumption of use in this way will save the mark from revocation, as long as that use is itself genuine. This appears from the proviso to sub-section 46(3), which states that any commencement or resumption of use after the five years of non-use but within the period of three months before the application for revocation is made, is to be disregarded unless preparations for the commencement or resumption began at a time when the proprietor was unaware that the application for revocation might be made. This proviso is clearly designed to prevent a proprietor from being able to preserve his mark by hastily making preparations to use the mark, once he knows that an application for revocation may be made, merely to defeat that application. In any event, it would seem that, with or without the proviso, a court would be unlikely to find that any such use made after notice had been given of an application for revocation was genuine, so as to save the mark.

3.46   Sub-section 46(2) is similar to section 30(1) of the 1938 Act[21] and, if similarly construed, would seem to show that the requirement that the distinctive character of the mark should not be altered by the change in the mark from its form as registered will not entitle a proprietor to rely upon use of an unregistrable mark to protect the unused registered mark.

3.47   The second limb of sub-section 46(2) also had roots in the 1938 Act.[22] It is a straightforward provision ensuring that a mark which has been used in the United Kingdom only in the sense of being fixed here to goods (or the packaging of goods) intended solely for export, nonetheless is deemed to have been used within the United Kingdom.

3.48   An application for revocation may be made either to the Registrar, or to the court, and indeed must be made to the court where proceedings concerning the trade mark are already before the court.[23] Where the application is made to the Registrar, the procedure is governed by Rule 31. This makes detailed provisions for an exchange of statement and counter-statement, and then of evidence, as in the case of opposition proceedings under Rule 13. There is also provision for intervention in the proceedings by other interested parties (see Rule 31(5)). Rules 48 to 56 also apply to section 46 proceedings.

3.49   The effect of an application for revocation may vary according to the circumstances of the case. For instance, under sub-section 46(5), revocation may relate only to certain of

---

[21] See, *e.g. Huggars trade mark* [1979] F.S.R. 310 and *Neutrogena* [1996] R.P.C. 473 at 488–9

[22] s. 31.

[23] Again, please see the discussion of the use of s. 46 as a defence to a trade mark infringement action, in paras. 4.87–4.89 of Chap. 4, below.

the goods or services for which the trade mark is registered, where, perhaps, use has been made of the mark upon some goods covered by the registration but not others.

3.50   Under sub-section 46(6), the court or Registrar is also given powers to decide what is the appropriate date from which the rights of the proprietor shall be deemed to have ceased in relation to the mark. The usual rule would be that the cessation of his rights would date only from the date of the application for revocation, but by section 46(6)(b) the Registrar or court is given a discretion to order that the revocation be back-dated to any appropriate date.

3.51   Revocation pursuant to section 46(1)(a) or (b) can in any event be avoided if the proprietor is able to show that there were "proper reasons" for his non-use of the mark. This term is not defined, although some guidance may be found in decisions on section 26(3) of the 1938 Act, which had a similar provision based upon "special circumstances in the trade", such as an import ban.[24]

3.52   Finally, sub-sections 46(1)(a) and (b) also make it plain that the use which has been made by the proprietor need not have been use made personally by him, but will be sufficient if made by a licensee or another with his consent.

Genericism

3.53   Sub-section 46(1)(c) provides a rather different reason for revoking the registration of a trade mark. A mark may be revoked where it has become the common name for a product or service for which it is registered, and where the fact that it has become the common name is due to the acts or inactivity of the proprietor of the mark.[25]

3.54   Under sub-section 46(1) it is plain that only where the proprietor is in some way to blame for the loss of distinctiveness of the mark will revocation follow. The proprietor must, therefore, ensure that he does not make the mistake of using the mark as the name of the goods himself and does not permit others to use the mark in that way. This can be difficult where the mark is applied to an innovative product of some sort, such as "Shredded Wheat", "Aspirin", or "Escalator", all of which were originally trade marks but lost their distinctiveness by becoming the generic name of the goods.

Misleading marks

3.55   Lastly, under section 46(1)(d), a registration may be revoked if the mark has become liable "to mislead the public, particularly as to the nature, quality or geographical origin of his goods or services". Again, this provision bears a resemblance to section 32 of the 1938 Act by which a mark could be removed from the Register if it had become deceptive since registration by reason of some "blameworthy act" of the proprietor.[26] In

---

[24] See *Manus* (1949) 66 R.P.C. 71.
[25] To some extent this provision replaces s. 15 of the 1938 Act, although that section provided that a mark would become invalid where it became the generic name of the goods, regardless of the proprietor's responsibility for that change in the use of the name.
[26] See, *e.g. GE* [1973] R.P.C. 297.

this sub-section also, it is clear that the registration will not be revoked unless the misleading nature of the mark arises as a consequence of use made of the mark by the proprietor with his consent. It would seem that the question of whether the mark is liable to mislead the public, especially in the ways mentioned in the sub-section, would be considered in the light of similar considerations to those which would be applied under sub-section 3(3)(b) at the stage of application being made for registration.[27]

3.56 It also seems possible that revocation might be ordered under this sub-section where a proprietor had granted such widespread licenses of his mark, without imposing or maintaining any controls at all as to the nature or quality of the goods or services in relation to which the mark was to be used, that the mark had become misleading. It is worth noting that the wording of sub-sections 46(1)(c) and (d) is significantly different, in that generic marks can be removed by reason of the *acts* or *inactivity* of the proprietor but misleading marks can only be removed by reason of the *use* made of the mark by the proprietor or with his consent. Thus, for instance, inactivity in terms of failure to take action against persistent infringers would not be caught by sub-section (d).[28]

Invalidity of registration

3.57 Under section 47 of the Act, the registration of the mark may be declared invalid on the basis that the mark should not have been registered at all, either upon the grounds set out in section 3 or upon the grounds set out in section 5. There is no requirement in the section that the application for such a declaration should be made by a person having any particular sort of interest, although doubtless such applications as are made on the basis of earlier trade marks, or the other earlier rights referred to in section 5, will be made by the owners of or other persons interested in those rights. The oddity of the section is that whilst there may be a declaration of invalidity made, there does not appear to be any direct consequence upon the trade mark registration in terms of an order that the mark be removed from the Register.

3.58 Sub-section 47(1) is the provision dealing particularly with registrations made in breach of section 3. There is no point in reiterating here the terms of section 3, and the reader is asked to refer back to Chapter 2(7) above.

3.59 However, there are a few points which do need to be made specifically in relation to section 47(1). First, the wording of the section is such as to make it plain that, again, the decision as to whether to grant a declaration of invalidity is one which lies within the discretion of the tribunal. It has been suggested that this is not consistent with the provisions of the Directive which section 47 is intended to implement.[29] Secondly, the second part of sub-section 47(1) makes the sensible provision that where a mark was not distinctive when registered, but has become distinctive since registration in relation to the relevant goods or services, it shall not be declared invalid. This provision, therefore, is in

---

[27] See Chap. 2(5), above.
[28] See the Australian case of *New South Wales Dairy Corporation v. Murray Goulburn Co-Operative Co.* [1991] R.P.C. 144 at 162.
[29] See the notes to the *Current Law Statutes* edition of the Act pointing to the difference between the wording of s. 47 and of Art. 3(1) of the Directive.

many ways to be equated to the proviso to sub-section 3(1). Equally, the same test will apply as to the extent of distinctiveness required to satisfy the proviso; if *British Sugar*[30] is to be followed, a very high level of distinctiveness will be required.

3.60   Finally, it may be seen that section 47(1) does not appear to cover the position of a mark which was distinctive at the time of registration, but has become descriptive or misleading since registration. The only remedies for such a situation would appear to be found in sub-section 46(1)(c) or (d), and the limitations of those provisions have been discussed above.

3.61   Sub-section 47(2) makes similar provision in relation to marks which should not have been registered on the basis that they clashed with rights protected by section 5. Again, there is a similar point as to the discretionary nature of the remedy, given the wording of Article 4(1) of the Directive. The sub-section does not specify the time at which the conflict of marks or other rights falls to be assessed; it could be the date of the application for registration of the mark which is challenged, the date of completion of the registration, or, possibly, the date of application for the declaration. The second of these dates seems to be most compelling, as the Registrar ought to have been able to assess the situation as at the date of registration at least.

3.62   Sub-section 47(2) provides specifically that no declaration of invalidity shall be made where the owner of the relevant earlier mark or right has consented to the proprietor's registration of his mark. Most declarations of invalidity would presumably be sought by an owner of an earlier right, but this provision may have some limited effect in preventing, for example, a licensee of an earlier registered mark from seeking a declaration of invalidity, where his licensor had consented to its registration.

3.63   Sub-section 47(3), like sub-section 46(4) provides that the declaration may be sought either from the Registrar or the court, save where proceedings are already pending in relation to the trade mark in court, when the application must be made to the court. Sub-section 47(4) provides that the Registrar himself may apply to the court for a declaration of invalidity where the registration was achieved in bad faith.

3.64   Like sub-section 46(5), the declaration of invalidity may affect certain of the goods or services for which the mark is registered but not others. Under sub-section 47(6) where a declaration of invalidity is made, the registration, logically, is to be deemed never to have been made. However, past transactions are not to be affected by such a declaration.

3.65   Finally, it must be mentioned that where the later mark being attacked was registered on the grounds of honest concurrent user pursuant to section 7 (or presumably section 12(2) of the 1938 Act), this will provide no defence to an application for a declaration of invalidity under section 47(2).

3.66   The 1994 Act applies in relation to marks registered prior to October 1, 1994 as if the 1994 Act had been in force at all material times, except that no objection to the validity

---

[30]   [1996] R.P.C. 281 and see discussion in Chap. 2, paras. 2.71–2.72.

of such an existing registration may be taken on the grounds specified in sub-section 5(3), as such grounds were not grounds for objection under the 1938 Act.[31]

Section 60: marks registered by an agent

3.67 Where an agent or representative applies for registration of a mark which is owned by another, and that other is the owner of the mark in another Paris Convention country, the proprietor may oppose the application. If the application is granted without opposition by the proprietor, then the proprietor may subsequently apply for a declaration of invalidity of registration or apply to have his name substituted as proprietor of the registered mark. He may also restrain by injunction any use of the mark in the United Kingdom which is not authorised by him. By sub-section 60(6), any application for a declaration of invalidity or for rectification must be made within three years of the proprietor becoming aware of the registration, and similarly he will not be entitled to an injunction if he has acquiesced for three years or more in the agent's use of the mark. This section implements Article 6*septies* of the Paris Convention.

(8) ACQUIESCENCE

3.68 Section 48 provides a statutory "defence" of acquiescence which implements Article 9 of the Directive. This form of statutory acquiescence presumably will co-exist with the usual equitable type of acquiescence which is described in the section on defences to infringement in Chapter 4(7) below.

3.69 Section 48(1) provides that where the proprietor of an earlier trade mark or any other earlier right (presumably as defined by section 5(4)), has acquiesced in the *use* of a registered trade mark in the United Kingdom for a continuous period of five years, that proprietor shall not be entitled either to apply for a declaration that the registration of a later mark is invalid or to oppose the use of that later mark on the goods or services upon which it has been used.

3.70 The possibility of raising this defence of acquiescence will not, therefore, arise until the later mark has been registered for at least five years and will not arise then unless it has also been used for five years. Moreover, the proprietor of the earlier mark or right must have been aware of that use for a continuous period of five years, otherwise he could not be said to have acquiesced in it.

3.71 Once the conditions of use/acquiescence have been established, then the proprietor of the earlier mark or right effectively loses his rights to remove the later trade mark from the Register or to oppose its use. Presumably, the wording of (b) is intended to prevent proceedings being taken against the use of the later trade mark. It is noteworthy that this provision affects not only registered and unregistered trade marks, but other intellectual property rights such as copyright, design rights and registered designs. The only saving for the proprietors of such rights who have acquiesced in this way for this period will be if they

---

[31] See para. 18 of Sched. 3.

are able to show that the registration of the later trade mark was applied for in bad faith.[32]

3.72   On the other hand, sub-section 48(2) also provides that where there has been a period of five years' use of the later trade mark in which the proprietor of the earlier right has acquiesced, the proprietor of the *later* mark is not entitled to oppose the use of the earlier mark either, on the basis of his trade mark registration.

3.73   Proprietors of all such earlier marks and rights therefore need to be vigilant in the protection of their rights if they are not to fall foul of section 48. It is not clear what steps, short of proceedings for a declaration of invalidity or infringement, would be sufficient to show that there had been no acquiescence within the meaning of this section. It is possible that there will be cases in which damaging confusion is caused by the later registered mark, but the proprietor of the earlier right is not in a position to bring infringement or revocation proceedings. It remains to be seen whether he can protect his position by correspondence indicating that he does not acquiesce in the use of the later mark.

(9) APPEALS

3.74   Section 76 of the Act deals generally with appeals from decisions of the Registrar, including appeals against decisions involving an exercise of his discretion. The appeal may be brought to the High Court or to the "appointed person", who is usually a specialist Queen's Counsel appointed by the Lord Chancellor pursuant to section 77 of the Act. By sub-section 76(3) where the appeal is made to the appointed person he may refer it to the court if there is a point of general legal importance involved or if the parties or Registrar so request. This possibility of referring the matter straight to the court is important since there is no appeal from a decision of the appointed person (see sub-section 76(4)).

3.75   The procedure for appeals to the High Court is set out in Order 100 of the Rules of the Supreme Court. The procedure for an appeal to the appointed person is set out in Rules 57 to 59, which do not need further comment here, save to say that the provisions of Rule 48(2) as to giving notice of a hearing date and Rules 49 to 55 as to evidence, hearings, the appointed person's powers, and costs apply to appeals to the appointed person as they do to hearings before the Registrar.

(10) COLLECTIVE AND CERTIFICATION MARKS

3.76   A collective mark is a mark used to identify the goods or services of the members of an association which will be the proprietor of the mark. The members of the association must use the collective mark in accordance with regulations which must be filed with the Registrar. Such members who are authorised users of the collective mark obtain rights similar to those of a licensee of an ordinary mark in respect of bringing infringement proceedings.

3.77   The basic provision for collective marks is found in section 49 of the Act, with all the details as to registration, invalidity, etc., found in Schedule 1 of the Act.

---

[32]   On this point, please see the discussion of s. 3(6) in Chap. 2(7), above.

3.78 Such marks are new to English law and may consist of all types of signs, including signs indicating the geographical origin of the goods or services upon which they are to be used, as long as this does not prevent the use of such signs in accordance with honest practices in industrial or commercial matters.[33]

3.79 Otherwise, the provisions of Schedule 1 as to registrability reflect those of the main body of the Act. Sections 46 and 47 apply to collective marks, with some additional grounds for revocation to be found in paragraphs 13 and 14 of Schedule 1. There is no particular alteration of the rules on infringement, except for a specific rule relating to the right of an authorised user of the collective mark to bring proceedings in his own name, which is dealt with by paragraph 12 of Schedule 1.

3.80 It remains to be seen how attractive collective marks may be in the United Kingdom. The advantage which they have over certification marks is that their use may be restricted to members of the association which is the proprietor of the mark, whereas certification marks can be used by any person who satisfies the conditions of use of the mark.

3.81 Certification marks are dealt with by section 50 of the Act and Schedule 2. A certification mark is defined as "a mark indicating that the goods or services in connection with which it is used are certified by the proprietor . . . in respect of origin, material, mode of manufacture of goods or performance of services, quality, accuracy or other characteristics". It is not entirely clear how this provision is designed to apply in the light of the absolute grounds for refusal of registration which are set out in section 3(1) of the Act. The only specific point covered by Schedule 2 is in relation to marks indicating geographic origin.[34]

3.82 Certification marks have existed under English law for many years; examples are "Woolmark", the "Kite" mark of the British Standards Institute, and "Stilton". As in the case of collective marks, regulations as to the use of the mark must be filed with the Registrar and approved by him before the application can go ahead. The applicant for the mark cannot be someone carrying on a business involving supply of goods or services of the kind certified, but must, therefore, presumably be some sort of regulatory body or association.

3.83 Certification marks are, unlike any others, not intended to have any functions indicating the origin of goods, but only indications of their geographic origin, quality or other characteristics, etc. Under the 1938 Act, the public interest element in certification marks was reflected in the requirement that the mark should be available to any trader who was able to comply with the Regulations governing its use. It is thought that this requirement will be continued under the 1994 Act, although this is not reflected in the Rules published to date.

---

[33] See para. 3 of Sched. 1.
[34] See para. 3.

(11) COMMUNITY TRADE MARK REGULATION

3.84 As described in Chapters 1 and 7, the territorial limitations of trade marks have long posed a problem in the context of the objectives of the European Union.

3.85 These difficulties led, on the one hand, to the numerous decisions on the enforce-ability of trade mark rights and dealings in trade mark rights which are discussed in Chapters 1 and 7. On the other hand, they have led to attempts to control the effects of national intellectual property laws by regulatory and harmonising legislation.

3.86 In particular, it was seen that there was a need for a unified trade mark system to overcome the hindrances to free trade and free circulation caused by the presence of separate national trade marks systems within the Community. The various Community institutions have taken their own steps to seek to mitigate the effects of the national restrictions of trade mark rights, however where no unjustified restriction on trade is being caused by the use of a trade mark right, but its essential function is merely being properly protected, and where there is no anti-competitive agreement splitting the market, then the restrictions inherent in national trade mark rights could not prevent them from having such effects.

3.87 The decision was therefore taken that it would be wise to provide for such rights to be granted upon a Community basis for all of the Community's territory. Work on the creation of a Community Trade Mark ("CTM") began as early as 1959 but it was not until 1976 that a detailed draft was produced in the form of the "Memorandum on Creation of an EEC Trade Mark",[35] which is the basis of the current Regulation. Subsequently, it was decided to accompany the Community trade mark with harmonisation of national trade mark laws and, many years of negotiation and drafting later, the harmonisation Directive was adopted on December 21, 1988. The Community Trade Mark Regulation 40/94 was adopted on December 20, 1993. The essential aim of the Regulation is set out in its third recital:

> "Whereas the barrier of territoriality of the rights conferred on proprietors of trade marks by the laws of the Member States cannot be removed by approximation of laws; whereas in order to open up unrestricted economic activity in the whole of the common market for the benefit of undertakings, trade marks need to be created which are governed by a uniform Community law directly applicable in all Member States."

And by the fifth recital:

> "Whereas the Community law relating to trade marks nevertheless does not replace the laws of the Member State on trade marks; whereas it would not in fact appear to be justified to require undertakings to apply for registration of their trade marks as Community trade marks; whereas national trade marks continue to be necessary for those undertakings which do not want protection of their trade marks at Community level;"

[35] Published in the *Bulletin of the European Communities*, Supplement 8/76.

3.88   In other words, the aim of the Regulation is to provide a single, unified trade mark which may be applied for and take effect throughout the Community, but such marks are to co-exist with national trade marks, since it is accepted that not every proprietor would wish to own or be able to achieve registration of a Community trade mark.

3.89   The Regulation provides a very comprehensive code, covering, in brief, a definition of what may be registered as a CTM or a collective CTM, a definition of the rights conferred by registration, comprehensive provisions as to the processing of applications and subsequent alteration, renewal, etc., of registrations, the control of dealings in CTMs, invalidity proceedings of various kinds, appeals (including appeals to the European Court of Justice), provision for various proceedings to be heard in national courts nominated for that purpose, and a host of rules relating to the establishment and organisation of the Community Trade Mark Office ("CTMO", also known as the Office for the Harmonisation of the Internal Market (Trade marks and Designs), or "OHIM"). The Implementing Regulation was adopted on December 13, 1995.[36]

3.90   It is impossible in a work of this size to deal with the Regulation in detail but the bulk of the rules relating to applications for CTMs will be found in the Implementing Regulation itself. The major provisions of the Regulation (as implemented) may be summarised as follows[37]:

  (a)   The nature of a CTM is set out in Article 1(2). It is to have "a unitary character. It shall have equal effect throughout the Community; it shall not be registered, transferred or surrendered or be the subject of a decision revoking the rights of the proprietor or declaring it invalid, nor shall its use be prohibited, save in respect of the whole Community."

      This provision shows both the strength and weaknesses of the Regulation. On the one hand, it may be attractive to large enterprises to have trade marks which are valid throughout the Community and to be able to apply for those marks in one place alone. On the other hand, such marks would be useless to very many small or medium-sized enterprises whose base of operations is geographically limited. Such enterprises are unlikely to wish to have to go to the trouble of finding a trade mark which is registrable throughout the Community, since it will be seen that a CTM cannot be registered where a prior conflicting right exists in just one of the Member States.

      Similarly, proprietors may be wary of choosing a CTM due to the danger that invalidity in one member state only will cause loss of the mark throughout the Community.

      Another potential weakness of the CTM system is that it is, apparently, anticipated that there will be a very large proportion of opposed applications in the CTMO and this will render the process of registration slow and expensive. Unless there is a genuine need for a Community wide registration, the proprietor may

---

[36] Regulation 2868/95: [1995] O.J.L.303/1.
[37] A more detailed discussion of the Community trade mark may be found at Chap. 14 of Annand & Norman, *Blackstone's Guide to the Trade Mark Act 1994*.

consider it easier, quicker and cheaper to pursue however many national registrations he really needs.

(b) Article 4 of the Regulation defines the signs which may be registered as a CTM and this definition is almost identical to that of Article 2 of the Directive and seemingly the same in substance to section 1(1) of the 1994 Act. Article 6 provides that a CTM may be obtained only by registration. Rules 1–5 of the Implementing Regulation set out the details, both of the mark and of the applicant, which must be specified in the application for registration. Rules 6-8 deal with claims to priority.

(c) Articles 7 and 8 set out the grounds upon which registration of a CTM may be refused. Article 7 sets out absolute grounds for refusal which are substantially the same as those found in Article 3 of the Directive and section 3 of the 1994 Act,[38] and Article 8 of the Regulation sets out relative grounds for refusal which are very similar to the grounds in Article 4 of the Regulation and section 5 of the 1994 Act.

However, there is one difference in relation to the rights protected by sub-section 5(4) of the Act. The nearest provision is Article 8(4) whereby a CTM may be opposed by the proprietor of "a non-registered trade mark or of another sign used in the course of trade of more than mere local significance ... to the extent that ... that sign confers on its proprietor the right to prohibit the use of the subsequent trade mark." This begs the question of what will be the meaning given to the phrase "mere local significance" but otherwise would appear to cover unregistered trade marks, protectable in the United Kingdom by a passing off action. There is no equivalent to the protection granted to copyright and other such rights by sub-section 5(4) of the 1994 Act.

One more important difference between the provisions of the Regulation and the 1994 Act lies in the effect of discovering that there is a conflicting prior right. Whereas the 1994 Act, at present,[39] provides that where the Registrar finds a conflict of this kind he shall refuse the registration of the mark, under the Regulation the rights of the proprietor of the earlier mark can only be protected on opposition being brought by him against the registration, or alternatively by bringing invalidity proceedings under Article 52 after the CTM has been registered.

Owners of prior rights may be in some difficulty in knowing that they have to oppose an application, unless they are vigilant in scrutinising the CTM bulletin, since it seems that the only such proprietors who would be informed of the pending application are the proprietors of earlier CTMs (see Article 39(6)).[40] Proprietors of other prior rights which may give a basis for opposition will have to watch the CTM bulletin so as to bring opposition proceedings in time. Where the opportunity for opposition is missed, or does not apply, such as in the case of prior copyrights or other industrial property rights, the proprietor will have to seek instead a declaration of invalidity of the CTM under Article 52, after it has been registered.

---

[38] See Rule 11 of the Implementing Regulation.
[39] See the potential for alteration of the system in s. 8 of the Act.
[40] Although the *applicant* for the CTM would be advised of all the prior rights, whether national registered marks or prior CTMs, under the search procedure set by Art. 39 of the Regulation.

Opposition procedures are set out in Rules 15–22 of the Implementing Regulation.

(d) Article 9 describes the rights conferred by a CTM, which are very similar to the rights conferred by Article 5 of the Directive and section 9 of the Act. These rights are subject to Article 12 which provides similar defences to those of section 11 of the 1994 Act. Article 13 of the Regulation also provides for the exhaustion of CTMs in terms similar to section 12 of the 1994 Act. The question of what amounts to infringement of the CTM is to be governed by the national law of the country where the infringement occurs (by Article 14) and Title X of the Regulation provides for infringement actions to be heard in the appropriate national courts, with Article 93 in particular specifying the appropriate jurisdiction for a CTM infringement action.

(e) Dealings in CTMs are covered by Articles 16 to 22. A CTM must be assigned in its entirety but may be licensed for some or all of the goods or services for which is registered and for the whole or just part of the Community. The adoption of the exhaustion theory in Article 13 is designed to prevent any division of the territory between licensees creating artificial barriers to trade.

(f) Article 25 deals with the filing of applications for a CTM which may be made either at the CTMO which is at Alicante in Spain, or at a national trade mark office. The U.K. Registry charges a £15 handling fee for dealing with such applications, but the application fees as such must be remitted (in ECUs) directly to Alicante. The CTMO will use 5 working languages: English, French, German, Italian and Spanish. Articles 26 to 45 deal with procedures for registration. Article 40 provides for publication of an application which has been accepted by the CTMO[41] and Article 42 provides for opposition on any of the grounds set out in Article 8. Article 41 also provides for the filing of observations by third parties, as under section 38 of the 1994 Act.

(g) CTMs will be registered for a period of 10 years and may be renewed for further 10 year periods (see Articles 46 and 47). CTMs may be surrendered (Article 49) or may be revoked for non-use or other reasons similar to those set out in section 46 of the 1994 Act (by Article 50).[42] Alternatively, the CTM may be declared invalid under Article 51, on the basis that the CTM was registered in breach of Articles 5 or 7 or because the registration was made in bad faith. Article 52 sets out the basis upon which a CTM may be declared invalid by reason of a clash with a variety of earlier rights, whether registered or unregistered trade marks or other rights. Article 53 provides a similar provision to section 48 of the 1994 Act in relation to acquiescence.

(h) Title VII of the Regulation deals with appeals, there is an internal Board of Appeal and actions may then be taken to the European Court of Justice.[43]

(i) Title VIII provides for registration of Community collective marks, similar to national collective marks but Community wide.[44]

---

[41] See Rule 12.
[42] See Rules 29–41.
[43] See Rules 48–51.
[44] See Rules 42–43.

(j) The Regulation contains very comprehensive provisions as to the creation and organisation of the CTMO which, as stated above, is in Alicante in Spain.

3.91 The CTMO is now open; application forms may be obtained through the U.K. Registry and may be submitted directly to the CTMO in Alicante or via the Registry in the United Kingdom. It remains to be seen how attractive such marks will be and this may well depend in part upon the scale of fees which may be charged as well as upon the rapidity of the procedures adopted pursuant to the Regulation. The basic cost for an application in up to three classes is ECU 975; further classes above three will cost ECU 200 per class; the registration then costs ECU 1100 and a renewal, ECU 2500. At the time of writing an ECU is worth about 80 pence, so that the basic fee for registration would be around £1,660, and for a renewal, £2,000. By way of comparison, a trade mark application in the United Kingdom currently costs £225, plus £125 for each class over one. Depending upon the cost of registration in the chosen Member States, therefore, the CTM might be expensive for a few but good value for more states. In any event, the greater test of the CTM system will doubtless be whether the attraction of having a unitary mark throughout the Community outweighs the potential disadvantages of that unitary mark being destroyed in its entirety by invalidity in one Member State alone.

3.92 One aspect of the system which has caused a certain amount of apprehension is the provision for infringement actions to be heard before the national courts of Member States. Except in the most blatant cases of infringement, the courts will naturally have to determine whether or not there is a conflicting similarity between the two marks, and difficulty may well arise as national definitions of this concept differ. For instance, in the recent *Deutsche Renault* case in the ECJ[45] it was pointed out that whereas in Germany there was a clash between the marks "Quattro" and "Quadra", the same marks co-existed upon the U.K. Register. Linguistic differences between Member States may also have an effect upon the result of such a case. As a result, it is feared that there may well be some "forum shopping" to the extent that the rules allow this.

(12) INTERNATIONAL CONVENTIONS

3.93 The difficulties and expense of obtaining a trade mark registration in the United Kingdom are mirrored to a greater or lesser extent in many other countries. Where a number of national registrations need to be pursued, delays, procedural hurdles and multiplying costs, quite apart from barriers of language, may present a formidable obstacle to an enterprise seeking to extend the protection of its trade mark beyond the frontiers of its state of origin. In order to facilitate international trade, a series of international conventions have been concluded, which are intended to simplify the acquisition of intellectual property rights by foreign nationals.

The Paris Convention for the Protection of Industrial Property (Paris Union)

3.94 The Paris Union of 1883 constituted the first attempt to overcome the real obstacles placed in the way of foreign nationals wishing to register industrial property rights of any

---

[45] [1995] 1 C.M.L.R. 461 at para. 23 of the Opinion of Tesauro A.-G.

kind.[46] The major provision of the Paris Convention is Article 2, which provides for the "national treatment" by all Member States of all nationals of the other Member States of the Union, which is to say that all of those nationals shall enjoy the same rights, advantages and protection as nationals of the state in which protection is sought. The second important element of the Paris Union system was the establishment of a right of priority[47] to run in the case of trade marks for six months from the date of application for the mark in the proprietor's country of origin. This effectively gives the proprietor six months in which to effect the registration of his rights in the other states of the Union. This right of priority is now reflected in section 35 of the 1994 Act.

3.95 The other important provisions of the Paris Convention which are incorporated in the 1994 Act are the protection for well-known trade marks which may be found in part in section 56[48] and in the inclusion of well-known trade marks in the definition of earlier trade marks in section 6(1).[49] The provisions of Article 6*septies* of the Convention are reflected in section 60 of the 1994 Act, as to applications for registration made by an agent of a proprietor of the mark in a Convention country.[50]

3.96 Otherwise, the Paris Convention does not have direct force or effect in the United Kingdom, nor are there any steps which may be taken to rely upon it or to seek to enforce it here, save as specifically incorporated into English law in relation to trade marks by the 1994 Act.

The Madrid Agreement

3.97 This is a much more important agreement to United Kingdom trade mark owners, not so much in the form of the Madrid Agreement itself but in the form of the Protocol to the Agreement which was signed in 1989 and which came into force in 1996.

3.98 The Madrid Agreement, which first came into being in 1891 and was periodically updated, provided a system whereby a national of a member country of the arrangement who had registered a trade mark in any contracting state could make a single international application, to be submitted to his national trade mark office and forwarded to the international office at Geneva, specifying those countries party to the arrangement in which he would wish to have his mark registered.

3.99 There were a number of serious drawbacks to the arrangement as first drafted and although these were mitigated by various revisions, neither the United States nor the United Kingdom ever ratified the Agreement, and membership was limited to about 30 countries altogether.

---

[46] In the 1967 Stockholm text, Article 1 extends protection to patents, utility models, industrial designs, trade marks, service marks, trade names, and indications of source: "industrial property shall be understood in the broadest sense".
[47] Art. 4(A)(1).
[48] See discussion at paras. 4.81 *et seq.* of Chap. 4.
[49] See discussion in Chap. 2, para. 2.111.
[50] See para. 3.67 above.

3.100   As a result of the unsatisfactory performance of the Madrid Agreement, a Protocol was adopted on June 27, 1989 which effectively provides an alternative system for international registrations.

3.101   The Protocol came into force on April 1, 1996.[51] It required ratification by four member countries before it could come into effect, and by the end of February 1996 there had been nine ratifications: China, Cuba, Denmark, Finland, Germany, Norway, Spain, Sweden and the United Kingdom. The U.K. Registry has been accepting applications under the Madrid Protocol since January 1996, all of which took the opening date of April 1, 1996 as their filing date. The procedure for registration of a trade mark at the International Bureau is governed by the "Common Regulations" adopted under the Protocol, which also came into force on April 1, 1996. The original Madrid Agreement will remain in force alongside the Madrid Protocol although ultimately the Protocol will replace the Agreement, when the Protocol will have been in operation for at least 10 years. As the United Kingdom does not seem likely to become a member of the Agreement, the discussion below is confined to indicating the scope of the Protocol.

3.102   Article 2 of the Protocol provides that where an application has been made for registration of a mark, or where a mark has been registered in a person's home state (which must of course be a contracting state) that person may apply for an international registration. Equally, it will be possible to apply for an international registration where there is an application for registration of a Community trade mark. The international registration is effected by making the appropriate application to one's national trade mark office (or the CTMO) which will then forward the application to the International Bureau.[52] A handling fee of £40 will be charged by the U.K. Registry for dealing with the Madrid application.[53] The basic registration fee charged by WIPO is 653 Swiss Francs for a mark in up to three classes in monochrome, 903 SF where it is reproduced in colour, with a further 72 SF for each additional class. Each contracting state is entitled to make an individual charge for examination and renewal and so far a number of members (including the United Kingdom) intend to make such individual charges.

3.103   Article 3 provides that applications shall be made on a form to be prescribed by the Common Regulations and must include predictable details of the home registration, including the goods and services in respect of which the protection of the mark is claimed. Under Article 3(4) the International Bureau will immediately register the marks filed in accordance with Article 2 and the registration will bear the date on which the international application was received in the home trade mark office, as long as it was received by the International Bureau within two months from that date. The International Bureau then notifies all national trade mark offices concerned and the mark will be published in a periodical to be issued by the International Bureau, the *WIPO Gazette of International Trade Marks*.

---

[51] By virtue of S.I. 1996 No. 714.
[52] An explanatory guide to making an international application was published as a Supplement to the *Trade Mark Journal* on March 27, 1996, setting out the administrative side of applications and giving some details of fees.
[53] See the relevant Fees Order, S.I. 1996 No. 715.

3.104 By Article 4, from the date of registration at the International Bureau, the protection of the mark in each of the contracting states will be the same as if the mark had been deposited directly in that contracting state. However, Article 5(1) gives each national office a right to refuse to register the international registration in its territory, but only on a basis upon which it would refuse to register a national application. Where there is such a refusal, the applicant will have the same remedies as if the mark had been applied for directly at that national office. Each national state has 12 months to decide whether to refuse the registration, although there is an option for countries to extend that period to 18 months.

3.105 Registration of a mark at the International Bureau is for a term of 10 years with a possibility of renewal for further 10 year periods (Articles 6 and 7). However, one of the continuing difficulties with the Madrid Protocol is that, despite the fact that the procedure enables a trade mark proprietor to acquire a number of national trade mark registrations, these registrations do not immediately have a validity which is independent of the initial registration in the home state. Under Article 6, the protection resulting from the international registration may not be relied upon where, within a period of five years from the date of the international registration, any application upon which the international registration was based is rejected, or any registration upon which the international registration was based is revoked, cancelled or otherwise invalidated. If that "central attack" is successful, the proprietor of the international registration may seek to transform the international registration into national registrations, and if he makes such an application within the three months following the cancellation of the international registration, he will keep his priority date. It will only be once the international registration has been in place for five years that the registration will become independent of the home application or registration, so that each national registration would have to be attacked separately. However, the possibilty of continuing to maintain a number of national registrations even where the home registration has been lost represents a clear benefit of the Protocol system.

3.016 As the system creates a series of national marks, questions of infringement will be dealt with under the laws of each contracting state.

3.107 Section 54 of the 1994 Act gave the Secretary of State powers to make necessary orders to give effect in the United Kingdom to the Madrid Protocol and sub-section 54(2) listed a number of matters to be dealt with by those Regulations. These were dealt with by the Trade Marks (International Registrations) Order 1996,[54] which deals with entitlement to and effects of an international registration (they are largely treated as U.K. registrations by paragraphs 4, 5, 7, 13 and 14 in particular), and numerous administrative matters affecting international registrations in the United Kingdom. Paragraph 22 deals with applications for international registration made by United Kingdom nationals, etc., through the U.K. Registry.

3.108 The benefit of the Madrid system over the Community trade mark system is exactly this possibility of achieving a number of national registrations through one single

[54] S.I. 1996 No. 714.

application, yet not being faced with the possibility of rejection of the application as a whole because of objections legitimately raised in only one of the contracting states. Equally, the benefit is that once the five year period has safely passed, even the revocation of the mark in the home territory will not affect the validity of the other national registrations.

CHAPTER 4

INFRINGEMENT OF TRADE MARKS

(I) THE PROTECTION OF TRADE MARKS

4.1   As described in Chapter 1 above, a trade mark's ability to fulfil its economic and legal functions depends upon its distinctiveness and upon its ability to identify the goods or services upon which it is used, and to stimulate and maintain goodwill. The proprietor therefore requires his valuable property right to be protected from incursions by competitors, which can only be achieved by that right being exclusive. Whether or not the mark is registered, the law offers the trade mark proprietor redress against acts of his competitors which would lead the public to confuse their goods with his own. The various remedies available are described in Chapter 6; broadly, these include the important right to obtain an injunction to prevent the repetition of the acts of which complaint is made as well as a right to financial compensation in the form of damages or an account of profits and to delivery up or destruction of the infringing goods.

4.2   In order to protect his mark in this way, the proprietor must exercise vigilance. First, he must take care in the way in which he, his licensees, agents and distributors use and, in particular, advertise the mark. Under no circumstances must the proprietor allow the mark to be used as the name of the goods by the trade, so as to be liable to attack for having become generic.[1] Secondly, the proprietor must keep a careful eye on the market and on the *Official Journal* from the Trade Marks Registry, to be ready to take prompt action either for infringement and passing off or to bring opposition proceedings, if delay and acquiescence are not to ruin future chances of keeping the exclusivity of the mark. As the Community Trade Mark becomes of importance in the future, it will also become necessary to monitor applications for CTMs so as to avoid international as well as national conflicts. It is vital that conflicting marks should be discovered and opposed, if possible, before they become established as defensible concurrent rights.[2]

4.3   As already explained, there exists a dual protection in the United Kingdom against damaging forms of imitation of trade marks in the form of the statutory action for infringement, where marks are registered, and the common law action for passing off, which may be brought *whether or not* marks are registered. Under the 1938 Act, there was a very clear distinction between infringement and passing off proceedings. Under the 1938 Act, to summarise, it was sufficient to prove title to the trade mark by showing a valid registration, whilst one could only complain of infringements upon the goods or services for which the mark was registered. One therefore had to rely upon passing off in order to complain of the unauthorised use of a confusingly similar mark upon other goods or services, but in passing off actions one had also to prove that one had a goodwill in the mark.

4.4   These distinctions have been blurred in the 1994 Act, since for some sorts of infringement actions one will have to prove not simply title to the registered mark, but also

---

[1] See discussion of s. 46(1)(c) at paras. 3.53 *et seq.* of Chap. 3, above.
[2] See Chap. 3(8), above.

a reputation in the United Kingdom, and in some cases there may be infringement by use of an identical or similar mark upon similar goods to those for which the plaintiff's mark is registered. Passing off is considered in Chapter 5 below.

4.5 However, it is important to realise that the two actions may be complementary; this was often the case when the 1938 Act was in force, and may well still be the case today, even with the broadening of infringement actions. Trade mark proprietors may still often be well advised to bring an action based both upon their registered marks and upon passing off.

4.6 Actions for trade libel or malicious falsehood may sometimes also arise where there are problems with trade mark rights. Actions of this nature fall outside the scope of this book.[3] Broadly speaking, such actions may protect cases where untrue statements are made in relation to goods or services which damage the plaintiff's trade reputation. Such cases have succeeded, for instance, where advertisements alleged that the defendant alone used the true recipe for particular goods[4] and where out-dated goods were knowingly sold under the plaintiff's mark.[5]

4.7 There are two final points to bear in mind before going into the details of infringement actions. First, it is always important to seek to take action in relation to a perceived infringement as rapidly as is possible. As a general rule, it may be easier to persuade a court that a mark which has yet to be put into use is likely to cause confusion or deception than it is to persuade a court, where a mark is already in use but no instances of confusion have come to light, that confusion is likely to occur. Considerations of delay are also important in the field of interlocutory injunctions, which are discussed in Chapter 6 below.

4.8 Secondly, for the near future at least, it is important to note that whilst sections 9 to 12 of the 1994 Act apply to marks registered under the 1938 Act, it is not an infringement of such an existing registered mark or a mark which is substantially the same as an existing registered mark to continue[6] after October 31, 1994 any use which did not amount to infringement of the existing registered mark under the old law (see paragraph 4 of Schedule 3 of the 1994 Act). Where the use of the mark of which complaint is made commenced before October 31, 1994, it will therefore, be necessary to show that the defendant's activities would have amounted to infringement under the 1938 Act if a claim to trade mark infringement under the 1994 Act is to be made.[7]

---

[3] See, *e.g.* Kerly (12th ed.), Drysdale & Silverleaf, *Passing Off Law and Practice*, (2nd ed.) *Clerk & Lindsell on Torts*, (17th ed.)
[4] *Thorley's Cattle Food Co. v. Massam* (1880) 14 Ch. D. 763.
[5] *Wilts United Dairies Limited v. Robinson & Sons Limited* [1958] R.P.C. 94; this action also succeeded in passing off.
[6] "The provision in speaking of continuance of a use is referring to what is regarded commercially as a continued use" *per* Jacob J. in *Northern & Shell Plc v. Conde Nast* [1995] R.P.C. 117 at 127.
[7] *ibid.*

(2) Infringement under the 1938 Act

4.9 Under the 1938 Act, an action for infringement could be brought only by the proprietor of a validly registered trade mark, or by his registered user under the provisions of section 28(3) where the proprietor himself had failed to bring an infringement action within two months of being called upon to do so. The right to bring the action depended only upon the title conferred by the registration, which would have had effect from the date of the application but which could not be relied upon until completion of the application.[8]

4.10 Section 4 of the 1938 Act defined the right given by registration and what amounted to infringement of the registered mark. Over the years, a large number of pejorative comments have been made about the section, all of which were undoubtedly justified in the light of the long-winded and confusing manner in which the section was phrased.[9]

4.11 Despite the intricacy of its wording, it seems safe to say that section 4 entitled the proprietor of the mark to the exclusive use of his mark upon the goods or services for which it was registered, which right included the right to prevent use of a confusingly similar mark upon those[10] goods or services by anyone lacking his consent.

4.12 The test for confusing similarity has already been discussed in Chapter 2 above and the comments made there apply equally to cases of infringement. As a general rule, it may be said again that what was important in terms of confusing similarity was whether the essential feature(s) of the plaintiff's mark had been used by the defendant, whether with or without further distinguishing material. One nice example is *"Ford's Eureka Shirts/Foster's Improved Eureka Shirts".*[11] Under the 1938 Act, the sort of use of the mark which could amount to infringement was restricted to any "printed or other visual representation of the mark."[12] Importantly, this excluded merely oral use of the mark, for example in radio or television advertisements or simply in the course of business.

4.13 There were a number of difficulties in construing section 4(1). For instance, the section described the use of the mark which could be complained of as being use "in relation to" the relevant goods or services. This quite clearly covered use directly upon the goods in the form of labelling or packaging and it also covered use in advertisements or other trade documentation.[13] However, it was less clear whether it covered use of the mark as the name of a shop or business selling goods or providing services covered by the registration.[14]

---

[8] See *Henry Denny & Sons Limited v. United Biscuits (U.K.) Limited* [1981] F.S.R. 114 and *McGregor-Doniger Inc v. Stirling McGregor Limited* [1981] F.S.R. 299.
[9] See, *e.g.* Megarry J. in *British Northrop v. Texteam Blackburn Limited* [1974] R.P.C. 57.
[10] As an example of how strictly this rule might be construed, see *Hovis Limited v. Spillers Limited* [1953] R.P.C. 51 in which a registration for flour was deemed not to cover use on bread, despite the obvious potential for confusion. See also the more recent case of *Unilever v. Johnson Wax* [1989] F.S.R. 145 in which a lavatory cleaner did not infringe a registration for common soap and detergents.
[11] *Ford v. Foster* (1872) L.R. 7 Ch. 611.
[12] See s. 68(2).
[13] *Cheetah Trade Mark* [1993] F.S.R. 263.
[14] See, *e.g. Furnitureland Limited v. Harris* [1989] F.S.R. 536 and *Autodrome trade mark* [1969] R.P.C. 564.

Comparative advertising

4.14 Sub-section 4(1)(b) led to even more difficulty due to its obscure wording. To summarise the sub-section, it extended the definition of infringement to use which "imports a reference" to the proprietor or a registered user, or the goods or services protected by the registration. Essentially, the sub-section was probably intended to cover and was judicially construed as covering cases of comparative advertising. The leading case on the point was *Bismag Limited v Amblins (Chemists) Limited*.[15] *Bismag* was a clear case of comparative advertising, in which the defendant had produced a table comparing the composition of the plaintiff's products and its own medicines which were competitively priced. The Court of Appeal found that although clearly there was no confusion as to origin, to constitute infringement in a traditional sense, the defendant's acts were caught by sub-section 4(1)(b).

4.15 Similarly in *British Northrop v Texteam Blackburn*,[16] there was a reference to goods as being approved by "engineers of many years' experience in the manufacture of Northrop parts", where Northrop was the plaintiff's mark. It was found that section 4(1)(b) was applicable.

4.16 A distinction was drawn in the case of *Pompadour Laboratories v. Fraser*[17] where the defendants advertised their own products by saying that they had "manufactured hair lacquer for *Pompadour Laboratories Limited* for several years". In the infringement action, which would in any case have failed because the plaintiffs' trade mark Pompadour covered not hair lacquer but shampoos and hair cream, it was held that the defendants had used only the plaintiff's trade name, and not its mark, so that it did not fall under section 4(1)(b).

4.17 In the more recent case of *Duracell v. Ever Ready*[18] the defendants made reference to Duracell Batteries Limited when comparing the parties' respective products. The plaintiff owned the trade mark "Duracell". It was held, on the hearing of a motion, that infringement was arguable since there was a reference to the goods, not just to the proprietor.

4.18 In *Chanel Limited v. Triton Packaging Limited*,[19] the comparative "advertisement" was a table in a manual sent out to the defendant's numerous distributors, which set out the plaintiff's trade marks alongside the defendant's code numbers for its "smell-alike" perfumes. The Court of Appeal held that there was a breach of section 4(1)(b).

4.19 Lastly, in *Compaq Computer Co v. Dell Computer Co Limited*,[20] the defendant had advertised its computers by using photographs of its own computers alongside similar photographs of the plaintiffs' computers, accompanied with a text which claimed that

[15] [1940] Ch. 667; (1940) 57 R.P.C. 209.
[16] See n.9, above.
[17] [1966] R.P.C. 7.
[18] [1989] F.S.R. 71.
[19] [1993] R.P.C. 32.
[20] [1992] F.S.R. 93.

Dell's systems were "basically the same as Compaq's", but much cheaper.[21] It was held that as both advertisements used the plaintiff's registered mark as a trade mark in respect of the plaintiff's personal computers, there was a clear case of infringement.

Trade mark use

4.20 Under both sub-section 4(1)(a) and 4(1)(b), it was necessary that the use complained of was "trade mark use" of the plaintiffs' mark. That is to say, the use had to be use which in some way indicated that the mark was being used so as to indicate a connection in the course of trade between the marked goods or services and the plaintiff. Thus, for example, the proprietors of the trade mark "Treets" for confectionery who also manufactured miniature versions of their Mars Bars in "fun size" bags, objected to the sale by the defendants of "Treat Size" packets of sweets. However, the defendants were held not to be infringing the mark "Treets" not only because it was found that in all the circumstances confusion or deception was unlikely to occur, but also because the use made of the phrase "Treat Size" was unlikely to be taken as being a trade mark use of a phrase. The judge considered that members of the public clearly identified items of confectionery

An example of merchandising of Coca-Cola products. 'Coca-cola', 'Coke' and the design of the contour bottle are registered trade marks of The Coca-Cola Company. 'Coca-Cola' merchandise produced under licence by The Barling Group. This image is reproduced with kind permission of The Coca-Cola Company and The Barling Group.

[21] It was alleged that false representations were made as to the quality, etc., of the parties' respective goods and that the adverts also made unfavourable comparisons between the service offered by each party, which led to Compaq suing additionally for trade libel/injurious falsehood.

by reference to the name of the particular product and would see the phrase "Treat Size" as merely an indication of the size of the particular chocolate bar or bag of sweets they were buying.[22]

4.21 Another example of non-trade mark use of a phrase occurred where a slogan identical to a mark was used as a slogan upon a T-shirt. This was found to be use by way of decoration rather than by way of identification of origin.[23] Similarly, the use of the word "Mothercare" in a book title was held not to be trade mark use of the plaintiff's mark.[24]

4.22 The cases under section 4(1)(b) also required the use of the trade mark to be use in a trade mark sense, even if the goods in relation to which the mark was being used were in fact the plaintiff's goods. Such was the case in *Bismag* and in *Duracell*.[25]

Sub-section 4(2): disclaimers

4.23 Not surprisingly, the exclusive right granted by sub-section 4(1) was to be subject to any conditions or limitations or disclaimer registered in relation to the trade mark.

Sub-section 4(3): genuine goods

4.24 This sub-section provided a more substantive and important exception to the generality of the exclusive right granted in sub-section 4(1). The proprietor of a mark could prevent the use of a deceptively similar mark to his own upon goods for which his registration was valid, as long as the goods were not particular goods to which the trade mark had been applied by or with the express or implied consent of the trade mark proprietor or a registered user. This rule gave statutory effect to the so-called "exhaustion theory"[26] which in effect provides that a trade mark proprietor can only control the initial marketing or release of his goods on to the market and cannot seek subsequently to restrain other dealings with them, at least in the context of trade mark law.

4.25 There have been a number of cases showing the different aspects of this sub-section. First, in *Revlon Inc. v. Cripps & Lee Limited*,[27] the Court of Appeal held that where shampoos had been marketed in the United States by one subsidiary of the large Revlon group, those products when imported and sold in the United Kingdom under the same Revlon mark were deemed to have been sold under that mark with the consent of all of the companies in the group. This was the case despite the fact that the products had been sold in the United States upon the express condition that they should not be re-sold. The

---

[22] *Mars Limited v. Cadbury Limited* [1987] R.P.C. 387.
[23] *Unidoor Limited v. Marks and Spencer Plc* [1988] R.P.C. 275: the plaintiff's mark was registered in Class 25 for articles of clothing and the defendant's use of the words "Coast to Coast" had been as a slogan underneath the larger words "Marine Girl".
[24] *Mothercare U.K. Limited v. Penguin Books Limited* [1988] R.P.C. 113.
[25] See also the interesting case of *Montana Wines Limited v. Villa Maria Wines Limited* [1985] R.P.C. 412, a case of comparative advertising in New Zealand, where there was found to be infringement by the comparative advertising, although relief was refused due to the application of the New Zealand equivalent to the special "defence" of s. 5(2) of the 1938 Act, on which see paras. 4.32 *et seq.*, below.
[26] See discussion in the context of European law in paras. 7.52 *et seq.* below.
[27] [1980] F.S.R. 85.

majority in the Court of Appeal found that, although there had been the group consent, the *United Kingdom* mark had not actually been applied to the goods by the proprietor or the registered user in the United Kingdom, but only the *United States* mark by the American co-member of the group. Such consent was, however, sufficient for section 4(3), given the group structure involved.

4.26 A rather different result was reached in the case of *Colgate-Palmolive Limited v. Markwell Finance Limited*[28] in which objection was raised by Colgate to the importation of toothpaste made for the Brazilian market. It had been made to a different formula from that used in the United Kingdom and had been sold initially by a Brazilian subsidiary of Colgate which was not entitled to export its goods outside certain South American countries. It was again held that section 4(3)(a) did not apply, since the proprietor of the United Kingdom mark had not applied the United Kingdom mark to the Brazilian goods as the intention was that the goods should be sold only in Brazil (or possibly certain other South American countries). It was an important factor in the decision that the quality and composition of the Brazilian goods were markedly inferior as well as different from the goods usually sold under the Colgate mark in the United Kingdom, if only to show that the goods were never destined for the U.K. market.[29]

4.27 Section 4(3)(a) was also successfully relied upon where goods had been legitimately marked but not yet marketed. For instance, in *Accurist Watches v. King*[30] a defendant was entitled to rely upon his retention of title clause so as to sell watches that had been marked with the trade mark by a registered user who had become insolvent.

4.28 The protection offered by section 4(3)(a) also extended to retailers of marked goods sold as second-hand or re-conditioned products. However, such re-conditioning had not to be so extensive as to amount to rebuilding of the product.[31]

4.29 Finally, section 4(3)(a) had also to be considered in conjunction with section 8 of the 1938 Act, which provided a defence to use of a mark where it constituted "any bona fide description of the character or quality" of the marked goods. Thus, use of the mark upon goods to indicate that they contained components properly marked with that mark was no infringement.

Sub-section 4(3)(b): accessories/spare parts

4.30 This provided rather a similar exception to that of sub-section 4(3)(a) in relation to use of the mark so as to indicate the suitability of the goods to which it was applied for use as accessories or for spare parts. For example, this would permit one to indicate the various sizes and shapes of dust-bags for vacuum cleaners which were suitable for use on

---

[28] [1989] R.P.C. 497.
[29] See Slade L.J. at pp. 517 and 527 and see comments in *Northern & Shell v. Conde Nast* [1995] R.P.C. 117 at 124 – note that the latter case followed *Revlon* and distinguished *Colgate*. Would the case have been decided differently if there had been no difference in quality and no ban on export to the U.K.? Perhaps, especially given the limited effects of s. 12 of the 1994 Act, on which see below.
[30] [1992] F.S.R. 80.
[31] See, *e.g. Rolls Royce Motors v. Zanelli* [1979] R.P.C. 148; *IBM v. Phoenix* [1994] R.P.C. 251.

a Hoover product, a Vax product or whatever. The sub-section was in any event construed quite strictly, as may be seen from the case of *British Northrop*.[32]

Section 6: contractual limitations

4.31 This section provided some means for a proprietor of a mark to control the manner in which the goods bearing the mark might be treated after leaving his possession or control. The proprietor might enter into a contract in writing with a purchaser of the goods restricting what could be done with them after the purchase, and any breach of such restriction would amount to an infringement unless a third party had obtained the goods and had purchased them in good faith before receiving notice of the contractual obligation. Such limitations might control the application of the mark to altered or re-packaged goods, the application of a second mark, etc. By such means the proprietor could circumvent certain of the difficulties discussed above, as long as he could persuade his purchaser to restrict his commercial freedom in this way.

Section 5: Part B marks

4.32 Under section 5, marks registered in Part B of the Register were accorded the same exclusive rights as those registered in Part A, subject only to sub-section 5(2). This strange sub-section provided that no injunction or other relief would be granted to a plaintiff who was the proprietor of a Part B mark in any action for infringement, other than one under section 6:

"if the defendant establishes to the satisfaction of the Court that the use of which the plaintiff complains is not likely to deceive or cause confusion or to be taken as indicating a connection in the course of trade between the goods and some person having the right either as proprietor or as registered user to use the trade mark."

4.33 Clearly, this excluded Part B marks from being infringed by comparative advertising. However, apart from that clear exclusion, it was often difficult to see precisely how the section 5(2) "defence" was to be proved, and in truth it was of limited use.[33]

4.34 It seems possible that since the wording of sub-section 5(2) was not to preclude there being an infringement in such a case, but merely to preclude the plaintiff from obtaining the usual relief in relation to that infringement of his mark, section 5(2) will now be of historical interest only. This is because under paragraph 2 of Schedule 3 of the 1994 Act, all marks, whether in Part A or Part B of the Register, which were in existence when the 1994 Act came into force, were to be transferred into the new Register, and paragraph 4 of the Schedule, especially paragraph 4(2), applies to all existing marks. That sub-paragraph provides that it shall be no infringement under the new Act to continue "any use which did not amount to infringement of the existing registered mark under the old law." If all the factors of infringement were present in relation to a Part B mark, strictly on

---

[32] [1974] R.P.C. 57.
[33] For a recent case showing the limitations of s. 5(2) see *Provident Financial Plc v. Halifax Building Society* [1994] F.S.R. 81 where (on motion) the building society was not able to satisfy the burden of proof upon it to show that no-one would connect the services it wished to offer with anyone but itself.

the wording of sub-paragraph 4(2) it would seem that further consideration of sub-section 5(2) of the 1938 Act should have become irrelevant. However, there must be room to doubt whether one would be able to persuade a court that it would be right to grant remedies in respect of infringements which commenced before October 31, 1994 when such infringements could not have been remedied under the 1938 Act by reason of sub-section 5(2).

(3) DEFENCES TO INFRINGEMENT UNDER THE 1938 ACT

4.35   Having looked at the principles of infringement under the 1938 Act, it is necessary to look also into the various defences which might have been available to allegations of such infringement.

(a) Challenge to the validity of the plaintiff's registration

4.36   When faced with an allegation of infringement of a registered trade mark, it was possible to respond by counterclaiming for rectification of the Register. Such rectification could be sought upon a number of different bases, according to the circumstances of the case. For instance, it was possible to challenge the mark on the basis that it ought never to have been registered at all, perhaps because it was never distinctive, upon the grounds set out in section 32(1) of the Act. However, such grounds would not have been available against a Part A mark which had been registered for more than seven years, by virtue of section 13 of the Act, unless it was possible to show that the registration had been obtained by fraud or that the trade mark offended against the provisions of section 11.[34] Section 32(1) was also held recently to permit rectification of the Register on the grounds that a trade mark had been abandoned by its proprietor.[35]

4.37   Alternatively, it was possible to challenge the plaintiff's mark on the basis of non-use, which again could give rise to rectification of the Register under section 26 of the 1938 Act. Where the application for rectification concerned a mark which had been on the register for less than five years and one month, it was necessary to show not just that the mark had not been used, but also that the proprietor had lacked the necessary intention to use the mark when it was registered.

4.38   If rectification was possible on the grounds either of section 32 or section 26(1), this could obviously provide a defence to the infringement action, but only in relation to the future. Thus, an injunction would not be granted to prevent future infringements, where the plaintiff's mark was to be deleted from the Register. However, it was held that the order for rectification would not have retrospective effect, so that the defendant might be liable for damages in respect of infringements committed prior to the order for rectification. On the other hand, where rectification was ordered for non-use, it was hard to see what damage the proprietor of the registered mark might have suffered in the interim.[36]

---

[34] See Chap. 2(7) and (8), above.
[35] *Second Sight Limited v. Novell U.K. Limited* [1995] R.P.C. 423 at 431.
[36] *ibid.*

Balcombe J. in "*Nerit*"[37] found that an order under section 26 of the 1938 Act did not have retrospective effect, so that remedies could in theory be granted to the plaintiff in relation to prior infringements. However, he pointed out that an injunction would not be granted to restrain future infringements and that where the mark had not been used as was the case in "*Nerit*" it would not be appropriate to grant either an inquiry as to damages or an account of profits.

(b) No infringement

4.39 Obviously, a defence might often be based upon an argument that there was no infringement either because the goods or services of the defendant were not the same as those for which the plaintiff's mark was registered, or on the grounds that the marks were not "nearly resembling" so as to cause confusion.[38] Naturally, if the defendant's mark had been in use for some time prior to the issue of the proceedings, and yet the plaintiff was unable to plead examples of confusion, the defendant might well have a reasonable chance of convincing the court that confusion was not likely to occur.

(c) Concurrent right

4.40 It was a defence to show that the defendant had a perfectly legitimate right to use his own mark, despite any rights which the plaintiff might have.

4.41 First, it was a good defence under section 4(4) to show that one was merely exercising a right to use one's own mark given by registration. So, if two or more similar marks were for any reason registered concurrently, for instance under section 12(2), neither could succeed in an infringement action against the other. The defence would only succeed insofar as the defendant was using his mark strictly upon the goods for which it was registered and in the manner in which it was registered, and in particular in accordance with any conditions of use imposed upon it.[39]

4.42 In *Neutrogena*,[40] the defendants raised by way of defence a combination of sections 4(4) and 30(1) of the 1938 Act, seeking to say that their use of "Neutralia" was, by virtue of section 30(1), equivalent to use of their registration of "Nutralia" so that they could rely upon section 4(4). This argument was rejected by Jacob J., who considered that the difference between the two names was such as to affect the identity of the mark; it was significant that the defendants did not wish to use "Nutralia".

4.43 In relation to unregistered trade marks, section 7 of the 1938 Act provided that the owner of a registered trade mark could not bring an infringement action to restrain the use

---

[37] *Imperial Group Limited v. Philip Morris & Co.* [1980] F.S.R. 146 (1st instance decision; see [1982] F.S.R. 72 for C.A.).

[38] See discussion of confusing similarity in Chap. 2(7).

[39] See, *e.g. Eli Lilly & Co. Limited v. Chelsea Drug Chemical Co. Limited* [1966] R.P.C. 14 in which the defendant's mark was registered as ECONOCIL-VK but had been used in the form econoCIL-VK. The plaintiffs were the registered proprietors of the mark V-CIL-K. An injunction was granted against use mixing upper and lower case, but with the proviso that the defendant could use the mark in the form Econocil-VK.

[40] *Neutrogena Corp v. Golden Limited* [1966] R.P.C. 473 at 488–9

of a similar trade mark where the latter had been continuously used from before the date of first use or registration (whichever was earlier) of the registered mark. Logically, therefore, this meant that where a trade mark had been registered in ignorance of other established rights, the mere registration of the mark would not give the proprietor any right to complain of use of the earlier mark. However, some extension was given to the rights of the proprietor of a registered mark by section 30(2) of the 1938 Act, which deemed use of one of a series of marks to be use of the others for all the purposes of the 1938 Act.[41]

(d) Bona fide use of one's own name

4.44 It was also a good defence that the defendant was merely making bona fide use of his own name, under section 8 of the 1938 Act. A similar defence existed where the person was making use of the name of his place of business. It seems that the test under section 8 was not an objective one, but a subjective one of the actual honesty or dishonesty of the defendant in the manner in which he chose, or chose to use, the name in dispute.[42] Section 8 extended to the use of a company's name and possibly also to the use of the name of the firm, as long as it was fully established. The protection extended to successors in title to the business of the original "name".

4.45 Sub-section 8(b) protected the use by any person of any "bona fide description of the character or quality of his goods" as long as that description would not be likely to be taken as importing a reference.

(e) Estoppel, acquiescence or delay

4.46 As with all forms of action, it was possible to raise a defence based upon estoppel, acquiescence or delay in the appropriate circumstances; these are not matters which were special to trade mark law in any way and the usual equitable principles applied.

4.47 Essentially, these defences relied upon a claim that the plaintiff's behaviour had been such that he should, for one reason or another, be denied relief. The defendant might be able to say, for example, that the plaintiff knew of his use of the mark, but either consented to it or led the defendant in some other way to believe that he would not object to it, so that in reliance upon that indication, the defendant spent time and money in building up his business under that mark.[43] In general terms, delay did not give grounds of defence to an infringement action, unless the mere lapse of time was accompanied by acts amounting to consent or acquiescence or acts upon which estoppel could be based.

4.48 However, of course, there was (and is) a limitation period in relation to trade mark infringement actions, which would prevent relief being sought in relation to acts which

---

[41] See for example the position in *Portakabin Limited v. Powerblast Limited* [1990] R.P.C. 471, in which long-standing use of "Portablast" and then "Portoblast" by the defendant pre-dated the plaintiffs registered marks "Porta" (the only ones pleaded as having been infringed) but did not pre-date use of the plaintiff's other marks, "Portakabin" and "Portasilo", so that the s. 7 defence failed.

[42] See *Baume v. Moore* [1958] R.P.C. 226, applied, though criticised, in *Provident Financial Plc v. Halifax Building Society* [1994] F.S.R. 81. And see *Guccio Gucci SpA v. Paolo Gucci* [1991] F.S.R. 89.

[43] Generally on the principles of estoppel see Chap. 5 of *Snell's Equity*, (29th ed., 1990).

occurred more than six years prior to the commencement of the proceedings. Moreover, where there had been a delay of a period in excess of the tortious limitation period, the court might well be reluctant to enforce the registration or to find the necessary likelihood of confusion, unless the evidence was very compelling.

(4) INFRINGEMENT UNDER THE 1994 ACT

Section 9: Rights conferred by a trade mark

4.49 Section 9 of the 1994 Act simply states that the proprietor of a registered trade mark has exclusive rights in the trade mark, which are infringed by the use of the trade mark in the United Kingdom without his consent. This part of sub-section 9(1) must be construed in accordance with section 103(2), which, as stated before, defines use as any kind of use, and not just as a graphic representation of the mark. Sub-section 9(1) goes on to state that the acts amounting to infringement, where they are done without the proprietor's consent, are specified in section 10. Consent of the proprietor in this respect must mean either the consent of the proprietor himself, or indirect consent through the intermediary of a licensee or agent.

4.50 The exclusive rights which are granted in the mark take effect from the date of filing of the application for registration (see section 40(3)) but, as under the 1938 Act, the proprietor is not entitled to bring infringement proceedings before the trade mark is actually registered.[44] Sub-section 9(3) also provides that, despite the exclusive rights taking effect from the date of application, no offence under section 92 of the 1994 Act is committed by anything done before the date of publication of the registration.

4.51 One last general point to note is that proceedings for infringement can be brought either by the proprietor himself or, in certain circumstances, by an exclusive licensee. Please see discussion of the rights which may be conferred upon licensees in Chapter 7(9) and (10) below.

Section 10: Definition of infringement

4.52 The various sub-sections of section 10 are closely related to the sub-sections of section 5, that is to say the relative grounds for refusal to register a trade mark which were discussed at length in Chapter 2(8) above. The similarity between the relative grounds for refusing to register a mark and the basis of infringement of the mark is a further change from the old law. Under the 1938 Act, as I hope will by now be clear, the Registry applied a wider test in assessing a mark's likelihood of confusion with other marks than was applied by the courts in deciding whether or not there was infringement of the registered mark pursuant to sections 4 and 5 of the 1938 Act. The essential difference was that under sections 11 and 12 of the 1938 Act, the relative grounds for refusal included similarity to

---

[44] See *Henry Denny & Sons v. United Biscuits* [1981] F.S.R. 114 and para. 4.9, above as to the 1938 Act position.

marks registered for goods of the same description as those for which registration of the later mark was sought, but under sections 4 and 5 there was infringement of a trade mark only where the alleged infringer used the confusingly similar mark upon the identical goods or services to those for which the earlier mark was registered. That distinction is not maintained in the 1994 Act and the broadening of the infringement action under the 1994 Act is one of the more significant changes that the Act has brought about. Actions for infringement of a registered trade mark may, as a result of the innovations in the 1994 Act, be much closer to passing off actions.

4.53   Each of sub-sections 10(1) to (3) refers to use of a sign "in the course of trade" which may amount to infringement. This phrase is fairly self-explanatory, and sub-section 103(1) also defines "trade" as including any business or profession. However, none of the sub-sections of section 10 refer to the infringing use being use of the sign in a "trade mark sense" and it is not clear whether this is a necessary requirement of infringement under the new Act. Clearly it was such a requirement in relation to the 1938 Act, as discussed above.[45] This question was addressed whilst the Bill was going through Parliament and an amendment was proposed seeking to insert in the 1994 Act some equivalent to section 68(2) of the 1938 Act, which defined a trade mark as "a mark used or proposed to be used in relation to goods for the purpose of indicating ... a connection in the course of trade between the goods and .... [the] proprietor or ... registered user ....". That amendment was rejected by Lord Strathclyde upon the basis that the Act implicitly only applied to trade mark use of signs.[46] That may indeed be the intention behind the Act, and would be consistent with the recognised function of a trade mark as indicating the origin of goods or services, but it is perhaps more difficult to read that construction into the Act whilst lacking an equivalent to section 68(2), as sections 9 and 10 merely refer to "use" of the trade mark.

4.54   At the time of writing, this question has been raised in two cases. First, in *Bravado Merchandising Services v. Mainstream Publishing*[47] the question arose in relation to an alleged infringement in a book title "A Sweet Little Mystery — Wet Wet Wet — The Inside Story", where the name of the pop group "Wet Wet Wet" was registered in Class 16 for books. There counsel conceded that, on the basis of the Parliamentary debate, there had to be trade mark use of the mark, and reliance was placed on *Mothercare*.[48] However, in *British Sugar*, Jacob J. held first that the *Pepper v. Hart* principle ought not to apply where the Act in question was implementing a Directive, but that one should look instead to the Directive itself,[49] and secondly, that he found no reason to restrict infringement to cases of trade mark use of the mark in the light of the wording of Article 5 of the Directive. Instead, he found that the same practical effect would be achieved by applying the defence available under section 11(2).[50] He concluded, on the wording of sections 9(1) and 10:

[45] See above and in particular the cases of *Mars GB v. Cadbury and "Mothercare/Othercare"* at nn. 22–4, above.
[46] See *Hansard*, H.L. Vol. 552, col. 733 (February 24, 1994).
[47] [1996] F.S.R. 205.
[48] n. 24, above.
[49] [1996] R.P.C. 281 at 292 and see para. 1.21 of Chap. 1.
[50] See paras. 4.98 *et seq.*, below.

"It is said that s.9(1) ... is providing an overriding requirement that there be trade mark use ....

I can see no reason so to limit the provisions of section 10. That is not to say a purely descriptive use is an infringement. It is not, but not because it does not fall within s.10 but becasue it falls within s.11(2) ... s.10 ... merely requires the court to see whether the sign registered as a trade mark is used in the course of trade and then to consider whether that use falls within one of the ... sub-sections."

He commented that in the *Wet Wet Wet* case, the use of the mark was to refer to the group, rather than in relation to the goods covered by the registration.[51]

4.55 This construction of the Act clearly represents a change from the old law. It is clearly consistent with the broad wording of section 10 itself, which, as pointed out above, merely refers to *use* of a *sign*, not use of a trade mark. However, it remains to be seen whether the defence provided by section 11(2) will cover every type of case in which the use being made by the defendant is not trade mark use, in the sense described above.

The products at issue in the British Sugar plc v. James Robertson Ltd case, reproduced by kind permission of British Sugar plc and James Robertson & Sons Ltd.

---

[51] *ibid.* at pp. 291 and 299 respectively.

Sub-section 10(1): Identical mark/identical goods

4.56 Sub-section 10(1) is straightforward in prohibiting the use of an identical mark to the registered mark upon goods or services for which the mark is registered.

Please see the comments in relation to sub-section 5(1) in Chapter 2 above.

4.57 Please also see the section relating to the comparison to be made between marks in paragraphs 2.94–2.101 of Chapter 2 above. As under the 1938 Act, there may at times be difficulties in deciding whether particular goods or services are covered by the registration sought to be protected, but this is a matter to be decided in the light of each particular case.

Sub-section 10(2): Identical or similar marks/identical or similar goods

4.58 This sub-section again reflects the wording of sub-section 5(2). It covers cases where the marks are identical but the goods or services are only similar, where the marks are similar but the goods or services are identical and cases where the marks are similar and the goods or services are similar. As is the position under sub-section 5(2), the criteria for assessing the likelihood of confusion will be the same as those applied under the 1938 Act, so that the marks will be compared in notional fair use, if they are not already being used, or in the circumstances in which they are actually used, if both are being used. This continuity of application of the old law was confirmed both in *Origins*[52] in which it was held that the comparison between the marks for the purposes of section 10 would be in notional fair use and in *Wagamama*.[53] Moreover, in *British Sugar*[54], Jacob J. urged caution in the application of section 10(2), since: "Otherwise, however narrow the specification, the actual protection will be wide."

Similarity causing confusion

4.59 Again, as in relation to sub-section 5(2) there will be no infringement unless the similarity between the marks and/or the goods or services is such as to create a likelihood of confusion on the part of the public.

4.60 It seems unlikely that section 10(2) will be found to cover the case of "look-alike" brands, that is to say, goods the get-up of which is designed to be a "deliberate imitation of brand leader goods",[55] since such look-alikes generally adopt features of trade dress which are unlikely to be registered. If, however, the trade-dress or packaging copied by the look-alike were to be registered, then the proprietor would need to show that there was a likelihood of confusion despite the usual practice of the look-alike clearly bearing

---

[52] *Origins Natural Resources Limited v. Origin Clothing Limited* [1995] F.S.R. 280, a decision under both the 1938 and the 1994 Acts.

[53] *Wagamama Limited v. City Centre Restaurants Plc* [1995] F.S.R. 213; also in *British Sugar*, see n. 49, above.

[54] *ibid.* at p. 295.

[55] Certainly, it was not the intention of the Government that the Act *should* cover look-alikes, this question was addressed on several occasions as the Bill went through Parliament, and consistently rejected, see, *e.g.* *Hansard* H.C. Vol. 241 col. 668 (April 18, 1994), whence this definition of a look-alike from Sir Dudley Smith MP.

the name of its manufacturer or retailer (many such look-alikes are supermarket "own-brands"). Possibly, one such type of confusion might be found to exist and fall within the ambit of sub-section 10(2), if the consumer were led to believe that the use of the brand leader's trade dress meant that the goods had been manufactured by the brand leader for the supermarket. Some brand leaders (*e.g.* Kelloggs) have taken active steps to advertise the fact that they do not manufacture for others, but recently it has been reported that Heinz is to make baked beans for supermarkets to sell as own-brand lines, and it is possible that this fact might lead to confusion for other brand leaders too.

4.61 Again, confusion is defined as including "the likelihood of association with the trade mark" and the reader is asked to refer back to the comments made in relation to likelihood of association under section 5(2) in Chapter 2 above. In the *Wagamama* case,[56] Laddie J. held that the phrase "likelihood of confusion" in the 1994 Act did not have the extended meaning apparently given to its equivalent under the Benelux Uniform trade mark law, but referred only to the type of "association as to origin" already known to English law,[57] that is to say, the type of confusion which amounts to a belief "that the alleged infringer's goods were associated with the proprietor's goods or services, for example that they were an extension of the range of goods made by the proprietor".[58]

Evidence of infringement

4.62 The question of confusing similarity is one for the judge to decide. It is not a matter upon which a witness of any kind can be definitive. Even if the marks are prima facie similar, there may often be some difficulty in proving that there is the necessary likelihood of confusion or that there have been instances of actual confusion. If ordinary members of the public can be found who can be shown to have been confused, theirs will generally be the best evidence available.[59]

4.63 Alternatively, and especially on the hearing of an interlocutory motion, the court may be prepared to give weight to evidence from trade witnesses, either as to their own confusion, or as to the particular circumstances of their trade which render it likely that members of the public would be confused.[60] In *IBM v. Phoenix International Computers*

---

[56] See n. 50, above.

[57] He cited, by way of example, *Ravenhead Brick Co Limited v. Ruabon Brick Co Limited* (1937) 54 R.P.C. 341, in which the plaintiff's mark was "Rus" for bricks; it was found on the evidence that use of the mark "Sanrus" by the defendant would be taken as being use of a word invented by the plaintiff to describe some new product, although the decision is seen by Kerly (*op. cit.*) at para. 17–08 as an example of a case in which the defendant's mark would be seen as a variation in the detail of a familiar mark, rather than a case of "association" as such. Contrast the passing off cases discussed below.

[58] *ibid.* at 721.

[59] In *Wagamama*, for instance, it is clear that the judge's own impressions of the similarity of the marks were reinforced by the clear evidence of confusion on the part of a small number of witnesses called.

[60] See, *e.g.* some *dicta* in *Taittinger SA v. Allbev* [1993] F.S.R. 641 at 663 approving *Guccio Gucci SpA v. Paolo Gucci* [1991] F.S.R. 89 in which Browne-Wilkinson V.-C. held that he could hear evidence from the trade as to likelihood of confusion amongst their customers: "Plainly it is my decision as to whether or not people will be confused, but why should I be required to make that decision on the basis of my own lack of information, rather than on the basis of expert advice from those who can tell me what the experience in that market is . . ." but note that this was a *quia timet* action in which, naturally, no actual confusion had yet occurred.

Limited,[61] Ferris J. said that where there is a specialised market, evidence from those in the trade as to what is usual will be essential. However, if it is not a specialist field and the judge feels that he is as well qualified as anyone else to assess the likelihood of confusion, he may do so without hearing such trade evidence.[62]

4.64   Many attempts have been made over the last few years to rely upon survey evidence to establish a likelihood of confusion, with only intermittent success. The problem has often been that the questions asked were found by the court to be leading or simply misleading or nonsensical,[63] but in a few notable cases the evidence from properly conducted surveys has been important in helping the court to reach a decision.[64] It has been suggested that where a survey is carried out, it is most likely to be of use to the court if some of those taking part in the poll are able to give direct evidence in court.[65]

Sub-section 10(3): Dissimilar goods, but damage to the mark

4.65   This sub-section reflects sub-section 5(3) (please see discussion at paragraphs 2.132–2.137 above) with the difference that the extent of the protection is offered only to registered trade marks. It covers situations where an identical or similar mark is used in relation to goods which are not similar to those for which the mark is registered and again depends on the mark having a reputation in the United Kingdom. To infringe, the use of the mark must be made without due cause and must take unfair advantage of or be detrimental to the distinctive character or repute of the registered mark. Again, see the discussion in Chapter 2 as to the probable meaning of these various phrases. To reiterate, there is considerable doubt as to the sorts of damaging activities which would be caught by this sub-section. In particular, there is the difficulty of knowing whether it applies only to infringing use of the mark which amounts to use of the mark in a "trade mark sense" as discussed above. If so, then it may be that the extension of the old law apparently offered by this sub-section is limited. However, if not then, for example, the use of a mark with some sort of reputation, even if not a famous mark, upon goods for which it is not registered, in some sort of promotional manner, rather than use in a trade mark sense, may be deemed to be an infringement.[66] On the other hand, if Knox J.'s judgment in *BASF Plc v. CEP (U.K.) Plc*[67] is correct (which it is submitted makes a good deal of practical sense of what is otherwise a deeply unsatisfactorily worded provision) then reliance on sub-section 10 will, in any event, be limited to cases where there is some confusion between the marks.

---

[61] [1994] R.P.C. 251, applying *GE* [1973] R.P.C. 297 at 321.
[62] See Blackburne J. in *Dalgety Spillers Foods Limited v. Food Brokers Limited ("Pot Noodles")* [1994] F.S.R. 504.
[63] See, *e.g. Tetrosyl* [1980] F.S.R. 68; *Imperial Group Plc v. Philip Morris Limited* [1984] R.P.C. 293, in which Whitford J. set out the criteria for an acceptable survey; *Scott Limited v. Nice-Pak Products Limited* [1989] F.S.R. 100, C.A.; *United Biscuits (U.K.) Limited v. Burtons Biscuits Limited* [1992] F.S.R. 14.
[64] See, *e.g. Lego System Aktieselskab v. Lego M Lemelstrich Limited* [1983] F.S.R. 155; *"Jif"* [1990] R.P.C. 341.
[65] See comments made by Jacob J. in *Neutrogena* [1996] R.P.C. 473 at 485–6
[66] On this basis cases such as *Unidoor v. Marks and Spencer* [1988] R.P.C. 275 and *Mothercare U.K. v. Penguin Books* [1988] R.P.C. 113, discussed at para. 4.21 above, would have succeeded.
[67] October 26, 1995 (unreported).

Sub-section 10(4): Definition of use of a sign

4.66   This sub-section provides a list of ways in which a person may use a sign for the purposes of infringement. It is important to note that the list of uses given is not exhaustive. On the other hand, it may be construed by the courts in accordance with the traditional *ejusdem generis* rule, which broadly means that where one has a list of examples of use which is not intended to be exhaustive, other kinds of use may be caught, but only if they are of the same nature as those already listed by way of example.

4.67   Certain of the uses listed in sub-section (4) are self-explanatory infringing uses of the trade mark, and show no alteration in the law from the position under the 1938 Act as discussed above. Thus, fixing the mark to the goods or their packaging, importing or exporting goods under the mark or using it on business papers or in advertising, are all acts which would previously have been acts of infringement and continue to be so. Most of the acts listed under (b) would also have constituted infringements under the 1938 Act, and are rather obvious acts of infringement, for example, offering goods for sale under the mark. It is possible that the words "stocks [goods] . . . .under the sign, or offers or supplies services under the sign" would cover the position, probably not covered by the 1938 Act,[68] of use of the trade mark as the name of a business and/or upon the fascia of a shop.

4.68   Again, as under the old law, the time at which confusion occurs need not necessarily be at the point of sale of the goods or services, but it is sufficient if the use of the confusingly similar mark leads to confusion at a later stage. This means that reliance upon the use of other distinguishing material to show that there is no likelihood of confusion may not amount to a defence, if there may be post-sale confusion once those other distinguishing marks have been removed.[69]

Sub-section 10(5): Application of a mark by printers, etc.

4.69   This sub-section is new to the 1994 Act, but reflects previous case-law which suggested that printing labels for use on infringing goods was an infringement capable of being restrained by an injunction.[70] Sub-section (5) makes it plain that it is only an infringement where the defendant knew or had reason to believe that the application of the mark was unauthorised. This brings in elements which are familiar in the context of copyright infringement actions and it may well be that the tests which have been applied over the years in relation to "secondary" copyright infringements will be applied by analogy in relation to sub-section 10(5).[71] Most recently, in this context, it has been held that there is a distinction to be made between knowledge of facts from which a reasonable person would arrive at the belief that an article was an infringing copy (as required under section 23 of the Copyright, Designs and Patents Act 1988) and mere knowledge of

[68] Please see references at n. 14, above.
[69] See, *e.g.* post-sale confusion by use of a mark consisting of a tab sewn into a pocket seam on jeans: *Levi Strauss v. Kimbyr Investments Limited* [1994] F.S.R. 335 (a New Zealand decision applying *Aristoc v. Rysta* [1945] A.C. 68). By way of contrast, it seems that post-sale confusion will not found a passing off action: see, *e.g. Hodgkinson & Corby Limited v. Wards Mobility Services Limited* [1995] F.S.R. 169.
[70] See para. 14–08 of Kerly.
[71] See, *e.g. LA Gear Inc v. Hi-Tech Sports Plc* [1992] F.S.R. 121.

assertions of fact (*i.e.* in the form of a letter of complaint from the plaintiff) the truth of which the defendant is unable to ascertain from his own knowledge.[72] If *Hutchison* was correctly decided, then the similarity of wording between sections 23 of the Copyright, Designs and Patents Act 1988 and sub-section 10(5) of the 1994 Act would suggest that a defendant would need to have some personal knowledge of the fact of infringement, or at least of the use to which the labels or packaging which are being produced are to be put, in order to fall within this sub-section. This may restrict its usefulness. However, perhaps such personal knowledge might be found to arise where the defendant was asked to apply a well-known mark to goods having no obvious connection with the recognised owner of that mark.

Sub-section 10(6): Comparative advertising

4.70   The first part of this sub-section excludes use of the mark upon or in relation to genuine goods of the trade mark proprietor or any of his licensees from being infringing use. It thus reflects the position under sub-section 4(3)(a) of the 1938 Act, discussed above.[73]

4.71   However, the section is also intended to ensure that comparative advertising, in which the advertiser uses the plaintiff's registered mark to refer to the plaintiff's goods may be legitimate. Moreover, it should be noted that neither of the words "comparative" or "advertising" actually appear in the sub-section, so that *non-advertising* uses of the mark may well be covered by it, such as use on packaging. To this extent, there is a clear difference between the 1938 and 1994 Acts.

4.72   The proviso to sub-section 10(6) – which is not directly derived from the Directive, but is "home-grown"[74] – is designed to ensure that comparative advertising can be controlled by the proprietor of the registered mark so as to ensure that no unfair use is made of his mark. The hope is to balance the interests of consumers in being provided with information to facilitate a choice between goods or services of various proprietors,[75] and the rights of the trade mark owner to ensure that his mark is not used in such a way as to diminish its goodwill, in particular where the comparison which is made is unfair or untruthful in some way. The White Paper on the Reform of Trade Mark Law, which preceded the 1994 Act, put the matter this way: "while comparative advertising is regarded as more acceptable than it used to be, at least in some fields, it is still generally felt that an advertiser should not be free to ride on the back of a competitor's trade mark."[76]

4.73   Bearing in mind that general intention, it is unfortunate that the wording of sub-section 10(6) is unclear, and possibly tautologous. It is necessary that the use which is

---

[72] See *Hutchison Personal Communications Limited v. Hook Advertising Limited* [1995] F.S.R. 365.
[73] At paras 4.14 *et seq.* and see article by Lewin [1994] E.I.P.R. 91.
[74] *per* Laddie J. in *Barclays Bank Plc v. RBS Advanta*, [1996] R.P.C. 307.
[75] Apparently, however, there is little empirical evidence to show that comparative advertising does actually benefit consumers, since even where it is not misleading, it tends to be one-sided, or simply to confuse the consumer: see article by Mills, [1995] E.I.P.R. 417.
[76] See para. 3.28 of the White Paper of the Law Reform Committee, Cm. 1203 (1990).

made of the mark be "in accordance with honest practices in industrial or commercial matters". This phrase is, naturally, not defined and does not come from the Directive, but from Article 10bis of the Paris Convention for the Protection of Industrial Property, which is entitled "Unfair Competition". This provides:

"(2) Any act of competition contrary to honest practices in industrial or commercial matters constitutes an act of unfair competition.

(3) The following in particular shall be prohibited:
1. All acts of such a nature as to create confusion by any means whatever with the establishment, the goods or the industrial or commercial activities of a competitor;
2. False allegations in the course of trade of such a nature as to discredit the establishment, the goods, or the industrial or commercial activities, of a competitor;
3. Indications or allegations the use of which in the course of trade is liable to mislead the public as to the nature, the manufacturing process, the characteristics, the suitability for their purpose, or the quantity, of the goods."[77]

4.74 Recital 6 of the Directive provided that it should not exclude the application to trade mark law of national rules on unfair competition. Of course, the Paris Convention has never had direct effect in this country, since the Convention binds only the Crown and has not, as such, been incorporated into domestic law. No domestic unfair competition law has existed in the United Kingdom other than in the indirect form of the more specific torts of passing off, trade libel, etc., or under some specific relevant statute, such as, perhaps, the Trade Descriptions Act 1968.

4.75 First, the court may have to decide which "practices" (if any) are relevant. In the general field of advertising, this may not be too difficult, since there are a number of controls upon advertising which are of general application. For instance, misleading advertisements are controlled by a statutory instrument[78] which imposes a duty upon the Director General of Fair Trading, the IBA and the Cable Authority to consider and deal with complaints as to misleading advertisements, in line with E.C. Council Directive 84/450 relating to misleading advertising. Article 3 of that Directive dealt with the definition of a misleading advertisement and provided that account is to be taken of all relevant circumstances, all the features of the advertisement and any information contained in it, in particular concerning the characteristics of goods or services, such as their availability, nature, composition, fitness for purpose, use, specification, geographic or commercial origin, or the results and material features of tests carried out on them. Thus, for example, unbalanced or inaccurate references to comparative tests carried out on competing products in comparative advertising could breach this particular yardstick. Similarly, Article 3(b) deals with advertisements which are misleading as to the price or conditions upon which goods are supplied or services provided, and Article 3(c) similarly prohibits advertisements which are misleading as to the identity, assets, qualifications, or

---

[77] The Paris Convention is conveniently to be found in App. 12 to Kerly.
[78] Control of Misleading Advertisements Regulations 1988 (S.I. 1988, No. 915).

other rights of the advertiser.[79] There are equally controls upon the content of advertisements, enforced by industry watchdogs, such as the British Code of Advertising Practice;
subject to what is said in paragraph 4.77 below, these may be of relevance.

4.76   To date, because of the terms of the 1938 Act, there has in any event been relatively
little use made of comparative advertising which has not been deemed to be an infringement of trade mark rights and it may therefore be difficult to say that any particular type
of comparative advertising is in line with industry practices in relation to such advertisements. However, in those fields where comparative advertising has been accepted by
mutual consent, of course, it will be possible to point to the parameters set by the industry
practice, for example, the practice in the car trade of comparing the performance of
various models of cars. As time goes on, practices which are generally deemed acceptable
may evolve in relation to other particular types of industry or commerce.

4.77   However, it seems that the court will not consider itself bound by any such industry
practices, regulations or codes of practice, since these could result in differing standards of
honesty being applied in different industries.[80] Compliance with such an agreed code of
practice alone may not, therefore, resolve the issue of honesty in the advertiser's favour
for the purposes of the proviso to sub-section 10(6).

4.78   In *Barclays Bank Plc v. RBS Advanta*,[81] Laddie J. held that the essential test was the
honesty of the comparative advertisement:

> "... there will be no infringement unless the use of the registered mark is not in
> accordance with honest practices ... this test is objective. This part of the proviso simply
> means that if the use is considered honest by members of a reasonable audience, it will
> not infringe. ... If ... a reasonable reader is likely to say, on being given the full facts,
> that the advertisement is not honest, for example because it is significantly misleading,
> then the protection from trade mark infringement is removed."

Similarly, in *Vodafone Group Plc v. Orange Personal Communications*,[82] Jacob J. held:

> "If a comparison is significantly misleading on an objective basis to a substantial
> proportion of the reasonable audience, it is not an 'honest practice' within the
> section."

4.79   Thus, the test to be applied is an objective one. Given the peculiarities which may
occur where a subjective construction is given to a concept such as honesty, there is much
to be said for an objective standard.[83]

---

[79] For a useful summary of the provisions, see *Halsbury's Laws* (4th ed.), Vol. 51. para. 8.92.
[80] See *Barclays Bank Plc v. RBS Advanta* [1996] R.P.C. 307 at 315–316.
[81] *ibid.* at p. 315.
[82] July 10, 1996, Jacob J., unreported.
[83] Contrast the position in relation to bona fide use of one's own name, under s. 8 of the 1938 Act, for example,
see *Provident Financial PLC v. Halifax Building Society* [1994] F.S.R. 81 esp. at 93.

4.80   Moreover, on this construction of the phrase "in accordance with honest practices in industrial or commercial matters", it is difficult to see what further test must be passed if the advertisement is not "without due cause" to take "unfair advantage of, or [be] detrimental to, the distinctive character or repute of the trade mark." It seems clear from the wording of the sub-section that the two parts to the proviso are intended to be cumulative, yet virtually any kind of use of the registered mark which would take unfair advantage or be detrimental to the distinctive character or repute of the registered trade mark would be unlikely to be in accordance with honest practices in industrial or commercial matters. At the most, "... the use must either give some advantage to the defendant or inflict some harm on the character or repute of the registered mark which is above the level of *de minimis.*" [83a] Moreover, the use, as in sub-section 5(3) of the Act, of the phrase "without due cause" before the reference to the unfair advantage/detriment to the mark is, again, difficult to construe sensibly as adding anything to the sense of the proviso.

4.81   The facts of *Barclays Bank Plc v. RBS Advanta* were that the defendant had distributed advertising literature for its credit card which included a brochure carrying a comparative table of fees and interest rates for various credit cards, including the "Barclaycard Standard Visa". "Barclaycard" is a registered trade mark. It was held, on the hearing of an interlocutory motion, that it was most unlikely that any reasonable reader would take the view that the advertisement was not honest, as, read as a whole, it truly reflected the defendant's view that the package of benefits offered by its card offered a better deal to the customer. An interlocutory injunction was therefore refused.

4.82   In *Vodafone Group Plc v. Orange Personal Communications*, the plaintiffs objected to the defendants' use of the slogan "On average, Orange users save £20 every month", and the saving was expressly stated to be in comparison with Vodafone's equivalent tariffs.[83b] It was held that had the slogan been misleading, it would have taken advantage of the distinctive character or repute of the Vodafone mark as it would have been meaningless if no-one had heard of Vodafone. However, after examining carefully the way in which the comparison had been worked out, including various "assumptions" as to relevant use enabling the "average" to be stated, it was held that the slogan was objectively honest and would not have misled "the ordinary reader".

4.83   Perhaps it may also be helpful to look at some of the reported cases under the 1938 Act relating to comparative advertising, to see how they might be treated under the 1994 Act. The case of *Bismag*[84] concerned a straightforward comparative table of an analysis of

---

[83a] *Per* Laddie J. in *Barclays Bank Plc v. RBS Advanta*, n.80 above at p. 316. This part of subs. 10(6) comes from Art. 5(5) of the Directive, but see the criticism of its wording at p. 316 of *Barclays v. Advanta*, echoed by Jacob J. in *Vodafone Group Plc v. Orange Personal Communications*, n.82 above. Please also see paras. 2.132 *et seq.* of Chap. 2 above, in which the question of unfair advantage, etc., is discussed.

[83b] n.82 above. One relevant point was that the action was brought only by the Vodafone companies, although the advertisement of which they complained had also referred to Cellnet. Cellnet did not sue. The judge also considered it relevant to the question of honesty that the campaign was adopted by various service providers dealing in all three networks.

[84] (1940) 57 R.P.C. 209.

the parties' respective magnesia tablets, showing the price difference between them. Assuming that the analysis which had been carried out by or on behalf of the defendants in that case was accurate and was accurately set out in the advertisement, it would seem that the publication of such a table, or the material contained in such a table in some other form, would not now be an infringement of the registered mark. In *Chanel*,[85] the comparative table which had been produced by the defendant indicated which of its products (described by their code numbers) were intended to be equivalent to the plaintiff's products. This was more of a borderline case, since the advertisement was presumably accurate, in so far as it went, but of course supported the defendant's intentions of producing a perfume so similar in smell to the plaintiff's famous brands as to be mistaken (in use, if not at the time of purchase) for those brands. Unless deemed to be "detrimental" to the repute of the plaintiff's mark it is doubtful if this would have exceeded the bounds of permissible comparative advertising under the 1994 Act.[86]

4.84 One case which clearly would have fallen on the wrong side of the proviso in sub-section 10(6) was the case of *Compaq*[87] in which the text of the comparative advertisements was misleading. For instance, the defendant claimed in the advertisements that the parties' respective computer systems shown in the advertisements were "basically and essentially the same". This was found not to be true, as the parties' respective systems were materially different in essential features. Similarly, the comparisons made between the prices of the two systems were also found to be misleading, in that the defendant had made no allowance for the fact that discounts would usually be given from the quoted retail prices. These misrepresentations in the advertisements would seem likely to have infringed each part of the proviso to sub-section 10(6). First, they would seem unlikely to have been able to be justified as being honest in any objective sense. Secondly, they were in breach of advertising practice and were misleading within the definition given by Directive 84/450. Thirdly, the advertisements could have been said to have taken unfair advantage of the repute of the Compaq mark by indicating that Dell products were equivalent to Compaq products when they were not (surely, riding on the back of Compaq's reputation) and, finally, would have been detrimental to Compaq's repute in suggesting that the Dell products were equivalent but cheaper, when they were not.

4.85 All of the difficulties with comparative advertising *may* perhaps be resolved in the relatively near future, as the Council of Ministers has now approved a draft of an E.U. Directive on the subject,[88] in the form of a Directive amending Directive 84/450. This would, once brought into force, largely replace section 10(6), unless, that is, the terms of that sub-section are deemed to comply with the final version of the Directive as they stand, which seems possible.[89]

---

[85] *Chanel Ltd v. Triton Packaging Ltd* [1993] R.P.C. 32.
[86] It is interesting to see that the commentaries on the new Act differ in their views as to whether or not this would be an infringement. Morcom (*A Guide to the Trade Marks Act 1994* at p. 40) and Annand and Norman (*Blackstone's Guide to Trade Marks Act 1994* at p. 160), suggest that it would, whilst the *Current Law Statutes* annotation suggests that it would not.
[87] *Compaq Computer Corp v. Dell Computer Corporation Ltd* [1992] F.S.R. 93.
[88] See draft at [1994] O.J. C136/4.
[89] See article by Meyer-Harport [1995] Ent. L.R. 195.

(5) THE SEA-LION MARK EXAMPLE

4.86 Let us return to the example taken in Chapter 1 of the mark "sea-lion" chosen for soaps in Class 3, and look at possible infringements of the marks, obviously, subject to the risk of having an invalid or partially invalid registration, the wider the specification of goods for the mark, the wider the protection may be:

1. Use of the word "sea-lion" upon soap would be a clear infringement falling within section 10(1), *i.e.* an identical mark for identical goods.
2. Use of the word "sea-lion" upon toothpaste ought to be an infringement falling within sub-section 10(2), being use of the identical mark upon similar goods to those covered by the registration, applying the old tests amended as suggested in *British Sugar* (see above). One cannot be categorical in saying that this would be an infringement, however, since the sub-section also requires that the similarity between the marks and/or goods should be such as to give rise to a likelihood of confusion. It seems improbable that confusion could be avoided in these circumstances, but the possibility would have to be examined, if necessary, in the light of the manner in which the alleged infringer was using the mark.
3. Use of a similar sea-lion device in relation to toothpaste could also be an infringement within sub-section 10(2) as long as the two devices were sufficiently similar. Here the court would have to look not only to the similarity of the devices themselves, but also to the overall likelihood of confusion as in example 2 above.
4. Use of a similar sea-lion device in relation to lip-salve might pose a slightly more tricky problem, because of the greater difference between the goods for which the mark is registered and the goods upon which the alleged infringer is using them. Here, it seems that the court would be required to decide in all the circumstances whether confusion between the two would be likely and, if the sea-lion device or the series of sea-lion marks had acquired some sort of reputation by use, it seems quite likely that in this case there would be a likelihood of association between the marks, in that it might be thought that the owner of the original sea-lion mark had licensed this use, even if there was not "traditional" confusion as to origin.
5. Use of a device consisting of a walrus or maybe a seal would also pose more difficulty. The question would be whether the devices were sufficiently similar as to be likely to be confused or associated one with the other, and here the court would probably have recourse to the test of the essential idea of the mark, being in the one case a sea-lion and in the other a walrus/seal, but the result might well be different if the manner and style of the execution of the two devices was so similar as to overcome the difference between the animals, given the test of "imperfect recollection" by the consumer. Here, the seal mark would probably be at greater risk than the walrus mark.
6. Use of the word "sea-lion" or, indeed, a similar sea-lion device, upon jelly sweets might fall within sub-section 10(3) if the sea-lion mark had acquired a reputation in the United Kingdom and the alleged infringer's use could be deemed to be detrimental to the distinctive character or repute of the sea-lion mark or in some way took an unfair advantage of it. Detriment of this kind might be established where for instance the sea-lion mark had been used in relation to soaps, etc., for

children, and the mark had established a reputation as being used in relation to very pure, hypo-allergenic goods free from harmful additives or colourings. If the sweets being sold by the defendant under the same mark were crammed full of additives and E-numbers, possibly it could be said that this would have a detrimental effect upon the reputation of the registered sea-lion mark.

7. If it had proved impossible to register the sea-lion shaped soap, and the use made of the mark had been made only in relation to a standard rectangular soap tablet, what would be the position if use were made of a sea-lion shaped soap by an alleged infringer, even under a significantly different name? These would clearly be identical goods to those for which the mark is registered, but would this be use of a "sign" which is similar to the sea-lion word or device mark? In other words, can a shape be similar to a name? If the right test to apply is to consider what is the essential feature of the device, then it is suggested that this would be a similar trade mark, since the essential feature of each of them would be the sea-lion. In any event, the question would also have to be asked as to whether there was a likelihood of confusion by reason of the defendant's use of that shape, and this might depend upon the way in which he was using it, if it was already on sale.

8. Would the situation described in 7 above be different if the proprietor of the sea-lion trade mark had in fact used the word and the device in relation to sea-lion shaped cakes of soap, despite its failure to register that shape as a trade mark? To the extent that the marks are to be compared in "notional fair use" this actual use might not be relevant. But if, as seems likely, given the court's need to look for a likelihood of confusion, the court would look at the surrounding circumstances, then it is suggested that the fact that the sea-lion word or device may have become connected in the mind of the public with sea-lion shaped cakes of soap would strengthen the case considerably, whatever steps the alleged infringer had taken to differentiate the two products.

9. In each case, what would have been the position had the sea-lion mark been an "existing trade mark", that is to say, one registered prior to October 31, 1994 and it was discovered that these infringements had also commenced prior to that date and were mere continuations of existing uses of the allegedly infringing marks? Under the old Act, as discussed in Chapter 2, only the sea-lion word and device mark could have been registered. Use of either of those marks, or marks confusingly similar to either of them upon soap (whether in the form of a simple cake of soap, a sea-lion-shaped cake of soap or liquid soap) would have been an infringement, so that action could now be taken against the alleged infringer. However, the other uses discussed above would not have been infringements under the 1938 Act, due to the limitation of section 4(1) to use upon goods for which the mark was registered, and as a result no infringement action could now be brought against such "infringements".

(6) PROTECTION OF WELL-KNOWN TRADE MARKS: SECTION 56

4.87 The 1994 Act introduces to English law a special protection for well-known trade marks. This statutory form of relief, which bears some resemblance to the common law passing off action, is innovative in that a mark can be protected here whether or not its proprietor carries on business or has any goodwill in the United Kingdom.

4.88 Sub-section 56(1) defines a well-known trade mark, entitled to protection under Article 6bis of the Paris Convention, as "a mark which is well-known in the United Kingdom as being the mark of a person" who is a national of a Convention country or established in a Convention country "whether or not that person carries on business or has any goodwill, in the United Kingdom." The sub-section therefore envisages marks being well-known here even when they have not been used here either at all or to such an extent as to found a goodwill.[90]

4.89 Where such a mark exists, its proprietor is entitled to restrain by injunction the use of an identical or substantially similar trade mark in relation to identical or similar goods or services, where the use is likely to cause confusion. Most of the elements of this sub-section are clear, given the discussions earlier in this work as to the meaning of identical or similar marks and identical or similar goods.[91]

4.90 The right to the injunction will arise where there is sufficient similarity of marks/goods or services *and* a likelihood of confusion. Naturally, where the proprietor is relying upon a well-known mark which has not established a goodwill in the United Kingdom (where there is such goodwill, presumably a passing off action would be more attractive to the proprietor) the likelihood of confusion would not lead to a likelihood of damage or, at any rate, quantifiable damage, and this is not a requisite factor in the application of the section. In this respect, proceedings under section 56(2) differ from passing off proceedings (damage is a requisite ingredient of the tort, see Chapter 5 below). Indeed, the sub-section makes no provision for the award of damages where rights are "infringed" in this way, and the only relief which may be sought is an injunction.

4.91 There are two provisos to sub-section 56(2), first, that the right may be lost where the proprietor acquiesces in the use of the "infringing" mark (see section 48). Secondly, as in the case of infringements of United Kingdom registered trade marks, nothing in sub-section 56(2) affects the continuation of any use of a trade mark begun before the commencement of the Act. Sub-section 56(3), refers to the *bona fide* use of such a trade mark begun before October 31, 1994 and there is no guidance as to the meaning of these words in this context. In particular, it is not clear whether a subjective or objective test of bona fides would be applied.[92]

(7) DEFENCES TO INFRINGEMENT UNDER THE 1994 ACT

4.92 Many of the defences to infringement which were available under the 1938 Act are similar to those which may apply in the case of infringements under the 1994 Act.

---

[90] Passing off has generally made a distinction between mere reputation and a protectable goodwill acquired by trading here – contrast, *e.g.* "*Crazy Horse*" [1967] R.P.C. 581 with *Maxim's Limited v. Dye* [1977] F.S.R. 364; [1977] 1 W.L.R. 1155.
[91] See especially the discussion of confusing or deceptive similarity of marks at paras. 2.94 *et seq.* of Chap. 2 and the discussion of s. 5 of the Act, at 2.110 *et seq.*
[92] See again the comments in *Provident Financial Plc v. Halifax Building Society* [1994] F.S.R. 81 at 93.

(i) Challenge to the validity of the plaintiff's registration

4.93   As was the case with section 46 of the 1938 Act, section 72 of the 1994 Act deems a registration of a trade mark to be prima facie evidence of the validity of the original registration. However, this does not preclude a challenge to that registration at a later date. Registrations may be revoked under section 46 of the Act for non-use, or for a variety of other reasons which are discussed in Chapter 3 above. Sub-section 46(4) anticipates that an application for revocation may be made where proceedings concerning the trade mark are pending in the High Court, and in that case the application for revocation must be made to the Court, and will be made by way of counterclaim.

4.94   Sub-section 46(6) resolves the position in relation to the retrospective effect of such revocation, by providing that where the registration of a trade mark is revoked to any extent the rights of the proprietor may be deemed to have ceased to that extent as from either the date of the application for revocation or, if the court is satisfied that the grounds for revocation existed at an earlier date, that date. Thus, if the grounds for revocation are that the mark was liable to mislead the public, and had been for some time prior to the application for revocation, it seems likely that the court would order that the date by which it had become misleading should be the date for the effect of revocation. This may mean, in appropriate cases, that not only will no injunction be granted in relation to the future, but no remedy will be available to the proprietor of the revoked mark for past infringements.[93]

4.95   Similarly, in the context of infringement proceedings, a counterclaim may be made for the registration of the trade mark to be declared invalid pursuant to section 47 of the 1994 Act.[94] Where it is found that the registered mark was registered in breach of sections 3 or 5, sub-section 47(6) provides that the effect of the declaration of invalidity is that the registration shall be deemed never to have been made. In other words, in such cases, the effect of the finding of invalidity will be wholly retrospective, precluding any relief being granted to the proprietor of the invalid mark. Please note that section 48 may also be relevant in such cases.[95]

(ii) No infringement

4.96   Just as under the 1938 Act, it will obviously always be open to a defendant to claim that the particular acts which are alleged to constitute infringement do not amount to infringement under the 1994 Act. As before, there will almost always be scope to argue that a mark which is similar to the registered mark is not confusingly similar to it, and such arguments may have a better chance of success if the marks have been used concurrently without good evidence of confusion having come to the attention of the proprietor of the registered mark.

---

[93] See *Second Sight Limited v. Novell U.K. Limited* [1995] R.P.C. 423 at 428 to 429.
[94] See paras. 3.57 *et seq.* above.
[95] See paras. 3.68 *et seq.* above.

4.97   Alternatively, it may be possible to claim that the acts complained of have been carried out with the consent of the proprietor of the mark, at least in cases where the infringement proceeedings are being brought by a licensee.[96]

(iii) Concurrent right

4.98   Sub-section 11(1) states that a registered trade mark is not infringed by the use of another's registered trade mark. This section therefore equates to sub-section 4(4) of the 1938 Act.[97] The section specified that the protection only extends to use of the defendant's mark upon the goods or services in respect of which it is registered, and, again, this represents no change over the previous law. However, under the 1938 Act, it was possible to seek to rely upon the provision of sub-section 30(1), to claim that use of a mark slightly different to the defendant's registered mark amounted to use of the registered mark, so that the Defendant could plead section 4(4).[98] There is no full equivalent to section 30(1) in the 1994 Act, save in relation to revocation proceedings under section 46.[99]

4.99   Sub-section 11(1) also goes on to make reference to section 47 of the 1994 Act, which deals with declarations of invalidity. The sub-section does not spell out the position, but it seems clear by the reference which is made to sub-section 47(6) that what is meant is that if the defendant's mark is declared invalid under section 47, presumably in such a case because of its clash with the plaintiff's earlier registered mark, then the defendant's registration will by sub-section 47(6) be deemed never to have been made. The temporary validity of the defendant's registration would, therefore, give no defence to an infringement action in relation to any period, whether at the time when it was registered or not.

Section 11(3): unregistered concurrent rights

4.100   Sub-section 11(3) deals with concurrent rights which are not registered. However, the section is significantly different from section 7 of the 1938 Act and, in some ways, is much narrower than section 7. The sub-section is based on Article 6(2) of the Directive, in which reference is made to the slightly strange concept, so far as English law is concerned, of the use of a mark in a particular locality.

4.101   The sub-section protects earlier, unregistered trade mark rights or other signs which have been used continuously by the proposed defendant or his predecessor in title from before the date of first use or registration (whichever is earlier) of the registered mark. To this extent, the sub-section is like section 7 and will presumably be applied in the same manner.[1] Of course, there may be some difficulty in following the decisions under section 7, given the much broader definition of infringement contained in the 1994 Act. Nonetheless, the principle appears to be clear that registration of a trade mark should not interfere with the continuation of use of unregistered local marks of earlier provenance.

---

[96] See, *e.g. Northern & Shell Plc v. Conde Nast* [1995] R.P.C. 117, and as to the rights of exclusive licensees see Chap. 7(8).
[97] On which see paras. 4.40 *et seq.* above.
[98] This defence was unsuccessfully pleaded in *Neutrogena* [1996] R.P.C., see section on defences to the 1938 Act above.
[99] See para. 3.43 above.
[1]   See paras. 2.144 *et seq.*, above.

4.102 However, the reference to the marks being used in a particular locality appears to restrict the use of this sub-section in two ways. First, it seems clear that the defence will only apply to use in the particular locality in which use has previously been established. So the proprietor of the earlier right will not be entitled to expand the geographical area in which he exploits his mark by reliance upon the use made of the mark earlier in his initial locality. Such expansion would appear to be deemed an infringement.

4.103 Secondly, it also seems clear that this sub-section will not protect the use of an earlier unregistered mark which is used throughout the United Kingdom, as the reference to the earlier right being a right "which applies only in that locality" would appear to exclude this possibility. Therefore, the proprietor of an unregistered mark which has been used throughout the United Kingdom before use or registration of the registered mark began will have no protection under this sub-section. His only protection (assuming that he missed the opportunity to oppose the registration of the mark) would seem to be to seek a declaration of invalidity of the registered mark, under section 47, so that the registration of the later mark will be deemed never to have been made. Again, it must be remembered that the right to apply under section 47 may be affected by acquiescence for a continuous period of five years or more, under section 48.

(iv) Honest use of own name, or other indications

4.104 Sub-section 11(2) is in many ways equivalent to section 8 of the 1938 Act.[2] Along with the provisions of section 3, especially 3(1)(c), this sub-section is designed to ensure that honest traders may make use of terms which they might perfectly fairly want to use.[3]

4.105 Under sub-section 11(2) there is no infringement when use is made of a number of kinds of descriptive terms (discussed below) as long as such use is "in accordance with honest practices in industrial or commercial matters." This phrase has already been discussed in relation to sub-section 10(6) on comparative advertising and it is not therefore intended to discuss it in detail here. However, it does seem clear from the use of this phrase in this context that the test of honesty for the purposes of this sub-section must be an objective one, rather than a subjective one. There could be no reason otherwise to refer to honest *practices*, if one would look to the honesty of the individual trader in relation to the acts complained of. This sub-section therefore differs, it seems, from section 8 of the 1938 Act.

4.106 Sub-section 11(2)(a) provides, as did section 8(a) of the 1938 Act, that there is no infringement where the defendant is using his own name. This provision, as before, would appear to include use of a company name or even the name of an established business or firm, as well as the name of an individual. It remains to be seen whether it is consistent with "honest practices in industrial or commercial matters" to continue to make use of one's own name, and in particular a company or business name which could be changed, if one

---

[2] See paras. 4.44 *et seq.*, above.
[3] This phrase is taken from the judgment of Whitford J. in *Have a Break Trade Mark* [1993] R.P.C. 217, where he was considering the appropriate test for registrability of a slogan.

subsequently discovers that confusion is being caused with a registered trade mark. Use of one's business address is also protected.

4.107 Sub-section 11(2)(b) provides a similar defence in respect of the use of indications of the "kind, quality, quantity, intended purpose, value, geographical origin, time of production of goods or of rendering of services, or other characteristics of goods or services." Section 8(b) of the 1938 Act covered descriptive references to the character or quality of the goods or services and it is clear that this sub-section extends that provision substantially, but keeps within the ambit of seeking to protect a trader's right to make honest use of a descriptive term applicable to his goods or services. Presumably, if an infringement would only occur where the use of the descriptive term was in some trade mark sense,[4] then the protection offered by this sub-section would be for such trade mark use. This was not how section 8(b) of the 1938 Act was applied[5] and, indeed, it is difficult to see why protection should be granted for use of such terms as trade marks, as opposed to descriptive terms, if the boundaries of registrability are to be set according to a test of whether registration of a descriptive term would exclude honest traders from *describing* their goods or services in appropriate terms.

4.108 Sub-section 11(2)(c) provides that it is no infringement to use a trade mark "where it is necessary to indicate the intended purpose of a product or service (in particular, as accessories or spare parts)". This is similar to section 4(3) of the 1938 Act. Construing this sub-section in the light of the requirement that any such use be made in accordance with honest practices, it would seem that it should be reasonably easy to establish whether use of the trade mark is necessary in any particular case. All of sub-section 11(2) is based upon Article 6(1) of the Directive.

(v) Exhaustion of rights: section 12

4.109 Section 12(1) provides that it is no infringement to use a registered trade mark in relation to goods which have been put on the market anywhere in the European Economic Area under that trade mark by the proprietor or with his consent. This gives statutory effect to the doctrine of exhaustion of rights which has been developed over a number of years by the European Court of Justice and which is discussed more fully in Chapter 7. The rule arises out of the principle of free circulation of goods and services, so that where goods have been put on the market with the consent of a proprietor, his rights in relation to the trade mark are deemed to have been exhausted, despite the territorial limitations of national trade marks. This may be contrasted with the position as it existed under section 4(3)(a) of the 1938 Act as construed in, for example, the *Revlon* case.[6] The use of the term "with his consent" makes it plain that the exhaustion of the proprietor's rights may occur where the initial marketing of the trade mark's products has been done by a licensee or any other authorised distributor and need not have been done by the proprietor himself.

---

[4] See paras. 4.53 *et seq.*, above, and see especially *British Sugar Plc v. James Robertson & Sons Ltd* [1996] R.P.C. 281.
[5] See *Portakabin Limited v. Powerblast Limited* [1990] R.P.C. 471 at 483.
[6] [1980] F.S.R. 85.

4.110 There are exceptions to the rule under section 12(1). First, sub-section 12(2) provides that sub-section (1) does not apply where there are legitimate reasons for the proprietor opposing further dealings in the goods, in particular where the condition of the goods has been changed or impaired after they have been put on the market. This proviso again stems from the European law precedents on this subject, on which see the discussion in Chapter 7(13) and, in particular, the string of pharmaceuticals cases where parallel imports of trade marked products have been prohibited where there were potentially dangerous alterations to the goods. The reference to the reasons of the proprietor being "legitimate" again stems from the European law precedents on this subject, since the European Court of Justice has made it plain that a trade mark proprietor will not be able to rely upon differences between his trade marks in different Member States if it can be shown that those differences arose out of the proprietor's wish to partition the market.[7]

4.111 It must be noted, however, that section 12 only applies to parallel imports of goods which have been first marketed somewhere within the European Economic Area, and the previous law as to exhaustion of rights in relation to goods sold outside that area will presumably still apply.

(vi) European defences

4.112 Apart from the specific defence based on exhaustion of rights, when faced with an allegation of infringement of trade mark there may be other defences to be raised based upon European Community law, for instance, a claim that the plaintiff is disentitled from enforcing his trade mark right as an abuse of a dominant position contrary to Article 86. However, it must be said that, to date, the so-called "Euro-Defences" have not met with much success in the context of trade mark law in the United Kingdom courts.

(vii) Estoppel, acquiescence and delay

4.113 As discussed in relation to the 1938 Act above, it is always open to a defendant in a trade mark infringement action to raise defences based not strictly upon the Act itself, but upon general equitable principles. To this extent, it may be possible to claim that the plaintiff is disentitled by reason of his actions, his conduct or his inactivity to the relief which he seeks. These defences have been discussed above, and, with one exception, do not need to be discussed further here as they do not depend upon the wording of the 1994 Act itself.

4.114 The exception is section 48 of the Act which deals specifically with acquiescence, which would seem to make it most unlikely that a claim based on general equitable principles of acquiescence would be considered in addition to a section 48(2) claim. Section 48 is discussed in Chapter 3(8) above.

---

[7] See, *e.g.* Case 3/78, *Centrafarm BV v. American Home Products Corp*: [1978] E.C.R. 1823; [1979] 1 C.M.L.R. 326 and see paras. 7.52 *et seq.* below.

CHAPTER 5

PASSING OFF

(1) INTRODUCTION

5.1 The common law action for passing off is left untouched by the 1994 Act. Passing off actions, in one guise or another, predated the first registered trade mark law and have continued to coexist with the law of registered marks ever since.

5.2 The great advantage that passing off actions have over the protection offered to registered trade marks is the flexibility of the concept, which as a common law action, relatively unhampered by precise definitions, has adapted itself to the needs of commerce over the years. In many ways, passing off is the nearest equivalent to the laws of unfair competition which exist elsewhere, and although a passing off action cannot stretch to the full extent of a law against unfair competition, it may be used as a means of ensuring fair trading.[1]

---

[1] See Lord Morris in *Parker-Knoll Limited v. Knoll International Limited* [1962] R.P.C. 265 at 278.

5.3 The simplest definition of the traditional basis of the passing off action is that "nobody has any right to represent his goods as the goods of somebody else".[2] However, this rather simple definition, whilst probably accurate for the better part of this century, may now be somewhat too narrow to cover more recent developments and extensions to the law of passing off. Perhaps these days a better definition (if such it can be called) is "[t]he principle that no man is entitled to steal another's trade by deceit."[3]

5.4 The classic form of passing off as a misrepresentation that one's goods are somebody else's has now to be seen merely as a particular manner of committing a wrong "included in a wider genus".[4] Today it is generally accepted that the best definition of the basis of a passing off action was given by Lord Diplock in the *Advocaat* case.[5] He held that it was:

> "possible to identify 5 characteristics which must be present in order to create a valid cause of action for passing off: (i) a misrepresentation (ii) made by a trader in the course of trade, (iii) to prospective customers of his or ultimate consumers of goods or services supplied by him, (iv) which is calculated to injure the business or goodwill of another trader (in the sense that this is a reasonably foreseeable consequence) and (v) which causes actual damage to the business or goodwill of the trader by whom the action is brought or (in a *quia timet* action) will probably do so".

5.5 In *Advocaat*, Lord Diplock also approved the speech of Lord Parker in *Spalding v. Gamage*[6] in which Lord Parker had said:

> "The basis of a passing off action being a false representation by the defendant, it must be proved in each case as a fact that the false representation was made ... The more common cases, where the representation is implied in the use or imitation of the mark, trade mark or get-up with which the goods of another are associated in the minds of the public ... The point to be decided is whether, having regard to all the circumstances of the case, the use by the defendant in connection with the goods of the mark, name, or get-up in question impliedly represents such goods to be the goods of the plaintiff, or the goods of the plaintiff of the particular class or quality".

5.6 It seems to be generally accepted[7] that these definitions do not lay down any cast-iron definition of what amounts to passing off, or what must be proved before a passing off action will succeed. However, they do show the general scope of a passing off action.

5.7 More recently, in "*Jif*"[8] two Law Lords sought to simplify the definition of passing off somewhat, whilst accepting the definition which had been given in *Advocaat*. Lord

---

[2] *per* Halsbury L.C. in *Reddaway v. Banham* [1896] A.C. 199 at 204.
[3] *per* Lord Oliver in "*Jif*" [1990] R.P.C. 340; [1990] 1 W.L.R. 491.
[4] *per* Lord Diplock in the leading case of *Erven Warnink BV v. J. Townend & Sons (Hull) Limited* [1979] A.C. 731 at 742; [1979] F.S.R. 397 at 404 ("*Advocaat*").
[5] *ibid.* at 742 and 405.
[6] (1915) 32 R.P.C. 273.
[7] See, *e.g.* p. 4 of Wadlow, *The Law of Passing Off* (2nd ed., 1994).
[8] See n. 3, above.

The products at issue in the "jif lemon" case, reproduced from Reports on the Patent Cases by kind permission of Her Majesty's Stationary Office

Defendants' Mark II Lemon

Defendants' Mark III lemon

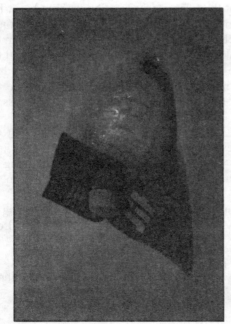

Jif lemon

Defendants' Mark I lemon

Jauncey reduced the definition to the classic "trinity" of (1) a reputation on the part of the plaintiff, (2) a misrepresentation by the defendant and (3) a likelihood that the plaintiff will thereby suffer damage. The same "trinity" of criteria was reiterated by Lord Oliver.[9]

5.8 It could be said that Lord Diplock's five point definition can, in any event, be "boiled down" to the classic "trinity" of reputation, misrepresentation and damage. Each of these three will now be examined relatively briefly and the reader is referred to specialist works on passing off for further details as to the historical development of the tort which may throw further light upon its current scope and definition.[10]

(2) REPUTATION OR GOODWILL

5.9 It may be somewhat misleading to suggest that it is sufficient for the purposes of bringing a passing off action to have a reputation in the United Kingdom. This is probably not the case, but what is required is that the plaintiff should have acquired a *goodwill* in the name or other distinguishing indicia which he would wish to protect by the passing off action, it being accepted that goodwill can be built up only in relation to a business.

5.10 The first question to answer, therefore, is whether the plaintiff has a business benefiting from a protectable goodwill. All kinds of businesses can be protected, but some kind of commercial activity does need to be carried on by the plaintiff before the court will accept that he or it has a protectable goodwill. For instance, a political party does not carry on a business and does not have a protectable goodwill.[11] On the other hand, where a charity carries on certain trading activities, goodwill may be established and therefore be protectable.[12] Even the fund-raising activities of a charity may qualify it for protection by a passing off action in an appropriate case.[13]

5.11 If it can be established that there is a business in the United Kingdom, it may suffice for that business to be locally based. In *Brestian v. Try*[14] for instance, a hairdresser managed to prevent another from using the same name "Charles of London" when his own reputation was based on salons in London, Wembley and Brighton and the defendant's business was in Tunbridge Wells. The geographical separation of the businesses was not sufficient to exclude the possibility of confusion as customers might travel or the businesses might expand. Moreover, where there is only a local goodwill, it may still be possible to obtain a nationwide injunction.[15]

---

[9] The same adoption of the "trinity" was followed by Nourse L.J. in *Consorzio Del Prosciutto di Parma v. Marks & Spencer Plc* [1991] R.P.C. 351.
[10] See, *e.g.* Wadlow (above) and Drysdale & Silverleaf, *Passing Off Law and Practice* (2nd ed.).
[11] See *Kean v. McGivan* [1982] F.S.R. 119.
[12] *e.g. British Legion v. British Legion Club (Street) Limited* (1931) 48 R.P.C. 555; *The Law Society v. The Society of Lawyers* (1996) I.P.D. 19049.
[13] See *British Diabetic Assoc. v. Diabetic Society* [1996] F.S.R. 1 at 10.
[14] [1958] R.P.C. 161.
[15] See *Chelsea Man Menswear Limited v. Chelsea Girl Limited* [1987] R.P.C. 189.

Foreign goodwill

5.12   On the other hand, it seems that there is still a requirement that there be a goodwill to be protected in the United Kingdom. There are numerous cases in which well known foreign plaintiffs have sought to obtain relief in the United Kingdom against defendants seeking to use identical or confusingly similar names to their own or to the names of their businesses. The results of such cases have differed according to whether or not there had been some actual business done here. For instance, if the plaintiff has an agent or representative here, doing business here, then there will be a goodwill here, too. Alternatively, it may suffice if the foreign plaintiff has a number of existing customers in this country.[16] Where there has been no trading at all here, despite a strong foreign reputation, relief will generally be refused.[17]

5.13   Where there is a well known foreign mark or name, which enjoys a reputation here, but has no goodwill here, then it may be that the difficulties of bringing a passing off action by reason of this line of authority will be of historic interest only, as an action might now be brought instead under section 56 of the Trade Marks Act 1994.

5.14   The business in question must not only exist, but have reached a stage in its development where it has acquired some sort of reputation which will be built up into goodwill. It is a question of fact in each case as to whether such acts as have been taken to use the name or mark in question and to bring it to the notice of the public is sufficient to have established the goodwill for a passing off action.

5.15   Usually, it is necessary to have started actually trading under the name or get-up, etc. Quite a short period of trading will suffice in some circumstances, particularly if the launch of the new business, product, etc., is accompanied by substantial advertising.[18]

Pre-trading reputation

5.16   It is not certain whether an action may be brought for passing off before trading commences. However, if acts have been carried out in preparation for the launch of a new product, including pre-launch publicity and advertising, it may be that such an action would succeed, although this would depend upon the facts. Where rival publishers both intended to launch new magazines under the name "Leisure News" the Court of Appeal found that neither of them had acquired a sufficient reputation or goodwill to justify a claim for passing off, despite a certain amount of pre-launch trade publicity.[19]

---

[16]   See, *e.g. SA Des Anciens Etablissements Panhard et Levassor v. Panhard Levassor Motor Co* [1901] 2 Ch. 513; or *Globelegance v. Sarkissian* [1974] R.P.C. 603.

[17]   See, *e.g. Athletes Foot Marketing Associates Limited v. Cobra Sports Limited* [1980] R.P.C. 343.

[18]   Contrast the extreme case of *Stannard v. Reay* [1967] R.P.C. 589 (where a mere three weeks use in a small area was sufficient to build up a reputation for a mobile fish and chip van) with *County Sound PLC v. Ocean Sound Limited* [1991] F.S.R. 367, (in which six months of transmission of a radio programme under the name "The Gold AM" was not sufficient to establish a reputation in such a descriptive name).

[19]   See *Marcus Publishing PLC v. Hutton-Wild Communications Limited* [1990] R.P.C. 576.

Residual goodwill

5.17   On the other hand, where a business has ceased trading, it may retain some residual goodwill for a period after the business has closed down. However, the residual goodwill will only be protected where the plaintiff has not abandoned his goodwill but intends to resume the business at some stage. It will be a matter of degree in each case as to whether the plaintiff's link with the goodwill has become so remote as to have lost its right to protection.[20]

(3) SHARED REPUTATION

5.18   In the case of certain types of name, it is possible for the reputation in the name or mark to be shared. This is a very old principle.[21] The most interesting recent cases on this point have all concerned alcoholic drinks. Individual producers of champagne,[22] sherry[23] and whisky[24] have all been found to have the necessary share in a joint reputation to prevent the use of the shared mark on goods lacking the necessary geographical origin or traditional mode of production to which such mark could properly be applied. The name "champagne" could not, therefore, be used in relation to Spanish sparkling wine. However, where an attempt was made to prevent the term "sherry" being used in relation to wine manufactured in the United Kingdom from rehydrated grape juice imported from a number of different countries, it was held that use of the name "sherry" by itself would be misleading, but that the plaintiff's long acquiescence in the use of the term "British sherry" was such as to disentitle it to an injunction.

5.19   In the *Advocaat* case,[25] the House of Lords restrained the use of the name "Advocaat" on any drink other than that made according to a traditional recipe, as used by the plaintiff and others. The action was therefore used to protect the reputation of the product as much as that of the particular trader and it seems from the judgment that any one who set up production of Advocaat according to that traditional recipe would be entitled to use the name, regardless of whether the product was made in the Netherlands (traditional source of the product) or anywhere else.[26] The larger the class of traders sharing the goodwill, the harder it will be to prove the existence of the reputation, but:

> "It is the reputation that that type of product itself has gained in the market by reason of its recognisable and distinctive qualities that has generated the relevant goodwill. So if one can define with reasonable precision the type of product that has acquired the reputation, one can identify the members of the class entitled to share in the goodwill as being all those traders who have supplied and still supply to the

[20] Contrast *Ad-Lib Club v. Granville* [1972] R.P.C. 673 with *Norman Kark Publications v. Odhams Press Limited* [1962] R.P.C. 163.
[21] See, *e.g. Dent v. Turpin* (1861) 2 J. & H. 139 which held that either of two watchmakers with separate reputations in the name Dent might sue another for use of the same name.
[22] *Bollinger v. Costa Brava Wine Co Limited* [1960] R.P.C. 16.
[23] *Vine Products Limited v. Mackenzie & Co Limited* [1969] R.P.C. 1.
[24] *John Walker & Sons Limited v. Henry Ost & Co Limited* [1970] R.P.C. 489.
[25] See n. 4, above.
[26] See speech of Lord Diplock.

English market a product which possesses those recognisable and distinctive qualities".[27]

(4) SIGNS WHICH MAY BE PROTECTED

5.20   The variety of signs which may be protected in a passing off action certainly include all of those which may be registered as trade marks even under the 1994 Act and goes wider than that in many respects.

5.21   Names of any kind can obviously be protected, whether they are names which have some relation to the proprietor, invented names, or names given to a product or service. There have been numerous cases in which a reputation has been found in a name by which a product has become known, whether or not this was the name actually applied to the product by the proprietor.

Descriptive marks

5.22   Other word marks may also be protected. As in the case of registered trade marks, it will generally be much easier to prove that a fancy or invented word mark is distinctive than it will be to prove that there is a reputation/goodwill in a descriptive mark, whether the description relates to character, quality or nature of the product or services or to some geographical connotation.

5.23   Such descriptive marks do pose particular problems for their proprietors, since the courts will not accept that there can be a goodwill attaching to them unless they have acquired a "secondary meaning", so that the mark has come to distinguish the plaintiff's goods from those of others, even if it has not lost its primarily descriptive nature.[28] Furthermore, marks which are primarily descriptive may also be more difficult to protect than marks which are primarily distinctive in terms of proving the necessary misrepresentation. There have been a number of cases in which it has been held that minor differences between the names of the parties have sufficed to distinguish between them, where the plaintiff's mark was primarily descriptive.[29]

5.24   Where a descriptive term is used as part of the name applied to a product, in addition to the name of the proprietor, it has generally been impossible to prevent the use of the descriptive name by others in conjunction with their names.[30]

---

[27] *ibid.*, and see Chap. 1 on the functions of trade marks.

[28] See, *Burberrys v. Cording & Co Limited* (1909) 26 R.P.C. 693.

[29] See, *e.g. Office Cleaning Services Limited v. Westminster Window & General Cleaners Limited* (1946) 63 R.P.C. 39: the plaintiffs traded as "Office Cleaning Services". The defendants started trading as "Office Cleaning Association". Held, the plaintiffs could not obtain a monopoly in such a descriptive title and the difference between the two titles was sufficient to distinguish the businesses.

[30] See, *e.g. Horlick's Malted Milk Co v. Summerskill* (1917) 34 R.P.C. 63: the plaintiff could not prevent the sale of "Hedley's malted milk" on the basis of its reputation in the name "Horlicks Malted Milk", malted milk was a descriptive term and the distinctiveness resided only in the name Horlicks; similarly in *McCain International Limited v. Country Fair Foods Limited* [1981] R.P.C. 69, the owners of the name "McCain oven chips" whose product was innovatory and who had coined the phrase "oven chips" to describe it, were not able to prevent the defendants from selling their version of the product under the names "Country Fair oven chips" and "Birds Eye oven chips".

5.25 It is irrelevant whether the public has any knowledge of the identity of the proprietor of the mark, as long as it can be shown that the public recognises the mark, name, get-up, etc., as identifying a particular product.[31]

Publications

5.26 The names of publications, such as magazines, in particular, may be capable of being protected by an action for passing off, but again this is an area in which names tend to be very descriptive. In the case of magazines or periodicals, in particular, very small differences between the names may be sufficient on the facts to distinguish the parties' publications. Small differences between the names will be more likely to be taken as distinguishing the products if there are differences in get-up between them as well, or indeed differences in nature.[32]

5.27 The names or images of fictional characters, or cartoon characters, can also be protected, see further paragraph 5.39 below.

Get-up

5.28 Get-up can also be protected by a passing off action, whether get-up of goods or of a business. The "*Jif*" lemon case is probably the high point of protection of get-up for goods, where the House of Lords considered that the lemon-shaped, yellow plastic bottle used by the plaintiff over many years as a container for its lemon juice had become so distinctive that shoppers would disregard the fact that lemon juice contained in a similar container bore a completely different label, with a completely different name upon it. It was found, on the evidence, that members of the public would rely upon the lemon-shaped container in making their purchases, believing that such a container indicated that the product was the plaintiff's product. In other words, it was found that the plastic lemon-shaped container had acquired a secondary significance.[33]

5.29 Otherwise, generally get-up or packaging can be protected where it has become sufficiently distinctive, and this is an area in which a combination of features may become capable of being protected, even where there may be difficulties in obtaining such protection under the 1994 Act. However, it is very much more difficult to protect "get-up" which consists of some attribute of the goods themselves, rather than their packaging.[34]

---

[31] *e.g. Edge & Sons Limited v. William Niccolls & Sons Limited* [1911] A.C. 693; 28 R.P.C. 582.
[32] See, *e.g. Morning Star Cooperative Society Limited v. Express Newspapers Limited* [1979] F.S.R. 113; publishers of "Morning Star" could not prevent the publication of "Daily Star"; similarly in *Management Publications Limited v. Blenheim Exhibitions Group Plc* [1991] F.S.R. 348 and 550, "Management Today" would not be connected with "Security Management Today". Contrast to *Morgan-Grampian PLC v. Training Personnel Limited* [1992] F.S.R. 267; publishers of series of magazines "What's New in ... " could prevent "What's New in Training". See discussion of these cases in para. 6.20, below.
[33] See "*Jif*" [1990] R.P.C. 341 at 414.
[34] See, *e.g. Politechnika Ipari Szovetkezet v. Dallas Print Transfer Limited* [1982] F.S.R. 529; the Rubik's cube (which had been copied) was not associated with the plaintiff.

5.30 It may be somewhat easier to protect the get-up of business premises, where the plaintiff's business has established a very distinctive decor, consisting of a combination of features, which had been copied by the defendant.[35]

(5) MISREPRESENTATION

5.31 The variety of kinds of misrepresentation which may be prevented by a passing off action is also very wide. Such misrepresentations may consist of the kind of uses of the plaintiff's marks or other indicia which would amount to infringement of a trade mark, were the sign registered. Thus, using the same or a confusingly similar name or mark may well be an actionable misrepresentation, if it causes confusion. The misrepresentation may be a direct one, that the defendant is the plaintiff, or is selling the plaintiff's goods or providing the same services as the plaintiff, or it may be more indirect and cover the situation where the use of the plaintiff's distinguishing signs is such as to imply some connection in the course of trade to the plaintiff such as an agency or licence.[36] Of course, such a representation will only be actionable at all if it is a misrepresentation. It is not a misrepresentation to state truthfully that there was some connection in the past between the parties, although care must be taken with the way in which such a connection is expressed, so that there is no effective misrepresentation.

5.32 It is not passing off to describe one's goods or services as being a "substitute for" or "the same as" the plaintiff's goods or services (if this is true), but it may be passing off to suggest that the defendant's goods or services are the same as those which have been "shown on television" by the plaintiff[37] or to claim that certain tests carried out on the plaintiff's goods had in fact been carried out on the defendant's goods.[38]Such misleading or untruthful advertisements would, of course, today be caught by the various regulations on advertisements which are discussed in relation to comparative advertising in chapter 5 above.

5.33 The relevant misrepresentation may also be a more subtle one which would indicate some business relationship between the parties. Such was the case in *Associated Newspapers Plc v. Insert Media Limited*[39] in which it was held that the introduction of unauthorised advertising material between the pages of magazines constituted a mis-representation that the publication, so altered, was that of the plaintiffs and that the inserts were connected or associated with the plaintiffs and their publication.[40] See further the discussion of "likelihood of association" in Chapter 2(8) above.

---

[35] See *My Kinda Town Limited v. Soll* [1983] R.P.C. 15 and 407: it was held at first instance that the striking similarity between the decor of the defendant's restaurant and the plaintiff's restaurant was likely to contribute to the confusion caused by the similarity of the names. However, in the Court of Appeal these arguments were rejected upon the basis of the way the case had been put in the pleadings. Cases in which copying of get-up has *not* amounted to passing off include *Dalgety Spillers Foods Limited v. Food Brokers Limited* [1994] F.S.R. 504 ("*Pot Noodles*"); it was found that the plaintiff's getup was distinctive but that the defendant's getup was not close enough to cause confusion.

[36] As to a misrepresentation of agency see *Sony KK v. Saray Electronics (London) Limited* [1983] F.S.R. 302.

[37] *Copydex Limited v. Noso Products Limited* (1952) 69 R.P.C. 38.

[38] *Plomien Fuel Economiser Company Limited v. National School of Salesmanship Limited* (1943) 60 R.P.C. 209.

[39] [1990] 1 W.L.R. 900.

[40] See especially *ibid.*, at 908.

(6) Reverse passing off

5.34 One rather different sort of misrepresentation which was held to amount to passing off was found in the case of *Bristol Conservatories Limited v. Conservatories Custom Built Limited*.[41] In this case, the defendant's salesman had showed prospective customers a portfolio of photographs of conservatories, indicating that they showed examples of the defendant's goods and workmanship. The photographs were in fact photographs of conservatories built by the plaintiff. It was held that this constituted a passing off, since the defendant by its misrepresentations, was seeking to induce customers to purchase conservatories from the defendant in the belief that they would be obtaining a conservatory from the same source as that shown in the photograph. It seems that the basis of the decision was that showing the photographs to the prospective customers created the goodwill that the defendants at once misappropriated.[42] There would be no misrepresentation if the defendant merely said that he could produce goods or workmanship, etc., equivalent to that shown to the prospective customer.[43]

(7) Necessity for confusion

5.35 Whatever the nature of the misrepresentation made by the defendant, there will be no passing off unless the misrepresentation causes confusion in the minds of the public. This must be a question of fact, to be considered in all the circumstances of the case and upon the evidence before the court.[44]

5.36 Moreover, any misrepresentation which may be made must take effect at the point of sale, that is to say prior to the purchase of the goods or services. For instance in *Bostick Limited v. Sellotape*[45] the plaintiff based its case of passing off upon the colour of the product produced by the defendant in competition to the plaintiff's blue "Blu-tack". It was held there was no passing off as the colour of the defendant's product could not be seen until after it had been taken out of the packet. For the purposes of an interlocutory injunction, Blackburne J. was not impressed by the unlikely possibility that there might be confusion in respect of repeat purchases, if not in relation to initial purchases.[46]

(8) Common field of activity

5.37 There was a long string of passing off cases in which it was held that it was necessary to have a "common field of activity" between the businesses of the parties before there

---

[41] [1989] R.P.C. 455 and see also *John Robert Powers School Inc. v. Tessensohn* [1995] F.S.R. 947 (C.A. Singapore).

[42] *ibid.* 464 to 465.

[43] *per* Laddie J. in *Leec Limited v. Morquip Limited* (1996) I.P.D. 19043.

[44] See discussion of confusing or deceptive similarity in Chap. 2(8), above and discussion of the evidence required in trade mark infringement actions in Chap. 4(4).

[45] [1994] R.P.C. 556.

[46] See also *Hodgkinson & Corby Limited v. Wards Mobility Services Limited* [1995] F.S.R. 254: no confusion where product would be purchased through a professional, who would know the source of supply.

could be passing off.[47] However, the impact of this doctrine was greatly lessened by the judgment of Falconer J. in *Lego*[48] in which it was held that the common field of activity was essentially no more than an indication of the likelihood of confusion between the parties' goods leading to a likelihood of damage. In the Lego case, the makers of the well known plastic children's Lego toys were successful in preventing the use of the name "Lego" upon plastic garden irrigation equipment, which had legitimately been made under that name in Israel. It was held that the public might think that the plaintiff had expanded its business into that field or had licensed the use of its name upon the defendant's goods (in other words that there was a likelihood of association) and it was further held that such confusion could lead to damage because the plaintiff would lose the possibility of licensing or franchising another trader to use the mark Lego in the gardening equipment field.[49]

5.38   The question of whether there is a need for a common field of activity between the parties really only goes, it is suggested, to being able to show the necessary likelihood of confusion and of damage.

Character merchandising

5.39   The common field of activity doctrine was applied in early cases relating to the use of the names of real or fictional characters by unauthorised defendants, so as to deprive the plaintiffs of an opportunity of protecting their names by a passing off action.[50] However, the courts will now recognise the fact that the public is aware of the widespread use of character merchandising licences to licence the use of names or photographs of pop stars or other famous people[51] and the names or images of popular cartoon or fictional characters upon all sorts of goods and services. This recognition of the realities of character merchandising was most clearly made in the *Ninja Turtles* case.[52] In this case the defendant had made drawings of humanoid turtle characters similar in appearance to the plaintiff's cartoon characters and began to licence these drawings to various garment manufacturers. The plaintiffs did not manufacture or market any goods themselves but were the owners of the copyright in original drawings of the characters. The major part of their business consisted of making and marketing cartoons and Turtles films. However, their business also included the merchandising of those characters and a significant part of their income arose from such activities. It was held that the latter facts would be well known to the public in general and that the public would connect goods bearing the defendant's turtles with the plaintiffs. Damage would be caused either by a genuine loss of royalties or by the depreciation of the image caused by fixing the copy turtle pictures to inferior goods.

---

[47] See, *e.g. McCulloch v. Lewis A May* (1947) 65 R.P.C. 58; *Wombles Limited v. Wombles Skips* [1975] F.S.R. 488.

[48] *Lego System Aktieselskab v. Lego M Lemelstrich Limited* [1983] F.S.R. 155.

[49] *ibid.*, at 194.

[50] See *Wombles* n.49 above; *Taverner Rutledge Limited v. Trexalpalm* [1977] R.P.C. 275; [1975] F.S.R. 479; *Lyngstad v. Anabas Products Limited ("Abba")* [1977] F.S.R. 62. Contrast to the position under registered trade mark law, see para. 2.87 and *Rawhide* [1962] R.P.C. 133.

[51] Or even the football league! see *Football Assoc. Premier League v. Graymore Marketing Limited* [1995] E.I.P.R. D/15, (1995) I.P.D. 18016.

[52] *Mirage Studios v. Counter-Feat Clothing Co Limited* [1991] F.S.R. 145.

(9) DAMAGE

5.40 This brings us on to the final necessary element of the tort, which is that the defendant's acts will not only cause confusion but will also cause damage to the plaintiff. The common field of activity cases mentioned above refused relief to the plaintiff not only because it was considered that there would be no real confusion, but also because the distinction in the activities of the parties led the court to think there would be no damage caused to the plaintiff. Decisions such as *Lego*, the *Turtles* case and the case of *Insert Media*[53] indicate that the courts will now take a realistic view of the likelihood of damage being caused to a plaintiff, even where he does not trade directly in the relevant field.[54]

5.41 However, of course, damage in the general run of cases will be much more likely to occur where there is a direct loss of sales caused by the defendant's activities. This may be because the defendant is diverting custom from the plaintiff to himself. Alternatively there may be loss of sales where the defendant's acts impinge upon the reputation of the plaintiff's mark, goods and/or services. This may be the case particularly where the defendant's goods or services are inferior to those of the plaintiff.[55]

"Dilution"

5.42 One new area of damage which has been recognised recently by the courts, relates to the difficulties which may be caused by a loss of exclusivity, by erosion or swamping of the distinctiveness of the plaintiff's mark and by dilution. Swamping of distinctiveness may occur where the plaintiff's mark is used upon a small scale in relation to high quality goods and the defendant's mark would be used on a large scale on lower quality goods.[56]

5.43 The relevance of dilution was recognised in the *Elderflower Champagne* case.[57] The defendants had produced a drink which they had called "Elderflower Champagne". It was sold in bottles of the same shape, size and colour as champagne, with labels and wired corks similar to those used for champagne, but the content of the bottles was a carbonated soft drink containing elderflower cordial. It sold for about £2.45 per bottle. The plaintiffs sued in a representative capacity on behalf of the producers of genuine champagne, and the Court of Appeal found that there had been a misrepresentation that the defendants' product was champagne or in some way associated with champagne. It was found that there would be confusion in that some members of the public would be deceived so that they would buy elderflower champagne in the belief that it was real champagne, and that there would be others who would be confused into thinking that the defendants' product had some association with genuine champagne, if it was not actually champagne. The plaintiffs' counsel put the head of damage in this way:

> "If the defendants continue to market their product, there would take place a
> blurring or erosion of the uniqueness that now attends the word 'champagne', so that

---

[53] See nn. 48, 52 and 39 above respectively.
[54] See for example *Blazer Plc v. Yardley & Company Limited* [1992] F.S.R. 501.
[55] See, *e.g. Chelsea Man v. Chelsea Girl* [1987] R.P.C. 189.
[56] See, *e.g. Parfums Givenchy SA v. Designer Alternatives Limited* [1994] R.P.C. 243 (the argument was made in the context of trade mark infringement, although passing off had also been pleaded).
[57] *Taittinger v. Allbev* [1993] F.S.R. 641.

the exclusive reputation of the champagne houses will be debased ... if the defendants are allowed to continue to call their product Elderflower Champagne, the effect will be to demolish the distinctiveness of the word champagne, and that would inevitably damage the goodwill of the champagne houses."[58]

5.44   Peter Gibson L.J. referred to the speech of Lord Diplock in *Advocaat*[59] in which he had referred to the "debasement of reputation" of advocaat and agreed that it was obvious that erosion of the distinctiveness of the name champagne would be a form of damage to the plaintiffs' goodwill.[60] Sir Thomas Bingham put the matter another way[61]:

> "The first plaintiffs' reputation and goodwill in the description Champagne derive not only from the quality of their wine and its glamorous associations, but also from the very singularity and exclusiveness of the description, the absence of qualifying epithets and imitative descriptions. Any product which is not Champagne but is allowed to describe itself as such must inevitably, in my view, erode the singularity and exclusiveness of the description Champagne and so cause the first plaintiffs damage of an insidious but serious kind."

He found, in effect, that allowing the defendants to make such use of the name champagne would be but the thin end of a wedge, so that subsequently any other fizzy fruit cordial might be marketed by reference to the description champagne. The damage to the plaintiffs, minimal in the case of the defendants' drink alone, would then be "incalculable but severe".

5.45   *Taittinger* does not represent a significant change in the law of passing off in relation to what may amount to an actionable misrepresentation, since the sort of representation described by the Court of Appeal is similar to the kinds of "association" already discussed, but the case is more interesting on the question of damage. It had already been suggested in *Bulmer v. Bollinger*,[62] where the plaintiffs were seeking declarations that they were entitled to use the expressions "champagne cider" and "champagne perry" that there could be damaging effects from such an association. Gough L.J. held:

> "In my view there can be a passing off of goods without representing that they are actually the well-known goods which the plaintiff produces or a new line which he is supposed to have started. It is sufficient in my view if what is done represents the defendant's goods to be connected with the plaintiffs in such a way as would lead people *to accept them on the face of the plaintiff's reputation*. Thus for example it would be sufficient if they were taken to be made under licence, or under some trading arrangement which would give the plaintiff some control over them". [emphasis added]

He went on to find[63]:

[58]   Argument summarised by Peter Gibson L.J. at 669.
[59]   [1979] A.C. 731 at 740.
[60]   *ibid.*, at 670.
[61]   *ibid.*, at 678.
[62]   *H.P. Bulmer Limited v. J. Bollinger SA* [1978] R.P.C. 79.
[63]   *ibid.*, at 126.

"The possibility of members of the public thinking that this is a new cheap Champagne product cannot be ruled out, and that impression if created, could well be very damaging to the Champagne goodwill."

5.46 This seems to have been the reason for the decision in *Taittinger* also, given the extracts quoted above, and it is suggested that this does not represent a significant change in, for example, extending passing off to cases where there is no confusion caused by the misrepresentation, but instead makes it plain that the damage which the misrepresentation may cause may not be in terms of loss of sales or even direct damage to reputation, but may be some more intangible damage to the reputation of the famous mark.[64] These cases show that the kind of damage which it may be necessary to show in order to succeed in a passing off action need not be very direct or specific.

(10) INNOCENCE OR FRAUD

5.47 Although passing off may have had its roots historically in the tort of deceit, which does include elements of fraud, a fraudulent or dishonest intention on the part of the defendant has not formed an element of the law of passing off in modern times. Indeed, it is quite clear that passing off can be committed by a wholly innocent defendant and such innocence will not even preclude the defendant from having to pay damages.[65]

5.48 However, where it can be shown that the defendant did have the dishonest intention of appropriating to himself some of the benefit of the plaintiff's reputation or goodwill, the courts will be inclined to find that he has succeeded in achieving that aim. Lord Cozens-Hardy M.R. put it famously thus: "If you find a defendant who is a knave, you may presume he is not a fool".[66]

5.49 There is no doubt that in cases where the court considers that there is an intention to cash in on the plaintiff's reputation and goodwill, it will be more inclined to find that deception will occur. This was exactly the case in *Elderflower Champagne*.[67]

(11) DEFENCES

5.50 Most defences in relation to passing off actions really amount to countering the elements of the plaintiff's case, either by showing that the plaintiff does not have the necessary reputation or goodwill or by showing that there has been no misrepresentation[68] or no confusion caused by any misrepresentation made by the defendant. The defendant may also be able to show that damage is unlikely to arise by reason of the confusion, if any.

---

[64] Just as described by Frank Schechter in (1927) 40 Harvard L.R. 813 all those years ago ... Indeed, there may be grounds to doubt whether any dilution law protects marks where there is no confusion at all; see the discussion in Martino, *Trade Mark Dilution* (1996).

[65] See *County Sound PLC v. Ocean Sound Limited* [1991] F.S.R. 367; *Gillette U.K. v. Eden West Limited* [1994] R.P.C. 279.

[66] *Claudius Ash Sons & Co Limited v. Invicta Manufacturing Co Limited* (1911) 28 R.P.C. 597 at 603.

[67] See n. 57, above.

[68] See, *e.g. IBM v. Phoenix International Computers Limited* [1994] R.P.C. 251; could the defendant sell cards genuinely made by IBM, to which it had made various alterations, as "reworked IBM cards"? Held, this defence was arguable.

5.51   There is a narrow defence available to a defendant in a passing off action that he is merely making bona fide use of his own name. It does not seem that this defence is as wide as that offered by section 11 of the 1994 Act, since it appears that it applies only to individuals or to well established companies, and it certainly does not apply to new businesses. Moreover, it seems that the defendant may only use the name as a trade name and not as a mark for his goods or services.[69] The essential elements to the defence have been summarised as follows:

> "The defendant must be using his own full name; he must do nothing more that causes confusion with the plaintiff; he must act honestly; he must in general be an actual person; and he must not be using the name so as to describe his goods".[70]

5.52   The difficulty is that the leading case on the subject, *Parker-Knoll*, is unclear and does not fully answer the question of whether use of one's own name as a trade name can be distinguished from use as a trade mark. Lord Denning alone suggested there was no such distinction, but the majority did not fully deal with the point.

---

[69] See the discussion in *Parker-Knoll Limited v. Knoll International Limited* [1962] R.P.C. 265.
[70] See Wadlow, *The Law of Passing Off* (2nd ed., 1994), at 483.

Chapter 6

REMEDIES FOR INFRINGEMENT OF TRADE MARK AND PASSING OFF

(1) Introduction

6.1 A large number of different remedies for infringement of trade marks are available. Many of these are also available in cases of passing off. There are remedies available against the defendant, which are first and foremost injunctions to prevent repetition of the acts of infringement or passing off and, secondly, pecuniary remedies in the form of an inquiry as to damages or an account of profits. These were always available to a trade mark proprietor or a proprietor of unregistered rights protected by passing off, and are now confirmed in relation to registered marks by section 14(2). Next, there are remedies available in relation to the goods and/or the infringing marks upon the goods or other articles, including packaging, such remedies include an order for erasure or obliteration of infringing marks, or, if necessary, an order for destruction of the infringing goods, or alternatively an order for delivery up of infringing goods, material or articles.

6.2   These remedies are available under the 1994 Act to the proprietor of the registered mark and, in certain circumstances prescribed by sections 30 and 31 of the Act, to his licensees. For a discussion on the rights of licensees to bring proceedings in relation to infringement, please see discussion in Chapter 7(9) and (10) below.

Vital: interim (urgent) injunctions

6.3   Before going on to deal with the various remedies available in more detail, there is one point to be made which cannot be stressed too greatly. Almost always, the major concern of the proprietor of a mark which is being infringed or which is the subject of passing off is to stop the defendant from carrying out the acts complained of urgently. It is possible to obtain an interim, that is to say, a temporary injunction from the High Court if the plaintiff proprietor moves quickly enough and if the circumstances merit such immediate relief. The availability of these interlocutory injunctions is the greatest weapon in the trade mark proprietor's armoury, and it cannot be stressed too greatly how important it is on discovering an infringement or a threatened infringement to seek advice at once and to ensure that the possibility of obtaining interlocutory relief is immediately considered and pursued if appropriate.

6.4   Delay can be fatal to an application for interlocutory relief and it cannot be judged in advance how long a period of delay may be acceptable in any particular case, since this will depend upon all the circumstances, many of which may well not be known to the plaintiff at the outset. It is therefore vital for a trade mark proprietor to move as swiftly as he can to take advice as to whether interlocutory relief is appropriate to his case and to pursue that relief if he can. The bottom line is that in the vast majority of cases where an interlocutory injunction is granted in favour of a plaintiff, that puts an end to the acts or threatened acts of infringement and there is never a trial of the action.

(2) INJUNCTIONS

6.5   An injunction is an order of the court requiring the defendant (and others through whom he might act, such as his employees or agents) either to refrain from doing certain specified acts, or to carry out certain specified acts. Obviously, in the case of trade mark infringement or passing off, the type of injunction most generally sought is one to restrain the defendant from carrying out the acts of infringement or passing off. However, other mandatory orders may be sought, perhaps more commonly at an interlocutory stage, such as, for example, the disclosure of the defendant's customer list or the names of his suppliers.[1] Alternatively, an order might be made that a defendant change its company name or trade name, and amend all business documentation accordingly, where the use of the name amounts to an infringement or an act of passing off.

---

[1] One can even seek a discovery order against someone who is not himself an infringer, but who has "got mixed up in the tortious acts of others", to give any relevant information which may be in his possession: see, *e.g.* *Norwich Pharmacal Co v. Commissioners of Customs & Excise* [1974] A.C. 133.

6.6 Whether the injunction which is sought is interlocutory or final, it may often be a difficult matter to decide precisely what wording is appropriate to restrain the defendant from continuing acts of infringement or passing off, but otherwise leaving him free to run his business without infringement. At the interlocutory stage, the terms of the injunction should be specifically directed to those acts which it is alleged constitute the acts of infringement or passing off and should not merely say that the defendant should not infringe the plaintiff's trade mark or commit acts of passing off, since this begs the question of the plaintiff's entitlement to the order at all. The principle is that the defendant should know with a reasonable degree of certainty what is or what is not permitted pending the trial of the action.[2]

6.7 As to the wording of a permanent form of injunction, this will again depend upon the circumstances of the case. An absolute prohibition against infringement of a registered trade mark is not unusual. However, in cases of passing off, it may be that the mark or other sign being used by the defendant would not cause the confusion complained of if used in a way that would prevent the actionable misrepresentation arising. It is not unknown for the injunction in such cases to be granted subject to the limitation that the injunction only covers use of the plaintiff's mark which is made "without clearly distinguishing" the defendant's goods or services from the plaintiff's goods or services. Naturally, such a qualified injunction may represent something of a hollow victory to the plaintiff and is apt to lead to further disputes between the parties as to whether any steps taken by the defendant to distinguish his goods or services from the plaintiff's are sufficient to avoid a breach of the order.

6.8 The principles to be applied in seeking an interlocutory injunction are quite different from those relating to the grant of a permanent injunction after success at trial. I shall deal with them separately, and take interlocutory injunctions first, partly because they are far more important in the context of most trade mark or passing off cases than are permanent injunctions, and partly because an interlocutory injunction naturally comes first.

(3) INTERLOCUTORY INJUNCTIONS

6.9 An interlocutory injunction is, as stated above, probably the most important remedy available to a trade mark proprietor. Where an infringement or an act of passing off is discovered or threatened, the interlocutory injunction offers an opportunity of stopping the defendant in his tracks, sometimes extremely quickly. In cases of real urgency, an application for interlocutory relief can be made *ex parte*, that is to say without giving notice (or without giving formal notice, at least) to the defendant and the length of time which will be taken between discovering the infringement and obtaining one's injunction will depend in part upon the speed with which the plaintiff is able to act and to provide any necessary information or evidence to his lawyers and in part upon judicial availability. However, where counsel is able to persuade the court of the urgency of the application

---

[2] See *Video Arts Limited v. Paget Industries Limited* [1988] F.S.R. 501; *The Staver Co. Inc. v. Digitext Display Limited* [1985] F.S.R. 512.

which is to be made, it is not particularly unusual for such applications to be made on the day advice is first sought, or at least within a few days of seeking advice. It may not even be necessary to issue a writ first, as long as the plaintiff undertakes to do so "forthwith", *i.e.* as soon as possible after the hearing.

6.10   Generally, if an *ex parte* application is not required, the procedure will be as follows: the plaintiff will issue a writ and a further document called a Notice of Motion in which he sets out the specific order which he would wish the court to make on an interlocutory basis, that is to say until after the trial. That document will be supported by evidence in the form of affidavits or affirmations sworn on behalf of the plaintiff and incorporating whatever supporting documentation is appropriate. All of those documents will be served upon the defendant, who needs to be given two clear days' notice of the application. In cases of urgency, that period can be abridged by the court.

6.11   What happens upon the first hearing of the motion depends on the circumstances of the case. If the defendant does not appear, then the plaintiff will make his application and seek his order from the judge. If the defendant does appear, he may indicate that he wishes to put in evidence in answer and the matter will then be adjourned until the evidence is complete and a hearing date can be found. When that happens, the plaintiff may wish for some protection in the meantime. Sometimes, defendants are prepared to offer an undertaking, possibly in a form which is somewhat less restrictive than the order sought in the Notice of Motion, which may satisfy the plaintiff or, possibly, the judge. If the plaintiff is not satisfied with any undertaking which is offered, then an application will be made at that first hearing date to the judge for an interlocutory order lasting only until the full hearing of the motion.

6.12   One further possibility which the court may consider in an appropriate case, is to order that the action proceed to "a speedy trial". This would mean that instead of having an exchange of written evidence followed by a hearing of a motion at which only interim relief would be granted, the parties proceed instead to a rapid preparation for a full trial of the action. The usual theoretical time limits are ordered to be squeezed to a minimum, with the matter being listed for trial as early as possible. Depending upon the parties' ability to keep to an often optimistic timetable, and also upon the state of the lists in the Chancery Division of the High Court, it is sometimes possible to have a speedy trial in almost the same time as the hearing of a substantial interlocutory motion. A speedy trial may be an appropriate alternative where it seems that it would be particularly important to hear oral evidence or where it is clear from both parties' points of view that an interlocutory order would not have the effect of determining the dispute between the parties and there is some urgency in having a final determination of the dispute.

6.13   The possibility of seeking interlocutory relief is generally very attractive to the proposed plaintiff. However, there are two financial considerations. First, it may be quite expensive to seek interlocutory relief, if the motion develops into a full-blown battle between the parties, with an exchange of voluminous evidence and a hearing lasting several days. Obviously, if the plaintiff is successful in obtaining the motion, those costs may well have been well spent and he is likely to get an order for costs against the defendant in one form or another.[3]

6.14 The second financial consideration relates to what is called the "cross-undertaking in damages". The court recognises that in granting an interlocutory injunction, some damage may well be caused to the defendant, which damage obviously would have been wrongly caused to him if he succeeds in his defence at trial. In order to mitigate the effects of granting such an injunction, therefore, the court generally requires a plaintiff to offer a cross-undertaking in damages, which is an undertaking that he will pay to the defendant any damages which the court may find the defendant has suffered by reason of the order which was made against him. The requirement to offer such a cross-undertaking may be very off-putting to a plaintiff in a small way of business or with limited means who is faced with a large, corporate defendant whose claim for damages under the cross-undertaking might be very substantial.

6.15 The court will require to see evidence of the plaintiff's means and his ability to pay any damages which may be assessed under the cross-undertaking and will weigh his ability to pay against the likely measure of such damages. In appropriate cases, the court may require the plaintiff to give some security for the cross-undertaking. On the other hand, the court will not refuse an injunction merely on the grounds of the plaintiff's inability to meet a cross-undertaking in damages, if to refuse the injunction would be to do an injustice, and this means that a legally-aided plaintiff can still obtain an injunction in such circumstances.[4]

Cyanamid principles

6.16 The general principles which apply in cases of trade mark infringement and passing off are the same[5] and it has been generally accepted for some years that the principles to be applied are those adopted in the case of *American Cyanamid Co. v. Ethicon Limited*.[6] As discussed below, it may be that a recent case, *Series 5 Software*, will mean that some of those principles will need to be re-assessed or amended.

6.17 According to *American Cyanamid*, the principles to be applied in deciding whether to grant an interlocutory injunction are as follows:

(a) *Arguable case*

This, it must be said, is the part of the *Cyanamid* decision most affected by the *Series 5* judgment discussed below. Subject to that caveat, under *Cyanamid*, the first quesion to ask is: has the plaintiff established that he has a "good arguable claim" to the relief he seeks?

---

[3] It is extremely rare for an order to be made for costs to be paid forthwith; much more usually the order would be "plaintiff's costs in cause" which means that the plaintiff will get his costs of the motion if he wins at trial, but will not have to pay the defendant's costs of the motion if the plaintiff loses at trial.
[4] See, *e.g. Allen v. Jambo Holdings* [1980] 1 W.L.R. 1252.
[5] See *County Sound Plc v. Ocean Sound Limited* [1991] F.S.R. 367.
[6] [1975] A.C. 396; [1975] R.P.C. 513; this happened to be a patent case in which the House of Lords set out the basic principles relating to interlocutory injunctions in all kinds of cases.

To put it another way, has the plaintiff shown "that there is a serious question to be tried"? The plaintiff does not need to show that he has such a strong case that he is likely to win at trial, but he does need to show that his claim is not frivolous, vexatious or so weak that it would be wrong to grant any injunction without having a full hearing of the evidence. Kerly suggests that even a 20 per cent chance of success at trial would suffice to pass this test,[7] but 20 per cent seems rather a low threshold where the court is persuaded that the result of the interlocutory application may, in effect, be final and that the matter will never go to a full trial. This is very frequently the case in infringement or passing off actions, where the defendant would never wish to revert to use of a name or mark which he had been prevented from using by an interlocutory injunction, if between that time and the trial of the action, perhaps one or even two years later, he had invested time, money and effort in building up a non-infringing mark or name.[8]

The amount of evidence which a plaintiff needs to bring before the court will obviously vary according to the circumstances of the case. In the case of an infringement action, obviously the plaintiff will need to prove his title to the registered mark, and where he relies upon the reputation as well as the registration he will need to show that he has made sufficient use of the mark to have acquired a protectable reputation. The same obviously applies to cases of passing off. The evidence will then need to cover the actions of the defendant of which complaint is made, showing the actual or threatened infringement or misrepresentation, as the case may be, and where actual confusion is necessary, providing details of any known instances of confusion. Naturally, where action is taken very swiftly, either before the defendant has started using the mark, etc., or where he has only been using it for a very short time, there may well be no evidence of confusion which will have come to the plaintiff's notice. In many ways, therefore, speed can be a benefit to the plaintiff in this respect also, since the court might not expect the plaintiff to have discovered instances of confusion to put before it at the outset of the activity of which he complains. The court will therefore have to look at the plaintiff's mark and/or reputation and the acts complained of and simply assess the likelihood of confusion. Where, on the other hand the defendant's activity has been going on for some time, a lack of evidence of confusion may be damaging to a plaintiff's case.

(b) *Damages an inadequate remedy*

Assuming that the plaintiff does show that he has an arguable case, he will then have to show the court that damages awarded at an eventual trial would not be an adequate remedy for him. In cases of infringement of trade mark or passing off, it is commonly possible to show that there may be an incalculable element of damage that would be caused by the defendant's actions, and this will be the case particularly if the defendant's goods or services can be shown to be inferior to those of the plaintiff. Where, for example, the type of confusion complained of is a likelihood of association, such as a belief that the defendant's goods or services have been licensed by the plaintiff, this consideration of the quality of the defendant's goods or services may be particularly important.[9]

---

[7] See *Kerly's Law of Trade Marks and Trade Names*, (12th ed., 1986) at para. 15–66.
[8] See, *e.g. Elan Digital Systems Limited v. Elan Computers Limited* [1984] F.S.R. 373 at 386.
[9] See, *e.g. Mirage Studios v. Counter-feat Clothing Co. Limited* [1991] F.S.R. 145.

Where it can be shown that damages would be an adequate remedy, an injunction will not normally be granted, save if it is clear that the defendant could not pay the damages in any event.

(c) *Damages sufficient for the defendant*

The court will then consider the converse situation: would damages be a sufficient remedy to the defendant if an injunction were granted but the defendant were to succeed at trial? If so, then obviously, again assuming the plaintiff could satisfy such an award of damages, an injunction will be granted. However, again, it is generally the case that a defendant can find some element of unquantifiable damage where he is to be prevented from starting or continuing with a planned expansion to his business or new business venture.

(d) *Balance of convenience*

If the court reaches this stage, then it will seek to settle the matter upon a consideration of the "balance of convenience". This amounts to a comprehensive consideration of all the circumstances of the case and an attempt to weigh up the competing claims of each side and the likely effects of granting or not granting an injunction upon each side. This process has been described as "choosing the course which appears to involve the least risk of causing injustice in the sense of causing uncompensatable damage to a party who is refused an injunction which should have been granted or injuncted when the injunction should have been refused".[10] A whole multitude of factors may be considered by the court in seeking to achieve this balance of convenience and to do the best it can, in the absence of the full evidence, to do the least injustice. Such factors can include the parties' respective positions in the market place in terms of size, market share and length of establishment of the business, the effect of any injunction or the refusal of injunction on their business, and the parties' general approach to the proceedings, and in particular any delay which may have occurred in the plaintiff's application to the court.

Delay

The stage which the defendant has reached in its plans or activities may be vital.[11] It is frequently for this reason that delay on the part of the plaintiff can be fatal to his application for interlocutory relief. If the delay has been such that the defendant has made progress in his steps towards taking the action complained of, which it would be difficult or damaging to alter, or if the defendant has, during the period of the plaintiff's delay, actually started the activities complained of or has consolidated those activities, the prejudice caused to the defendant by the delay may be such as to tip the balance of convenience in the defendant's favour.

It is because the question of delay is related to the prejudice caused to the defendant that it is impossible to say precisely how much delay may be fatal to an application for interlocutory relief. In some cases, a few days delay is too much, if the plaintiff ought to

---

[10] *per* Hoffmann J. in *Management Publications Limited v. Blenheim Exhibitions Group Plc* [1991] F.S.R. 348 at 352.
[11] See, *e.g. Blazer v. Yardley* [1992] F.S.R. 501.

have been able to move more rapidly and those few days were vital to the defendant.[12] Upon the whole, it may be said that a delay of more than a month may require some good explanation on the part of the plaintiff, although there are many cases in which delay of a few months has not been fatal to the application for interlocutory relief, depending on the circumstances of the case.[13] The effects of delay may be mitigated if the defendant is well aware of the plaintiff's genuine intentions to issue proceedings if forced to do so.

Any excessive delay may also be seen by the court as indicating something of a lack of genuine concern on the part of the plaintiff to protect its marks. For instance, in *Gala of London v. Chandler*[14] an injunction was refused where the plaintiff had delayed in bringing its proceedings and had sought to relaunch its own unused mark in the interim, using the "spoiling tactics" of selling goods under that mark at knock-down prices. Not surprisingly, perhaps, no injunction was granted where the merits were so adversely affected by the plaintiff's unmeritorious behaviour.

(e) *Status quo*

Lastly, if the court finds the balance of convenience equal between the parties the solution it is likely to prefer is to preserve the status quo, which is to say to preserve the state of affairs existing immediately preceding the issue of the writ or, if there has been some unreasonable delay between the issue of the writ and the motion, the period immediately preceding the motion.[15] In appropriate circumstances, it may be possible sometimes to argue that the status quo should be taken at some slightly earlier time, where, for example, there has been a letter before action written shortly before the issue of the writ and the defendant took some precipitate action upon receipt of the letter.[16] Preserving the status quo need not necessarily favour a plaintiff, where the defendant's activities are well advanced at the relevant time.[17]

(f) *Strength of case*

If all else is equal, then the court will, as a last resort, look to the strength of the plaintiff's case, in deciding whether or not to grant the interlocutory injunction.

Post Cyanamid

6.18   Since *Cyanamid* it has been generally accepted that all the matters set out above needed to be considered when deciding whether or not to grant interlocutory relief. However, for some time, there has been some anxiety felt (if not expressed) that the requirement only to show an arguable case was not necessarily wholly appropriate, when it seemed likely (as in many intellectual property cases) that the interlocutory decision would end the case one way or the other. In those circumstances, there was some concern

---

[12] See, *e.g. The Financial Times Limited v. Evening Standard Co. Limited* [1991] F.S.R. 7 where only about 11 days delay was too long.
[13] See *CPC (United Kingdom) Limited v. Keenan* [1986] F.S.R. 527: delay caused by genuine and laudable attempts to settle without litigation was no bar to injunction.
[14] [1991] F.S.R. 294.
[15] See *Garden Cottage Foods v. Milk Marketing Board* [1984] A.C. 130.
[16] See para. 6.15 of Drysdale and Silverleaf *Passing off Law and Practice* (2nd ed.).
[17] See *Blazer v. Yardley* n. 11, above.

that the judges should look more to the merits of the claim and the defence, and there was certainly some perception that judges were indeed assessing the merits of cases, even when paying lip service to *American Cyanamid* principles. In *Series 5 Software Limited v. Clarke*,[18] Laddie J., in a carefully reasoned judgment, analysed *Cyanamid* and the case-law preceding it, as well as the contemporaneous interlocutory House of Lords decision in *Hoffmann LaRoche v. Sec. of State for Trade*.[19] He came to the view that the House of Lords:

> " ... did not intend ... to exclude consideration of the strength of the cases in most applications for interlocutory relief. .... what is intended is that the courts should not attempt to resolve difficult issues of fact or law on an application for inter-locutory relief. If, on the other hand, the court is able to come to a view as to the strength of the parties' cases on the credible evidence then it can do so ... If it is apparent ... that one party's case is much stronger than the other's then that is a matter the court should not ignore."

He concluded that the major factors which the court may bear in mind on interlocutory applications are:

> "(a) the extent to which damages are likely to be an adequate remedy for each party and the ability of the other party to pay, (b) the balance of convenience, (c) the maintenance of the status quo, (d) any clear view the court may reach as to the relative strength of the parties' cases."

6.19   There are innumerable reported cases of decisions made on an interlocutory basis in cases of trade mark infringement or passing off. Almost all of them turn solely upon their own facts and the extent to which they give guidance for the future is limited. However, it may be helpful to compare some of these decisions. For example, one can compare two decisions in 1991, each of which related to magazine titles, always a fruitful source of revenue for intellectual property lawyers!

6.20   The first of these was *Management Publications Limited v Blenheim Exhibitions Group Plc*.[20] The plaintiff had been publishing a magazine called "Management Today" since 1966, and it was found that the magazine had a well-established reputation and a circulation exceeding 100,000 copies per month. The defendants had organised two annual fire and security exhibitions and then had launched a monthly magazine called "Security Management Today" which was distributed free to about 30,000 people. The plaintiff sued for passing off and produced evidence, upon the interlocutory motion, from three people who said they had been confused. Hoffmann J. held that there might be some confusion in the minds of the public that the two magazines were published by the same publishers and that such supposed association might cause damage to the plaintiff's goodwill. That is to say, he found that there was an arguable case to answer. He then found that damages would not be an adequate remedy to either side. He found that the balance of convenience

---

[18]   [1996] F.S.R. 273.
[19]   [1975] A.C. 295.
[20]   [1991] F.S.R. 348.

was for refusing an injunction. Refusal would lead to only a small likelihood of the plaintiff suffering damage until trial, but, on the other hand, granting an injunction against the defendant would in practice be the end of the matter, since the defendant would have to change the name of its magazine immediately and there would be no point in it reverting to the name "Security Management Today" if it succeeded in its defence at trial.

6.21   In *Morgan-Grampian Plc v. Training Personnel Limited*[21] the plaintiff was the publisher of a series of 10 magazines with titles commencing "What's New In . . . . . . ". The defendant had since February 1989 published a fortnightly magazine called "Training Personnel". From about March 1989 the defendant's magazine had included a section called "What's New In Training" and in July 1991 the defendant changed the title of the magazine to "What's New In Training". When the plaintiff sought an interlocutory injunction against the change in the main title of the defendant's magazine, it succeeded. Mummery J. held that there was a risk of confusion and a serious issue to be tried. In considering the balance of convenience he found the deciding factor was that if an injunction were granted, there would be nothing to prevent the defendant from continuing to use the title and format which it had used up until July 1991. The learned judge distinguished *Management Publications v. Blenheim* on the basis that the defendant could easily revert to using its prior title and its losses, if it succeeded in its defence at trial, would be relatively easily quantified and would be more easily ascertainable than any damage the plaintiff might suffer if the injunction were refused.

(4) PERMANENT INJUNCTIONS

6.22   Where an infringement action or passing off action goes to trial, then the injunction will again be the most important remedy to be sought. The court will not grant relief which is wholly unnecessary and the plaintiff therefore needs to show that further infringements are threatened or are likely to occur. It is not necessary to show that there has been infringement in the past, since proceedings may be brought on a *quai timet* basis (that is to say, before the defendant commences his acts of infringement or passing off) but it is necessary to show a continuing threat of infringement or passing off.

6.23   The innocence of the defendant's acts and the absence of fraud are not grounds for refusal of a claim for an injunction.[22] If the defendant offers no undertaking to the plaintiff prior to the trial, whether in correspondence or in the defence, an injunction may be granted.[23]

6.24   If a permanent injunction is granted, steps may be taken by the court if necessary to enforce its terms. There are a number of procedures available where a defendant breaches an injunction, such as committal to prison for contempt of court or sequestration of his assets. Alternatively the court may impose fines for a breach of an injunction, but all of these remedies require that the order be properly served upon the defendant, including its directors if the defendant is a company and, obviously it is vital to ensure that the wording of the order is sufficiently precise.

[21] [1992] F.S.R. 267.
[22] *Millington v. Fox* (1838) 3 My. & Cr. 338.
[23] See *Fram v. Morton* (1923) 40 R.P.C. 33.

(5) Pecuniary remedies

6.25   There are two kinds of pecuniary remedy available in infringement or passing off actions. The plaintiff may wish to claim damages from the defendant and in all kinds of intellectual property cases it is the general rule that damages are not assessed at trial but are assessed at a subsequent, separate hearing. There are two different kinds of such hearing, in which the monetary compensation to be paid to the plaintiff will be assessed in two different ways. First, there is an inquiry as to damages, which looks to the damage suffered by the plaintiff as a result of the defendant's acts, and secondly there is an account of profits, in which the court assesses the profits which the defendant has made by reason of his acts of infringement or passing off, and he must pay those assessed profits to the plaintiff.

6.26   The remedies of an inquiry as to damages or an account of profits are alternative ones. It is for the plaintiff to choose which course he prefers to pursue, subject to the rule that an account of profits is an equitable remedy, which the court has a discretion to refuse to grant. Such a refusal might occur where the defendant has been found to be an innocent infringer. By contrast, damages are available as of right and whether or not the defendant's behaviour was innocent.[24]

6.27   If the plaintiff has the choice of an inquiry as to damages or an account of profits, there may be a question as to what information should be made available to him in order for him to decide which remedy would be better for him. The difficulty may be that where the trial of liability has been split from the question of the quantum of damages/account of profits, as is usual in trade mark cases and in passing off, discovery of relevant documentation will generally have been restricted to documents concerning liability and the plaintiff may even at the end of a successful trial have no very clear idea as to which of an inquiry as to damages or an account of profits would be the better remedy to pursue. It has recently been held in a copyright infringement case that the choice may be postponed until after there has been discovery as to quantum.[25] Lightman J. ordered that the defendants were to provide the plaintiff with an audited schedule detailing information concerning sales, amounts in stock and so on within two months and thereafter the plaintiff was to have seven days to choose which of the two remedies it preferred to pursue. Lightman J. isolated four principles which applied in circumstances such as these:

(1)   a plaintiff can seek in the alternative damages or an account of profits, but he cannot obtain judgment for both;

(2)   once judgment had been entered, either for damages or an account of profits, any claim for the alternative remedy is forever lost;

(3)   a party should in general not be required to elect unless and until he is able to make an informed choice, otherwise the right is meaningless;

(4)   the exercise of the right of election should not be unreasonably delayed to the prejudice of the defendant.

---

[24] *See Gillette UK v. Edenwest Limited* [1994] R.P.C. 279.
[25] See *Island Records Limited v. Tring International Plc* [1995] F.S.R. 560.

6.28   Finally, if the plaintiff decides to seek an inquiry as to damages, rather than an account of profits, the court will only order such an inquiry if it finds that there is sufficient evidence of special damage to justify the costs of an inquiry. This is the case even though the plaintiff would be at risk as to those costs. In *McDonald's Hamburgers Limited v. Burgerking (UK) Limited*[26] the Court of Appeal held that the mere fact that an injunction has been granted does not establish that damage has been suffered by the plaintiff and the court has a degree of discretion to refuse an inquiry if it is satisfied that it would be a fruitless exercise.[27]

(a) Assessment of damages

6.29   If an inquiry as to damages is ordered, then further procedural steps have to be taken to pursue the claim, with further discovery if necessary, culminating in a hearing which generally takes place before a Master of the High Court. In pursuing the inquiry, the onus is upon the plaintiff to show that he has suffered loss which was caused by the defendant's wrongdoing. In *Spalding v. Gamage*[28] the claim was for the plaintiff's lost profit on the sales made by the defendant and for further damages for loss of reputation. The principle appears to have been accepted by the Court of Appeal, although the plaintiff's figures certainly were not. The court will not presume that the plaintiff's loss is necessarily calculable by reference to sales made by the defendant, but it will be necessary to show that the plaintiff would have made those sales himself in view of all the circumstances of the case and of the trade.[29]

6.30   In patent or copyright infringement cases it is common for damages to be assessed upon the basis of a notional licence fee, that is to say the sum which the plaintiff would have charged the defendant had the infringing use been licensed. This basis of calculation of damages has yet to be accepted in relation to a trade mark infringement or passing off case. It was argued recently in *Dormeuil Freres SA v. Feraglow Limited*[30] where there had been consent to an order for an inquiry as to damages for infringement. The plaintiffs claimed that 75 per cent of the sales made by the defendant had led to a direct loss of sales by the plaintiff and claimed that the defendant should pay a royalty on the remaining 25 per cent of its sales at 28 per cent of the gross price of the defendant's goods. This notional licence fee was based upon a single transaction in which the plaintiff had licensed the manufacture of some of its cloth by a third party. The matter was heard in the context of an application for an interim payment by the plaintiff and it was held that there was no authority for this royalty basis of assessment of damages and that such a basis for damages would be difficult to reconcile with the rule (mentioned above) that not every sale made by the defendant can necessarily be attributed to the plaintiff.[31]

---

[26] [1987] F.S.R. 112.
[27] *per* Fox L.J. at 118; and see also *Second Sight Limited v. Novell U.K. Limited* [1995] R.P.C. 423 at 436.
[28] *Spalding v. Gamage* (1918) 35 R.P.C. 101.
[29] See the patent case of *Watson, Laidlaw & Co. Limited v. Pott, Cassells & Williamson* (1914) 31 R.P.C. 104.
[30] [1990] R.P.C. 449.
[31] This view of the notional licence fee was reinforced in *Second Sight Limited v. Novell U.K. Limited* [1995] R.P.C. 423 at 436.

6.31   The plaintiff may also claim damages which are not based directly on loss of sales or loss of profit, in particular damages for injury to the plaintiff's reputation where the infringing goods were of an inferior or different quality.[32] An additional head of damage may be the cost of having pursued inquiries in relation to the infringements or passing off, whether in terms of seeking discovery against innocent third parties, or in having pursued inquiries in relation to foreign suppliers, manufacturers or other infringers.[33]

6.32   The damages can only be recovered for infringements which were committed in the six years prior to the issue of the writ.[34]

6.33   A plaintiff may seek to recover interest on any damages by virtue of the Supreme Court Act 1981. Generally, the court will award damages at a commercial rate, over whatever period it considers to be appropriate. VAT may also be payable on any sum paid by way of settlement.[35]

6.34   The costs of the inquiry will be reserved until the end of the inquiry itself. This means that a plaintiff will be at risk as to his costs, and if it turns out that the inquiry was a fruitless exercise, he may be penalised as to the costs wasted on the inquiry.

6.35   Lastly, note the effects of sub-sections 30(6) and 31(6) on taking the losses of all relevant parties into account when assessing the damages and ensuring that the damages are held in appropriate shares for each party. See further the discussion in Chapter 7 below.

(b) Account of Profits

6.36   As stated above, this is an equitable and discretionary remedy which will not be granted against an innocent infringer and may also be refused to a plaintiff who has delayed in bringing his action after becoming aware of the infringement.[36]

6.37   The principle upon which the court will grant an account of profits has been stated to be "that where one party owes a duty to another, the person to whom that duty is owed is entitled to recover from the other party every benefit which that other party has received by virtue of his fiduciary position if in fact he has obtained it without the knowledge or consent of the party to whom he owed the duty."[37]

6.38   The purpose of ordering an account of profits has been said to be "to prevent an unjust enrichment of the defendant by compelling him to surrender those profits, or those

---

[32] See *Spalding v. Gamage*, n. 28, above.
[33] See, *e.g. Morton-Norwich Products Inc. v. Intercen Limited* (No. 2) [1981] F.S.R. 337 and see *Dormeuil* at n. 30, above.
[34] Limitation Act 1980, s. 2.
[35] See *Cooper Chasney Limited v. Commissioners of Customs and Excise* [1992] F.S.R. 298.
[36] For instance, in *Lever Brothers, Portsunlight Limited v. Sunnywhite Products Limited* (1949) 66 R.P.C. 84, where the plaintiff had learned of the defendant's infringement in August 1946 but had not written a letter before action until April 1947, the account of profits was ordered to be taken from the date of the letter before action.
[37] *per* Lloyd-Jacob J. in *Electrolux Limited v. Electrix Limited* (1953) 70 R.P.C. 158 at 159. Again, this was a case in which there had been substantial delay by the plaintiff which affected its right to the account.

parts of the profits, actually made by him which were improperly made and nothing beyond this."[38] The purpose of the account is not, therefore, to punish the defendant, but to ensure that all profits which he made by use of the infringing matter or the act of passing off should be passed on to the plaintiff. "Before specifying the form of the account, the court therefore should, I think, initially ask itself this question: what categories of the relevant profits or parts of such profits ought to be treated as having been properly made by the defendants? The facts of many particular cases may justify the conclusion that the whole of the relevant profits should be so treated."

6.39   Of course, in many cases, only part of the profits depends upon the infringing acts. *My Kinda Town* was a case in which the defendant had used various elements of get-up distinctive of the plaintiff's restaurant, but it was solely the use by the defendant of the name of the business which the judge had found to be unjustified in law. Slade J. held that it was necessary to ascertain how much of the profits made by the defendants over the relevant period were properly attributable to the use of the name; profits made by the defendants by the sale of meals to customers who were not confused were not attributable to the use and should not be passed on to the plaintiff. This case clearly illustrates the difficulties which may be experienced in seeking to take an account of profits, since the account may be directed to be taken months or even years after the infringing acts and at that stage it may be very difficult to distinguish between profits made by the infringing use and profits made legitimately.

6.40   Again, generally, the costs of taking the account of profits will be reserved until it is clear that the plaintiff will recover a substantial amount through the account.

6.41   Again, the profits claimed may only be awarded in respect of the six years prior to the issue of the writ.

6.42   And, as in the case of an inquiry as to damages, the court must take into account the relative positions of proprietors and licensees of trade marks.[39]

(6) DELIVERY UP AND OBLITERATION OF OFFENDING MARKS OR SIGNS

6.43   An order for delivery up of infringing goods or for the obliteration of infringing marks or signs upon goods or other materials has always been a remedy available in both cases of trade mark infringement and passing off. As far as passing off is concerned, it is still governed by the common law, but in relation to trade mark infringements this remedy is now dealt with by the 1994 Act, sections 15 to 19. The substance of the common law remedy is the same as under the Act, and will not be dealt with separately.

6.44   Section 15 provides for the remedies which may be ordered against an infringer in relation to infringing goods, material or articles in his possession, custody or control. Infringing goods, material or articles are defined in section 17 as goods which, or the

---

[38] This quotation and the next come from the judgment of Slade J. in *My Kinda Town Limited v. Soll* [1982] F.S.R. 147 at 156.

[39] See ss. 30(6) and 31(6) and paras. 7.23 and 7.28 of Chap. 7, below.

packaging of which, bear a sign identical or similar to the registered trade mark, where the application of the sign to the goods or packaging was an infringement of the mark, or the goods are proposed to be imported into the United Kingdom and the application of the sign in the United Kingdom to them or to their packaging would be an infringement or where the sign has otherwise been used in relation to the goods in such a way as to infringe. The application of this section may be relatively simple where the goods were manufactured and/or marked in the United Kingdom. However, the position is somewhat more complicated where the goods are imported, or are to be imported, and where they would have been marked abroad. Sub-section 17(2)(b) depends on making certain assumptions as to the circumstances in which the mark was applied to the goods or packaging. Similar provisions under the Copyright Act 1956 were construed to mean that one must look to the actual person who marked the goods (in the case of copyright infringement, made the infringing article) and look at his hypothetical position had he carried out those acts in the United Kingdom.[40] It would therefore seem that in relation to this sub-section the court will need to decide whether the person who applied the marks to the goods or packaging abroad would have infringed the trade mark had he carried out the same acts in the United Kingdom.

6.45   Sub-section 17(3) provides that nothing in sub-section (2) shall affect the importation of goods which can lawfully be imported into the United Kingdom by virtue of an enforceable Community right. This presumably means that genuine parallel imports cannot be affected by these provisions, in line with section 12 of the Act. This does leave open the question, however, as to the position in relation to other parallel imports which do not have a Community origin and it is not clear whether the position in *Revlon v. Cripps & Lee*[41] will still apply.

6.46   Sub-section 17(4) defines infringing material as any material bearing an identical or similar sign to the mark which is used for labelling, packaging, generally as business papers or for advertising, in any case in such a way as to infringe the registered mark, or material which is intended so to be used. Sub-section 17(5) defines infringing articles as articles specifically designed or adapted for making copies of a sign identical or similar to the mark and where the person having them in his possession, custody or control knows or has reason to believe that they are to be used to produce infringing goods or material.

6.47   Sub-section 15(1) provides that the infringer may be ordered to have the offending sign erased, removed or obliterated from any infringing goods, material or articles in his possession, custody or control. It seems plain from the wording of the sub-section that it is only if it is not reasonably practicable for the offending sign to be erased, removed or obliterated, that an order would be made under sub-section 15(1)(b) that the infringing goods, material or articles be destroyed. Whichever of these remedies is most appropriate will obviously depend upon the circumstances of the case. There may be many cases in which it is possible for the offending mark easily to be removed from the defendant's goods, particularly in the case of labelling or packaging, but it may be very much more difficult to do this where the mark is directly upon the articles. Sub-section 15(2) gives the

---

[40] See, *e.g. CBS Limited v. Charmdale Record Distributors Limited* [1981] Ch. 91.
[41] [1980] F.S.R. 85; see also para. 4.25 of Chap. 4, above.

court the power to order delivery up to such persons as the court may direct where the infringer does not comply with an order made under section 15(1), so that the erasure, etc., which has been ordered can be carried out.

6.48   Section 16 provides a mechanism for seeking an order for delivery up of infringing goods, material or articles which someone other than an infringer has in his possession in the course of a business. By analogy with section 99 of the Copyright, Designs and Patents Act 1988, it would seem that such a person might be wholly innocent of the infringing nature of the goods, materials or articles in his possession, yet still be the subject of an order under this section.[42] Moreover, the *Lagenes* case would suggest that any issue as to whether or not the goods, material or articles are infringing may be decided at a later stage, and the fact that it has not yet been established that they are infringing copies is no bar to the exercise of the jurisdiction to order such delivery up.[43] Nonetheless, it seems probable that the court would require to be satisfied that there is at the very least a good arguable case that the goods, etc., are infringing goods before an order would be made against an innocent person under this section.

6.49   Sub-section 16(2) imposes two restrictions on the generality of the power given by sub-section 16(1). First, no such order is to be made after the end of the six year limitation period which is provided by section 18.[44] Secondly, no order is to be made unless the court also makes or considers that it could make an order under section 19. Section 19 provides that where infringing goods, etc., have been delivered up under section 16, an application may be made for an order that they be destroyed or forfeited to such persons as the court may think fit. Alternatively an application may be made for a decision that no such order should be made.

6.50   Presumably, the first sort of order would be sought by the trade mark proprietor and the latter sought by someone having an interest in the goods. Sub-sections 19(2) and (4) provide respectively that the court should consider whether there are other adequate remedies available to the trade mark proprietor, before exercising the powers under section 19 and that the court must make such order as seems just bearing in mind the various people interested in the goods. Sub-section 19(3) provides that rules of court shall deal with proceedings under this section and provides in particular that notice shall be served on the persons having an interest in the goods, material or articles. Sub-section 19(5) provides that if no order is to be made for destruction or forfeiture of the goods then they are to be returned to the person in whose possession, etc., they were before the order for delivery up was enforced.

(7) SECTION 89 NOTICE

6.51   Where a trade mark owner or licensee of a trade mark has reason to believe that infringing goods, materials or articles are to be imported into the United Kingdom, he may notify the Commissioners of Customs and Excise in writing that he is a proprietor/licensee

---

[42] See in relation to the 1988 Act *Lagenes Limited v. It's At (UK) Limited* [1991] F.S.R. 492 at 504.
[43] See *ibid.*, at 505 of the judgment of Ferris J.
[44] The section is more complicated than this, but is also self-explanatory.

of the trade mark and that the infringing items are expected to arrive in the United Kingdom either from outside the European Economic Area or from within that area but not having been entered for free circulation within it. The proprietor/licensee is to provide information to the Customs pursuant to the Trade Marks (Customs) Regulations 1994 to enable the Customs to carry out their powers pursuant to section 89. The information to be supplied is fairly predictable; the proprietor/licensee needs to give details of the mark, the infringing goods, material or articles upon which it is believed to be found, the details of the place and method of exportation and expected date of arrival, etc. By the notice, the proprietor requests the Customs to treat the goods, etc., as prohibited goods and when a notice is in force under section 89, the importation of the goods is prohibited if effected otherwise than for private and domestic use (see sub-section 89(2)).

(8) CERTIFICATE OF CONTESTED VALIDITY

6.52　One side-product of litigation in which the validity of a registered mark is contested, may be that if the court finds that the trade mark is validly registered, the court may give a certificate to that effect. The only benefit of such a certificate, however, is that it gives better protection to the proprietor in relation to his costs of any further proceedings relating to the validity of the mark.[45]

(9) CRIMINAL OFFENCES UNDER THE 1994 ACT

6.53　Sections 92 to 98 deal with a variety of criminal offences in relation to registered trade marks. The most important of these is probably section 92 which defines the offences of applying to goods or material a sign identical to or likely to be mistaken for a registered trade mark, or making or having possession of articles likely to be used for making copies of such signs.

6.54　The forerunner of this section was section 58A of the 1938 Act which was inserted by section 300 of the Copyright, Designs and Patents Act 1988. Although quite similar in many respects to the provisions of section 92, section 58A contained a provision, sub-section (3)(b), that an offence would be committed only if the prosecution could prove that the defendant intended that "... the goods in question should be accepted as connected in the course of trade" with the trade mark proprietor or his licensee, or, in other words "... that a trader intends that a consumer should believe that the goods were genuine."[46] Where goods were sold at "rock-bottom" prices, a prosecution might well fail upon this basis. Similarly, there were difficulties in pursuing similar prosecutions under the Trade Descriptions Act 1968.

6.55　Two particular decisions under the previous law lay behind the new provision of section 92. First, in *Kent County Council v. Price*[47] the defendant had been selling a variety of T-shirts bearing copies of famous name trade marks. The T-shirts were sold at a very low price and the trader had displayed disclaimer notices describing the goods as "brand

---

[45] See generally, s. 73.
[46] See Mr McLoughlin M.P., *Hansard* Vol. 241 col. 661. (April 18, 1994).
[47] [1993] C.L.Y. 484; [1993] E.I.P.R. D/224.

copies" and had in addition told his customers that his were cheap copies of the branded goods. The Divisional Court held that he was not liable for a false trade description under the 1968 Act. In the rather similar case of *R. v. Veys*[48] the defendant was selling T-shirts and badges with a logo very like that of Manchester Football Club outside the Club grounds. The T-shirts had ribald slogans on the back. It was held that even though there was a trade mark infringement, as there was no express or implied indication that the goods were connected in the course of trade with the Football Club, there was no false trade description and no offence committed.

6.56   It is clear from the Parliamentary debates relating to section 92 that it was intended on the one hand to catch such behaviour whilst, on the other, to preclude offences being committed innocently. It remains to be seen whether this is how section 92 will be applied.

6.57   Each of sub-sections 92(1), (2) and (3) relates to offences which are committed if the offender acts "with a view to gain for himself or another, or with intent to cause loss to another, and without the consent of the proprietor". In the majority of cases, it must be assumed that someone selling spuriously marked goods does so at the very least with an intention of achieving some gain for himself, regardless of his intentions with regard to the trade mark proprietor. By sub-section 92(4) no offence would be committed under any of sub-sections (1) to (3) unless the goods in relation to which the acts are carried out are goods in respect of which the trade mark is registered, or the goods differ but the trade mark has a reputation in the United Kingdom, so that the use of the sign will take unfair advantage of or be detrimental to the distinctive character or the repute of the trade mark. This latter provision is intended to catch cases where famous name marks are used on goods for which the proprietor has no registration, and whilst it may not always be easy to show any detriment to the character or repute of the trade mark, it may be easier to show an unfair advantage being taken of the repute of the famous name mark.

6.58   Each of sub-sections 92(1) to (3) also requires that the sign in question is "a sign identical to, or likely to be mistaken for, a registered trade mark". It was clearly the intention of Parliament that by using this wording, rather than the wording of section 10 of the Act, a stricter test would be applied as to the likelihood of confusion between the sign used by the defendant and the registered mark. Just how different the test may be remains to be seen. It also remains to be seen whether this wording would cure the perceived defect in the prior law as demonstrated by the cases of *Price* and *Veys*. It will presumably depend on how the court is going to assess whether a sign is "likely to be mistaken for a registered trade mark", whether the question simply falls to be considered upon a straightforward comparison of the marks or whether all of the surrounding circumstances must be taken into account. If the latter is the case, then possibly using a disclaimer as did Mr Price would preclude an offence from being committed. However, is the matter to be proved on a balance of probabilities (the civil test) or beyond a reasonable doubt (the criminal one)? The Act does not say.

---

[48] [1993] E.I.P.R. D/223.

6.59 Sub-section 92(1) describes a variety of ways in which an offence may be committed in relation to goods. Where all of the matters discussed above have been satisfied an offence would be committed where the defendant applies to goods, or their packaging, a sign identical to, or likely to be mistaken for, a registered mark or sells, lets for hire, offers or exposes for sale or hire or distributes goods bearing or having packaging bearing such a sign or where the defendant has in his possession, custody or control in the course of a business any such goods with a view to doing any such things by himself or by another. Sub-section 92(2) provides for an offence to be committed in relation to the application of such an "infringing" sign to material intended to be used for labelling, packaging or business papers or for advertising or where the defendant uses such business material in the course of the business or has such material in his possession custody or control in the course of the business with a view to doing anything by himself or by another which would be an offence. Under sub-section 92(3) it is an offence to make an article specifically designed or adapted for making copies of a sign identical to, or likely to be mistaken for, a trade mark or to have such an article in one's possession, custody or control in the course of a business. This sub-section does, however, have the further requirement that an offence will only be committed where the person knows or has reason to believe that the article has been or is to be used to produce goods or material for labelling or packaging goods, etc. This proviso would seem to have somewhat limited scope, since such articles must generally be obviously designed for such a purpose.

6.60 Sub-section 92(5) provides that it is a defence for someone to show that he believed on reasonable grounds that the use of the sign in the manner in which it was used or was to be used was not an infringement of the mark. What seems to be strange about this sub-section is that it refers to infringement, and thus presumably the civil test of infringement under section 10, rather than to the higher test to be applied under the previous sub-sections of section 92 itself. Where the marks and/or the goods are not identical, therefore, it may be that there will be room to argue that the reasonableness of the defendant's belief depends upon the strength of a likelihood of confusion between the marks.[49]

6.61 Finally, sub-section 92(6) provides the penalties for committing an offence under section 92 which are:

(a) on summary conviction, imprisonment for up to 6 months or a fine of up to the statutory maximum[50] and

(b) on conviction in the Crown Court, an unlimited fine or imprisonment for up to 10 years.

(10) ENFORCEMENT BY LOCAL AUTHORITIES

6.62 By section 93 a duty is imposed on every local weights and measures authority to enforce section 92 within their area. Various specific powers given to such officers by the Trade Descriptions Act 1968 are given to them in relation to the enforcement of section 92, including a power to make test purchases, and a power to enter premises and inspect

---

[49] See the commentary on s. 92 by Rawlinson in [1995] E.I.P.R. 54.
[50] Currently £5,000.

and seize goods and documents. The ability of local officers to enforce the provisions of section 92 will no doubt depend upon the other calls upon their resources.

(11) FALSIFICATION OF REGISTER

6.63   Section 94 makes it an offence for a person to make a false entry in the trade marks register, knowing or having reason to believe it is false. By sub-section 94(2) it is also an offence to produce a document which falsely purports to be a copy of an entry in the register.

(12) FALSELY REPRESENTING TRADE MARK AS REGISTERED

6.64   Section 95 provides that it is an offence falsely to represent a mark as a registered trade mark or to make a false representation as to the goods or services for which a mark is registered knowing or having reason to believe the representation is false. Sub-section 95(2) provides that the use of the word registered or any symbol importing a reference to registration (this is presumably a reference to the sign consisting of an "R" in a circle) is deemed to be a representation as to registration but it will be a defence to the offence to show that the mark is in fact registered elsewhere than in the United Kingdom for the goods or services in question. In *Second Sight Limited v. Novell (U.K.) Limited*[51] the defendant had used the symbol and the word "registered" beside its mark "Tuxedo" which was not registered in the United Kingdom. Lightman J held that the true question under section 95(2) is "whether it is sufficient that the reference is consistent with registration elsewhere and this registration elsewhere in fact does exist."[52]

(13) FORFEITURE

6.65   Section 97 provides that where any person has come into possession of goods, material or articles such as are described in section 92(1) to (3) in connection with the investigation of an offence, that person may apply for an order for the forfeiture of the goods, material or articles. Obviously, such a person may include a trading standards officer who may be holding such goods, material or articles pursuant to the exercise of his powers under section 93.

6.66   Sub-section 97(2) provides that an application may be made to any court which has heard proceedings relating to the goods, material or articles, whether under section 92 or under the Trade Descriptions Act 1968 or any offence involving dishonesty or deception,[53] or by way of complaint to a Magistrates' Court. The court shall make an order for forfeiture only if it is satisfied that a relevant offence (again as defined in sub-section 97(8)) has been committed. However, by sub-section 97(4) the court may *infer* that such an offence has been committed if it is satisfied that such an offence has been committed in relation to goods, material or articles which are *representative* of the goods which it is sought to forfeit. It appears from this sub-section that there is no requirement that

---

[51] [1995] R.P.C. 423.
[52] See in particular *ibid.* at 437.
[53] See subs. 97(8).

anybody should have been convicted of any relevant offence before forfeiture can be ordered, although the court must be satisfied that someone has committed some such offence in relation to goods, etc., of which these goods are representative.

6.67 By sub-section (6), the court may order that the forfeited goods be destroyed. By sub-section (7), the court may order the release of the items to such persons as the court may specify on condition that the person causes the offending sign to be erased, removed or obliterated and pays any costs ordered against him.

6.68 Section 98 makes similar provisions in relation to Scotland.

(14) THREATS ACTIONS UNDER SECTION 21

6.69 The provisions of section 21 do not properly fall within the description of remedies for trade mark infringement, as the section provides a remedy where a person threatens another with proceedings for infringement for registered trade mark and a person aggrieved (not necessarily the person threatened) complains that the threat was un-justified.

6.70 Sub-section 21(1) provides that a person aggrieved may bring proceedings for relief under this section where a person threatens another with proceedings for infringement of registered trade mark, *other than* in relation to the application of the mark to goods or their packaging or the importation of goods to which the mark has been applied or the supply of services under the mark. In other words, the section does not cover threats made to a "primary" infringer. However, it does seem that where the threat is made to, for example, a distributor of marked products, it is not just the distributor who might be a person aggrieved for the purposes of sub-section (1) but the supplier of the goods in question might be able to seek relief under this section.

6.71 Sub-section (2) provides that the relief which may be applied for is a declaration that the threats were unjustifiable, an injunction against the continuation of the threats and damages for any loss which has been suffered. The person who has made the threats needs to make good his claim that the acts in respect of which proceedings were threatened constitute an infringement of registered trade mark. However, by sub-section (3) the defence will not succeed if the registration is invalid or liable to be revoked.

CHAPTER 7

ASSIGNMENT AND LICENSING OF MARKS

(1) INTRODUCTION

7.1 Section 22 of the Act provides that a registered trade mark is personal property and it can therefore be dealt with or transmitted in the manner of any other property right, subject only to the specific provisions of the Act. Under the 1938 Act, the assignment and licensing of registered trade marks was carefully controlled, or at least intended to be carefully controlled, in the hope that the Registrar would be able to protect the public interest against confusion. These restrictions had for some years been considered to be very out of date and were not always strictly applied, and the new Act reflects the view that it is for a proprietor of a registered mark to ensure that his dealings with his trade mark do not render it confusing, first, so as to protect his own goodwill, and secondly so as to avoid the possibility of the mark becoming misleading and liable to be revoked under section 46.[1]

(2) ASSIGNMENTS

7.2   Under section 24, therefore, a mark may be assigned whether with or without the goodwill of a business in relation to which it has previously been used. Sub-section 24(2) also permits partial assignments, that is to say assignments limited to certain of the goods or services for which the mark is registered or in relation to particular uses or a particular area.[2] The very real limitations upon such partial assignments will be the potential difficulties of having a number of different proprietors using the same mark in different localities within the United Kingdom or upon different goods. In extreme cases, this could be a recipe for misleading the public such that an application for revocation under section 46 could follow.[3] It may be unsatisfactory that such adverse effects of a partial assignment or a series of such assignments may be left to be dealt with only in this indirect way.[4]

(3) FORMALITIES

7.3   Sub-section 24(3) provides that an assignment will not be effective unless it is in writing and signed by or on behalf of the assignor or his personal representative. This presumably means that the assignment will not affect the rights of third parties in any way. However, if there is a binding agreement to assign the mark, the position is that the proposed assignee is entitled to call upon the proposed assignor to execute the assignment, and is able to bring proceedings for specific performance of the agreement to assign if the proposed assignor failed to complete the assignment.

7.4   By section 27 of the Act, an application for registration of a trade mark is treated as an object of personal property in just the same way as a complete registration and an application may be assigned in the same manner as a registered mark.

(4) REGISTRATION OF ASSIGNMENTS

7.5   An assignment of a trade mark (and indeed of an application for a mark) is a "registrable transaction" within the meaning of section 25 of the Act. There is much to be said for speedy registration of assignments, since the assignment may be ineffective in some respects until registration has been made. Sub-section 25(3) provides that until an application has been made to register the assignment it is ineffective against a person acquiring "a conflicting interest" in the mark in ignorance of the assignment. Further, by

---

[1]   See Chap. 3(7) at paras. 3.39 *et seq.*.
[2]   Such partial assignments are well known in the field of copyright, so that at least it should not prove difficult to draft the terms of such assignments.
[3]   That is assuming that the use of the mark by each of the separate owners, following upon a partial assignment or assignments, would amount to use by the proprietor deemed to fall within section 46(1)(d). This remains to be seen.
[4]   Contrast subss. 22(4) to (6) of the 1938 Act.

sub-section 25(4,) unless the application for registration of the assignment is made within six months of the assignment, or the court is satisfied that there was good reason for the delay in registration, the assignee is not entitled to damages or an account of profits in respect of any infringement of the trade mark occurring after the date of the assignment and before the registration of its particulars. The wording of sub-section 25(4) would seem to imply, although not spell out, that an assignee who has the benefit of an assignment in writing complying with section 24(3), but who has not registered the assignment at the Trade Marks Registry, will be able to bring proceedings for infringement despite the lack of registration of the assignment. Otherwise, the proviso in sub-section 25(4) restricting the remedies available to him in such an infringement action would not be necessary.

7.6   The entry of an assignment upon the Register must be made pursuant to Rules 34 and 35. The form needs to be accompanied by appropriate documentary evidence, in the case of assignment this would doubtless be a sufficient copy of the executed assignment, and the Registrar will want to see evidence of any necessary stamp duty having been paid (see Rule 35(3)).

(5) ASSIGNMENT OF UNREGISTERED MARKS

7.7   Sub-section 24(6) provides that nothing in the Act is to affect the assignment or other transmission of an unregistered trade mark as part of the goodwill of a business. This is a change from the previous law, in which special provisions were made for the assignment of unregistered marks alongside registered marks. This means that there is no statutory control over the assignment of unregistered trade marks and it seems that the old common law rule that such a mark could only be assigned together with the goodwill of the business in relation to which it had been used will be maintained. This makes a good deal of sense, as it was always difficult to understand how an unregistered mark could be severed from the goodwill annexed to it in any realistic way.

7.8   Sections 24 and 25 of the 1994 Act apply to assignments made prior to commencement: see paragraph 8 of Schedule 3.

(6) LICENSING OF TRADE MARKS

7.9   Under the old law, licensing of trade marks was strictly controlled because of the concern that application and use of the mark by a multiplicity of legitimate users might render the mark deceptive or lead to confusion as to the origin of the goods. This initial wariness was tempered where it could be shown that the proprietor of the mark was exerting sufficient control over his licensees to ensure that confusion and deception would not occur.[5]

7.10   The 1938 Act provided for the first time a statutory framework for licensing. It created a fairly complicated system under which the details of users of registered trade marks had to be registered, with safeguards designed to ensure that the registered user's use of the mark would not lead to confusion or deception. The Registrar was given power

---

[5] *e.g.* "*Manus*" (1949) 66 R.P.C. 71.

to approve the terms upon which the licence was granted and could refuse to register a user if he felt that the licence might work against the public interest.[6] In order to protect the origin function of the mark, the 1938 Act deemed the use made of the mark by the registered user to be use by the proprietor.[7] This deeming provision had two effects: it would protect the mark from being struck off the Register for non-use where the proprietor had only made use of the mark vicariously through his licensees, and equally it had the effect of deeming any common law rights which might arise as a result of the registered user's use of the mark to belong to the registered proprietor.

7.11   These provisions were more ignored than respected, and for many years licensing of registered as well as unregistered trade marks has taken place without such licences necessarily being registered at the Trade Marks Registry. Such licences were held to be valid, as long as they did not lead to confusion or deception[8] and for many years, there was an intention to bring the registered user system into line with the common law and practice.[9]

7.12   Article 8(1) of the Directive provided that a trade mark might be licensed for some or all of the goods or services for which it is registered and for the whole or for part of the territory of the Member State concerned, on an exclusive or non-exclusive basis. Article 8(2) provided that where a licensee contravened any provision in his licence, the proprietor might bring infringement proceedings against him. Article 10(3) of the Directive also provided, as had section 28(2) of the 1938 Act, that use of the trade mark by a licensee would be deemed to constitute use by the proprietor.

7.13   The 1994 Act puts into effect Article 8(1), but does not make any specific provision bringing into effect either Article 8(2) or Article 10(3), save perhaps in the context of revocation proceedings under section 46.

(7) SECTION 28

7.14   Licensing in general is dealt with by section 28 of the Act which, like section 24, provides that a licence may be limited to use upon some but not all of the goods or services for which the mark is registered, or may be limited to use of the trade mark in a particular manner or a particular locality. Again, wholly uncontrolled use of the mark upon a variety of goods by different parties or in different ways might run the risk of rendering the mark liable to revocation under sub-section 46(1)(d).[10] The liberalisation of licensing of trade marks stems from the belief that the proprietor of a mark will realise that it is in his own best interests to ensure that the mark remains capable of fulfilling its function as an indicator of origin (or even as a guarantee of the quality or composition of the goods) so that proprietors will be unlikely to deal with their marks in such a way as to render them confusing or liable to mislead the public through an uncontrolled series of licences.

---

[6] See s. 28 and in particular subs. 28(5) of the 1938 Act.
[7] By s. 28(2).
[8] See for example *Bostitch* [1963] R.P.C. 183 and for further discussion see Chap. 3 of Wilkof, *Trade Mark Licensing* (1995).
[9] See the Mathys Committee Report on *British Trade Mark Law and Practice* Cmnd. 5601 at para. 180 (1974).
[10] See discussion in paras. 3.39 of Chap. 3(7), above.

7.15 This may be so. However, it does depend upon licences being drafted sufficiently carefully to ensure that the trade mark proprietor is able to control the use made of the mark by the licensee and to put a stop to any unlicensed or inappropriate use within a fairly short period. In particular, as there is no direct implementation of Article 10(3) of the Directive in the 1994 Act, so as to make it plain that use by a licensee of the registered mark which breaches the licence agreement constitutes infringement of the mark, rather than a breach of contract, it might be worthwhile providing that this is the effect of breach in the licence agreement itself. As a matter of principle it would seem that any unlicensed use must be an infringement, so that Article 10(3) may not need to have been specifically implemented, but perhaps there is something to be said for attempting to avoid arguments on this basis.

7.16 Under sub-section 28(2) it is provided that a licence will not be effective unless it is in writing, signed by or on behalf of the grantor. This represents a change from the previous common law position, when a licence could be made orally. However, as there will be no infringement of a mark if use is made of it with the consent of the proprietor,[11] it may still be that there will be scope for oral licences of registered trade marks, albeit such licences obviously would not be registrable under the Act. In any event, the grant of a licence, whether oral or in writing, does not confer any right of property in the licensee. All that he obtains is a permission or consent to use the mark and this appears to be so whether or not the licence is an exclusive one.[12]

7.17 Sub-section 28(3) provides that a licence is binding on a successor to the interest of the licensor, unless the licence provides otherwise. Normally, the position is that nothing in a trade mark licence would prevent the assignment of the licensor's interest, but it is common for a trade mark licence to provide that the licensee shall not be able to assign his interest under the licence, or at least that he shall not be able to do so without the prior consent in writing of the licensor. Such a provision is generally inserted to ensure that a trade mark proprietor is able to continue to exert any necessary controls over his licensees. Sub-section 28(4) provides that a licensee may be given permission in the licence to grant sub-licences. Obviously, it is a matter for the parties to agree whether or not any sub-licensing would have to be made with the consent of the trade mark proprietor. Sub-section 28(4) goes on to provide that references in the Act to a licence or licensee include references to a sub-licence or sub-licensee.

(8) REGISTRATION OF LICENCES

7.18 Licences of trade marks are also registrable transactions within the meaning of section 25 and sub-sections 3 and 4 of that section apply to licences as they do to assignments (see discussion above). In particular, however, sub-section 25(3)(d) provides that until the application has been made to register the licence, the person claiming to be a licensee does not obtain the protection of sections 30 or 31, which are the sections conferring rights upon licensees to take infringement proceedings. Similarly, sub-section

---

[11] See the wording of s. 9(1).
[12] See *Northern & Shell Plc v. Conde Nast* [1995] R.P.C. 117.

25(4) would exclude a licensee from obtaining damages or an account of profits where the application to register the licence had not been made timeously.

(9) LICENSEES' RIGHTS OF ACTION

7.19 Section 30 makes general provisions as to the rights of licensees in the case of infringement. Its provisions can apply to both exclusive and non-exclusive licences, but do not apply to exclusive licences where, or to the extent that, an exclusive licensee has the right to bring proceedings in his own name by virtue of section 31.[13] Sub-section 30(7) might seem to conflict with the second sentence of sub-section 30(1). However, this is not the case, if it is right to say that sub-section (7) means that references to "the proprietor" in the earlier sub-sections of section 30 may, where appropriate, be references to an exclusive licensee, and references to a licensee are to the sub-licensee of an exclusive licensee.[14]

7.20 The rights which are granted to a licensee by sub-sections 30(2) to (5) may be excluded by the terms of the licence. If they are not so excluded, then by sub-section (2) a licensee is entitled to call upon the proprietor of the registered trade mark to take infringement proceedings if he becomes aware of any infringement of the mark which affects his, that is to say the licensee's, interests. By sub-section 30(3), if the proprietor either refuses to bring infringement proceedings or fails to do so within two months after being asked to do so by the licensee, the licensee may bring the proceedings in his own name as if he were the proprietor. Neither of the two sub-sections specifies how the licensee is to "call on" the proprietor to take this action, nor what constitutes a sufficient refusal to do so. Presumably, however, the licensee will be wise to make this demand to the proprietor in writing and to ask for a response in writing also.

7.21 It is important to note that there is no exception to sub-section 30(3) in relation to interlocutory proceedings.[15] Generally, the proprietor or licensee of a registered trade mark will wish (and need) to bring an application for interlocutory relief as soon as possible after learning of the infringing use of the trade mark. In the context of an application for interlocutory relief, a delay of two months can be important or even crucial, if during that period the defendant incurs expenditure in preparing for the launch of, or building up, his infringing use of the mark and starts to build up a goodwill in the infringing mark. Unfortunately, there is no provision for interlocutory relief to be sought by a licensee prior either to the refusal from the proprietor to take infringement proceedings when asked, or the expiry of the period of two months from the date when he was asked to take those infringing proceedings. Thus, two months of inactivity on the part of a disinterested proprietor may cause serious problems to a licensee. This inadequacy in the provision would obviously not be problematic if a prompt request by the licensee to the proprietor for action were met with a prompt response. Therefore, in his own interests, a licensee should act as quickly as he can in making a request to his proprietor and should ask specifically that the proprietor should make his response as rapidly as possible so that

---

[13] Please see discussion below, paras. 7.25 *et seq.*
[14] See para. 4.50 of *Wilkof on Trade Mark Licensing*, above.
[15] As to which see further in Chap. 6(3).

valuable time is not lost. Alternatively, provision could be made in the licence agreement itself as to the manner in which these two sub-sections should be exercised, setting out a rapid time-table. Obviously, this would not guarantee compliance, but it might help to concentrate a licensor's mind if delay on his part would amount to a breach of contract. Alternatively, conceivably a licensee could stipulate that where the proprietor refuses or fails to initiate infringement proceedings within a specified period after notice from the licensee, the latter would be irrevocably appointed as the proprietor's attorney for the purpose of bringing such proceedings in the proprietor's name.

7.22 Under sub-section 30(4) where a licensee takes his own infringement proceedings, he cannot proceed to trial without having joined the proprietor either as his co-plaintiff or as a defendant. He is, however, entitled to seek interlocutory relief before having joined the proprietor. This provision is reminiscent of a similar provision in the Copyright, Designs and Patents Act 1988.[16] It must be anticipated that a proprietor who takes an active interest in his trade mark will wish to be joined as co-plaintiff and therefore to have some control of the proceedings. A proprietor who is not interested may be added, whether or not he consents, as a defendant, but if he is added as a defendant he will not be made liable for any costs in the action unless he takes an active part in the proceedings.[17]

7.23 Sub-section 30(6) provides that where the proprietor of a mark brings infringement proceedings, any loss suffered or likely to be suffered by his licensee will be taken into account and the court may give directions, in effect, that the proprietor is to hold the proceeds of any award of damages or other pecuniary remedy in whole or in part on behalf of his licensee. As it is anticipated by this section that the action will be brought by the proprietor, it would seem that this provision would apply even where no licensee was a party to the proceedings. There is no reciprocal provision that where the infringement proceedings are brought by the licensee any losses of the proprietor are to be taken into account; this is yet another matter which might be dealt with in a well drafted licence agreement.

(10) EXCLUSIVE LICENCES

7.24 Sub-section 29(1) defines an exclusive licence as one which authorises the licensee to use a registered trade mark in the manner authorised by the licence to the exclusion of all other persons including his licensor. Such licenses can be partial or limited, like any other licence. Thus, a proprietor can divide up the exclusive use of his trade mark rights by territory or according to different goods or services within the registration, as he pleases. Obviously, again, a proprietor must take care when granting such licences that he retains sufficient control over the way in which the licensee will use the mark to ensure that the mark will not be open to challenge. Sub-section 29(2) provides that an exclusive licensee shall have the same rights against a successor in title to his licensor who is bound by the licence as he had against the original licensor. This provision may be contrasted with sub-section 28(3) where such will be the case unless the licence otherwise provides.

[16] s. 5.102.
[17] By subs. 30(5).

7.25   The general provisions of section 30, as has been indicated above, may apply to exclusive licences, unless section 31 is brought into play. Sub-section 31(1) provides that the exclusive licence may provide "that the licensee shall have to such extent as may be provided by the licence, the same rights and remedies in respect of matters occurring after the grant of the licence *as if the licence had been an assignment*" [emphasis added]. As a result, where such provision has been made, the licensee will be entitled to bring infringement proceedings against any person other than the proprietor in his own name. However, by sub-section 31(2) those rights and remedies will be concurrent with those of the proprietor. By providing that the exclusive licensee has rights against everybody *except* the proprietor and has rights concurrent with the proprietor, section 31 actually makes it plain that the rights granted to the exclusive licensee are *not* the same as if he had been granted a partial assignment of the rights. Where an assignment is granted, the assignor does not maintain any rights to bring proceedings in relation to infringements committed after the date of the assignment, nor is the assignee prevented from suing the assignor if the latter continues to make use of the mark. The description of the rights granted to the exclusive licensee as being the same as if the licence had been an assignment is therefore inaccurate.

7.26   Sub-section 31(3) provides that a defendant may avail himself of any defence which would have been available to him if the action had been brought by the proprietor of the mark, rather than by the exclusive licensee, and this obviously covers cases where the defendant has been granted a licence, or has the consent of the proprietor to make the use of the mark of which complaint is made. It seems possible that a trade mark proprietor could give consents which are binding upon the licensee despite the exclusivity of the licence.[18] Such consents would be binding and effective against both the proprietor and the exclusive licensee. This is because the licensee does not acquire a property right in the mark, regardless of the wording of section 31(1). In such circumstances, it would seem that the only remedy available to the aggrieved exclusive licensee would be dependent upon the terms of his contract with the proprietor, since it is likely that the granting of such consent by the proprietor would be a breach of the exclusive licence agreement.[19]

7.27   Sub-section 31(4) provides that where the infringement concerns matters in which the proprietor and the exclusive licensee have concurrent rights of action, whichever of them brings the proceedings must join the other either as a co-plaintiff or as a defendant. Thus, for example, if the exclusive licence covered some of the goods for which the mark was registered but not others, but all of the goods were similar goods to those upon which the infringing mark was being used, it would seem that the proprietor and the exclusive licensee would each have the right to bring infringement proceedings. In those circumstances, they would either need to agree to be co-plaintiffs, or he who issued proceedings first would have to join the other as defendant. However, the proviso to sub-section (4) ensures that either of them could seek interlocutory relief without needing to join the other. In the case of section 31, there is no requirement that the licensee call upon the proprietor to take action before issuing his own infringement proceedings. Conceivably,

---

[18] See *Northern & Shell plc v. Conde Nast* [1995] R.P.C. 117.
[19] Note that in *Northern & Shell ibid.*, there was indeed a contractual dispute which was not decided at the hearing before Jacob J. in December 1994.

where their rights of action are concurrent, this could lead to confusion if the proprietor and the exclusive licensee do not co-operate. Since the question of the exclusive licensee's rights to bring proceedings in his own name will clearly be a matter for discussion at the time of the negotiation of the exclusive licence agreement, these are questions which could usefully be addressed then.

7.28   Sub-sections (5) and (6) deal with the situation where both proprietor and exclusive licensee are parties to the proceedings. Where one of them has been joined as a defendant by the other he is not to be made liable for any costs in the action unless he takes part in the action, as is provided in the cases of actions under section 30. Where the court is to assess the damages for any proceedings in which there are concurrent rights of action, the court must take into account the terms of the licence, and any pecuniary remedy awarded or available to either of the parties in respect of the infringement, which presumably means any order for an inquiry as to damages or an account of profits which has not yet resulted in a payment. It is specifically provided that where one party has been granted an award of damages, no account of profits shall be directed and vice versa. If an account of profits is directed, the profits must be apportioned appropriately, subject to any agreement between the parties. The last paragraph of sub-section (6) provides that the sub-section is to apply whether or not the proprietor and the licensee are both parties to the action (which will of course be the norm in the light of sub-section (4), but need not be the case if the court dispenses with the need to join both parties pursuant to that sub-section). If they are not both parties, the court may give appropriate directions as under sub-section 30(6), as to the sharing of any proceedings of any pecuniary remedy.

7.29   Sub-section 31(7) provides that where the proprietor of a mark applies for an order for delivery up under section 16 of the Act and an exclusive licensee has a concurrent right of action in respect of the relevant infringement, the proprietor must notify the exclusive licensee of the proposed delivery up and the court may make any order it considers appropriate if the licensee applies to it in respect of such delivery up, having regard to the terms of the licence.

7.30   Sub-section 31(8) provides specifically that all of sub-sections 31(4) to (7) may be varied by the agreement of the parties. For example, it is not uncommon for licences to make provision as to the sharing of any damages which may be recovered in infringement proceedings.

(II) COMBINATION LICENCES OF TRADE MARKS AND OTHER RIGHTS

7.31   There are many fields in which it is common to grant combination licences, that is to say licences in which the licensee is granted a right to make use of a number of different intellectual property rights belonging to the licensor. Such combination licences can occur in many different situations. For example, it is common to have combined patent, know-how, copyright and trade mark licences, where a distributor is to be entitled to manu-facture products made according to a patent, with the benefit of the patentee's know-how, and possibly also with the benefit of his copyright, when such products will be sold under the licensor's trade mark, possibly utilising elements of trade dress or packaging which are also protected by a combination of copyright and trade mark rights, the latter being registered or unregistered.

7.32 A multiplicity of intellectual property rights may also need to be licensed where a franchise is granted. Franchises may include a patent licence, but perhaps more often consist of a combination of licences of know-how, copyright and trade mark rights (sometimes unregistered marks and signs which could only be protected by the law of passing off in the United Kingdom) dealing with the manner in which the business is to be run, the products to be stocked, the design of the outlets and the marks or other distinguishing indicia to be used in the outlets and upon the goods.[20]

7.33 Again, where merchandising rights are granted, especially in relation to popular fictional characters, cartoons, etc., a copyright licence will probably be needed in addition to a trade mark licence. Whilst in the past such rights were given rather short shrift by the English courts,[21] merchandising rights are now recognised here.[22]

7.34 Where such combination licences are granted, it is necessary to take into account the provisions of all relevant statute law, such as the 1994 Act and the Copyright, Designs and Patents Act 1988, as well as to take care to comply with all relevant European Community legislation and to seek to take advantage of any of the Block Exemption Regulations which have been produced by the European Commission in relation to licensing of intellectual property rights.[23]

(12) BASIC PROVISIONS OF A LICENCE AGREEMENT

7.35 In this section, some broad guidance is given as to the most essential terms to include in a trade mark licence. It is not intended that this summary should be taken as conclusive or exhaustive in any way, especially since the scope of necessary provisions may vary enormously depending upon the type of arrangement envisaged.[24] The reader, whether as proposed licensor or licensee, is urged to consider carefully what protection he might need and to take appropriate advice.

(a) Parties

7.36 It may sound ridiculous to make a point about the parties to the agreement, but this is a matter which, in commercial reality, is often easily confused, especially where negotiations take place with an individual, who might be acting in his personal capacity or as a partner or director. What is particularly important where a registered mark is concerned is, of course, to know that the purported licensor is indeed entitled to grant the

---

[20] Generally on franchising see Adams and Prichard Jones, *Franchising* (3rd ed.)
[21] See, *e.g. Wombles Limited v. Wombles Skips Limited* [1975] F.S.R. 488 or *"Kojak"* [1975] F.S.R. 479, and *"Abba"* [1977] F.S.R. 62.
[22] See *Mirage Studios v. Counter-feat Clothing Co Limited* [1991] F.S.R. 145, the Teenage Ninja Turtles case in which an injunction was granted on the basis of copyright infringement and passing off.
[23] *e.g.* Regulation 1983/83 on exclusive distribution agreements, Regulation 1984/83 on exclusive purchasing agreements, Regulation 2349/84 on patent licences, Regulation 4087/88 on franchise agreements, Regulation 556/89 on know-how licensing agreements; see further part (13) below.
[24] See, *e.g.* comments in paras. 7.14, 7.15, 7.17, 7.20–7.23, 7.27 and 7.30, above.

intended licence, whether as trade mark proprietor or as a licensee (exclusive or not) who has power to grant sub-licences. If an intervening licence is involved, obviously the proposed sub-licensee needs to know that his proposed licence is permitted, and that any necessary consent to the sub-licensing has been or will be obtained.

7.37 It is also necessary to make provision about possible changes of party. It is usual for the licensor to be completely free to assign his interest in the mark, but a licensee may well be restricted as to his rights to assign or sub-licence. The extent of his rights to do so should be clearly spelled out, together with any mechanism required for approval by the licensor.

(b) The rights to be licensed

7.38 Where the licence is just of a single registered trade mark, the definition of the rights granted will be a simple matter. However, where there is an unregistered mark, or a combination of a registered mark and certain unregistered elements of get-up, or a combination of trade mark and other intellectual property rights, then the definition of the rights granted may require careful thought. Both parties may wish to provide for the licensee to use any variations which may be made to the mark or its get-up over the term of the agreement or any improvements in associated know-how, etc. Where the licence involves the use of know-how or confidential information, it is common for restrictions to be imposed on their use by the licensee both during and after the term of the licence, to the extent that this is permissible,[25] and the licensor may well also require the licensee to allow him the benefit of improvements, etc., made by the licensee.

7.39 Commonly, the licensor will wish to control carefully the manner in which the licensee uses the mark, and may require to see and approve samples of packaging, advertising, etc., prior to use. There may well be controls as to what use the licensee can make of his own name or mark alongside the licensed mark.[26]

7.40 It is also, obviously, vital to make it plain whether the licence is exclusive or non-exclusive and to define the rights of the parties in the case of infringements by third parties. See paragraphs 7.19–30, above.

(c) Territory

7.41 The licence should specify whether the licensee is to be able to use the mark in a specified territory only, or anywhere he pleases. Clearly, if the licensor does attempt to impose territorial exclusivity upon either himself or any particular licensee, any restrictions imposed may well clash with national or E.C. rules on exhaustion of rights. In particular, where the exclusivity imposes import or export bans, etc., such terms may well

---

[25] See comments as to relevant E.C. law rules below.
[26] And see para. 7.15, above.

fall foul of the E.C. competition rules, so as to be void and to render the parties liable to fines for breach of Article 85.[27]

(d) Goods or services

7.42 It is necessary to define with some care the range of goods or services upon which the mark and any associated rights are to be used. The licensor will generally be well advised to impose strict quality controls upon the licensee, and should have the right to see samples of goods, both at the outset and at regular (or irregular) intervals during the term. The licensor may want access to the licensee's premises to inspect goods, but should in any event make plain the result of any breach of quality conditions. The licensor may also wish to control any sub-contracting of manufacture by the licensee.

(e) Royalties

7.43 What royalties are to be paid is clearly a matter for negotiation; there may be a sliding scale depending upon turnover and/or a minimum royalty. The licence should require the licensee to keep adequate records of relevant transactions and make adequate provision for the submission of regular accounts by the licensee, and for the inspection of the licensee's books by the licensor.

(f) Term

7.44 The initial term of the agreement will be easily settled, and should be a fixed period rather than open-ended, save in unusual cases. Provision will then need to be made for the extension or renewal of the term and it must be decided whether notice will be needed, and if so how long before the end of the initial term. If renewal is to be allowed, it must also be specified whether the renewed licence will contain the same term as to renewal as did the initial licence, so as to allow multiple or indefinite renewals. If renewal is to depend upon or open the way to alterations in royalty tariffs, then a proper mechanism for such change must be included (rather as in a good rent review clause).

7.45 It is equally important to specify how the licence may be brought to an end. If it is by simple expiry of the licence period, or by agreement, then it is usual to allow for some "sell-off" period for legitimately marked stock after termination. Such sales obviously need to be subject to proper controls and to the prior terms on accounting, royalties, etc.

7.46 Licences also commonly provide for termination upon the licensee going into liquidation, etc., and there need to be terms dealing with the consequences of such termination, especially in relation to unsold marked stock. Termination for breach is a very important area to consider carefully at the outset. There need to be clear provisions for giving notice of breach, and the consequences of failure to remedy any remediable breach. Where the breaches are fundamental and/or irremediable, then it must be decided whether the licensor is to have the right immediately to determine the licence, and, if so,

---

[27] See further part (13) below.

whether he needs first to serve any notice upon the licensee. If the licence is determined in this way, what is to become of stocks, etc?

(g) Miscellaneous

7.47   If the parties to the licence are based in different countries, even within the E.U., it is sensible to provide for a forum for the resolution of disputes between them, whether in terms of an arbitration clause or an exclusive jurisdiction clause. The governing law of the agreement should also be agreed. The licence should state how notices are to be served upon each party.

(13) The effect of European Community law on assignments and licences

(a) Introduction

7.48   The incompatibility of intellectual property rights and the aims of the Community (now the European Union) has already been mentioned. Essentially, there is an obvious clash between the monopolistic rights granted by national intellectual property laws and the major Treaty objectives of free movement of goods and services, freedom of competition and, now, unification into a single market. The obvious concern was that the exercise of national intellectual property rights could create barriers to the free circulation of goods and services within the Community.

7.49   The difficulty arose in this way: Article 222 of the Treaty of Rome protects national laws governing the ownership of property. National property rights such as trade marks should not, therefore, be affected by Community legislation. However, the anti-competitive effects of common ways of exercising intellectual property rights and the resulting barriers to free trade and the unification of the market raised by national intellectual property rights have been tackled by the Commission and the European Court of Justice by the application of two areas of Community law, namely on the one hand, the rules as to the free circulation of goods themselves (Article 30 *et seq*) and on the other the rules controlling anti-competitive behaviour (Articles 85 and 86). As discussed in Chapter 1 above, in considering the role of trade marks, in particular, in the context of these Treaty provisions, the European Court of Justice has developed its own theory as to the function of trade marks and has drawn a distinction between the protection of the essential function of a trade mark, and its improper exercise by seeking to protect a monopoly position.

7.50   Article 30 of the Treaty of Rome prohibits "quantitative restrictions on imports and all measures having equivalent effect . . . .". This catches all forms of national legislation, including national intellectual property laws. However, Article 36 then provides an exception to that prohibition:

> "the provisions of Articles 30 to 34 shall not preclude prohibitions or restrictions on imports, exports or goods in transit justified on the grounds of . . . . . . the protection of industrial and commercial property. Such prohibitions or restrictions shall not,

however, constitute a means of arbitrary discrimination or a disguised restriction on trade between Member States."

In applying Article 36, therefore, the ECJ has sanctioned the exercise of trade mark rights in cases where it amounted to no more than the proper exercise of such rights necessary to protect their essential function, but qualified this right by a requirement that such apparent exercise of those rights should not amount to a disguised restriction on trade.

7.51   Article 85 is aimed at preventing anti-competitive agreements or concerted practices. To summarise, it prohibits all agreements or concerted practices which may affect trade between Member States and which have as their object or effect the prevention, restriction or distortion of competition within the Common Market. By Article 85(2), agreements or concerted practices which are prohibited by Article 85(1) are automatically void. However, Article 85(3) provides that certain agreements or concerted practices which would fall within Article 85(1) but which contribute to improving the production or distribution of goods, or promote technical or economic progress, may be exempted from the effects of Article 85(2). Such exemption may be sought individually or may be found by bringing an agreement within the terms of one of a number of "block exemption" Regulations relating to a variety of kinds of agreements, many of which affect trade mark licences in particular.

The exhaustion theory

7.52   The first cases involving trade marks to come before the ECJ were not surprisingly based on Article 85.[28] The anti-competitive agreements at issue included or were reinforced by the separate proprietorship of national rights in one trade mark, intended to partition off each national market by making it possible to oppose parallel imports. The Court invariably held that national trade mark rights could not be used in this way, adopting the exhaustion theory already found in some national laws.[29] Essentially, this amounted to finding that the sale of the products under the mark in one Member State[30] by one party exhausted his associates' rights in the mark, so that they could not exercise the exclusive rights conferred by their national trade mark registration. Once the goods had been legitimately sold under that mark by a connected proprietor, the proprietor of the mark in the importing state lost his otherwise exclusive right to the mark and was precluded from prohibiting the parallel imports.

7.53   However, in later cases, the Court placed more emphasis upon the identity of the product and the need for it to reach consumers in its original condition. This was made particularly clear in the *Hoffmann-La Roche* case in 1978,[31] where the parallel importers

---

[28] See, *e.g.* Joined Cases 56 & 58/64 *Etablissements Consten Sarl & Grundig-Verkaufs GmbH v. E.C. Commission*: [1966] E.C.R. 299; [1966] C.M.L.R. 418; Case 40/70 *Sirena Srl v. Eda Srl* [1971] E.C.R. 69; [1971] C.M.L.R. 260; Case 192/73, *Van Zuylen Freres v. Hag AG*: [1974] E.C.R. 731; [1974] 2 C.M.L.R. 127; Case 78/70, *Deutsche Grammophon GmbH v. Metro-SB-Grossmarkte*: [1971] E.C.R. 487; [1971] C.M.L.R. 631.

[29] For a summary of national laws see E.C. Commissions's working paper 111/D/1424/79 by Professor Beier and Dr von Muhlendahl.

[30] Exhaustion did not apply where first marketing was outside the E.U.

[31] Case 102/77, *Hoffmann-La Roche v. Centrafarm Vertriebsgesellschaft Pharmazeutischer Erzeugnisse mbH* [1978] E.C.R. 1139 [1978] 3 C.M.L.R. 217.

Centrafarm had been repackaging and remarking (with the identical mark) pharmaceutical products they had legitimately acquired in the United Kingdom, for resale in the Netherlands. The Court held that such repackaging could only be prevented by the trade mark proprietor where it adversely affected the "original condition" of the product.[32]

7.54   The difficulty of reconciling the need to protect inherently monopolistic rights with the rules freeing the market from artificial restraints was clearly seen in another case involving the repackaging of pharmaceutical products by Centrafarm: *American Home Products*.[33] The essential difference between this and the *Hoffmann–La Roche* case was that in this case the English and Dutch marks for the same[34] products differed. American Home Products claimed that its associated company's rights to the Dutch mark had not been exhausted, because the original sale had not been under the same mark. Centrafarm, on the contrary, claimed that its use of the Dutch mark was legitimate and actually avoided confusion on the part of the Dutch consumers, who would correctly associate the mark they had put onto the product with its usual producer.

7.55   The Court held that Centrafarm's action constituted an infringement of the Dutch proprietor's right to be the first to place goods upon the market under that mark, as there was no exhaustion in such a case. This finding was qualified, however, by requiring the national judge to ensure that the use of different marks for the same product in different Member States was not the result of a policy decision aimed at splitting-up the common market, *i.e.* a disguised restriction on trade.

7.56   Article 86 prohibits any abuse by one or more undertakings of a dominant position within the common market so far as it may affect trade between Member States. This provision has as yet been little considered in the context of trade mark rights, but may be an area which will become more important in the future, in the light of some recent decisions.

7.57   The analysis below does not seek to follow the long and complicated history of the ECJ's numerous decisions on intellectual property matters in chronological order, nor indeed at all comprehensively. Such an analysis would be beyond the bounds of this book.[35] However, the main points to be considered in relation to assignments on the one hand and licences on the other are considered below.

(b) Assignments

7.58   Some of the early ECJ decisions on the exercise of trade mark rights were of particular concern in relation to the assignment of trade marks. First, in *Sirena Srl v. Eda*

---

[32] At paras. 9–10 of the judgment, see also Case 1/81 *Pfizer v. Eurim Pharm GmbH* [1981] E.C.R. 2913; [1982] 1 C.M.L.R. 406; putting new packaging around the untouched original package was acceptable.

[33] Case 3/78, *Centrafarm BV v. American Home Products Corporation*: [1978] E.C.R. 1823; [1979] 1 C.M.L.R. 326.

[34] There were in fact minor differences in taste between the English and Dutch products, but they were substantially the same drug.

[35] The reader is recommended to see Bellamy & Child, *Common Market Law of Competition* (4th ed.) for a very comprehensive analysis of competition law, including both the Article 85/86 and Article 30/36 intellectual property decisions.

Srl[36] a Milanese court had referred to the ECJ various questions on the applicability of Articles 85 and 86 to an infringement action brought by the owners of the Italian trade mark "Prep" against importers of identically marked goods produced by German licensees of the American proprietors of the mark in Germany. The Italian plaintiffs had acquired their rights to the mark in 1937 by an assignment from the same American company. Despite the fact that the assignment had been made so many years before, even before the Treaty of Rome, it was found that the continued exercise of the national trade mark right by the Italian plaintiff was prohibited under Article 85. The manner in which the Court worded its decision made perfectly good sense in terms of Article 85 but seems iniquitous in the light of the date of the assignment.

7.59   The *Sirena* decision was mildly tempered by the European Court of Justice in *EMI Records v. CBS*[37] where Article 85 was applied to an agreement which was regarded as continuing to produce its effects where the existence of elements of a concerted practice could be inferred.

7.60   In the meantime, the Court had taken its decision in the case now commonly called "*HAG I*".[38] The facts of the *HAG* case were unusual and the results somewhat startling. HAG coffee was originally produced by a single German enterprise. In 1927 its Belgian production was transferred to a wholly-owned Belgian subsidiary company whose assets were sequestrated in 1944 as being enemy property. The shares were sold and eventually, in 1971, the trade mark was acquired by Van Zuylen. When, in 1972, the German company began to sell its coffee under the same HAG mark in Luxembourg, Van Zuylen sued for infringement. The questions referred to the European Court of Justice concerned Article 85 and Articles 30 *et seq*. The Court found, hardly surprisingly, that Article 85 could not be applied because there were no contractual links at all between the two holders of the rights. Although there had been an assignment to the Belgian subsidiary in the first place, that link had been severed by the sequestration. However, the Court applied the provisions of Article 30/36 and held that the importation of the German-marked goods into Luxembourg could not be prevented where the imported goods bore an identical mark of the same origin. The right to use the mark to prevent imports might only be exercised against infringers "lacking in any legal title".[39]

7.61   However, happily, the decisions in both *HAG I* and *Sirena* have been overtaken by more recent decisions of the European Court of Justice. First, in *HAG II*[40] the ECJ effectively reversed the decision in *HAG I*. In this case the German trade mark owner was seeking to prevent the importation of HAG marked coffee from the Benelux, where it had been legitimately marked by the Benelux owner of the same mark. The European Court of Justice expressly reversed the decision in *HAG I* and held that the trade mark proprietor could exercise his right under national law to prevent the importation of products marked in another Member State by the proprietor of the same mark there, even

[36] Case 40/70: [1971] E.C.R. 69; [1971] C.M.L.R. 260.
[37] Case 51/75: [1976] E.C.R. 811; [1976] 2 C.M.L.R. 235.
[38] Case 192/70, *Van Zuylen Freres v. HAG*: [1974] E.C.R. 731; [1974] 2 C.M.L.R. 127.
[39] See para. 10 of the judgment.
[40] Case C10/89, *SA CNL-Sucal NV v. HAG GF AG*: [1990] I E.C.R. 3711; [1990] 3 C.M.L.R. 571.

where the marks were of common origin, if the marks had fallen into separate ownership. The Court held:

> "For the trade mark to be able to fulfil [its] role it must offer a guarantee that all goods bearing it have been produced under the control of a single undertaking which is accountable for their quality ...
>
> ... the essential function of the mark ... is to give the consumer or final user a guarantee of the identity of the origin of the marked product by enabling him to distinguish, without any possible confusion, that product from others of a different provenance ...
>
> ... the determinant factor is the absence of any consent on the part of the proprietor of the trade mark ... to the putting into circulation in another Member State of similar products bearing an identical trade mark ... which are manufactured and marketed by an undertaking which is economically and legally independent of the proprietor ...
>
> ... the essential function of the mark would be compromised if the owner of the right could not exercise his option under national law to prevent the importation of the similar product under a name likely to be confused with his own mark ... ".[41]

7.62   This decision brought the ECJ's position on the function of trade marks of common historical origin into line with previous decisions taken in relation to marks of independent origin, under which a trade mark proprietor is entitled to exercise his trade mark rights to prevent the importation of similar goods produced independently and marketed under a confusingly similar mark of completely independent origin.[42] The Court defined the essential function of a trade mark to be to guarantee to the consumer the identity of origin of the product. It also justified its adoption of the exhaustion theory in cases of marks of common origin by the fact that sub-division of the mark would already have undermined this essential function, implying that the Court would not feel bound to protect this function of the mark where its proprietors did not.

7.63   Then, in *Ideal Standard*[43] the European Court of Justice effectively reversed the decision in *Sirena*. The facts were that the Ideal Standard mark had been registered in France and in Germany for sanitary fittings and for heating equipment. The original French and German owners were subsidiaries of a common American parent. From 1976 onwards the French subsidiary found itself in financial difficulty and after some insolvency proceedings the heating division of the company was sold, together with the trade mark

---

[41] *ibid.*, at paras. 13–16.
[42] See, *e.g.* Case 119/75, *Terrapin (Overseas) Limited v. Terranova Industrie CA Kapferer & Co*: [1976] E.C.R. 1039; [1976] 2 C.M.L.R. 482. The definition of "confusing similarity" in fact was a major issue outstanding after the *Terrapin* case, since it demonstrated the substantially different tests of confusing similarity adopted under national trade mark laws - a likelihood of confusion was found in Germany which probably would not have been found here. This was also an issue in the *Tanabe-Bayer* case, where complaint was made of the strictness of the German rules on confusing similarity: [1979] 2 C.M.L.R. 80. See also Case C-317/91, *Deutsche Renault AG v. Audi AG*: [1995] 1 C.M.L.R. 461 at 476; [1995] F.S.R. 738.
[43] Case C9/93, *IHT Internationale Heiztechnik GmbH v. Ideal-Standard GmbH*: [1994] I E.C.R. 2789; [1994] 3 C.M.L.R. 857.

registration for heating equipment. The first assignee had no links with the American parent company, neither did a subsequent further assignee. The defendant in these proceedings was importing heating equipment bearing the trade mark Ideal Standard into Germany, which had been manufactured in France by the French proprietor of the French trade mark. The real question for the European Court of Justice was whether the solution which it had reached in *HAG II* should also apply in the event of the division of ownership of the trade mark by a voluntary act. The Court found that it should, and that the exhaustion principle depended on the reality of any consent to the marketing of the goods under the mark sought to be protected. Where ownership of the two national marks had been properly divided, therefore, and whilst national trade mark laws permitted such assignments, they must be given effect so that the German trade mark proprietor was entitled to prevent the importation of the French marked products.

7.64   The result of these two more recent decisions is that where an assignment is a legitimate, commercial, arms' length transaction, which is not merely a disguised attempt at market partitioning, the division of the ownership of the rights will be given effect under European Community law as it will under any relevant national rules. It is worth noting, however, that in *Ideal Standard* the Court analysed the circumstances in which the assignment had been made in 1984, presumably in order to ensure that it really was a proper, commercial transaction and not one designed to achieve a partitioning of the French and German markets. Anyone either purchasing or selling a mark which is identical to marks previously held by one party or one group in more than one of the Member States would do well to bear this qualification to the rule in mind.

(c) Licences

7.65   The European Commission and the ECJ have been willing to accept that, in principle at least, trade mark licensing is a mode of fostering competition and economic growth, since often the trade mark proprietor will not be in a position directly to exploit his trade mark in all of the Member States for which it is registered, or even, necessarily, in the whole territory of any one Member State. Thus, using licensees and distributors may be the only realistic way of ensuring that the goods or services bearing that mark will be given the widest possible distribution. On the other hand, frequently a distributor will be taking an onerous job upon himself when he agrees to handle a manufacturer's products, if this means that he will have to carve out a niche in the market through his own efforts, where the mark is not already well established. As a consequence, a trade mark licensee or distributor may well be prepared to take on the distributorship only if he has sufficient protection to ensure that he is the only one who will reap the rewards of his own efforts. A distributor is likely to want to have some chance of real exclusivity in his territory, and to be protected from competition by the licensor and by fellow licensees or purchasers from them.

7.66   The exhaustion theory[44] developed by the ECJ deems trade marked goods which have been put on the market anywhere in the Community with the consent of the trade mark proprietor in the State of first marketing to exhaust the right of connected trade

---

[44] See above at paras. 7.52 *et seq.* and Chap. 1 and see s. 12 of the 1994 Act.

mark proprietors in all the other Member States to be the first to market goods under that mark in those states. In particular, this will stop a trade mark proprietor from objecting to "parallel imports" of products bearing "his" mark. The ECJ justified its adoption of the exhaustion theory upon the basis that it would be anti-competitive, and going beyond the protection necessary for the protection of the legitimate function of a trade mark, to seek to give a licensee full market protection.

7.67   The Commission and the ECJ have dealt with trade mark licences in two ways, where it has been felt necessary to control their perceived anti-competitive effects. First, some such licences have been dealt with by the application of the exhaustion theory and reference to Articles 30 to 36, especially in cases where the licensor and licensee(s) were not wholly independent parties but were parent and subsidiary or members of the same group of companies. Alternatively, where the parties to the trade mark licence have been fully independent, then the ECJ has applied Article 85 to the licence agreement on the basis that the agreement produced anti-competitive effects. Where Article 85 has been concerned, however, the Commission and the Court have recognised that there are potential benefits from trade mark licensing, in terms of improved distribution of the marked products and improved intra-brand competition. Such licences have, therefore in certain cases been granted either individual or block exemptions under Article 85(3).

7.68   I shall deal below with the position under Articles 30 to 36, and then Articles 85 and the exemptions, ending with a brief discussion of the extremely important block exemption Regulations which apply to various kinds of distribution agreements and licences. Where a trade mark licence is being contemplated either for the whole of one Member State or for more than one Member State, or for a significant part of the territory of one Member State, then the parties will need to take advice as to the applicability of these European law rules and bear in mind the possibility of bringing the terms of the licence within one of the block exemptions.

Articles 30 to 36

7.69   The principle that the theory of exhaustion of rights could be applied to trade mark rights as to other intellectual property rights was established in the case of *Centrafarm BV v. Winthrop BV*,[45] which was one of a string of cases involving the Centrafarm group. In this particular case it was held that the Dutch member of the group could not use its Dutch trade mark rights to prevent the importation into the Netherlands of products bearing a mark which had been legitimately applied to the goods and so marketed in the United Kingdom.

7.70   Please see the discussion in paragraphs 7.52–7.55 above for the circumstances in which the exhaustion theory may not apply, for example where re-packaging might have affected the condition or quality of the product.

---

[45] Case 16/74: [1974] E.C.R. 1183; [1974] 2 C.M.L.R. 480.

Article 85

7.71 There are a number of conditions which must be satisfied before Article 85 will apply. First, there must be an agreement or a concerted practice between undertakings or one or more than one association of undertakings. This means that there must be a degree of independence of the parties to the agreement or concerted practice. Secondly, of course, there must be an agreement or concerted practice, but in the case of trade mark licences this should not be hard to establish!

7.72 A more important qualification is that the agreement must have either as its object or, more probably, as its effect, the prevention or restriction or distortion of competition within the Common Market. This condition, as may be seen below, is not inevitably satisfied in the case of a trade mark licence, although it will frequently be the case. Lastly, the agreement must be such as to affect trade between Member States. This essentially means that it must be possible to foresee that the effect of the agreement may be to influence, directly or indirectly, the pattern of trade between Member States. This may be the case even if the agreement relates only to one Member State if, for example, there are provisions which might prevent the free flow of trade marked goods from or into that Member State. The question will not necessarily be answered by the fact that both parties to the agreement are within the same Member State or that all the performance of the agreement will take place in one Member State, if the structure of competition may be affected or the flow of trade could be affected by the agreement. On the other hand, if the agreement deals with conduct wholly in one Member State and there are no likely repercussions outside that State, there will not be the necessary effect upon inter-state trade.[46] Moreover, the likely effect on inter-state trade must be an appreciable one for Article 85 to apply: if the effect would be absolutely minimal, then there will be no infringement of this Article.[47]

7.73 There are a limited number of types of clause commonly inserted in trade mark licences, which have been held in the past not to fall within Article 85(1) at all, as not restricting competition. For instance, a term in a trade mark licence by virtue of which the licensor may exert quality control over the production and use of the mark by the licensee is not itself anti-competitive.[48] The realistic view seems to be taken that as a licence need not be granted at all, it must be open to the licensor to limit the licence he grants to use of the mark upon goods or services which meet his quality control standards. However, to take this approach to its logical conclusion would be to permit the licensor to impose unlimited restrictions upon the licensee, and this could not be countenanced under Article 85(1). On the contrary, numerous sorts of clauses which might commonly be imposed in trade mark licence agreements have been found to fall within Article 85(1). Any kind of clause which may have as its direct or indirect effect the prevention of parallel imports to or from the licensee's territory is likely to fall within Article 85(1). This could take the form of an obligation on the licensee not to export or sell within his territory for resale

---

[46] See Case 22/78 *Hugin v. Commission*: [1979] E.C.R. 1869; [1979] 3 C.M.L.R. 345.
[47] There are a number of Commission Notices giving guidance as to the relevant tests of market share, see generally paras. 2–139 to 2–146 of Bellamy & Child, *Common Market Law of Competition*, (4th ed. 1993).
[48] And such terms of quality control may be vital in a trade mark licence, if the licensee's use of the mark is not to render the mark deceptive. See Wilkof, *Trade Mark Licensing*.

outside it, or an obligation on the licensor not to export to or sell for export into the licensed territory.[49] Other clauses which may fall within the Article are obligations not to sell competing products or to obtain all supplies from the licensor. Various price controls may also fall within the Article. All in all, it would be an unusual trade mark licence which did not run the risk of falling within Article 85(1).

7.74 This is even more likely to be the case where there is a series of "vertical" distribution agreements, and particularly where they are franchise agreements. In the latter kind of case, the franchisee is often obliged to obtain all his supplies directly from the franchisor, to sell them under very specific conditions controlled by the licensor, to provide specialist staff and an after-sales service and to conform to the franchisor's "front of house" policies and pricing. Such agreements are particularly likely to restrict competition and to restrict intra-brand competition. If each distributor or franchisee must conform to the same rules as his co-distributors or licensees, there will be no possibility of competition between different sources of the same marked products or services. If the distributors or franchisees are in addition restricted from selling competing goods or offering competing services, then competition will suffer further.

7.75 Exclusive distribution networks or franchise networks can also hamper third parties from entering into competition in relation to the same or similar goods, as the number of distributors in a particular area may be limited or the qualifications for becoming a distributor may be onerous. Even discriminatory rebate policies may effectively prevent competition from non-selected distributors.[50]

7.76 It will therefore be an unusual trade mark licence or franchise agreement which does not fall initially within Article 85(1). The penalties for non-exempt infringement of Article 85(1) are heavy, the agreement may be deemed void and heavy fines may be imposed upon the parties to it by the Commission.

7.77 Happily, Article 85(3) allows agreements which would otherwise infringe Article 85(1) to be exempted from the effects of Article 85(2) where they nonetheless contribute to the production or distribution of goods or economic progress. Parties contemplating entering into a trade mark licence which is likely to come within Article 85(1) can seek to protect themselves in one of two ways. First, they may apply for a negative clearance from the European Commission.[51] Alternatively, the parties may seek to bring the terms of their licence agreement within one or more of the so-called block exemption Regulations which have been promulgated by the European Commission itself, and which cover a number of different kinds of distribution or licence agreements. There is no one such block exemption which applies to trade mark licences of all kinds, but a number of them may apply to particular kinds of trade mark licence and it is generally considered that if a licence agreement falls outside the precise scope of any one such exemption, but the restrictions imposed by it are restrictions which would be permitted pursuant to such a regulation, there is little danger of Article 85(2) being applied to the agreement.

---

[49] See one of the earliest decisions in this area Joined Cases 56 & 58/64, *Consten & Grundig*: [1966] E.C.R. 299; [1966] C.M.L.R. 418.
[50] See, *e.g.* Case 73/74, *Papiers Peints*: [1975] E.C.R. 1491; [1976] 1 C.M.L.R. 589.
[51] See Chap. 11 of Bellamy & Child, above.

7.78 These block exemptions need to be studied in detail in relation to any proposed licence agreement. The Commission brings out such Regulations intermittently in relation to specific fields of economic activity. They include:

> Regulation 1983/83 on exclusive distribution agreements.
> Regulation 1984/83 on exclusive purchasing agreements.
> Regulation 2349/84 on patent licensing.
> Regulation 4087/88 on franchise agreements.
> Regulation 556/89 on know-how licensing.

All of these block exemption regulations tend to follow the same pattern; they give two lists – a "white list" of acceptable clauses for such an agreement to qualify for the exemption given by the regulation and a "black list" of clauses which will not be acceptable. They may also include "grey lists" of clauses which may be acceptable if they are genuinely "necessary to protect the franchisor's industrial or intellectual property rights or to maintain the common identity and reputation of the franchised network".[52]

7.79 Taking the example of Regulation 4087/88 on franchise agreements, it may be seen that the white list includes an obligation on the franchisor not to grant further franchises to third parties within the franchisee's area nor to exploit the franchise itself in that area or an obligation on the franchisee to refrain from seeking customers from outside his own contract territory.[53] Further "white" restrictions may include protection of the franchisor's know-how, obligations on the franchisee to inform the franchisor of any experience gained in exploiting the franchise and an obligation to grant the franchisor and other franchisees an exclusive licence for that know-how. Similarly, an obligation of quite a different kind, not to assign the rights and obligations under the franchise agreement without the franchisor's consent is also in the "white" list.[54] The "grey" list includes an obligation upon the franchisee only to sell goods meeting the franchisor's quality requirements, or even to sell only goods manufactured by the franchisor or designated third parties where it will be difficult otherwise to apply objective quality specifications, and a common clause not to engage in a competing business in the territory where it has been active for a reasonable period after determination of the franchise agreement. Such a reasonable period may not exceed a year.[55] "Black" obligations include a refusal to permit the franchisee to determine his own sale prices or to permit the franchisee to challenge the validity of the intellectual property rights forming part of the franchise, without prejudice to the possibility for the franchisor to terminate the agreement in such a case.[56]

Article 86

7.80 Article 86 prevents abuses by an undertaking or group of undertakings having a dominant position within the Common Market or a substantial part of it. Such abuses may consist of imposing unfair purchase or selling prices or unfair trading conditions, limiting

---

[52] See Art. 3 of Regulation 4087/88.
[53] See Art. 2 of 4087/88.
[54] See Art. 3(2).
[55] See Art. 3(1).
[56] See Art. 5.

production or markets, etc. Article 86 has as yet played a very small role in the field of intellectual property licensing as, on the whole, the European Court of Justice has taken the view that the mere exercise of intellectual property rights cannot amount to an abuse of a dominant position.[57]

7.81   However, in *"Wilkinson Sword"*,[58] the Commission found an agreement concerning the sale and redistribution of worldwide trade mark rights fell under Article 86, because of the size of the purchaser's market share.

7.82   More recently, in *Magill*,[59] the ECJ held that a refusal to grant a licence by a copyright owner could, in certain circumstances, amount to an abuse of a dominant position. The case may be seen as having little immediate impact upon trade mark rights, but may nonetheless herald a shift in the Court's approach to the exercise of intellectual property rights.

---

[57] See, *e.g.* Case 238/87, *AB Volvo v. Eric Veng (U.K.) Limited*: [1988] E.C.R. 6211; [1989] 4 C.M.L.R. 122.
[58] *Warner-Lambert/Gillette and Eemland* [1993] 5 C.M.L.R. 559
[59] Joined Cases C-241/91P and C-242/91P, *RTE and TTP v. Commission*: [1995] 4 C.M.L.R. 718; and see commentary by Vinje in [1995] E.I.P.R. 297.

REGISTRABILITY UNDER THE 1938 ACT

(1) INTRODUCTION

A.1 Despite the fact that the 1994 Act enacts the Directive, in many respects, as may be seen from the main text, elements of the previous law remain relevant. Most of these remaining elements of pre-1994 law have been sufficiently covered in the relevant sections of this book.

A.2 Those unfamiliar with the 1938 Act may, however, find it of some further help to have here a summary of other elements of the 1938 Act relating to registrability, which may still be of relevance in dealing with the modern law. It should, however, be emphasised that this Appendix cannot cover every element of the old law.

(2) REGISTRABILITY UNDER THE 1938 ACT

Definition of a mark

A.3 The statutory definition of a mark for the purposes of the Trade Marks Act 1938 was found in section 68(1). A "mark includes a device, brand, heading, label, ticket, name, signature, word, letter, numeral or any combination thereof" whilst a "trade mark" was defined as " ... a mark used or proposed to be used in relation to goods for the purpose of indicating ... a connection in the course of trade between the goods and some person having the right either as proprietor or as registered user to use the mark."

A.4 To be a registrable mark, then, the sign had not only to fall within one of the categories in the first definition, but had to qualify as a trade mark by the use to which it was to be put.

Distinctiveness

A.5 There were two further hurdles to be cleared before a mark might be registered: the question of its distinctiveness, and the test for deceptiveness. The former was an objective criterion equivalent in some respects to the "absolute" grounds for refusal set out in section 3 of the 1994 Act, and intended to prevent traders from improperly registering for their exclusive use descriptive words inherently unsuited to distinguish one trader's goods from another's, or which another trader might genuinely wish or need to use to describe his products.

A.6 Under the 1938 Act, a sign had to qualify as a mark not only by falling within one of the categories of mark described in sections 9(1) and 68(1), which may be seen to have been broadly worded, but also by satisfying the demands of section 9(2), that the mark be "adapted ... to distinguish" (or, in the case of Part B marks, be "capable ... of distinguishing" under section 10). These latter requirements produced some strange results, denying registration to marks which had established truly distinctive reputations in use. As a result, the peculiarity of the 1938 Act was that a mark could be found to have become wholly distinctive in use, yet be deemed unregistrable as lacking an *inherent* ability/capacity to distinguish.[1] Surnames and geographical names were particularly subjected to stringent tests for distinctiveness for this reason (see paragraphs A.15–A.16 below), as were word marks deemed to have some reference to the "character" of the goods.

A.7 The separate test for deceptiveness was a mixture of objective and subjective tests; objective in ruling out marks which would or might mislead as to the qualities, composition, etc., of the product, subjective and comparative in the appraisal of the likelihood of confusion between a mark applied for and prior marks. These grounds for refusal of registration can broadly be likened to the absolute and relative grounds of refusal found respectively in sections 3(1) and 5 of the 1994 Act. One useful rule of thumb applied in relation to application under the 1938 Act in considering whether a mark was acceptable was whether the mark would be likely to cause difficulties to other traders, by preventing them from using terms common to the trade or generally descriptive of the products.[2]

Division of the Register

A.8 Under the 1938 Act the Trade Mark Register was divided into two parts, A and B, for which the Act provided separate qualifying provisions, sections 9 and 10 respectively. The difference between the wording and scope of the two sections was far from crystal clear, but the general idea was that Part B was used to register those marks which were marginally over-descriptive but which were (in practice) found to be distinctive, or which, if as yet unused, had some capacity of becoming distinctive in the future; Part B marks were effectively given the benefit of the doubt.

A.9 The real differences between the value of registrations in Part A and Part B were minimal, except that Part A registrations alone could become incontestable after seven years (subject in any event to intervening deceptiveness, see paragraph A.28 below.)

A.10 Part B marks were also granted less certain rights of exclusivity, as a special "defence" might be raised against an allegation of infringement of a Part B mark under section 5(2) of the 1938 Act. However, the defence was not easily made out in practice. All in all, the distinction between Part A and Part B registrations was unsatisfactory.[3]

A.11 It was perhaps not surprising that the distinction between the two parts of the Register was abolished by the 1994 Act; not only is there no equivalent distinction in the new Act, but by paragraph 2(1) of Schedule 3 of the new Act, all pre-existing Part A and Part B marks were transferred on the commencement of the new Act to the single Register.

---

[1] See especially *York* [1984] R.P.C. 231, H.L.
[2] See, *e.g. Have a Break trade mark* [1993] R.P.C. 217.
[3] See, *e.g. "Weldmesh" trade mark* [1966] R.P.C. 220: 100 per cent distinctiveness in fact not good enough to register descriptive mark in Part A.

A.12   The only continuing relevance of the distinction between Part A and Part B marks may arise in relation to infringement of marks which were originally in Part B, in those few cases where the section 5(2) "defence" may still be of relevance (see Chapter 4, paragraphs 4.32 *et seq.*)

Signs capable of being registered as marks

A.13   The list of signs set out in section 68(1) as being suitable for use as trade marks was echoed in the wording of section 9(1) of the 1938 Act with each category of mark listed increasing in its suitability for registration. To be registrable a mark had not only fit within one of the five parts of section 9(1) but had also to qualify as distinctive according to the conditions of section 9(2) and (3).[4]

- (a)   Names: see Chapter 2, paragraph 2.30;
- (b)   Signatures: see Chapter 2, paragraph 2.31;
- (c)   Invented words: see Chapter 2, paragraphs 2.32–3;
- (d)   Words having no direct reference to the character of the goods: see Chapter 2, paragraphs 2.34–40;
- (e)   Other distinctive marks: section 9(1)(e) was a catch-all provision covering marks which did not qualify for registration under heads (a) to (d) yet were in fact distinctive. This covered numerals, initials, devices, or other distinctive elements as well as word marks rejected under section 9(1)(c) or (d). However, such marks would not be registered without evidence of distinctiveness.

A.14   Sub-sections 9(2) and (3) defined distinctiveness. Sub-section 9(2) provided that a distinctive mark was one which was "adapted ... to distinguish" a trader's goods, that is one which is capable of identifying the goods to prevent them being confused with competing goods. The criteria for deciding whether a mark was distinctive were extended in section 9(3) to cover not only marks which were inherently adapted to distinguish the marked goods, but also those which had become so adapted through use or other circumstances. This second part of section 9(3) could be of vital importance to a trader whose mark was perhaps on the borderline of distinctiveness and descriptiveness in objective terms, such as a surname, but which had become distinctive in use.

A.15   Certain types of word marks which might have been expected to benefit from the permissibility of accepting *de facto* rather than inherent distinctiveness were nonetheless refused registration where the Registrar or court considered that the mark was inherently so ill-adapted to distinguish the goods that it could never become legally distinctive. Alternatively, marks might be found to be insufficiently distinctive to qualify for Part A registration, but just sufficiently distinctive to have a "capacity" to distinguish for registration in Part B.[5]

A.16   Certain words were considered incapable of ever losing their primarily descriptive meaning, whether referring to the nature or the qualities of the goods.[6] See discussion of "laudatory epithets" in Chapter 2, paragraph 2.38.

A.17   It was also possible to register slogans as marks under section 9(1)(e), if sufficiently distinctive, and if it appeared that they would be used in such a way that they would be taken as being used as a brand name (*i.e.* if used without any other "mark" which could be taken as being the trade mark for the goods).[7]

---

[4] See *"Monogram" trade mark* [1968] R.P.C. 246 and *York op. cit.*, n. 1.
[5] See, *e.g. Weldmesh Trade Mark*, n. 3, above.
[6] See, *e.g. "Yorkshire"* (1954) 71 R.P.C. 150; *"Chunky"* [1978] F.S.R. 322.
[7] See *"I Can't Believe it's Yogurt"* [1992] R.P.C. 533, distinguishing *Have a Break trade mark* [1993] R.P.C. 217 in which (in 1983) Whitford J. had refused registration of the phrase "Have a Break" as being merely part of Rowntree's advertising slogan for its Kit-Kat chocolate bars, and not indicating origin, so not a trade mark in its own right.

A.18   For discussion of registration of shapes, and colours see Chapter 2 paragraphs 2.46 and 2.59 respectively.

Disclaimers

A.19   Under section 14 of the 1938 Act, non-distinctive parts of a trade mark could be accepted for registration subject to a disclaimer (required to be made by the Registrar) of certain descriptive or non-distinctive parts of the mark. The mark was registered as a whole, but the exclusive rights given by registration would only apply to the distinctive parts, the essential features of the mark, not to non-distinctive words or designs and not to matter common to the trade.

A.20   Whether disclaimers served any very real purpose in preventing confusion in the market place must, of course, be doubted, since "disclaimers do not go into the market with the goods"[8] and the whole of the mark could be considered in the context of opposition proceedings.[9]

A.21   Changes have therefore been made in relation to disclaimers by the 1994 Act (see section 13 and para. 3.33 above).

In use or proposed to be used

A.22   Under the 1938 Act there was one further qualification for the mark to be registrable, satisfied not by reference to the characteristics of the mark itself but by the use to which the mark was to be put. This condition was found both in section 68(1) and in sections 9 and 10.

A.23   The mark had to be in use or proposed to be put into use. This was once again a protection against monopolies, as it prevented proprietors from taking out registrations for marks which they did not actually intend to use. See the *"Nerit"* case[10] discussed at Chapter 2, paragraph 2. 87. However, registration for use by a licensee sufficed.[11] A mark could legitimately be applied for by a distributor rather than a manufacturer, see *Radiation Limited's Application*.[12]

Restrictions on registration founded upon confusion or deception

A.24   The further restrictions added to the registrability of marks by sections 11 and 12 have been discussed fully in Chapter 2(8).

A.25   There was no direct equivalent to section 4 of the 1994 Act, so that section 11 was used to preclude from registration marks which falsely indicated a royal connection by use of the Royal arms, the words "Royal", "Imperial", "Crown", etc., or a representation of any member of the Royal family. Similarly, the use of the Navy's anchor device or the "Wings" device of the RAF were banned. The use of city arms, national flags or emblems and the names of living or recently deceased persons were not registrable as trade marks without the consent of the body, State or person concerned. Where a Royal Warrant had been granted, the manner in which the arms could be used was in any case strictly controlled.

A.26   However, the more important aspects of sections 11 and 12 were those which entailed a comparison between the mark applied for or indeed a registered mark and prior marks or other prior rights. There were differences in the scope of the two sections[13] and see Chapter 2.92 *et seq.*

---

[8] *"Ace"* (1948) 65 R.P.C. 238 at 241.
[9] *"Granada"* [1979] R.P.C. 303.
[10] *Imperial Group Limited v. Philip Morris & Co. Limited* [1982] F.S.R. 72 and see *Palm trade mark* [1992] R.P.C. 258.
[11] *"Bostitch"* [1963] R.P.C. 183.
[12] (1930) 47 R.P.C. 37.
[13] The leading case on the differences between ss. 11 and 12 was *Smith Hayden & Co's Application* (1946) 63 R.P.C. 97, updated by *GE* [1973] R.P.C. 297.

Section 11 as grounds for rectification

A.27 Section 11 could be used not only to defeat an application for a mark but also subsequently when actual confusion or deception had arisen, giving grounds to expunge the deceptive mark from the Register. The application of section 11 could result in the rectification of the Register even where the two conflicting marks had both been registered for a number of years. For instance, in *Berlei v. Bali*[14] the Register was rectified after many years' use of the later mark, as it was found that at the time of registration there had been a possibility of deception or confusion which sufficed to invalidate Bali's registration.

A.28 In *GE* the almost identical marks of a British and an American company had been registered respectively in 1906 and 1907 for electrical goods. It was common ground that when registered the American mark was not likely to cause confusion. Later, though, as imports of the American products increased, the British company applied for rectification of the Register. The use to which section 11 might be put was exhaustively examined by Lord Diplock, and the vital question of the likelihood of the mark to cause confusion or deception was described as:

> "a hypothetical question, which first arises on an original application for registration. It looks to the future use of the matter as a trade mark and embraces any normal and fair use which as registered proprietor the applicant would be entitled to make of it in the ordinary course of trade."[15]

Thus, although bounded by the notion of normal and fair use, in applying section 11 one could look ahead beyond the immediate circumstances in which the mark would be used, so as to refuse to register marks which at a later date could result in two proprietors being entitled to use confusingly similar marks either on similar goods, in direct competition, or in circumstances which might lead to confusion.

A.29 However, where the initial registration of the contested mark had been valid, but subsequently the marks had actually come into conflict, the second mark could only be expunged from the Register where this deceptive situation was the result of some "blameworthy" act of the proprietor.[16] In any case, the court had a discretion whether or not to rectify the Register. In *GE*, in fact, no blame was attached to the American proprietors of the contested mark, so that rectification was refused.

A.30 Under section 13 of the 1938 Act, Part A marks became incontestable after seven years' registration, subject at all times to such a challenge under section 11.

A.31 Generally on section 12 (1) and (2) see Chapter 2, paragraphs 2.100–2.109 and 2.145 *et seq.* respectively.

A.32 For the purpose of section 12, a mark was deemed to be "already on the Register" even if renewal fees for it were overdue, and this situation continued for one year after the date of removal.[17] If, however, registration was refused because of similarities between the new mark and a prior mark which was not in current use, the applicant qualified as an "aggrieved person" in the sense of section 26(1) and could seek to have the Register rectified, so as to clear the way to register his own mark.[18]

---

[14] *Bali trade mark* [1969] R.P.C. 472 and see *Bali (No. 2)* [1978] F.S.R. 193 – refusal of Bali's application to register the mark; honest concurrent use was found, but the discretion to refuse registration was exercised.
[15] *GE* [1973] R.P.C. 297 at 321.
[16] *ibid.*, at 335.
[17] By s. 20, and see *Runner trade mark* [1978] R.P.C. 402.
[18] *e.g. Trina trade mark* [1977] R.P.C. 131.

Section 12(3)

A.33   This section applied where neither one of two confusingly similar marks had been registered (as opposed to section 12(2) where one such mark was already registered).[19] Section 12(3) was used where there were conflicting pending applications and a variety of procedures could be followed depending on the closeness of the marks. Sometimes, it was possible to obtain mutual consents to the applications before advertisement and acceptance. Alternatively, a sort of mutual opposition procedure might be put into effect to decide which of the marks should be accepted.

A.34   The agreements which might be reached under section 12(3) included limitations as to the mode of use, colour and territory of use of the marks, as well as restrictions to particular goods. In *Lion Brand*,[20] for instance, separate applications were made by two companies for very similar marks, both marks having already been in use; one party's area of use was larger than, and allegedly included, the other's. The Court was initially loath to apply section 12(3) because of the strong likelihood of confusion which would be against the public interest, but was prepared to register both marks once agreement had been reached between the proprietors to vary the manner in which each would use the mark.

Defensive registrations

A.35   Under section 27 of the 1938 Act, it was possible for the proprietor of a "well-known" trade mark which consisted of an invented word or words to register the mark in relation to goods, notwithstanding a lack of any intention to use the mark on those goods, if the strength of the mark's reputation was such that use on those goods "would be likely to be taken as indicating a connection in the course of trade" between those goods and the goods on which his mark was actually used/the proprietor. This provision was so restrictively worded as to be little used, and there is no directly equivalent provision in the 1994 Act, doubtless because of the wider scope of a registration in terms both of section 5(2) and (3) and section 10(2) and (3).

---

[19] See *Caravillas trade mark* [1981] R.P.C. 381.
[20] *Bainbridge & Green & Co's Application* (1940) 57 R.P.C. 248.

MATERIALS

(1)   Trade Marks Act 1994

CHAPTER 26

ARRANGEMENT OF SECTIONS

Interpretation

Other general provisions

An Act to make new provision for registered trade marks, implementing Council Directive No. 89/104/EEC of 21st December 1988 to approximate the laws of the Member States relating to trade marks; to make provision in connection with Council Regulation (EC) No. 40/94 of 20th December 1993 on the Community trade mark; to give effect to the Madrid Protocol Relating to the International Registration of Marks of 27th June 1989, and to certain provisions of the Paris Convention for the Protection of Industrial Property of 20th March 1883, as revised and amended; and for connected purposes. [21st July 1994]

PART I
REGISTERED TRADE MARKS

Introductory

Trade marks

1.—(1) In this Act a "trade mark" means any sign capable of being represented graphically which is capable of distinguishing goods or services of one undertaking from those of other undertakings.

A trade mark may, in particular, consist of words (including personal names), designs, letters, numerals or the shape of goods or their packaging.

(2) References in this Act to a trade mark include, unless the context otherwise requires, references to a collective mark (see section 49) or certification mark (see section 50).

Registered trade marks

2.—(1) A registered trade mark is a property right obtained by the registration of the trade mark under this Act and the proprietor of a registered trade mark has the rights and remedies provided by this Act.

(2) No proceedings lie to prevent or recover damages for the infringement of an unregistered trade mark as such; but nothing in this Act affects the law relating to passing off.

Grounds for refusal of registration

Absolute grounds for refusal of registration

3.—(1) The following shall not be registered—
(a) signs which do not satisfy the requirements of section 1(1),
(b) trade marks which are devoid of any distinctive character,
(c) trade marks which consist exclusively of signs or indications which may serve, in trade, to designate the kind, quality, quantity, intended purpose, value, geographical origin, the time of production of goods or of rendering of services, or other characteristics of goods or services,
(d) trade marks which consist exclusively of signs or indications which have become customary in the current language or in the *bona fide* and established practices of the trade:

Provided that, a trade mark shall not be refused registration by virtue of paragraph (b), (c) or (d) above if, before the date of application for registration, it has in fact acquired a distinctive character as a result of the use made of it.

(2) A sign shall not be registered as a trade mark if it consists exclusively of—
(a) the shape which results from the nature of the goods themselves,
(b) the shape of goods which is necessary to obtain a technical result, or
(c) the shape which gives substantial value to the goods.

(3) A trade mark shall not be registered if it is—
(a) contrary to public policy or to accepted principles of morality, or
(b) of such a nature as to deceive the public (for instance as to the nature, quality or geographical origin of the goods or service).

(4) A trade mark shall not be registered if or to the extent that its use is prohibited in the United Kingdom by any enactment or rule of law or by any provision of Community law.

(5) A trade mark shall not be registered in the cases specified, or referred to, in section 4 (specially protected emblems).

(6) A trade mark shall not be registered if or to the extent that the application is made in bad faith.

Specially protected emblems

4.—(1) A trade mark which consists of or contains—
(a) the Royal arms, or any of the principal armorial bearings of the Royal arms, or any insignia or device so nearly resembling the Royal arms or any such armorial bearing as to be likely to be mistaken for them or it,
(b) a representation of the Royal crown or any of the Royal flags,
(c) a representation of Her Majesty or any member of the Royal family, or any colourable imitation thereof, or
(d) words, letters or devices likely to lead persons to think that the applicant either has or recently has had Royal patronage or authorisation,
shall not be registered unless it appears to the registrar that consent has been given by or on behalf of Her Majesty or, as the case may be, the relevant member of the Royal family.

(2) A trade mark which consists of or contains a representation of—
(a) the national flag of the United Kingdom (commonly known as the Union Jack), or
(b) the flag of England, Wales, Scotland, Northern Ireland or the Isle of Man,
shall not be registered if it appears to the registrar that the use of the trade mark would be misleading or grossly offensive.

Provision may be made by rules identifying the flags to which paragraph (b) applies.

(3) A trade mark shall not be registered in the cases specified in—
section 57 (national emblems, &c. of Convention countries), or
section 58 (emblems, &c. of certain international organisations).

(4) Provision may be made by rules prohibiting in such cases as may be prescribed the registration of a trade mark which consists of or contains—
(a) arms to which a person is entitled by virtue of a grant of arms by the Crown, or

(b) insignia so nearly resembling such arms as to be likely to be mistaken for them,
unless it appears to the registrar that consent has been given by or on behalf of that person.

Where such a mark is registered, nothing in this Act shall be construed as authorising its use in any way contrary to the laws of arms.

(5) A trade mark which consists of or contains a controlled representation within the meaning of the Olympic Symbol etc. (Protection) Act 1995 shall not be registered unless it appears to the registrar—

    (a) that the application is made by the person for the time being appointed under section 1(2) of the Olympic Symbol etc. (Protection) Act 1995 (power of Secretary of State to appoint a person as the proprietor of the Olympics association right), or

    (b) that consent has been given by or on behalf of the person mentioned in paragraph (a) above.*

Relative grounds for refusal of registration

5.—(1) A trade mark shall not be registered if it is identical with an earlier trade mark and the goods or services for which the trade mark is applied for are identical with the goods or services for which the earlier trade mark is protected.

(2) A trade mark shall not be registered if because—

    (a) it is identical with an earlier trade mark and is to be registered for goods or services similar to those for which the earlier trade mark is protected, or

    (b) it is similar to an earlier trade mark and is to be registered for goods or services identical with or similar to those for which the earlier trade mark is protected,

there exists a likelihood of confusion on the part of the public, which includes the likelihood of association with the earlier trade mark.

(3) A trade mark which—

    (a) is identical with or similar to an earlier trade mark, and

    (b) is to be registered for goods or services which are not similar to those for which the earlier trade mark is protected,

shall not be registered if, or to the extent that, the earlier trade mark has a reputation in the United Kingdom (or, in the case of a Community trade mark, in the European Community) and the use of the later mark without due cause would take unfair advantage of, or be detrimental to, the distinctive character or the repute of the earlier trade mark.

(4) A trade mark shall not be registered if, or to the extent that, its use in the United Kingdom is liable to be prevented—

    (a) by virtue of any rule of law (in particular, the law of passing off) protecting an unregistered trade mark or other sign used in the course of trade, or

    (b) by virtue of an earlier right other than those referred to in subsections (1) to (3) or paragraph (a) above, in particular by virtue of the law of copyright, design right or registered designs.

A person thus entitled to prevent the use of a trade mark is referred to in this Act as the proprietor of an "earlier right" in relation to the trade mark.

(5) Nothing in this section prevents the registration of a trade mark where the proprietor of the earlier trade mark or other earlier right consents to the registration.

Meaning of "earlier trade mark"

6.—(1) In this Act an "earlier trade mark" means—

    (a) a registered trade mark, international trade mark (UK) or Community trade mark which has a date of application for registration earlier than that of the trade mark in question, taking account (where appropriate) of the priorities claimed in respect of the trade marks,

    (b) a Community trade mark which has a valid claim to seniority from an earlier registered trade mark or international trade mark (UK), or

---

* Subsection (5) was inserted by the Olympic Symbol etc. (Protection) Act 1995.

    (c) a trade mark which, at the date of application for registration of the trade mark in question or (where appropriate) of the priority claimed in respect of the application, was entitled to protection under the Paris Convention as a well known trade mark.

    (2) References in this Act to an earlier trade mark include a trade mark in respect of which an application for registration has been made and which, if registered, would be an earlier trade mark by virtue of subsection (1)(a) or (b), subject to its being so registered.

    (3) A trade mark within subsection (1)(a) or (b) whose registration expires shall continue to be taken into account in determining the registrability of a later mark for a period of one year after the expiry unless the registrar is satisfied that there was no *bona fide* use of the mark during the two years immediately preceding the expiry.

Raising of relative grounds in case of honest concurrent use

    7.—(1) This section applies where on an application for the registration of a trade mark it appears to the registrar—
    (a) that there is an earlier trade mark in relation to which the conditions set out in section 5(1), (2) or (3) obtain, or
    (b) that there is an earlier right in relation to which the condition set out in section 5(4) is satisfied,
but the applicant shows to the satisfaction of the registrar that there has been honest concurrent use of the trade mark for which registration is sought.

    (2) In that case the registrar shall not refuse the application by reason of the earlier trade mark or other earlier right unless objection on that ground is raised in opposition proceedings by the proprietor of that earlier trade mark or other earlier right.

    (3) For the purposes of this section "honest concurrent use" means such use in the United Kingdom, by the applicant or with his consent, as would formerly have amounted to honest concurrent use for the purposes of section 12(2) of the Trade Marks Act 1938.

    (4) Nothing in this section affects—
    (a) the refusal of registration on the grounds mentioned in section 3 (absolute grounds for refusal), or
    (b) the making of an application for a declaration of invalidity under section 47(2) (application on relative grounds where no consent to registration).

    (5) This section does not apply when there is an order in force under section 8 below.

Power to require that relative grounds be raised in opposition proceedings

    8.—(1) The Secretary of State may by order provide that in any case a trade mark shall not be refused registration on a ground mentioned in section 5 (relative grounds for refusal) unless objection on that ground is raised in opposition proceedings by the proprietor of the earlier trade mark or other earlier right.

    (2) The order may make such consequential provision as appears to the Secretary of State appropriate—
    (a) with respect to the carrying out by the registrar of searches of earlier trade marks, and
    (b) as to the persons by whom an application for a declaration of invalidity may be made on the grounds specified in section 47(2) (relative grounds).

    (3) An order making such provision as is mentioned in subsection (2)(a) may direct that so much of section 37 (examination of application) as requires a search to be carried out shall cease to have effect.

    (4) An order making such provision as is mentioned in subsection (2)(b) may provide that so much of section 47(3) as provides that any person may make an application for a declaration of invalidity shall have effect subject to the provisions of the order.

    (5) An order under this section shall be made by statutory instrument, and no order shall be made unless a draft of it has been laid before and approved by a resolution of each House of Parliament.

No such draft of an order making such provision as is mentioned in subsection (1) shall be laid before Parliament until after the end of the period of ten years beginning with the day on which applications for Community trade marks may first be filed in pursuance of the Community Trade Mark Regulation.

(6) An order under this section may contain such transitional provisions as appear to the Secretary of State to be appropriate.

Effects of registered trade mark

Rights conferred by registered trade mark

9.—(1) The proprietor of a registered trade mark has exclusive rights in the trade mark which are infringed by use of the trade mark in the United Kingdom without his consent.

The acts amounting to infringement, if done without the consent of the proprietor, are specified in section 10.

(2) References in this Act to the infringement of a registered trade mark are to any such infringement of the rights of the proprietor.

(3) The rights of the proprietor have effect from the date of registration (which in accordance with section 40(3) is the date of filing of the application for registration):

Provided that—

(a) no infringement proceedings may be begun before the date on which the trade mark is in fact registered; and

(b) no offence under section 92 (unauthorised use of trade mark, &c. in relation to goods) is committed by anything done before the date of publication of the registration.

Infringement of registered trade mark

10.—(1) A person infringes a registered trade mark if he uses in the course of trade a sign which is identical with the trade mark in relation to goods or services which are identical with those for which it is registered.

(2) A person infringes a registered trade mark if he uses in the course of trade a sign where because—

(a) the sign is identical with the trade mark and is used in relation to goods or services similar to those for which the trade mark is registered, or

(b) the sign is similar to the trade mark and is used in relation to goods or services identical with or similar to those for which the trade mark is registered,

there exists a likelihood of confusion on the part of the public, which includes the likelihood of association with the trade mark.

(3) A person infringes a registered trade mark if he uses in the course of trade a sign which—

(a) is identical with or similar to the trade mark, and

(b) is used in relation to goods or services which are not similar to those for which the trade mark is registered,

where the trade mark has a reputation in the United Kingdom and the use of the sign, being without due cause, takes unfair advantage of, or is detrimental to, the distinctive character or the repute of the trade mark.

(4) For the purposes of this section a person uses a sign if, in particular, he—

(a) affixes it to goods or the packaging thereof;

(b) offers or exposes goods for sale, puts them on the market or stocks them for those purposes under the sign, or offers or supplies services under the sign;

(c) imports or exports goods under the sign; or

(d) uses the sign on business papers or in advertising.

(5) A person who applies a registered trade mark to material intended to be used for labelling or packaging goods, as a business paper, or for advertising goods or services, shall be treated as a party to any use of the material which infringes the registered trade mark if when he applied the mark he

knew or had reason to believe that the application of the mark was not duly authorised by the proprietor or a licensee.

(6) Nothing in the preceding provisions of this section shall be construed as preventing the use of a registered trade mark by any person for the purpose of identifying goods or services as those of the proprietor or a licensee.

But any such use otherwise than in accordance with honest practices in industrial or commercial matters shall be treated as infringing the registered trade mark if the use without due cause takes unfair advantage of, or is detrimental to, the distinctive character or repute of the trade mark.

Limits on effect of registered trade mark

11.—(1) A registered trade mark is not infringed by the use of another registered trade mark in relation to goods or services for which the latter is registered (but see section 47(6) (effect of declaration of invalidity of registration)).

(2) A registered trade mark is not infringed by—
- (a) the use by a person of his own name or address,
- (b) the use of indications concerning the kind, quality, quantity, intended purpose, value, geographical origin, the time of production of goods or of rendering of services, or other characteristics of goods or services, or
- (c) the use of the trade mark where it is necessary to indicate the intended purpose of a product or service (in particular, as accessories or spare parts),

provided the use is in accordance with honest practices in industrial or commercial matters.

(3) A registered trade mark is not infringed by the use in the course of trade in a particular locality of an earlier right which applies only in that locality.

For this purpose an "earlier right" means an unregistered trade mark or other sign continuously used in relation to goods or services by a person or a predecessor in title of his from a date prior to whichever is the earlier of—
- (a) the use of the first-mentioned trade mark in relation to those goods or services by the proprietor or a predecessor in title of his, or
- (b) the registration of the first-mentioned trade mark in respect of those goods or services in the name of the proprietor or a predecessor in title of his;

and an earlier right shall be regarded as applying in a locality if, or to the extent that, its use in that locality is protected by virtue of any rule of law (in particular, the law of passing off).

Exhaustion of rights conferred by registered trade mark

12.—(1) A registered trade mark is not infringed by the use of the trade mark in relation to goods which have been put on the market in the European Economic Area under that trade mark by the proprietor or with his consent.

(2) Subsection (1) does not apply where there exists legitimate reasons for the proprietor to oppose further dealings in the goods (in particular, where the condition of the goods has been changed or impaired after they have been put on the market).

Registration subject to disclaimer or limitation

13.—(1) An applicant for registration of a trade mark, or the proprietor of a registered trade mark, may—
- (a) disclaim any right to the exclusive use of any specified element of the trade mark, or
- (b) agree that the rights conferred by the registration shall be subject to a specified territorial or other limitation;

and where the registration of a trade mark is subject to a disclaimer or limitation, the rights conferred by section 9 (rights conferred by registered trade mark) are restricted accordingly.

(2) Provision shall be made by rules as to the publication and entry in the register of a disclaimer or limitation.

Infringement proceedings

Action for infringement

14.—(1) An infringement of a registrated trade mark is actionable by the proprietor of the trade mark.

(2) In an action for infringement all such relief by way of damages, injunctions, accounts or otherwise is available to him as is available in respect of the infringement of any other property right.

Order for erasure, &c. of offending sign

15.—(1) Where a person is found to have infringed a registered trade mark, the court may make an order requiring him—
  (a) to cause the offending sign to be erased, removed or obliterated from any infringing goods, material or articles in his possession, custody or control, or
  (b) if it is not reasonably practicable for the offending sign to be erased, removed or obliterated, to secure the destruction of the infringing goods, material or articles in question.

(2) If an order under subsection (1) is not complied with, or it appears to the court likely that such an order would not be complied with, the court may order that the infringing goods, material or articles be delivered to such person as the court may direct for erasure, removal or obliteration of the sign, or for destruction, as the case may be.

Order for delivery up of infringing goods, material or articles

16.—(1) The proprietor of a registered trade mark may apply to the court for an order for the delivery up to him, or such other person as the court may direct, of any infringing goods, material or articles which a person has in his possession, custody or control in the course of a business.

(2) An application shall not be made after the end of the period specified in section 18 (period after which remedy of delivery up not available); and no order shall be made unless the court also makes, or it appears to the court that there are grounds for making, an order under section 19 (order as to disposal of infringing goods, &c.).

(3) A person to whom any infringing goods, material or articles are delivered up in pursuance of an order under this section shall, if an order under section 19 is not made, retain them pending the making of an order, or the decision not to make an order, under that section.

(4) Nothing in this section affects any other power of the court.

Meaning of "infringing goods, material or articles"

17.—(1) In this Act the expressions "infringing goods", "infringing material" and "infringing articles" shall be construed as follows.

(2) Goods are "infringing goods", in relation to a registered trade mark, if they or their packaging bear a sign identical or similar to that mark and—
  (a) the application of the sign to the goods or their packaging was an infringement of the registered trade mark, or
  (b) the goods are proposed to be imported into the United Kingdom and the application of the sign in the United Kingdom to them or their packaging would be an infringement of the registered trade mark, or
  (c) the sign has otherwise been used in relation to the goods in such a way as to infringe the registered trade mark.

(3) Nothing in subsection (2) shall be construed as affecting the importation of goods which may lawfully be imported into the United Kingdom by virtue of an enforceable Community right.

(4) Material is "infringing material", in relation to a registered trade mark if it bears a sign identical or similar to that mark and either—
  (a) it is used for labelling or packaging goods, as a business paper, or for advertising goods or services, in such a way as to infringe the registered trade mark, or

(b) it is intended to be so used and such use would infringe the registered trade mark.

(5) "Infringing articles", in relation to a registered trade mark, means articles—

(a) which are specifically designed or adapted for making copies of a sign identical or similar to that mark, and

(b) which a person has in his possession, custody or control, knowing or having reason to believe that they have been or are to be used to produce infringing goods or material.

Period after which remedy of delivery up not available

18.—(1) An application for an order under section 16 (order for delivery up of infringing goods, material or articles) may not be made after the end of the period of six years from—

(a) in the case of infringing goods, the date on which the trade mark was applied to the goods or their packaging,

(b) in the case of infringing material, the date on which the trade mark was applied to the material, or

(c) in the case of infringing articles, the date on which they were made,

except as mentioned in the following provisions.

(2) If during the whole or part of that period the proprietor of the registered trade mark—

(a) is under a disability, or

(b) is prevented by fraud or concealment from discovering the facts entitling him to apply for an order,

an application may be made at any time before the end of the period of six years from the date on which he ceased to be under a disability or, as the case may be, could with reasonable diligence have discovered those facts.

(3) In subsection (2) "disability"—

(a) In England and Wales, has the same meaning as in the Limitation Act 1980;

(b) in Scotland, means legal disability within the meaning of the Prescription and Limitation (Scotland) Act 1973;

(c) In Northern Ireland, has the same meaning as in the Limitation (Northern Ireland) Order 1989.

Order as to disposal of infringing goods, material or articles

19.—(1) Where infringing goods, material or articles have been delivered up in pursuance of an order under section 16, an application may be made to the court—

(a) for an order that they be destroyed or forfeited to such person as the court may think fit, or

(b) for a decision that no such order should be made.

(2) In considering what order (if any) should be made, the court shall consider whether other remedies available in an action for infringement of the registered trade mark would be adequate to compensate the proprietor and any licensee and protect their interests.

(3) Provision shall be made by rules of court as to the service of notice on persons having an interest in the goods, material or articles, and any such person is entitled—

(a) to appear in proceedings for an order under this section, whether or not he was served with notice, and

(b) to appeal against any order made, whether or not he appeared;

and an order shall not take effect until the end of the period within which notice of an appeal may be given or, if before the end of that period notice of appeal is duly given, until the final determination or abandonment of the proceedings on the appeal.

(4) Where there is more than one person interested in the goods, material or articles, the court shall make such order as it thinks just.

(5) If the court decides that no order should be made under this section, the person in whose possession, custody or control the goods, material or articles were before being delivered up is entitled to their return.

(6) References in this section to a person having an interest in goods, material or articles include any person in whose favour an order could be made under this section or under section 114, 204 or

231 of the Copyright, Designs and Patents Act 1988 (which make similar provision in relation to infringement of copyright, rights in performances and design right).

Jurisdiction of sheriff court or county court in Northern Ireland

20. Proceedings for an order under section 16 (order for delivery up of infringing goods, material or articles) or section 19 (order as to disposal of infringing goods, &c.) may be brought—
 (a) in the sheriff court in Scotland, or
 (b) in a county court in Northern Ireland.
This does not affect the jurisdiction of the Court of Session or the High Court in Northern Ireland.

Remedy for groundless threats of infringement proceedings

21.—(1) Where a person threatens another with proceedings for infringement of a registered trade mark other than—
 (a) the application of the mark to goods or their packaging,
 (b) the importation of goods to which, or to the packaging of which, the mark has been applied, or
 (c) the supply of services under the mark,
any person aggrieved may bring proceedings for relief under this section.
 (2) The relief which may be applied for is any of the following—
 (a) a declaration that the threats are unjustifiable,
 (b) an injunction against the continuance of the threats,
 (c) damages in respect of any loss he has sustained by the threats;
and the plaintiff is entitled to such relief unless the defendant shows that the acts in respect of which proceedings were threatened constitute (or if done would constitute) an infringement of the registered trade mark concerned.
 (3) If that is shown by the defendant, the plaintiff is nevertheless entitled to relief if he shows that the registration of the trade mark is invalid or liable to be revoked in a relevant respect.
 (4) The mere notification that a trade mark is registered, or that an application for registration has been made, does not constitute a threat of proceedings for the purposes of this section.

Registered trade mark as object of property

Nature of registered trade mark

22. A registered trade mark is personal property (in Scotland, incorporeal moveable property).

Co-ownership of registered trade mark

23.—(1) Where a registered trade mark is granted to two or more persons jointly, each of them is entitled, subject to any agreement to the contrary, to an equal undivided share in the registered trade mark.
 (2) The following provisions apply where two or more persons are co-proprietors of a registered trade mark, by virtue of subsection (1) or otherwise.
 (3) Subject to any agreement to the contrary, each co-proprietor is entitled, by himself or his agents, to do for his own benefit and without the consent of or the need to account to the other or others, any act which would otherwise amount to an infringement of the registered trade mark.
 (4) One co-proprietor may not without the consent of the other or others—
 (a) grant a licence to use the registered trade mark, or
 (b) assign or charge his share in the registered trade mark (or, in Scotland, cause or permit security to be granted over it).
 (5) Infringement proceedings may be brought by any co-proprietor, but he may not, without the leave of the court, proceed with the action unless the other, or each of the others, is either joined as a plaintiff or added as a defendant.

A co-proprietor who is thus added as a defendant shall not be made liable for any costs in the action unless he takes part in the proceedings.

Nothing in this subsection affects the granting of interlocutory relief on the application of a single co-proprietor.

(6) Nothing in this section affects the mutual rights and obligations of trustees or personal representatives, or their rights and obligations as such.

Assignment, &c. of registered trade mark

24.—(1) A registered trade mark is transmissible by assignment, testamentary disposition or operation of law in the same way as other personal or moveable property.

It is so transmissible either in connection with the goodwill of a business or independently.

(2) An assignment or other transmission of a registered trade mark may be partial, that is, limited so as to apply—

  (a) in relation to some but not all of the goods or services for which the trade mark is registered, or

  (b) in relation to use of the trade mark in a particular manner or a particular locality.

(3) An assignment of a registered trade mark, or an assent relating to a registered trade mark, is not effective unless it is in writing signed by or on behalf of the assignor or, as the case may be, a personal representative.

Except in Scotland, this requirement may be satisfied in a case where the assignor or personal representative is a body corporate by the affixing of its seal.

(4) The above provisions apply to assignment by way of security as in relation to any other assignment.

(5) A registered trade mark may be the subject of a charge (in Scotland, security) in the same way as other personal or moveable property.

(6) Nothing in this Act shall be construed as affecting the assignment or other transmission of an unregistered trade mark as part of the goodwill of a business.

Registration of transactions affecting registered trade mark

25.—(1) On application being made to the registrar by—

  (a) a person claiming to be entitled to an interest in or under a registered trade mark by virtue of a registrable transaction, or

  (b) any other person claiming to be affected by such a transaction,

      the prescribed particulars of the transaction shall be entered in the register.

(2) The following are registrable transactions—

  (a) an assignment of a registered trade mark or any right in it;

  (b) the grant of a licence under a registered trade mark;

  (c) the granting of any security interest (whether fixed or floating) over a registered trade mark or any right in or under it;

  (d) the making by personal representatives of an assent in relation to a registered trade mark or any right in or under it;

  (e) an order of a court or other competent authority transferring a registered trade mark or any right in or under it.

(3) Until an application has been made for registration of the prescribed particulars of a registrable transaction—

  (a) the transaction is ineffective as against a person acquiring a conflicting interest in or under the registered trade mark in ignorance of it, and

  (b) a person claiming to be a licensee by virtue of the transaction does not have the protection of section 30 or 31 (rights and remedies of licensee in relation to infringement).

(4) Where a person becomes the proprietor or a licensee of a registered trade mark by virtue of a registrable transaction, then unless—

  (a) an application for registration of the prescribed particulars of the transaction is made before the end of the period of six months beginning with its date, or

    (b) the court is satisfied that it was not practicable for such an application to be made before the end of that period and that an application was made as soon as practicable thereafter,

he is not entitled to damages or an account of profits in respect of any infringement of the registered trade mark occurring after the date of the transaction and before the prescribed particulars of the transaction are registered.

    (5) Provision may be made by rules as to—

    (a) the amendment of registered particulars relating to a licence so as to reflect any alteration of the terms of the licence, and

    (b) the removal of such particulars from the register—

      (i) where it appears from the registered particulars that the licence was granted for a fixed period and that period has expired, or

      (ii) where no such period is indicated and, after such period as maybe prescribed, the registrar has notified the parties of his intention to remove the particulars from the register.

    (6) Provision may also be made by rules as to the amendment or removal from the register of particulars relating to a security interest on the application of, or with the consent of, the person entitled to the benefit of that interest.

Trust and equities

    26.—(1) No notice of any trust (express, implied or constructive) shall be entered in the register; and the registrar shall not be affected by any such notice.

    (2) Subject to the provisions of this Act, equities (in Scotland, rights) in respect of a registered trade mark may be enforced in like manner as in respect of other personal or moveable property.

Application for registration of trade mark as on object of property

    27.—(1) The provisions of sections 22 to 26 (which relate to a registered trade mark as an object of property) apply, with the necessary modifications, in relation to an application for the registration of a trade mark as in relation to a registered trade mark.

    (2) In section 23 (co-ownership of registered trade mark) as it applies in relation to an application for registration the reference in subsection (1) to the granting of the registration shall be construed as a reference to the making of the application.

    (3) In section 25 (registration of transactions affecting registered trade marks) as it applies in relation to a transaction affecting an application for the registration of a trade mark, the references to the entry of particulars in the register, and to the making of an application to register particulars, shall be construed as references to the giving of notice to the registrar of those particulars.

Licensing

Licensing of registered trade mark

    28.—(1) A licence to use a registered trade mark may be general or limited.

    A limited licence may, in particular, apply—

    (a) in relation to some but not all of the goods or services for which the trade mark is registered, or

    (b) in relation to use of the trade mark in a particular manner or a particular locality.

    (2) A licence is not effective unless it is in writing signed by or on behalf of the grantor.

    Except in Scotland, this requirement may be satisfied in a case where the grantor is a body corporate by the affixing of its seal.

    (3) Unless the licence provides otherwise, it is binding on a successor in title to the grantor's interest.

    References in this Act to doing anything with, or without, the consent of the proprietor of a registered trade mark shall be construed accordingly.

    (4) Where the licence so provides, a sub-licence may be granted by the licensee; and references in this Act to a licence or licensee include a sub-licence or sub-licensee.

Exclusive licences

29.—(1) In this Act an "exclusive licence" means a licence (whether general or limited) authorising the licensee to the exclusion of all other persons, including the person granting the licence, to use a registered trade mark in the manner authorised by the licence.

The expression "exclusive licensee" shall be construed accordingly.

(2) An exclusive licensee has the same rights against a successor in title who is bound by a licence as he has against the person granting the licence.

General provisions as to rights of licensees in case of infringement

30.—(1) This section has effect with respect to the rights of a licensee in relation to infringement of a registered trade mark.

The provisions of this section do not apply where or to the extent that, by virtue of section 31(1) below (exclusive licensee having rights and remedies of assignee), the licensee has a right to bring proceedings in his own name.

(2) A licensee is entitled, unless his licence, or any licence through which his interest is derived, provides otherwise, to call on the proprietor of the registered trade mark to take infringement proceedings in respect of any matter which affects his interests.

(3) If the proprietor—
 (a) refuses to do so, or
 (b) fails to do so within two months after being called upon,
the licensee may bring the proceedings in his own name as if he were the proprietor.

(4) Where infringement proceedings are brought by a licensee by virtue of this section, the licensee may not, without the leave of the court, proceed with the action unless the proprietor is either joined as a plaintiff or added as a defendant.

This does not affect the granting of interlocutory relief on an application by a licensee alone.

(5) A proprietor who is added as a defendant as mentioned in subsection (4) shall not be made liable for any costs in the action unless he takes part in the proceedings.

(6) In infringement proceedings brought by the proprietor of a registered trade mark any loss suffered or likely to be suffered by licensees shall be taken into account; and the court may give such directions as it thinks fit as to the extent to which the plaintiff is to hold the proceeds of any pecuniary remedy on behalf of licensees.

(7) The provisions of this section apply in relation to an exclusive licensee if or to the extent that he has, by virtue of section 31(1), the rights and remedies of an assignee as if he were the proprietor of the registered trade mark.

Exclusive licensee having rights and remedies of assignee

31.—(1) An exclusive licence may provide that the licensee shall have, to such extent as may be provided by the licence, the same rights and remedies in respect of matters occurring after the grant of the licence as if the licence had been an assignment.

Where or to the extent that such provision is made, the licensee is entitled, subject to the provisions of the licence and to the following provisions of this section, to bring infringement proceedings, against any person other than the proprietor, in his own name.

(2) Any such rights and remedies of an exclusive licensee are concurrent with those of the proprietor of the registered trade mark; and references to the proprietor of a registered trade mark in the provisions of this Act relating to infringement shall be construed accordingly.

(3) In an action brought by an exclusive licensee by virtue of this section a defendant may avail himself of any defence which would have been available to him if the action had been brought by the proprietor of the registered trade mark.

(4) Where proceedings for infringement of a registered trade mark brought by the proprietor or an exclusive licensee relate wholly or partly to an infringement in respect of which they have concurrent rights of action, the proprietor or, as the case may be, the exclusive licensee may not,

without the leave of the court, proceed with the action unless the other is either joined as a plaintiff or added as a defendant.

This does not affect the granting of interlocutory relief on an application by a proprietor or exclusive licensee alone.

(5) A person who is added as a defendant as mentioned in subsection (4) shall not be made liable for any costs in the action unless he takes part in the proceedings.

(6) Where an action for infringement of a registered trade mark is brought which relates wholly or partly to an infringement in respect of which the proprietor and an exclusive licensee have or had concurrent rights of action—

   (a) the court shall in assessing damages take into account—

      (i)   the terms of the licence, and

      (ii) any pecuniary remedy already awarded or available to either of them in respect of the infringement;

   (b) no account of profits shall be directed if an award of damages has been made, or an account of profits has been directed, in favour of the other of them in respect of the infringement; and

   (c) the court shall if an account of profits is directed apportion the profits between them as the court considers just, subject to any agreement between them.

The provisions of this subsection apply whether or not the proprietor and the exclusive licensee are both parties to the action; and if they are not both parties the court may give such directions as it thinks fit as to the extent to which the party to the proceedings is to hold the proceeds of any pecuniary remedy on behalf of the other.

(7) The proprietor of a registered trade mark shall notify any exclusive licensee who has a concurrent right of action before applying for an order under section 16 (order for delivery up); and the court may on the application of the licensee make such order under that section as it thinks fit having regard to the terms of the licence.

(8) The provisions of subsections (4) to (7) above have effect subject to any agreement to the contrary between the exclusive licensee and the proprietor.

Application for registered trade mark

Application for registration

32.—(1) An application for registration of a trade mark shall be made to the registrar.

(2) The application shall contain—

   (a) a request for registration of a trade mark,

   (b) the name and address of the applicant,

   (c) a statement of the goods or services in relation to which it is sought to register the trade mark, and

   (d) a representation of the trade mark.

(3) The application shall state that the trade mark is being used, by the applicant or with his consent, in relation to those goods or services, or that he has a *bona fide* intention that it should be so used.

(4) The application shall be subject to the payment of the application fee and such class fees as may be appropriate.

Date of filing

33.—(1) The date of filing of an application for registration of a trade mark is the date on which documents containing everything required by section 32(2) are furnished to the registrar by the applicant.

If the documents are furnished on different days, the date of filing is the last of those days.

(2) References in this Act to the date of application for registration are to the date of filing of the application.

Classification of trade marks

34.—(1) Goods and services shall be classified for the purposes of the registration of trade marks according to a prescribed system of classification.

(2)Any question arising as to the class within which any goods or services fall shall be determined by the registrar, whose decision shall be final.

Priority

Claim to priority of Convention application

35.—(1) A person who has duly filed an application for protection of a trade mark in a Convention country (a "Convention application"), or his successor in title, has a right to priority, for the purposes of registering the same trade mark under this Act for some or all of the same goods or services, for a period of six months from the date of filing of the first such application.

(2) If the application for registration under this Act is made within that six-month period—
  (a) the relevant date for the purposes of establishing which rights take precedence shall be the date of filing the first Convention application, and
  (b) the registrability of the trade mark shall not be affected by any use of the mark in the United Kingdom in the period between that date and the date of the application under this Act.

(3) Any filing which in a Convention country is equivalent to a regular national filing, under its domestic legislation or an international agreement, shall be treated as giving rise to the right of priority.

A "regular national filing" means a filing which is adequate to establish the date on which the application was filed in that country, whatever may be the subsequent fate of the application.

(4) A subsequent application concerning the same subject as the first Convention application, filed in the same Convention country, shall be considered the first Convention application (of which the filing date is that starting date of the period of priority), if at the time of the subsequent application—
  (a) the previous application has been withdrawn, abandoned or refused, without having been laid open to public inspection and without leaving any rights outstanding, and
  (b) it has not yet served as a basis for claiming a right of priority.

The previous application may not thereafter serve as a basis for claiming a right of priority.

(5) Provision may be made by rules as to the manner of claiming a right to priority on the basis of a Convention application.

(6) A right to priority arising as a result of a Convention application may be assigned or otherwise transmitted, either with the application or independently.

The reference in subsection (1) to the applicant's "successor in title" shall be construed accordingly.

Claim to priority from other relevant overseas application

36.—(1) Her Majesty may by Order in Council make provision for conferring on a person who has duly filed an application for protection of a trade mark in—
  (a) any of the Channel Islands or a colony, or
  (b) a country or territory in relation to which Her Majesty's Government in the United Kingdom have entered into a treaty, convention, arrangement or engagement for the reciprocal protection of trade marks,
a right to priority, for the purpose of registering the same trade mark under this Act for some or all of the same goods or services, for a specified period from the date of filing of that application.

(2) An Order in Council under this section may make provision corresponding to that made by section 35 in relation to Convention countries or such other provision as appears to Her Majesty to be appropriate.

(3) A statutory instrument containing an Order in Council under this section shall be subject to annulment in pursuance of a resolution of either House of Parliament.

Registration procedure

Examination of application

37.—(1) The registrar shall examine whether an application for registration of a trade mark satisfies the requirements of this Act (including any requirements imposed by rules).

(2) For that purpose he shall carry out a search, to such extent as he considers necessary, of earlier trade marks.

(3) If it appears to the registrar that the requirements for registration are not met, he shall inform the applicant and give him an opportunity, within such period as the registrar may specify, to make representations or to amend the application.

(4) If the applicant fails to satisfy the registrar that those requirements are met, or to amend the application so as to meet them, or fails to respond before the end of the specified period, the registrar shall refuse to accept the application.

(5) If it appears to the registrar that the requirements for registration are met, he shall accept the application.

Publication, opposition proceedings and observations

38.—(1) When an application for registration has been accepted, the registrar shall cause the application to be published in the prescribed manner.

(2) Any person may, within the prescribed time from the date of the publication of the application, give notice to the registrar of opposition to the registration.

The notice shall be given in writing in the prescribed manner, and shall include a statement of the grounds of opposition.

(3) Where an application has been published, any person may, at any time before the registration of the trade mark, make observations in writing to the registrar as to whether the trade mark should be registered; and the registrar shall inform the applicant of any such observations.

A person who makes observations does not thereby become a party to the proceedings on the application.

Withdrawal, restriction or amendment of application

39.—(1) The applicant may at any time withdraw his application or restrict the goods or services covered by the application.

If the application has been published, the withdrawal or restriction shall also be published.

(2) In other respects, an application may be amended, at the request of the applicant, only by correcting—

(a) the name or address of the applicant,

(b) errors of wording or of copying, or

(c) obvious mistakes,

and then only where the correction does not substantially affect the identity of the trade mark or extend the goods or services covered by the application.

(3) Provision shall be made by rules for the publication of any amendment which affects the representation of the trade mark, or the goods or services covered by the application, and for the making of objections by any person claiming to be affected by it.

Registration

40.—(1) Where an application has been accepted and—

(a) no notice of opposition is given within the period referred to in section 38(2), or

(b) all opposition proceedings are withdrawn or decided in favour of the applicant,

the registrar shall register the trade mark, unless it appears to him having regard to matters coming to his notice since he accepted the application that it was accepted in error.

(2) A trade mark shall not be registered unless any fee prescribed for the registration is paid within the prescribed period.

If the fee is not paid within that period, the application shall be deemed to be withdrawn.

(3) A trade mark when registered shall be registered as of the date of filing of the application for registration; and that date shall be deemed for the purposes of this Act to be the date of registration.

(4) On the registration of a trade mark the registrar shall publish the registration in the prescribed manner and issue to the applicant a certificate of registration.

Registration: supplementary provisions

41.—(1) Provision may be made by rules as to—
  (a) the division of an application for the registration of a trade mark into several applications;
  (b) the merging of separate applications or registrations;
  (c) the registration of a series of trade marks.

(2) A series of trade marks means a number of trade marks which resemble each other as to their material particulars and differ only as to matters of a non-distinctive character not substantially affecting the identity of the trade mark.

(3) Rules under this section may include provision as to—
  (a) the circumstances in which, and conditions subject to which, division, merger or registration of a series is permitted, and
  (b) the purposes for which an application to which the rules apply is to be treated as a single application and those for which it is to be treated as a number of separate applications.

Duration, renewal and alteration of registered trade mark

Duration of registration

42.—(1) A trade mark shall be registered for a period of ten years from the date of registration.

(2) Registration may be renewed in accordance with section 43 for further periods of ten years.

Renewal of registration

43.—(1) The registration of a trade mark may be renewed at the request of the proprietor, subject to payment of a renewal fee.

(2) Provision shall be made by rules for the registrar to inform the proprietor of a registered trade mark, before the expiry of the registration, of the date of expiry and the manner in which the registration may be renewed.

(3) A request for renewal must be made, and the renewal fee paid, before the expiry of the registration.

Failing this, the request may be made and the fee paid within such further period (of not less than six months) as may be prescribed, in which case an additional renewal fee must also be paid within that period.

(4) Renewal shall take effect from the expiry of the previous registration.

(5) If the registration is not renewed in accordance with the above provisions, the registrar shall remove the trade mark from the register.

Provision may be made by rules for the restoration of the registration of a trade mark which has been removed from the register, subject to such conditions (if any) as may be prescribed.

(6) The renewal or restoration of the registration of a trade mark shall be published in the prescribed manner.

Alteration of registered trade mark

44.—(1) A registered trade mark shall not be altered in the register, during the period of registration or on renewal.

(2) Nevertheless, the registrar may, at the request of the proprietor, allow the alteration of a registered trade mark where the mark includes the proprietor's name or address and the alteration is limited to alteration of that name or address and does not substantially affect the identity of the mark.

(3) Provisions shall be made by rules for the publication of any such alteration and the making of objections by any person claiming to be affected by it.

Surrender, revocation and invalidity

Surrender of registered trade mark

45.—(1) A registered trade mark may be surrendered by the proprietor in respect of some or all of the goods or services for which it is registered.

(2) Provision may be made by rules—
  (a) as to the manner and effect of a surrender, and
  (b) for protecting the interests of other persons having a right in the registered trade mark.

Revocation of registration

46.—(1) The registration of a trade mark may be revoked on any of the following grounds—
  (a) that within the period of five years following the date of completion of the registration procedure it has not been put to genuine use in the United Kingdom, by the proprietor or with his consent, in relation to the goods or services for which it is registered, and there are no proper reasons for non-use;
  (b) that such use has been suspended for an uninterrupted period of five years, and there are no proper reasons for non-use;
  (c) that, in consequence of acts or inactivity of the proprietor, it has become the common name in the trade for a product or service for which it is registered;
  (d) that, in consequence of the use made of it by the proprietor or with his consent in relation to the goods or services for which it is registered, it is liable to mislead the public, particularly as to the nature, quality or geographical origin of those goods or services.

(2) for the purposes of subsection (1) use of a trade mark includes use in a form differing in elements which do not alter the distinctive character of the mark in the form in which it was registered, and use in the United Kingdom includes affixing the trade mark to goods or to the packaging of goods in the United Kingdom solely for export purposes.

(3) The registration of a trade mark shall not be revoked on the ground mentioned in subsection (1)(a) or (b) if such use as is referred to in that paragraph is commenced or resumed after the expiry of the five year period and before the application for revocation is made:

Provided that, any such commencement or resumption of use after the expiry of the five year period but within the period of three months before the making of the application shall be disregarded unless preparations for the commencement or resumption began before the proprietor became aware that the application might be made.

(4) An application for revocation may be made by any person, and may be made either to the registrar or to the court, except that—
  (a) if proceedings concerning the trade mark in question are pending in the court, the application must be made to the court; and
  (b) if in any other case the application is made to the registrar, he may at any stage of the proceedings refer the application to the court.

(5) Where grounds for revocation exist in respect of only some of the goods or services for which the trade mark is registered, revocation shall relate to those goods or services only.

(6) Where the registration of a trade mark is revoked to any extent, the rights of the proprietor shall be deemed to have ceased to that extent as from—
  (a) the date of the application for revocation, or
  (b) if the registrar or court is satisfied that the grounds for revocation existed at an earlier date, that date.

Grounds for invalidity of registration

47.—(1) The registration of a trade mark may be declared invalid on the ground that the trade mark was registered in breach of section 3 or any of the provisions referred to in that section (absolute grounds for refusal of registration).

Where the trade mark was registered in breach of subsection (1)(b), (c) or (d) of that section, it shall not be declared invalid if, in consequence of the use which has been made of it, it has after registration acquired a distinctive character in relation to the goods or services for which it is registered.

(2) The registration of a trade mark may be declared invalid on the ground—
- (a) that there is an earlier trade mark in relation to which the conditions set out in section 5(1), (2) or (3) obtain, or
- (b) that there is an earlier right in relation to which the condition set out in section 5(4) is satisfied,

unless the proprietor of that earlier trade mark or other earlier right has consented to the registration.

(3) An application for a declaration of invalidity may be made by any person, and may be made either to the registrar or to the court, except that—
- (a) if proceedings concerning the trade mark in question are pending in the court, the application must be made to the court; and
- (b) if in any other case the application is made to the registrar, he may at any stage of the proceedings refer the application to the court.

(4) In the case of bad faith in the registration of a trade mark, the registrar himself may apply to the court for a declaration of the invalidity of the registration.

(5) Where the grounds of invalidity exist in respect of only some of the goods or services for which the trade mark is registered, the trade mark shall be declared invalid as regards those goods or services only.

(6) Where the registration of a trade mark is declared invalid to any extent, the registration shall to that extent be deemed never to have been made:

Provided that this shall not affect transactions past and closed.

Effect of acquiescence

48.—(1) Where the proprietor of an earlier trade mark or other earlier right has acquiesced for a continuous period of five years in the use of a registered trade mark in the United Kingdom, being aware of that use, there shall cease to be any entitlement on the basis of that earlier trade mark or other right—
- (a) to apply for a declaration that the registration of the later trade mark is invalid, or
- (b) to oppose the use of the later trade mark in relation to the goods or services in relation to which it has been so used,

unless the registration of the later trade mark was applied for in bad faith.

(2) Where subsection (1) applies, the proprietor of the later trade mark is not entitled to oppose the use of the earlier trade mark or, as the case may be, the exploitation of the earlier right, notwithstanding that the earlier trade mark or right may no longer be invoked against his later trade mark.

Collective marks

49.—(1) A collective mark is a mark distinguishing the goods or services of members of the association which is the proprietor of the mark from those of other undertakings.

(2) The provisions of this Act apply to collective marks subject to the provisions of Schedule 1.

Certification marks

50.—(1) A certification mark is a mark indicating that the goods or services in connection with which it is used are certified by the proprietor of the mark in respect of origin, material, mode of manufacture of goods or performance of services, quality, accuracy or other characteristics.

(2) The provisions of this Act apply to certification marks subject to the provisions of Schedule 2.

PART II

COMMUNITY TRADE MARKS AND INTERNATIONAL MATTERS

Community trade marks

Meaning of "Community trade mark"

51. In this Act—

"Community trade mark" has the meaning given by Article 1(1) of the Community Trade Mark Regulation; and

"the Community Trade Mark Regulation" means Council Regulation (EC) No. 40/94 of 20th December 1993 on the Community trade mark.

Power to make provision in connection with Community Trade Mark Regulation

52.—(1) The Secretary of State may by regulations make such provision as he considers appropriate in connection with the operation of the Community Trade Mark Regulation.

(2) Provision may, in particular, be made with respect to—

(a) the making of applications for Community trade marks by way of the Patent Office;

(b) the procedures for determining *a posteriori* the invalidity, or liability to revocation, of the registration of a trade mark from which a Community trade mark claims seniority;

(c) the conversion of a Community trade mark, or an application for a Community trade mark, into an application for registration under this Act;

(d) the designation of courts in the United Kingdom having jurisdiction over proceedings arising out of the Community Trade Mark Regulation.

(3) Without prejudice to the generality of subsection (1), provision may be made by regulations under this section—

(a) applying in relation to a Community trade mark the provisions of—

(i) section 21 (remedy for groundless threats of infringement proceedings);

(ii) sections 89 to 91 (importation of infringing goods, material or articles); and

(iii) sections 92, 93, 95 and 96 (offences); and

(b) making in relation to the list of professional representatives maintained in pursuance of Article 89 of the Community Trade Mark Regulation, and persons on that list, provision corresponding to that made by, or capable of being made under, sections 84 to 88 in relation to the register of trade mark agents and registered trade mark agents.

(4) Regulations under this section shall be made by statutory instrument which shall be subject to annulment in pursuance of a resolution of either House of Parliament.

The Madrid Protocol: international registration

The Madrid Protocol

53. In this Act—

"The Madrid Protocol" means the Protocol relating to the Madrid Agreement concerning the International Registration of Marks, adopted at Madrid on 27th June 1989;

"the International Bureau" has the meaning given by Article 2(1) of that Protocol; and "international trade mark (UK)" means a trade mark which is entitled to protection in the United Kingdom under that Protocol.

Power to make provision giving effect to Madrid Protocol

54.—(1) The Secretary of Sate may by order make such provision as he thinks fit for giving effect in the United Kingdom to the provisions of the Madrid Protocol.

(2) Provision may, in particular, be made with respect to—
  (a) the making of applications for international registrations by way of the Patent Office as office of origin;
  (b) the procedures to be followed where the basic United Kingdom application or registration fails or ceases to be in force;
  (c) the procedures to be followed where the Patent Office receives from the International Bureau a request for extension of protection to the United Kingdom;
  (d) the effects of a successful request for extension of protection to the United Kingdom;
  (e) the transformation of an application for an international registration, or an international registration, into a national application for registration;
  (f) the communication of information to the International Bureau;
  (g) the payment of fees and amounts prescribed in respect of applications for international registrations, extensions of protection and renewals.

(3) Without prejudice to the generality of subsection (1), provision may be made by regulations under this section applying in relation to an international trade mark (UK) the provisions of—
  (a) section 21 (remedy for groundless threats of infringement proceedings);
  (b) sections 89 to 91 (importation of infringing goods, material or articles); and
  (c) sections 92, 93, 95 and 96 (offences).

(4) An order under this section shall be made by statutory instrument which shall be subject to annulment in pursuance of a resolution of either House of Parliament.

The Paris Convention: supplementary provisions

The Paris Convention.

55.—(1) In this Act—
  (a) "the Paris Convention" means the Paris Convention for the Protection of Industrial Property of March 20th 1883, as revised or amended from time to time, and
  (b) a "Convention country" means a country, other than the United Kingdom, which is a party to that Convention.

(2) The Secretary of State may by order make such amendments of this Act, and rules made under this Act, as appear to him appropriate in consequence of any revision or amendment of the Paris Convention after the passing of this Act.

(3) Any such order shall be made by statutory instrument which shall be subject to annulment in pursuance of a resolution of either House of Parliament.

Protection of well-known trade marks: Article 6bis

56.—(1) References in this Act to a trade mark which is entitled to protection under the Paris Convention as a well known trade mark are to a mark which is well-known in the United Kingdom as being the mark of a person who—
  (a) is a national of a Convention country, or
  (b) is domiciled in, or has a real and effective industrial or commercial establishment in, a Convention country,
whether or not that person carries on business, or has any goodwill, in the United Kingdom.

References to the proprietor of such a mark shall be construed accordingly.

(2) The proprietor of a trademark which is entitled to protection under the Paris Convention as a

well known trade mark is entitled to restrain by injunction the use in the United Kingdom of a trade mark which, or the essential part of which, is identical or similar to his mark, in relation to identical or similar goods or services, where the use is likely to cause confusion.

This right is subject to section 48 (effect of acquiescence by proprietor of earlier trade mark).

(3) Nothing in subsection (2) affects the continuation of any *bona fide* use of a trade mark begun before the commencement of this section.

National emblems, &c. of Convention countries: Article 6ter

57.—(1) A trade mark which consists of or contains the flag of a Convention country shall not be registered without the authorisation of the competent authorities of that country, unless it appears to the registrar that use of the flag in the manner proposed is permitted without such authorisation.

(2) A trade mark which consists of or contains the armorial bearings or any other state emblem of a Convention country which is protected under the Paris Convention shall not be registered without the authorisation of the competent authorities of that country.

(3) A trade mark which consists of or contains an official sign or hallmark adopted by a Convention country and indicating control and warranty shall not, where the sign or hallmark is protected under the Paris Convention, be registered in relation to goods or services of the same, or a similar kind, as those in relation to which it indicates control and warranty, without the authorisation of the competent authorities of the country concerned.

(4) The provisions of this section as to national flags and other state emblems, and official signs or hallmarks, apply equally to anything which from a heraldic point of view imitates any such flag or other emblem, or sign or hallmark.

(5) Nothing in this section prevents the registration of a trade mark on the application of a national of a country who is authorised to make use of a state emblem, or official sign or hallmark, of that country, notwithstanding that it is similar to that of another country.

(6) Where by virtue of this section the authorisation of the competent authorities of a Convention country is or would be required for the registration of a trade mark, those authorities are entitled to restrain by injunction any use of the mark in the United Kingdom without their authorisation.

Emblems, &c. of certain international organisations: Article 6ter

58.—(1) This section applies to—
  (a) the armorial bearings, flags or other emblems, and
  (b) the abbreviations and names,
of international intergovernmental organisations of which one or more Convention countries are members.

(2) A trade mark which consists of or contains any such emblem, abbreviation or name which is protected under the Paris Convention shall not be registered without the authorisation of the international organisation concerned, unless it appears to the registrar that the use of the emblem, abbreviation or name in the manner proposed—
  (a) is not such as to suggest to the public that a connection exists between the organisation and the trade mark, or
  (b) is not likely to mislead the public as to the existence of a connection between the user and the organisation.

(3) The provisions of this section as to emblems of an international organisation apply equally to anything which from a heraldic point of view imitates any such emblem.

(4) Where by virtue of this section the authorisation of an international organisation is or would be required for the registration of a trade mark, that organisation is entitled to restrain by injunction any use of the mark in the United Kingdom without its authorisation.

(5) Nothing in this section affects the rights of a person whose *bona fide* use of the trade mark in question began before 4th January 1962 (when the relevant provisions of the Paris Convention entered into force in relation to the United Kingdom).

Notification under Article 6ter of the Convention

59.—(1) For the purposes of section 57 state emblems of a Convention country (other than the national flag), and official signs or hallmarks, shall be regarded as protected under the Paris Convention only if, or to the extent that—

(a) the country in question has notified the United Kingdom in accordance with Article 6*ter*(3) of the Convention that it desires to protect that emblem, sign or hallmark,

(b) the notification remains in force, and

(c) the United Kingdom has not objected to it in accordance with Article 6*ter*(4) or any such objection has been withdrawn.

(2) For the purposes of section 58 the emblems, abbreviations and names of an international organisation shall be regarded as protected under the Paris Convention only if, or to the extent that—

(a) the organisation in question has notified the United Kingdom in accordance with Article 6*ter*(3) of the Convention that it desires to protect that emblem, abbreviation or name,

(b) the notification remains in force, and

(c) the United Kingdom has not objected to it in accordance with Article 6*ter*(4) or any such objection has been withdrawn.

(3) Notification under Article 6*ter*(3) of the Paris Convention shall have effect only in relation to applications for registration made more than two months after the receipt of the notification.

(4) The registrar shall keep and make available for public inspection by any person, at all reasonable hours and free of charge, a list of—

(a) the state emblems and official signs or hallmarks, and

(b) the emblems, abbreviations and names of international organisations,

which are for the time being protected under the Paris Convention by virtue of notification under Article 6*ter*(3).

Acts of agent or representative: Article 6septies

60.—(1) The following provisions apply where an application for registration of a trade mark is made by a person who is an agent or representative of a person who is the proprietor of the mark in a Convention country.

(2) If the proprietor opposes the application, registration shall be refused.

(3) If the application (not being so opposed) is granted, the proprietor may—

(a) apply for a declaration of the invalidity of the registration, or

(b) apply for the rectification of the register so as to substitute his name as the proprietor of the registered trade mark.

(4) The proprietor may (notwithstanding the rights conferred by this Act in relation to a registered trade mark) by injunction restrain any use of the trade mark in the United Kingdom which is not authorised by him.

(5) Subsections (2), (3) and (4) do not apply if, or to the extent that, the agent or representative justifies his action.

(6) An application under subsection (3)(a) or (b) must be made within three years of the proprietor becoming aware of the registration; and no injunction shall be granted under subsection (4) in respect of a use in which the proprietor has acquiesced for a continuous period of three years or more.

Miscellaneous

Stamp duty

61. Stamp duty shall not be chargeable on an instrument relating to a Community trade mark or an international trade mark (UK), or an application for any such mark, by reason only of the fact that such a mark has legal effect in the United Kingdom.

PART III

ADMINISTRATIVE AND OTHER SUPPLEMENTARY PROVISIONS

The registrar

62. In this Act "the registrar" means the Comptroller-General of Patents, Designs and Trade Marks.

The register

63.—(1) The registrar shall maintain a register of trade marks.

References in this Act to "the register" are to that register; and references to registration (in particular, in the expression "registered trade mark") are, unless the context otherwise requires, to registration in that register.

(2) There shall be entered in the register in accordance with this Act—

(a) registered trade marks,

(b) such particulars as may be prescribed of registrable transactions affecting a registered trade mark, and

(c) such other matters relating to registered trade marks as may be prescribed.

(3) The register shall be kept in such manner as may be prescribed, and provision shall in particular be made for—

(a) public inspection of the register, and

(b) the supply of certified or uncertified copies, or extracts, of entries in the register.

Rectification or correction of the register

64.—(1) Any person having a sufficient interest may apply for the rectification of an error or omission in the register:

Provided that an application for rectification may not be made in respect of a matter affecting the validity of the registration of a trade mark.

(2) An application for rectification may be made either to the registrar or to the court, except that—

(a) if proceedings concerning the trade mark in question are pending in the court, the application must be made to the court; and

(b) if in any other case the application is made to the registrar, he may at any stage of the proceedings refer the application to the court.

(3) Except where the registrar or the court directs otherwise, the effect of rectification of the register is that the error or omission in question shall be deemed never to have been made.

(4) The registrar may, on request made in the prescribed manner by the proprietor of a registered trade mark, or a licensee, enter any change in his name or address as recorded in the register.

(5) The registrar may remove from the register matter appearing to him to have ceased to have effect.

Adaptation of entries to new classification

65.—(1) Provision may be made by rules empowering the registrar to do such things as he considers necessary to implement any amended or substituted classification of goods or services for the purposes of the registration of trade marks.

(2) Provision may in particular be made for the amendment of existing entries on the register so as to accord with the new classification.

(3) Any such power of amendment shall not be exercised so as to extend the rights conferred by the registration, except where it appears to the registrar that compliance with this requirement would involve undue complexity and that any extension would not be substantial and would not adversely affect the rights of any person.

(4) The rules may empower the registrar—

(a) to require the proprietor of a registered trade mark, within such time as may be prescribed, to file a proposal for amendment of the register, and

(b) to cancel or refuse to renew the registration of the trade mark in the event of his failing to do
     so.

(5) Any such proposal shall be advertised, and may be opposed, in such manner as may be
prescribed.

Powers and duties of the registrar

Power to require use of forms

66.—(1) The registrar may require the use of such forms as he may direct for any purpose relating
to the registration of a trade mark or any other proceeding before him under this Act.

(2) The forms, and any directions of the registrar with respect to their use, shall be published in the
prescribed manner.

Information about applications and registered trade marks

67.—(1) After publication of an application for registration of a trade mark, the registrar shall on
request provide a person with such information and permit him to inspect such documents relating
to the application, or to any registered trade mark resulting from it, as may be specified in the
request, subject, however, to any prescribed restrictions.

Any request must be made in the prescribed manner and be accompanied by the appropriate fee
(if any).

(2)Before publication of an application for registration of a trade mark, documents or information
constituting or relating to the application shall not be published by the registrar or communicated by
him to any person except—
   (a) in such cases and to such extent as may be prescribed, or
   (b) with the consent of the applicant;
but subject as follows.

(3) Where a person has been notified that an application for registration of a trade mark has been
made, and that the applicant will if the application is granted bring proceedings against him in
respect of acts done after publication of the application, he may make a request under subsection (1)
notwithstanding that the application has not been published and that subsection shall apply
accordingly.

Costs and security for costs

68.—(1) Provision may be made by rules empowering the registrar, in any proceedings before him
under this Act—
   (a) to award any party such costs as he may consider reasonable, and
   (b) to direct how and by what parties they are to be paid.

(2) Any such order of the registrar may be enforced—
   (a) in England and Wales or Northern Ireland, in the same way as an order of the High
        Court;
   (b) in Scotland, in the same way as a decree for expenses granted by the Court of Session.

(3) Provision may be made by rules empowering the registrar, in such cases as may be prescribed,
to require a party to proceedings before him to give security for costs, in relation to those
proceedings or to proceedings on appeal, and as to the consequences if security is not given.

Evidence before registrar

69. Provision may be made by rules—
   (a) as to the giving of evidence in proceedings before the registrar under this Act by affidavit or
        statutory declaration;
   (b) conferring on the registrar the powers of an official referee of the Supreme Court as regards
        the examination of witnesses on oath and the discovery and production of documents;
        and

(c) applying in relation to the attendance of witnesses in proceedings before the registrar the rules applicable to the attendance of witnesses before such a referee.

Exclusion of liability in respect of official acts

70.—(1) The registrar shall not be taken to warrant the validity of the registration of a trade mark under this Act or under any treaty, convention, arrangement or engagement to which the United Kingdom is a party.

(2) The registrar is not subject to any liability by reason of, or in connection with, any examination required or authorised by this Act, or any such treaty, convention, arrangement or engagement, or any report or other proceedings consequent on such examination.

(3) No proceedings lie against an officer of the registrar in respect of any matter for which, by virtue of this section, the registrar is not liable.

Registrar's annual report

71.—(1) The Comptroller-General of Patents, Designs and Trade Marks shall in his annual report under section 121 of the Patents Act 1977, include a report on the execution of this Act, including the discharge of his functions under the Madrid Protocol.

(2) The report shall include an account of all money received and paid by him under or by virtue of this Act.

Legal proceedings and appeals

Registration to be prima facie evidence of validity

72. In all legal proceedings relating to a registered trade mark (including proceedings for rectification of the register) the registration of a person as proprietor of a trade mark shall be prima facie evidence of the validity of the original registration and of any subsequent assignment or other transmission of it.

Certificate of validity of contested registration

73.—(1) If in proceedings before the court the validity of the registration of a trade mark is contested and it is found by the court that the trade mark is validly registered, the court may give a certificate to that effect.

(2) If the court gives such a certificate and in subsequent proceedings—
 (a) the validity of the registration is again questioned, and
 (b) the proprietor obtains a final order or judgment in his favour,
he is entitled to his costs as between solicitor and client unless the court directs otherwise.

This subsection does not extend to the costs of an appeal in any such proceedings.

Registrar's appearance in proceedings involving the register

74.—(1) In proceedings before the court involving an application for—
 (a) the revocation of the registration of a trade mark,
 (b) a declaration of the invalidity of the registration of a trade mark, or
 (c) the rectification of the register,
the registrar is entitled to appear and be heard, and shall appear if so directed by the court.

(2) Unless otherwise directed by the court, the registrar may instead of appearing submit to the court a statement in writing signed by him, giving particulars of—
 (a) any proceedings before him in relation to the matter in issue,
 (b) the grounds of any decision given by him affecting it,
 (c) the practice of the Patent Office in like cases, or
 (d) such matters relevant to the issues and within his knowledge as registrar as he thinks fit;

and the statement shall be deemed to form part of the evidence in the proceedings.

(3) Anything which the registrar is or may be authorised or required to do under this section may be done on his behalf by a duly authorised officer.

The court

75. In this Act, unless the context otherwise requires, "the court" means—
(a) in England and Wales and Northern Ireland, the High Court, and
(b) in Scotland, the Court of Session.

Appeals from the registrar

76.—(1) An appeal lies from any decision of the registrar under this Act, except as otherwise expressly provided by rules.

For this purpose "decision" includes any act of the registrar in exercise of a discretion vested in him by or under this Act.

(2) Any such appeal may be brought either to an appointed person or to the court.

(3) Where an appeal is made to an appointed person, he may refer the appeal to the court if—
(a) it appears to him that a point of general legal importance is involved,
(b) the registrar requests that it be so referred, or
(c) such a request is made by any party to the proceedings before the registrar in which the decision appealed against was made.

Before doing so the appointed person shall give the appellant and any other party to the appeal an opportunity to make representations as to whether the appeal should be referred to the court.

(4) Where an appeal is made to an appointed person and he does not refer it to the court, he shall hear and determine the appeal and his decision shall be final.

(5) The provisions of sections 68 and 69 (costs and security for costs; evidence) apply in relation to proceedings before an appointed person as in relation to proceedings before the registrar.

Persons appointed to hear and determine appeals

77.—(1) For the purposes of section 76 an "appointed person" means a person appointed by the Lord Chancellor to hear and decide appeals under this Act.

(2) A person is not eligible for such appointment unless—
(a) he has a 7 year general qualification, within the meaning of section 71 of the Courts and Legal Services Act 1990;
(b) he is an advocate or solicitor in Scotland of at least 7 years' standing;
(d) he is a member of the Bar of Northern Ireland or solicitor of the Supreme Court of Northern Ireland of at least 7 years' standing; or
(d) he has held judicial office.

(3) An appointed person shall hold and vacate office in accordance with his terms of appointment, subject to the following provisions—
(a) there shall be paid to him such remuneration (whether by way of salary or fees), and such allowances, as the Secretary of State with the approval of the Treasury may determine;
(b) he may resign his office by notice in writing to the Lord Chancellor;
(c) the Lord Chancellor may by notice in writing remove him from office if—
(i)   he has become bankrupt or made an arrangement with his creditors or, in Scotland, his estate has been sequestrated or he has executed a trust deed for his creditors or entered into a composition contract, or
(ii) he is incapacitated by physical or mental illness,
or if he is in the opinion of the Lord Chancellor otherwise unable or unfit to perform his duties as an appointed person.

(4) The Lord Chancellor shall consult the Lord Advocate before exercising his powers under this section.

Rules, fees, hours of business, &c.

Power of Secretary of State to make rules

78.—(1) The Secretary of State may make rules—
(a) for the purposes of any provision of this Act authorising the making of rules with respect to any matter, and
(b) for prescribing anything authorised or required by any provision of this Act to be prescribed,
and generally for regulating practice and procedure under this Act.
(2) Provision may, in particular, be made—
(a) as to the manner of filing of applications and other documents;
(b) requiring and regulating the translation of documents and the filing and authentication of any translation;
(c) as to the service of documents;
(d) authorising the rectification of irregularities of procedure;
(e) prescribing time limits for anything required to be done in connection with any proceeding under this Act;
(f) providing for the extension of any time limit so prescribed, or specified by the registrar, whether or not it has already expired.
(3) Rules under this Act shall be made by statutory instrument which shall be subject to annulment in pursuance of a resolution of either House of Parliament.

Fees

79.—(1) There shall be paid in respect of applications and registration and other matters under this Act such fees as may be prescribed.
(2) Provision may be made by rules as to—
(a) the payment of a single fee in respect of two or more matters, and
(b) the circumstances (if any) in which a fee may be repaid or remitted.

Hours of business and business days

80.—(1) The registrar may give directions specifying the hours of business of the Patent Office for the purpose of the transaction by the public of business under this Act, and the days which are business days for that purpose.
(2) Business done on any day after the specified hours of business, or on a day which is not a business day, shall be deemed to have been done on the next business day; and where the time for doing anything under this Act expires on a day which is not a business day, that time shall be extended to the next business day.
(3) Directions under this section may make different provision for different classes of business and shall be publsihed in the prescribed manner.

The trade marks journal

81. Provision shall be made by rules for the publication by the registrar of a journal containing particulars of any application for the registration of a trade mark (including a representation of the mark) and such other information relating to trade marks as the registrar thinks fit.

Trade mark agents

Recognition of agents

82. Except as otherwise provided by rules, any act required or authorised by this Act to be done by or to a person in connection with the registration of a trade mark, or any procedure relating to a registered trade mark, may be done by or to an agent authorised by that person orally or in writing.

The register of trade mark agents

83.—(1) The Secretary of State may make rules requiring the keeping of a register of persons who act as agent for others for the purpose of applying for or obtaining the registration of trade marks; and in this Act a "registered trade mark agent" means a person whose name is entered in the register kept under this section.

(2) The rules may contain such provision as the Secretary of State thinks fit regulating the registration of persons, and may in particular—
  (a) require the payment of such fees as may be prescribed, and
  (b) authorise in prescribed cases the erasure from the register of the name of any person registered in it, or the suspension of a person's registration.

(3) The rules may delegate the keeping of the register to another person, and may confer on that person—
  (a) power to make regulations—
     (i)   with respect to the payment of fees, in the cases and subject to the limits prescribed by the rules, and
     (ii) with respect to any other matter which could be regulated by the rules, and
  (b) such other functions, including disciplinary functions, as may be prescribed by the rules.

Unregistered persons not to be described as registered trade mark agents

84.—(1) An individual who is not a registered trade mark agent shall not—
  (a) carry on business (otherwise than in partnership) under any name or other description which contains the words "registered trade mark agent"; or
  (b) in the course of a business otherwise describe or hold himself out, or permit himself to be described or held out, as a registered trade mark agent.

(2) A partnership shall not—
  (a) carry on a business under any name or other description which contains the words "registered trade mark agent"; or
  (b) in the course of a business otherwise describe or hold itself out, or permit itself to be described or held out, as a firm of registered trade mark agents,
unless all the partners are registered trade mark agents or the partnership satisfies such conditions as may be prescribed for the purposes of this section.

(3) A body corporate shall not—
  (a) carry on a business (otherwise than in partnership) under any name or other description which contains the words "registered trade mark agent"; or
  (b) in the course of a business otherwise describe or hold itself out, or permit itself to be described or held out, as a registered trade mark agent,
unless all the directors of the body corporate are registered trade mark agents or the body satisfies such conditions as may be prescribed for the purposes of this section.

(4) A person who contravenes this section commits an offence and is liable on summary conviction to a fine not exceeding level 5 on the standard scale; and proceedings for such an offence may be begun at any time within a year from the date of the offence.

Power to prescribe conditions, &c. for mixed partnerships and bodies corporate

85.—(1) The Secretary of State may make rules prescribing the conditions to be satisfied for the purposes of section 84 (persons entitled to be described as registered trade mark agents)—
  (a) in relation to a partnership where not all the partners are qualified persons, or
  (b) in relation to a body corporate where not all the directors are qualified persons,
and imposing requirements to be complied with by such partnerships or bodies corporate.

(2) The rules may, in particular—
  (a) prescribe conditions as to the number or proportion of partners or directors who must be qualified persons;
  (b) impose requirements as to—

    (i)   the identification of qualified and unqualified persons in professional advertisements, circulars or letters issued by or with the consent of the partnership or body corporate and which relate to its business, and

    (ii) the manner in which a partnership or body corporate is to organise its affairs so as to secure that qualified persons exercise a sufficient degree of control over the activities of unqualified persons.

(3) Contravention of a requirement imposed by the rules is an offence for which a person is liable on summary conviction to a fine not exceeding level 5 on the standard scale.

(4) In this section "qualified person" means a registered trade mark agent.

Use of the term "trade mark attorney"

86.—(1) No offence is committed under the enactments restricting the use of certain expressions in reference to persons not qualified to act as solicitors by the use of the term "trade mark attorney" in reference to a registered trade mark agent.

(2) The enactments referred to in subsection (1) are section 21 of the Solicitors Act 1974, section 31 of the Solicitors (Scotland) Act 1980 and Article 22 of the Solicitors (Northern Ireland) Order 1976.

Privilege for communications with registered trade mark agents

87.—(1) This section applies to communications as to any matter relating to the protection of any design or trade mark, or as to any matter involving passing off.

(2) Any such communication—

    (a) between a person and his trade mark agent, or

    (b) for the purpose of obtaining, or in response to a request for, information which a person is seeking for the purpose of instructing his trade mark agent,

is privileged from, or in Scotland protected against, disclosure in legal proceedings in the same way as a communication between a person and his solicitor or, as the case may be, a communication for the purpose of obtaining, or in response to a request for, information which a person is seeking for the purpose of instructing his solicitor.

(3) In subsection (2) "trade mark agent" means—

    (a) a registered trade mark agent, or

    (b) a partnership entitled to describe itself as a firm of registered trade mark agents, or

    (c) a body corporate entitled to describe itself as a registered trade mark agent.

Power of registrar to refuse to deal with certain agents

88.—(1) The Secretary of State may make rules authorising the registrar to refuse to recognise as agent in respect of any business under this Act—

    (a) a person who has been convicted of an offence under section 84 (unregistered persons describing themselves as registered trade mark agents);

    (b) an individual whose name has been erased from and not restored to, or who is suspended from, the register of trade mark agents on the ground of misconduct;

    (c) a person who is found by the Secretary of State to have been guilty of such conduct as would, in the case of an individual registered in the register of trade mark agents, render him liable to have his name erased from the register on the ground of misconduct;

    (d) a partnership or body corporate of which one of the partners or directors is a person whom the registrar could refuse to recognise under paragraph (a), (b) or (c) above.

(2) The rules may contain such incidental and supplementary provisions as appear to the Secretary of State to be appropriate and may, in particular, prescribe circumstances in which a person is or is not to be taken to have been guilty of misconduct.

Importation of infringing goods, material or articles

Infringing goods, material or articles may be treated as prohibited goods

89.—(1) The proprietor of a registered trade mark, or a licensee, may give notice in writing to the Commissioners of Customs and Excise—
  (a) that he is the proprietor or, as the case may be, a licensee of the registered trade mark,
  (b) that, at a time and place specified in the notice, goods which are, in relation to that registered trade mark, infringing goods, material or articles are expected to arrive in the United Kingdom—
     (i) from outside the European Economic Area, or
     (ii) from within that Area but not having been entered for free circulation, and
  (c) that he requests the Commissioners to treat them as prohibited goods.
(2) When a notice is in force under this section the importation of the goods to which the notice relates, otherwise than by a person for his private and domestic use, is prohibited; but a person is not by reason of the prohibition liable to any penalty other than forfeiture of the goods.
(3) This section does not apply to goods entered, or expected to be entered, for free circulation in respect of which the proprietor of the registered trade mark, or a licensee, is entitled to lodge an application under Article 3(1) of Council Regulation (EEC) No. 3842/86 laying down measures to prohibit the release for free circulation of counterfeit goods.

Power of Commissioners of Customs and Excise to make regulations

90.—(1) The Commissioners of Customs and Excise may make regulations prescribing the form in which notice is to be given under section 89 and requiring a person giving notice—
  (a) to furnish the Commissioners with such evidence as may be specified in the regulations, either on giving notice or when the goods are imported, or at both those times, and
  (b) to comply with such other conditions as may be specified in the regulations.
(2) The regulations may, in particular, require a person giving such a notice—
  (a) to pay such fees in respect of the notice as may be specified by the regulations;
  (b) to give such security as may be so specified in respect of any liability or expense which the Commissioners may incur in consequence of the notice by reason of the detention of any goods or anything done to goods detained;
  (c) to indemnify the Commissioners against any such liability or expense, whether security has been given or not.
(3) The regulations may make different provision as respects different classes of case to which they apply and may include such incidental and supplementary provisions as the Commissioners consider expedient.
(4) Regulations under this section shall be made by statutory instrument which shall be subject to annulment in pursuance of a resolution of either House of Parliament.
(5) Section 17 of the Customs and Excise Management Act 1979 (general provisions as to Commissioners' receipts) applies to fees paid in pursuance of regulations under this section as to receipts under the enactments relating to customs and excise.

Power of Commissioners of Customs and Excise to disclose information

91. Where information relating to infringing goods, material or articles has been obtained by the Commissioners of Customs and Excise for the purposes of, or in connection with, the exercise of their functions in relation to imported goods, the Commissioners may authorise the disclosure of that information for the purpose of facilitating the exercise by any person of any function in connection with the investigation of prosecution of an offence under section 92 below (unauthorised use of trade mark, &c. in relation to goods) or under the Trade Descriptions Act 1968.

Offences

Unauthorised use of trade mark, &c. in relation to goods

92.—(1) A person commits an offence who with a view to gain for himself or another, or with intent to cause loss to another, and without the consent of the proprietor—
   (a) applies to goods or their packaging a sign identical to, or likely to be mistaken for, a registered trade mark, or
   (b) sells or lets for hire, offers or exposes for sale or hire or distributes goods which bear, or the packaging of which bears, such a sign, or
   (c) has in his possession, custody or control in the course of a business any such goods with a view to the doing of anything, by himself or another, which would be an offence under paragraph (b).
   (2) A person commits an offence who with a view to gain for himself or another, or with intent to cause loss to another, and without the consent of the proprietor—
   (a) applies a sign identical to, or likely to be mistaken for, a registered trade mark to material intended to be used—
      (i)   for labelling or packaging goods,
      (ii) as a business paper in relation to goods, or
      (iii) for advertising goods, or
   (b) uses in the course of a business material bearing such a sign for labelling or packaging goods, as a business paper in relation to goods, or for advertising goods, or
   (c) has in his possession, custody or control in the course of a business any such material with a view to the doing of anything, by himself or another, which would be an offence under paragraph (b).
   (3) A person commits an offence who with a view to gain for himself or another, or with intent to cause loss to another, and without the consent of the proprietor—
   (a) makes an article specifically designed or adapted for making copies of a sign identical to, or likely to be mistaken for, a registered trade mark, or
   (b) has such an article in his possession, custody or control in the course of a business,
knowing or having reason to believe that it has been, or is to be, used to produce goods, or material for labelling or packaging goods, as a business paper in relation to goods, or for advertising goods.
   (4) A person does not commit an offence under this section unless—
   (a) the goods are goods in respect of which the trade mark is registered, or
   (b) the trade mark has a reputation in the United Kingdom and the use of the sign takes or would take unfair advantage of, or is or would be detrimental to, the distinctive character or the repute of the trade mark.
   (5) It is a defence for a person charged with an offence under this section to show that he believed on reasonable grounds that the use of the sign in the manner in which it was used, or was to be used, was not an infringement of the registered trade mark.
   (6) A person guilty of an offence under this section is liable—
   (a) on summary conviction to imprisonment for a term not exceeding six months or a fine not exceeding the statutory maximum, or both;
   (b) on conviction on indictment to a fine or imprisonment for a term not exceeding ten years, or both.

Enforcement function of local weights and measures authority

93.—(1) It is the duty of every local weights and measures authority to enforce within their area the provisions of section 92 (unauthorised use of trade mark, &c. in relation to goods).
   (2) The following provisions of the Trade Descriptions Act 1968 apply in relation to the enforcement of that section as in relation to the enforcement of that Act—
      section 27 (power to make test purchases),
      section 28 (power to enter premises and inspect and seize goods and documents),
      section 29 (obstruction of authorised officers), and

section 33 (compensation for loss, &c. of goods seized).

(3) Subsection (1) above does not apply in relation to the enforcement of section 92 in Northern Ireland, but it is the duty of the Department of Economic Development to enforce that section in Northern Ireland.

For that purpose the provisions of the Trade Descriptions Act 1968 specified in subsection (2) apply as if for the references to a local weights and measures authority and any officer of such an authority there were substituted references to that Department and any of its officers.

(4) Any enactment which authorises the disclosure of information for the purpose of facilitating the enforcement of the Trade Descriptions Act 1968 shall apply as if section 92 above were contained in that Act and as if the functions of any person in relation to the enforcement of that section were functions under that Act.

(5) Nothing in this section shall be construed as authorising a local weights and measures authority to bring proceedings in Scotland for an offence.

Falsification of register, &c.

94.—(1) It is an offence for a person to make, or cause to be made, a false entry in the register of trade marks, knowing or having reason to believe that it is false.

(2) It is an offence for a person—
  (a) to make or cause to be made anything falsely purporting to be a copy of an entry in the register, or
  (b) to produce or tender or cause to be produced or tendered in evidence any such thing,
knowing or having reason to believe that it is false.

(3) A person guilty of an offence under this section is liable—
  (a) on conviction on indictment, to imprisonment for a term not exceeding two years or a fine, or both;
  (b) on summary conviction, to imprisonment for a term not exceeding six months or a fine not exceeding the statutory maximum, or both.

Falsely representing trade mark as registered

95.—(1) It is an offence for a person—
  (a) falsely to represent that a mark is a registered trade mark, or
  (b) to make a false representation as to the goods or services for which a trade mark is registered
knowing or having reason to believe that the representation is false.

(2) For the purposes of this section, the use in the United Kingdom in relation to a trade mark—
  (a) of the word "registered", or
  (b) of any other word or symbol importing a reference (express or implied) to registration,
shall be deemed to be a representation as to registration under this Act unless it is shown that the reference is to registration elsewhere than in the United Kingdom and that the trade mark is in fact so registered for the goods or services in question.

(3) A person guilty of an offence under this section is liable on summary conviction to a fine not exceeding level 3 on the standard scale.

Supplementary provisions as to summary proceedings in Scotland

96.—(1) Notwithstanding anything in section 331 of the Criminal Procedure (Scotland) Act 1975, summary proceedings in Scotland for an offence under this Act may be begun at any time within six months after the date on which evidence sufficient in the Lord Advocate's opinion to justify the proceedings came to his knowledge.

For this purpose a certificate of the Lord Advocate as to the date on which such evidence came to his knowledge is conclusive evidence.

(2) For the purposes of subsection (1) and of any other provision of this Act as to the time within which summary proceedings for an offence may be brought, proceedings in Scotland shall be deemed to be begun on the date on which a warrant to apprehend or to cite the accused is granted, if such warrant is executed without undue delay.

Forfeiture of counterfeit goods, &c.

Forfeiture: England and Wales or Northern Ireland

97.—(1) In England and Wales or Northern Ireland where there has come into the possession of any person in connection with the investigation or prosecution of a relevant offence—
- (a) goods which, or the packaging of which, bears a sign identical to or likely to be mistaken for a registered trade mark,
- (b) material bearing such a sign and intended to be used for labelling or packaging goods, as a business paper in relation to goods, or for advertising goods, or
- (c) articles specifically designed or adapted for making copies of such a sign,

that person may apply under this section for an order for the forfeiture of the goods, material or articles.

(2) An application under this section may be made—
- (a) where proceedings have been brought in any court for a relevant offence relating to some or all of the goods, material or articles, to that court;
- (b) where no application for the forfeiture of the goods, material or articles has been made under paragraph (a), by way of complaint to a magistrates' court.

(3) On an application under this section the court shall make an order for the forfeiture of any goods, material or articles only if it is satisfied that a relevant offence has been committed in relation to the goods, material or articles.

(4) A court may infer for the purposes of this section that such an offence has been committed in relation to any goods, material or articles if it is satisfied that such an offence has been committed in relation to goods, material or articles which are representative of them (whether by reason of being of the same design or part of the same consignment or batch or otherwise).

(5) Any person aggrieved by an order made under this section by a magistrates' court, or by a decision of such a court not to make such an order, may appeal against that order or decision—
- (a) in England and Wales, to the Crown Court;
- (b) in Northern Ireland, to the county court;

and an order so made may contain such provision as appears to the court to be appropriate for delaying the coming into force of the order pending the making and determination of any appeal (including any application under section 111 of the Magistrates' Courts Act 1980 or Article 146 of the Magistrates' Courts (Northern Ireland) Order 1981 (statement of case)).

(6) Subject to subsection (7), where any goods, material or articles are forfeited under this section they shall be destroyed in accordance with such directions as the court may give.

(7) On making an order under this section the court may, if it considers it appropriate to do so, direct that the goods, material or articles to which the order relates shall (instead of being destroyed) be released, to such person as the court may specify, on condition that that person—
- (a) causes the offending sign to be erased, removed or obliterated, and
- (b) complies with any order to pay costs which has been made against him in the proceedings for the order for forfeiture.

(8) For the purposes of this section a "relevant offence" means an offence under section 92 above (unauthorised use of trade mark, &c. in relation to goods) or under the Trade Descriptions Act 1968 or any offence involving dishonesty or deception.

Forfeiture: Scotland

98.—(1) In Scotland the court may make an order for the forfeiture of any—
- (a) goods which bear, or the packaging of which bears, a sign identical to or likely to be mistaken for a registered trade mark,
- (b) material bearing such a sign and intended to be used for labelling or packaging goods, as a business paper in relation to goods, or for advertising goods, or
- (c) articles specifically designed or adapted for making copies of such a sign.

(2) An order under this section may be made—

(a) on an application by the procurator-fiscal made in the manner specified in section 310 of the Criminal Procedure (Scotland) Act 1975, or

(b) where a person is convicted of a relevant offence, in addition to any other penalty which the court may impose.

(3) On an application under subsection (2)(a), the court shall make an order for the forfeiture of any goods, material or articles only if it is satisfied that a relevant offence has been committed in relation to the goods, material or articles.

(4) The court may infer for the purposes of this section that such an offence has been committed in relation to any goods, material or articles if it is satisfied that such an offence has been committed in relation to goods, material or articles which are representative of them (whether by reason of being of the same design or part of the same consignment or batch or otherwise).

(5) The procurator-fiscal making the application under subsection (2)(a) shall serve on any person appearing to him to be the owner of, or otherwise to have an interest in, the goods, material or articles to which the application relates a copy of the application, together with a notice giving him the opportunity to appear at the hearing of the application to show cause why the goods, material or articles should not be forfeited.

(6) Service under subsection (5) shall be carried out, and such service may be proved, in the manner specified for citation of an accused in summary proceedings under the Criminal Procedure (Scotland) Act 1975.

(7) Any person upon whom notice is served under subsection (5) and any other person claiming to be the owner of, or otherwise to have an interest in, goods, material or articles to which an application under this section relates shall be entitled to appear at the hearing of the application to show cause why the goods, material or articles should not be forfeited.

(8) The court shall not make an order following an application under subsection (2)(a)—

(a) if any person on whom notice is served under subsection (5) does not appear, unless service of the notice on that person is proved; or

(b) if no notice under subsection (5) has been served, unless the court is satisfied that in the circumstances it was reasonable not to serve such notice.

(9) Where an order for the forfeiture of any goods, material or articles is made following an application under subsection (2)(a), any person who appeared, or was entitled to appear, to show cause why goods, material or articles should not be forfeited may, within 21 days of the making of the order, appeal to the High Court by Bill of Suspension; and section 452(4)(a) to (e) of the Criminal Procedure (Scotland) Act 1975 shall apply to an appeal under this subsection as it applies to a stated case under Part II of that Act.

(10) An order following an application under subsection (2)(a) shall not take effect—

(a) until the end of the period of 21 days beginning with the day after the day on which the order is made; or

(b) if an appeal is made under subsection (9) above within that period, until the appeal is determined or abandoned.

(11) An order under subsection (2)(b) shall not take effect—

(a) until the end of the period within which an appeal against the order could be brought under the Criminal Procedure (Scotland) Act 1975; or

(b) if an appeal is made within that period, until the appeal is determined or abandoned.

(12) Subject to subsection (13), goods, material or articles forfeited under this section shall be destroyed in accordance with such directions as the court may give.

(13) On making an order under this section the court may if it considers it appropriate to do so, direct that the goods, material or articles to which the order relates shall (instead of being destroyed) be released, to such person as the court may specify, on condition that that person causes the offending sign to be erased, removed or obliterated.

(14) For the purposes of this section—

"relevant offence" means an offence under section 92 (unauthorised use of trade mark, &c. in relation to goods) or under the Trade Descriptions Act 1968 or any offence involving dishonesty or deception,

"the court" means—

(a) in relation to an order made on an application under subsection (2)(a), the sheriff, and

(b) in relation to an order made under subsection (2)(b), the court which imposed the penalty.

PART IV

MISCELLANEOUS AND GENERAL PROVISIONS

Miscellaneous

Unauthorised use of Royal arms, &c.

99.—(1) A person shall not without the authority of Her Majesty use in connection with any business the Royal arms (or arms so closely resembling the Royal arms as to be calculated to deceive) in such manner as to be calculated to lead to the belief that he is duly authorised to use the Royal arms.

(2) A person shall not without the authority of Her Majesty or of a member of the Royal family use in connection with any business any device, emblem or title in such a manner as to be calculated to lead to the belief that he is employed by, or supplies goods or services to, Her Majesty or that member of the Royal family.

(3) A person who contravenes subsection (1) commits an offence and is liable on summary conviction to a fine not exceeding level 2 on the standard scale.

(4) Contravention of subsection (1) or (2) may be restrained by injunction in proceedings brought by—

(a) any person who is authorised to use the arms, device, emblem or title in question, or

(b) any person authorised by the Lord Chamberlain to take such proceedings.

(5) Nothing in this section affects any right of the proprietor of a trade mark containing any such arms, device, emblem or title to use that trade mark.

Burden of proving use of trade mark

100. If in any civil proceedings under this Act a question arises as to the use to which a registered trade mark has been put, it is for the proprietor to show what use has been made of it.

Offences committed by partnerships and bodies corporate

101.—(1) Proceedings for an offence under this Act alleged to have been committed by a partnership shall be brought against the partnership in the name of the firm and not in that of the partners; but without prejudice to any liability of the partners under subsection (4) below.

(2) The following provisions apply for the purposes of such proceedings as in relation to a body corporate—

(a) any rules of court relating to the service of documents;

(b) in England and Wales or Northern Ireland, Schedule 3 to the Magistrates' Courts Act 1980 or Schedule 4 to the Magistrates' Courts (Northern Ireland) Order 1981 (procedure on charge of offence).

(3) A fine imposed on a partnership on its conviction in such proceedings shall be paid out of the partnership assets.

(4) Where a partnership is guilty of an offence under this Act, every partner, other than a partner who is proved to have been ignorant of or to have attempted to prevent the commission of the offence, is also guilty of the offence and liable to be proceeded against and punished accordingly.

(5) Where an offence under this Act committed by a body corporate is proved to have been committed with the consent or connivance of a director, manager, secretary or other similar officer of the body, or a person purporting to act in any such capacity, he as well as the body corporate is guilty of the offence and liable to be proceeded against and punished accordingly.

Interpretation

Adaptation of expressions for Scotland

102. In the application of this Act to Scotland—

"account of profits" means accounting and payment of profits;
"accounts" means count, reckoning and payment;
"assignment" means assignation;
"costs" means expenses;
"declaration" means declarator;
"defendant" means defender;
"delivery up" means delivery;
"injunction" means interdict;
"interlocutory relief" means interim remedy; and;
"plaintiff" means pursuer.

Minor definitions

103.—(1) In this Act—

"business" includes a trade or profession;
"director", in relation to a body corporate whose affairs are managed by its members, means any member of the body;
"infringement proceedings", in relation to a registered trade mark, includes proceedings under section 16 (order for delivery up of infringing goods, &c.);
"publish" means make available to the public, and references to publication—
  (a) in relation to an application for registration, are to publication under section 38(1), and
  (b) in relation to registration, are to publication under section 40(4);
"statutory provisions" includes provisions of subordinate legislation within the meaning of the Interpretation Act 1978;
"trade" includes any business or profession.

(2) References in this Act to use (or any particular description of use) of a trade mark, or of a sign identical with, similar to, or likely to be mistaken for a trade mark, include use (or that description of use) otherwise than by means of a graphic representation.

(3) References in this Act to a Community instrument include references to any instrument amending or replacing that instrument.

Index of defined expressions

104. In this Act the expressions listed below are defined by or otherwise fall to be construed in accordance with the provisions indicated—

account of profits and accounts (in Scotland)	section 102
appointed person (for purposes of section 76)	section 77
assignment (in Scotland)	section 102
business	section 103(1)
certification mark	section 50(1)
collective mark	section 49(1)
commencement (of this Act)	section 109(2)
Community trade mark	section 51
Community Trade Mark Regulation	section 51

Convention country	section 55(1)(b)
costs (in Scotland)	section 102
the court	section 75
date of application	section 33(2)
date of filing	section 33(1)
date of registration	section 40(3)
defendant (in Scotland)	section 102
delivery up (in Scotland)	section 102
director	section 103(1)
earlier right	section 5(4)
earlier trade mark	section 6
exclusive licence and licensee	section 29(1)
infringement (of registered trade mark)	sections 9(1)and (2) and 10
infringement proceedings	section 103(1)
infringing articles	section 17
infringing goods	section 17
infringing material	section 17
injunction (in Scotland)	section 102
interlocutory relief (in Scotland)	section 102
the International Bureau	section 53
international trade mark (UK)	section 53
Madrid Protocol	section 53
Paris Convention	section 55(1)(a)
plaintiff (in Scotland)	section 102
prescribed	section 78(1)(b)
protected under the Paris Convention	section 56(1)
—well-known trade marks	section 56(1)
—state emblems and official signs or hallmarks	section 57(1)
—emblems, &c. of international organisations	section 58(2)
publish and references to publication	section 103(1)
register, registered (and related expressions)	section 63(1)
registered trade mark agent	section 83(1)
registrable transaction	section 25(2)
the registrar	section 62
rules	section 78
statutory provisions	section 103(1)
trade	section 103(1)
trade mark	
—generally	section 1(1)
—includes collective mark or certification mark	section 1(2)
United Kingdom (references include Isle of Man)	section 108(2)
use (of trade mark or sign)	section 103(2)
well-known trade mark (under Paris Convention)	section 56(1)

Other general provisions

Transitional provisions

105. The provisions of Schedule 3 have effect with respect to transitional matters, including the treatment of marks registered under the Trade Marks Act 1938, and applications for registration and other proceedings pending under that Act, on the commencement of this Act.

Consequential amendments and repeals

106.—(1)The enactments specified in Schedule 4 are amended in accordance with that Schedule, the amendments being consequential on the provisions of this Act.
(2) The enactments specified in Schedule 5 are repealed to the extent specified.

Territorial waters and the continental shelf

107.—(1)For the purposes of this Act the territorial waters of the United Kingdom shall be treated as part of the United Kingdom.
(2) This Act applies to things done in the United Kingdom sector of the continental shelf on a structure or vessel which is present there for purposes directly connected with the exploration of the sea bed or subsoil or the exploitation of their natural resources as it applies to things done in the United Kingdom.
(3) The United Kingdom sector of the continental shelf means the areas designated by order under section 1(7) of the Continental Shelf Act 1964.

Extent

108.—(1) This Act extends to England and Wales, Scotland and Northern Ireland.
(2) This Act also extends to the Isle of Man, subject to such exceptions and modifications as Her Majesty may specify by Order in Council; and subject to any such Order references in this Act to the United Kingdom shall be construed as including the Isle of Man.

Commencement

109.—(1) The provisions of this Act come into force on such day as the Secretary of State may appoint by order made by statutory instrument.
Different days may be appointed for different provisions and different purposes.
(2) The references to the commencement of this Act in Schedules 3 and 4 (transitional provisions and consequential amendments) are to the commencement of the main substantive provisions of Parts I and III of this Act and the consequential repeal of the Trade Marks Act 1938.
Provision may be made by order under this section identifying the date of that commencement.

Short title

110. This Act may be cited as the Trade Marks Act 1994.

SCHEDULES

Schedule i
Collective marks

General

1. The provisions of this Act apply to collective marks subject to the following provisions.

Signs of which a collective mark may consist

2. In relation to a collective mark the reference in section 1(1) (signs of which a trade mark may consist) to distinguishing goods or services of one undertaking from those of other undertakings shall be construed as a reference to distinguishing goods or services of members of the association which is the proprietor of the mark from those of other undertakings.

Indication of geographical origin

3.—(1) Notwithstanding section 3(1)(c), a collective mark may be registered which consists of signs or indications which may serve, in trade, to designate the geographical origin of the goods or services.

(2) However, the proprietor of such a mark is not entitled to prohibit the use of the signs or indications in accordance with honest practices in industrial or commercial matters (in particular, by a person who is entitled to use a geographical name).

Mark not to be misleading as to character or significance

4.—(1) A collective mark shall not be registered if the public is liable to be misled as regards the character or significance of the mark, in particular if it is likely to be taken to be something other than a collective mark.

(2) The registrar may accordingly require that a mark in respect of which application is made for registration include some indication that it is a collective mark.

Notwithstanding section 39(2), an application may be amended so as to comply with any such requirement.

Regulations governing use of collective mark

5.—(1) An applicant for registration of a collective mark must file with the registrar regulations governing the use of the mark.

(2) The regulations must specify the persons authorised to use the mark, the conditions of membership of the association and, where they exist, the conditions of use of the mark, including any sanctions against misuse.

Further requirements with which the regulations have to comply may be imposed by rules.

Approval of regulations by registrar

6.—(1) A collective mark shall not be registered unless the regulations governing the use of the mark—

(a) comply with paragraph 5(2) and any further requirements imposed by rules, and

(b) are not contrary to public policy or to accepted principles of morality.

(2) Before the end of the prescribed period after the date of the application for registration of a collective mark, the applicant must file the regulations with the registrar and pay the prescribed fee.

If he does not do so, the application shall be deemed to be withdrawn.

7.—(1) The registrar shall consider whether the requirements mentioned in paragraph 6(1) are met.

(2) If it appears to the registrar that those requirements are not met, he shall inform the applicant and give him an opportunity, within such period as the registrar may specify, to make representations or to file amended regulations.

(3) If the applicant fails to satisfy the registrar that those requirements are met, or to file regulations amended so as to meet them, or fails to respond before the end of the specified period, the registrar shall refuse the application.

(4) If it appears to the registrar that those requirements, and the other requirements for registration, are met, he shall accept the application and shall proceed in accordance with section 38 (publication, opposition proceedings and observations).

8. The regulations shall be published and notice of opposition may be given, and observations may be made, relating to the matters mentioned in paragraph 6(1).

This is in addition to any other grounds on which the application may be opposed or observations made.

Regulations to be open to inspection

9. The regulations governing the use of a registered collective mark shall be open to public inspection in the same way as the register.

Amendment of regulations

10.—(1) An amendment of the regulations governing the use of a registered collective mark is not effective unless and until the amended regulations are filed with the registrar and accepted by him.

(2) Before accepting any amended regulations the registrar may in any case where it appears to him expedient to do so cause them to be published.

(3) If he does so, notice of opposition may be given, and observations may be made, relating to the matters mentioned in paragraph 6(1).

Infringement: rights of authorised users

11. The following provisions apply in relation to an authorised user of a registered collective mark as in relation to a licensee of a trade mark—

    (a) section 10(5) (definition of infringement: unauthorised application of mark to certain material);

    (b) section 19(2) (order as to disposal of infringing goods, material or articles: adequacy of other remedies);

    (c) section 89 (prohibition of importation of infringing goods, material or articles: request to Commissioners of Customs and Excise).

12.—(1) The following provisions (which correspond to the provisions of section 30 (general provisions as to rights of licensees in case of infringement)) have effect as regards the rights of an authorised user in relation to infringement of a registered collective mark.

(2) An authorised user is entitled, subject to any agreement to the contrary between him and the proprietor, to call on the proprietor to take infringement proceedings in respect of any matter which affects his interests.

(3) If the proprietor—

    (a) refuses to do so, or

    (b) fails to do so within two months after being called upon,

the authorised user may bring the proceedings in his own name as if he were the proprietor.

(4) Where infringement proceedings are brought by virtue of this paragraph, the authorised user may not, without the leave of the court, proceed with the action unless the proprietor is either joined as a plaintiff or added as a defendant.

This does not affect the granting of interlocutory relief on an application by an authorised user alone.

(5) A proprietor who is added as a defendant as mentioned in sub-paragraph (4) shall not be made liable for any costs in the action unless he takes part in the proceedings.

(6) In infringement proceedings brought by the proprietor of a registered collective mark any loss suffered or likely to be suffered by authorised users shall be taken into account; and the court may give such directions as it thinks fit as to the extent to which the plaintiff is to hold the proceeds of any pecuniary remedy on behalf of such users.

Grounds for revocation of registration

13. Apart from the grounds of revocation provided for in section 46, the registration of a collective mark may be revoked on the ground—

(a) that the manner in which the mark has been used by the proprietor has caused it to become liable to mislead the public in the manner referred to in paragraph 4(1), or

(b) that the proprietor has failed to observe, or to secure the observance of, the regulations governing the use of the mark, or

(c) that an amendment of the regulations has been made so that the regulations—

    (i) no longer comply with paragraph 5(2) and any further conditions imposed by rules, or

    (ii) are contrary to public policy or to accepted principles of morality.

Grounds for invalidity of registration

14. Apart from the grounds of invalidity provided for in section 47, the registration of a collective mark may be declared invalid on the ground that the mark was registered in breach of the provisions of paragraph 4(1) or 6(1).

SCHEDULE 2
CERTIFICATION MARKS

General

1. The provisions of this Act apply to certification marks subject to the following provisions.

Signs of which a certification mark may consist

2. In relation to a certification mark the reference in section 1(1) (signs of which a trade mark may consist) to distinguishing goods or services of one undertaking from those of other undertakings shall be construed as a reference to distinguishing goods or services which are certified from those which are not.

Indication of geographical origin

3.—(1) Notwithstanding section 3(1)(c), a certification mark may be registered which consists of signs or indications which may serve, in trade, to designate the geographical origin of the goods or services.

(2) However, the proprietor of such a mark is not entitled to prohibit the use of the signs or indications in accordance with honest practices in industrial or commercial matters (in particular, by a person who is entitled to use a geographical name).

Nature of proprietor's business

4. A certification mark shall not be registered if the proprietor carries on a business involving the supply of goods or services of the kind certified.

Mark not to be misleading as to character or significance

5.—(1) A certification mark shall not be registered if the public is liable to be misled as regards the character or significance of the mark, in particular if it is likely to be taken to be something other than a certification mark.

(2) The registrar may accordingly require that a mark in respect of which application is made for registration include some indication that it is a certification mark.

Notwithstanding section 39(2), an application may be amended so as to comply with any such requirement.

Regulations governing use of certification mark

6.—(1) An applicant for registration of a certification mark must file with the registrar regulations governing the use of the mark.

(2) The regulations must indicate who is authorised to use the mark, the characteristics to be certified by the mark, how the certifying body is to test those characteristics and to supervise the use of the mark, the fees (if any) to be paid in connection with the operation of the mark and the procedures for resolving disputes.

Further requirements with which the regulations have to comply may be imposed by rules.

Approval of regulations, &c.

7.—(1) A certification mark shall not be registered unless—
  (a) the regulations governing the use of the mark—
      (i)   comply with paragraph 6(2) and any further requirements imposed by rules, and
      (ii) are not contrary to public policy or to accepted principles of morality, and
  (b) the applicant is competent to certify the goods or services for which the mark is to be registered.

(2) Before the end of the prescribed period after the date of the application for registration of a certification mark, the applicant must file the regulations with the registrar and pay the prescribed fee.

If he does not do so, the application shall be deemed to be withdrawn.

8.—(1) The registrar shall consider whether the requirements mentioned in paragraph 7(1) are met.

(2) If it appears to the registrar that those requirements are not met, he shall inform the applicant and give him an opportunity, within such period as the registrar may specify, to make representations or to file amended regulations.

(3) If the applicant fails to satisfy the registrar that those requirements are met, or to file regulations amended so as to meet them, or fails to respond before the end of the specified period, the registrar shall refuse the application.

(4) If it appears to the registrar that those requirements, and the other requirements for registration, are met, he shall accept the application and shall proceed in accordance with section 38 (publication, opposition proceedings and observations).

9. The regulations shall be published and notice of opposition may be given, and observations may be made, relating to the matters mentioned in paragraph 7(1).

This is in addition to any other grounds on which the application may be opposed or observations made.

Regulations to be open to inspection

10. The regulations governing the use of a registered certification mark shall be open to public inspection in the same way as the register.

Amendment of regulations

11.—(1) An amendment of the regulations governing the use of a registered certification mark is not effective unless and until the amended regulations are filed with the registrar and accepted by him.

(2) Before accepting any amended regulations the registrar may in any case where it appears to him expedient to do so cause them to be published.

(3) If he does so, notice of opposition may be given, and observations may be made, relating to the matters mentioned in paragraph 7(1).

Consent to assignment of registered certification mark

12. The assignment or other transmission of a registered certification mark is not effective without the consent of the registrar.

Infringement: rights of authorised users

13. The following provisions apply in relation to an authorised user of a registered certification mark as in relation to a licensee of a trade mark—

(a) section 10(5) (definition of infringement: unauthorised application of mark to certain material);
(b) section 19(2) (order as to disposal of infringing goods, material or articles: adequacy of other remedies);
(c) section 89 (prohibition of importation of infringing goods, material or articles: request to Commissioners of Customs and Excise).

14. In infringement proceedings brought by the proprietor of a registered certification mark any loss suffered or likely to be suffered by authorised users shall be taken into account; and the court may give such directions as it thinks fit as to the extent to which the plaintiff is to hold the proceeds of any pecuniary remedy on behalf of such users.

Grounds for revocation of registration

15. Apart from the grounds of revocation provided for in section 46, the registration of a certification mark may be revoked on the ground—
(a) that the proprietor has begun to carry on such a business as is mentioned in paragraph 4,
(b) that the manner in which the mark has been used by the proprietor has caused it to become liable to mislead the public in the manner referred to in paragraph 5(1),
(c) that the proprietor has failed to observe, or to secure the observance of, the regulations governing the use of the mark,
(d) that an amendment of the regulations has been made so that the regulations—
  (i) no longer comply with paragraph 6(2) and any further conditions imposed by rules, or
  (ii) are contrary to public policy or to accepted principles of morality, or
(e) that the proprietor is no longer competent to certify the goods or services for which the mark is registered.

Grounds for invalidity of registration

16. Apart from the grounds of invalidity provided for in section 47, the registration of a certification mark may be declared invalid on the ground that the mark was registered in breach of the provisions of paragraph 4, 5(1) or 7(1).

SCHEDULE 3
TRANSITIONAL PROVISIONS

Introductory

1.—(1) In this Schedule—

"existing registered mark" means a trade mark, certification trade mark or service mark registered under the 1938 Act immediately before the commencement of this Act;
"the 1938 Act" means the Trade Marks Act 1938; and
"the old law" means that Act and any other enactment or rule of law applying to existing registered marks immediately before the commencement of this Act.

(2) For the purposes of this Schedule—
(a) an application shall be treated as pending on the commencement of this Act if it was made but not finally determined before commencement, and
(b) the date on which it was made shall be taken to be the date of filing under the 1938 Act.

Existing registered marks

2.—(1)Existing registered marks (whether registered in Part A or B of the register kept under the 1938 Act) shall be transferred on the commencement of this Act to the register kept under this Act and have effect, subject to the provisions of this Schedule, as if registered under this Act.

(2) Existing registered marks registered as a series under section 21(2) of the 1938 Act shall be similarly registered in the new register.

Provision may be made by rules for putting such entries in the same form as is required for entries under this Act.

(3) In any other case notes indicating that existing registered marks are associated with other marks shall cease to have effect on the commencement of this Act.

3.—(1) A condition entered on the former register in relation to an existing registered mark immediately before the commencement of this Act shall cease to have effect on commencement.

Proceedings under section 33 of the 1938 Act (application to expunge or vary registration for breach of condition) which are pending on the commencement of this Act shall be dealt with under the old law and any necessary alteration made to the new register.

(2) A disclaimer or limitation entered on the former register in relation to an existing registered mark immediately before the commencement of this Act shall be transferred to the new register and have effect as if entered on the register in pursuance of section 13 of this Act.

Effects of registration: infringement

4.—(1) Sections 9 to 12 of this Act (effects of registration) apply in relation to an existing registered mark as from the commencement of this Act and section 14 of this Act (action for infringement) applies in relation to infringement of an existing registered mark committed after the commencement of this Act, subject to sub-paragraph (2) below.

The old law continues to apply in relation to infringements committed before commencement.

(2) It is not an infringement of—

(a) an existing registered mark, or
(b) a registered trade mark of which the distinctive elements are the same or substantially the same as those of an existing registered mark and which is registered for the same goods or services,

to continue after commencement any use which did not amount to infringement of the existing registered mark under the old law.

Infringing goods, material or articles

5. Section 16 of this Act (order for delivery up of infringing goods, material or articles) applies to infringing goods, material or articles whether made before or after the commencement of this Act.

Rights and remedies of licensee or authorised user

6.—(1) Section 30 (general provisions as to rights of licensees in case of infringement) of this Act applies to licenses granted before the commencement of this Act, but only in relation to infringements committed after commencement.

(2) Paragraph 14 of Schedule 2 of this Act (court to take into account loss suffered by authorised users, &c.) applies only in relation to infringements committed after commencement.

Co-ownership of registered mark

7. The provisions of section 23 of this Act (co-ownership of registered mark) apply as from the commencement of this Act to an existing registered mark of which two or more persons were immediately before commencement registered as joint proprietors.

But so long as the relations between the joint proprietors remain such as are described in section 63 of the 1938 Act (joint ownership) there shall be taken to be an agreement to exclude the operation of subsections (1) and (3) of section 23 of this Act (ownership in undivided shares and right of co-proprietor to make separate use of the mark).

Assignment, &c. of registered mark

8.—(1) Section 24 of this Act (assignment or other transmission of registered mark) applies to transactions and events occurring after the commencement of this Act in relation to an existing registered mark; and the old law continues to apply in relation to transactions and events occurring before commencement.

(2) Existing entries under section 25 of the 1938 Act (registration of assignments and transmissions) shall be transferred on the commencement of this Act to the register kept under this Act and have effect as if made under section 25 of this Act.

Provision may be made by rules for putting such entries in the same form as is required for entries made under this Act.

(3) An application for registration under section 25 of the 1938 Act which is pending before the registrar on the commencement of this Act shall be treated as an application for registration under section 25 of this Act and shall proceed accordingly.

The registrar may require the applicant to amend his application so as to conform with the requirements of this Act.

(4) An application for registration under section 25 of the 1938 Act which has been determined by the registrar but not finally determined before the commencement of this Act shall be dealt with under the old law; and sub-paragraph (2) above shall apply in relation to any resulting entry in the register.

(5) Where before the commencement of this Act a person has become entitled by assignment or transmission to an existing registered mark but has not registered his title, any application for registration after commencement shall be made under section 25 of this Act.

(6) In cases to which sub-paragraph (3) or (5) applies section 25(3) of the 1938 Act continues to apply (and section 25(3) and (4) of this Act do not apply) as regards the consequences of failing to register.

Licensing of registered mark

9.—(1) Sections 28 and 29(2) of this Act (licensing of registered trade mark; rights of exclusive licensee against grantor's successor in title) apply only in relation to licences granted after the commencement of this Act; and the old law continues to apply in relation to licences granted before commencement.

(2) Existing entries under section 28 of the 1938 Act (registered users) shall be transferred on the commencement of this Act to the register kept under this Act and have effect as if made under section 25 of this Act.

Provision may be made by rules for putting such entries in the same form as is required for entries made under this Act.

(3) An application for registration as a registered user which is pending before the registrar on the commencement of this Act shall be treated as an application for registration of a licence under section 25(1) of this Act and shall proceed accordingly.

The registrar may require the applicant to amend his application so as to conform with the requirements of this Act.

(4) An application for registration as a registered user which has been determined by the registrar but not finally determined before the commencement of this Act shall be dealt with under the old law; and sub-paragraph (2) above shall apply in relation to any resulting entry in the register.

(5) Any proceedings pending on the commencement of this Act under section 28(8) or (10) of the 1938 Act (variation or cancellation of registration of registered user) shall be dealt with under the old law and any necessary alteration made to the new register.

Pending applications for registration

10.—(1) An application for registration of a mark under the 1938 Act which is pending on the commencement of this Act shall be dealt with under the old law, subject as mentioned below, and if registered the mark shall be treated for the purposes of this Schedule as an existing registered mark.

(2) The power of the Secretary of State under section 78 of this Act to make rules regulating practice and procedure, and as to the matters mentioned in subsection (2) of that section, is exercisable in relation to such an application; and different provision may be made for such applications from that made for other applications.

(3) Section 23 of the 1938 Act (provisions as to associated trade marks) shall be disregarded in dealing after the commencement of this Act with an application for registration.

Conversion of pending application

11.—(1) In the case of a pending application for registration which has not been advertised under section 18 of the 1938 Act before the commencement of this Act, the applicant may give notice to the registrar claiming to have the registrability of the mark determined in accordance with the provisions of this Act.

(2) The notice must be in the prescribed form, be accompanied by the appropriate fee and be given no later than six months after the commencement of this Act.

(3) Notice duly given is irrevocable and has the effect that the application shall be treated as if made immediately after the commencement of this Act.

Trade marks registered according to old classification

12. The registrar may exercise the powers conferred by rules under section 65 of this Act (adaptation of entries to new classification) to secure that any existing registered marks which do not conform to the system of classification prescribed under section 34 of this Act are brought into conformity with that system.

This applies, in particular, to existing registered marks classified according to the pre-1938 classification set out in Schedule 3 to the Trade Marks Rules 1986.

Claim to priority from overseas application

13. Section 35 of this Act (claim to priority of Convention application) applies to an application for registration under this Act made after the commencement of this Act notwithstanding that the Convention application was made before commencement.

14.—(1) Where before the commencement of this Act a person has duly filed an application for protection of a trade mark in a relevant country within the meaning of section 39A of the 1938 Act which is not a Convention country (a "relevant overseas application"), he, or his successor in title, has a right to priority, for the purposes of registering the same trade mark under this Act for some or all of the same goods or services, for a period of six months from the date of filing of the relevant overseas application.

(2) If the application for registration under this Act is made within that six-month period—
  (a) the relevant date for the purposes of establishing which rights take precedence shall be the date of filing of the relevant overseas application, and
  (b) the registrability of the trade mark shall not be affected by any use of the mark in the United Kingdom in the period between that date and the date of the application under this Act.

(3) Any filing which in a relevant country is equivalent to a regular national filing, under its domestic legislation or an international agreement, shall be treated as giving rise to the right of priority.

A "regular national filing" means a filing which is adequate to establish the date on which the application was filed in that country, whatever may be the subsequent fate of the application.

(4) A subsequent application concerning the same subject as the relevant overseas application, filed in the same country, shall be considered the relevant overseas application (of which the filing date is the starting date of the period of priority), if at the time of the subsequent application—
  (a) the previous application has been withdrawn, abandoned or refused, without having been laid open to public inspection and without leaving any rights outstanding, and
  (b) it has not yet served as a basis for claiming a right of priority.

The previous application may not thereafter serve as a basis for claiming a right of priority.

(5) Provision may be made by rules as to the manner of claiming a right to priority on the basis of a relevant overseas application.

(6) A right to priority arising as a result of a relevant overseas application may be assigned or otherwise transmitted, either with the application or independently.

The reference in sub-paragraph (1) to the applicant's "successor in title" shall be construed accordingly.

(7) Nothing in this paragraph affects proceedings on an application for registration under the 1938 Act made before the commencement of this Act (see paragraph 10 above).

Duration and renewal of registration

15.—(1) Section 42(1) of this Act (duration of original period of registration) applies in relation to the registration of a mark in pursuance of an application made after the commencement of this Act; and the old law applies in any other case.

(2) Sections 42(2) and 43 of this Act (renewal) apply where the renewal falls due on or after the commencement of this Act; and the old law continues to apply in any other case.

(3) In either case it is immaterial when the fee is paid.

Pending application for alteration of registered mark

16. An application under section 35 of the 1938 Act (alteration of registered trade mark) which is pending on the commencement of this Act shall be dealt with under the old law and any necessary alteration made to the new register.

Revocation for non-use

17.—(1) An application under section 26 of the 1938 Act (removal from register or imposition of limitation on ground of non-use) which is pending on the commencement of this Act shall be dealt with under the old law and any necessary alteration made to the new register.

(2) An application under section 46(1)(a) or (b) of this Act (revocation for non-use) may be made in relation to an existing registered mark at any time after the commencement of this Act.

Provided that no such application for the revocation of the registration of an existing registered mark registered by virtue of section 27 of the 1938 Act (defensive registration of well-known trade marks) may be made until more than five years after the commencement of this Act.

Application for rectification, &c.

18.—(1) An application under section 32 or 34 of the 1938 Act (rectification or correction of the register) which is pending on the commencement of this Act shall be dealt with under the old law and any necessary alteration made to the new register.

(2) For the purposes of proceedings under section 47 of this Act (grounds for invalidity of registration) as it applies in relation to an existing registered mark, the provisions of this Act shall be deemed to have been in force at all material times.

Provided that no objection to the validity of the registration of an existing registered mark may be taken on the ground specified in subsection (3) of section 5 of this Act (relative grounds for refusal of registration: conflict with earlier mark registered for different goods or services).

Regulations as to use of certification mark

19.—(1) Regulations governing the use of an existing registered certification mark deposited at the Patent Office in pursuance of section 37 of the 1938 Act shall be treated after the commencement of this Act as if filed under paragraph 6 of Schedule 2 to this Act.

(2) Any request for amendment of the regulations which was pending on the commencement of this Act shall be dealt with under the old law.

Sheffield marks

20.—(1) For the purposes of this Schedule the Sheffield register kept under Schedule 2 to the 1938 Act shall be treated as part of the register of trade marks kept under that Act.

(2) Applications made to the Cutlers' Company in accordance with that Schedule which are pending on the commencement of this Act shall proceed after commencement as if they had been made to the registrar.

Certificate of validity of contested registration

21. A certificate given before the commencement of this Act under section 47 of the 1938 Act (certificate of validity of contested registration) shall have effect as if given under section 73(1) of this Act.

Trade mark agents

22.—(1) Rules in force immediately before the commencement of this Act under section 282 or 283 of the Copyright, Designs and Patents Act 1988 (register of trade mark agents; persons entitled to describe themselves as registered) shall continue in force and have effect as if made under section 83 or 85 of this Act.

(2) Rules in force immediately before the commencement of this Act under section 40 of the 1938 Act as to the persons whom the registrar may refuse to recognise as agents for the purposes of business under that Act shall continue in force and have effect as if made under section 88 of this Act.

(3) Rules continued in force under this paragraph may be varied or revoked by further rules made under the relevant provisions of this Act.

SCHEDULE 4
CONSEQUENTIAL AMENDMENTS

General adaptation of existing references

1.—(1) References in statutory provisions passed or made before the commencement of this Act to trade marks or registered trade marks within the meaning of the Trade Marks Act 1938 shall, unless the context otherwise requires, be construed after the commencement of this Act as references to trade marks or registered trade marks within the meaning of this Act.

(2) Sub-paragraph (1) applies, in particular, to the references in the following provisions—

Industrial Organisation and Development Act 1947	Schedule 1, paragraph 7
Crown Proceedings Act 1947	section 3(1)(b)
Horticulture Act 1960	section 15(1)(b)
Printer's Imprint Act 1961	section 1(1)(b)
Plant Varieties and Seeds Act 1964	section 5A(4)
Northern Ireland Constitution Act 1973	Schedule 3, paragraph 17
Patents Act 1977	section 19(2)
	section 27(4)
	section 123(7)
Unfair Contract Terms Act 1977	Schedule 1, paragraph 1(c)
Judicature (Northern Ireland) Act 1978	section 94A(5)
State Immunity Act 1978	section 7(a) and (b)
Supreme Court Act 1981	section 72(5)
	Schedule 1, paragraph 1(i)
Civil Jurisdiction and Judgments Act 1982	Schedule 5, paragraph 2
	Schedule 8, paragraph 2(14) and 4(2)
Value Added Tax Act 1983	Schedule 3, paragraph 1
Companies Act 1985	section 396(3A)(a) or (as substituted by the Companies Act 1989) section 396(2)(d)(i)
	section 410(4)(c)(v)
	Schedule 4, Part I, Balance Sheet Formats 1 and 2 and Note (2)

	Schedule 9, Part I, paragraphs 5(2)(d) and 10(2)
Law Reform (Miscellaneous Provisions) (Scotland) Act 1985	section 15(5)
Atomic Energy Authority Act 1986	section 8(2)
Companies (Northern Ireland) Order 1986	article 403(3A)(a) or (as substituted by the Companies (No. 2) (Northern Ireland) Order 1990) article 403(2)(d)(i)
	Schedule 4, Part I, Balance Sheet Formats 1 and 2 and Note (2)
	Schedule 9, Part I, paragraphs 5(2)(d) and 10(2)
Consumer Protection Act 1987	section 2(2)(b)
Consumer Protection (Northern Ireland) Order 1987	article 5(2)(b)
Income and Corporation Taxes Act 1988	section 83(a)
Taxation of Chargeable Gains Act 1992	section 275(h)
Tribunals and Inquiries Act 1992	Schedule 1, paragraph 34.

Patents and Designs Act 1907 (c.29)

2.—(1) The Patents and Designs Act 1907 is amended as follows.

(2) In section 62 (the Patent Office)—

  (a) in subsection (1) for "this Act and the Trade Marks Act 1905" substitute "the Patents Act 1977, the Registered Designs Act 1949 and the Trade Marks Act 1994"; and

  (b) in subsections (2) and (3) for "the Board of Trade" substitute "the Secretary of State".

(3) In section 63 (officers and clerks of the Patent Office)—

  (a) for "the Board of Trade" in each place where it occurs substitute "the Secretary of State"; and

  (b) in subsection (2) omit the words from "and those salaries" to the end.

(4) The repeal by the Patents Act 1949 and the Registered Designs Act 1949 of the whole of the 1907 Act, except certain provisions, shall be deemed not to have extended to the long title, date of enactment or enacting words or to so much of section 99 as provides the Act with its short title.

Patents, Designs, Copyright and Trade Marks (Emergency) Act 1939 (c.107)

3.—(1) The Patents, Designs, Copyright and Trade Marks (Emergency) Act 1939 is amended as follows.

(2) For section 3 (power of comptroller to suspend rights of enemy or enemy subject) substitute—

"Power of comptroller to suspend trade mark rights of enemy or enemy subject

3.—(1) Where on application made by a person proposing to supply goods or services of any description it is made to appear to the comptroller—

  (a) that it is difficult or impracticable to describe or refer to the goods or services without the use of a registered trade mark, and

  (b) that the proprietor of the registered trade mark (whether alone or jointly with another) is an enemy or an enemy subject,

the comptroller may make an order suspending the rights given by the registered trade mark.

(2) An order under this section shall suspend those rights as regards the use of the trade mark—

  (a) by the applicant, and

  (b) by any person authorised by the applicant to do, for the purposes of or in connection with the supply by the applicant of the goods or services, things which would otherwise infringe the registered trade mark to such extent and for such period as the comptroller considers necessary to enable the applicant to render well-known and established some other means of describing or referring to the goods or services in question which does not involve the use of the trade mark.

(3) Where an order has been made under this section, no action for passing off lies on the part of any person interested in the registered trade mark in respect of any use of it which by virtue of the order is not an infringement of the right conferred by it.

(4) An order under this section may be varied or revoked by a subsequent order made by the comptroller".

(3) In each of the following provisions—
  (a) section 4(1)(c) (effect of war on registration of trade marks),
  (b) section 6(1)(c) (power of comptroller to extend time limits),
  (c) section 7(1)(a) (evidence as to nationality, &c.), and
  (d) the definition of "the comptroller" in section 10(1) (interpretation),
for "the Trade Marks Act 1938" substitute "the Trade Marks Act 1994".

Trade Descriptions Act 1968 (c.29)

4. In the Trade Descriptions Act 1968, in section 34 (exemption of trade description contained in pre-1968 trade mark)—
  (a) in the opening words, omit "within the meaning of the Trade Marks Act 1938"; and
  (b) in paragraph (c), for "a person registered under section 28 of the Trade Marks Act 1938 as a registered user of the trade mark" substitute ",in the case of a registered trade mark, a person licensed to use it".

Solicitors Act 1974 (c.47)

5.—(1) Section 22 of the Solicitors Act 1974 (preparation of instruments by unqualified persons) is amended as follows.

(2) In subsection (2)(aa) and (ab) (instruments which may be prepared by registered trade mark agent or registered patent agent) for ",trade mark or service mark" substitute "or trade mark".

(3) In subsection (3A) (interpretation)—
  (a) in the definition of "registered trade mark agent" for "section 282(1) of the Copyright, Designs and Patents Act 1988" substitute "the Trade Marks Act 1994"; and
  (b) in the definition of "registered patent agent" for "of that Act" substitute "of the Copyright, Designs and Patents Act 1988".

House of Commons Disqualification Act 1975 (c.24)

6. In Part III of Schedule 1 to the House of Commons Disqualification Act 1975 (other disqualifying offices), for the entry relating to persons appointed to hear and determine appeals under the Trade Marks Act 1938 substitute—

"Person appointed to hear and determine appeals under the Trade Marks Act 1994.".

Restrictive Trade Practices Act 1976 (c.34)

7. In Schedule 3 to the Restrictive Trade Practices Act 1976 (excepted agreements), for paragraph 4 (agreements relating to trade marks) substitute—

"4.—(1) This Act does not apply to an agreement authorising the use of a registered trade mark (other than a collective mark or certification mark) if no such restrictions as are described in section 6(1) or 11(2) above are accepted, and no such information provisions as are described in section 7(1) or 12(2) above are made, except in respect of—
  (a) the descriptions of goods bearing the mark which are to be produced or supplied, or the processes of manufacture to be applied to such goods or to goods to which the mark is to be applied, or

(b) the kinds of services in relation to which the mark is to be used which are to be made available or supplied, or the form or manner in which such services are to be made available or supplied, or

(c) the descriptions of goods which are to be produced or supplied in connection with the supply of services in relation to which the mark is to be used, or the process of manufacture to be applied to such goods.

(2) This Act does not apply to an agreement authorising the use of a registered collective mark or certification mark if—

(a) the agreement is made in accordance with regulations approved by the registrar under Schedule 1 or 2 to the Trade Marks Act 1994, and

(b) no such restrictions as are described in section 6(1) or 11(2) above are accepted, and no such information provisions as are prescribed in section 7(1) or 12(2) above are made, except as permitted by those regulations.".

Copyright, Designs and Patents Act 1988 (c.48)

8.—(1) The Copyright, Designs and Patents Act 1988 is amended as follows.

(2) In sections 114(6), 204(6) and 231(6) (persons regarded as having an interest in infringing copies, &c.), for "section 58C of the Trade Marks Act 1938" substitute "section 19 of the Trade Marks Act 1994".

(3) In section 280(1) (privilege for communications with patent agents), for "trade mark or service mark" substitute "or trade mark".

Tribunals and Inquiries Act 1992 (c.53)

9. In Part I of Schedule 1 to the Tribunals and Inquiries Act 1992 (tribunals under direct supervision of Council on Tribunals), for "Patents, designs, trade marks and service marks" substitute "Patents, designs and trade marks".

SCHEDULE 5
REPEALS AND REVOCATIONS

Chapter or number	Short title	Extent of repeal or revocation
1891 c. 50.	Commissioners for Oaths Act 1891.	In section 1, the words "or the Patents, Designs and Trade Marks Acts, 1883 to 1888,".
1907 c. 29.	Patents and Designs Act 1907.	In section 63(2), the words from "and those salaries" to the end.
1938 c. 22.	Trade Marks Act 1938.	The whole Act.
1947 c. 44.	Crown Proceedings Act 1947.	In section 3(1)(b), the words "or registered service mark".
1949 c. 87.	Patents Act 1949.	Section 92(2)
1964 c. 14.	Plant Varieties and Seeds Act 1964.	In section 5A(4), the words "under the Trade Marks Act 1938".
1967 c. 80.	Criminal Justice Act 1967.	In Schedule 3, in Parts I and IV, the entries relating to the Trade Marks Act 1938.
1978 c. 23.	Judicature (Northern Ireland) Act 1978.	In Schedule 5, in Part II, the paragraphs amending the Trade Marks Act 1938.
1984 c. 19.	Trade Marks (Amendment) Act 1984.	The whole Act.

1985 c. 6.	Companies Act 1985.	In section 396— (a) in subsection (3A)(a), and (b) in subsection (2)(d)(i) as inserted by the Companies Act 1989, the words "service mark,".
1986 c. 12.	Statute Law (Repeals) Act 1986.	In Schedule 2, paragraph 2.
1986 c. 39.	Patents, Designs and Marks Act 1986.	Section 2. Section 4(4). In Schedule 1, paragraphs 1 and 2. Schedule 2.
S.I. 1986/1032 (N.I. 6).	Companies (Northern Ireland) Order 1986.	In article 403— (a) in paragraph (3A)(a), and (b) in paragraph (2)(d)(i) as inserted by the Companies (No.2) (Northern Ireland) Order 1990, the words "service mark,".
1987 c. 43.	Consumer Protection Act 1987.	In section 45— (a) in subsection (1), the definition of "mark" and "trade mark"; (b) subsection (4).
S.I. 1987/2049.	Consumer Protection (Northern Ireland) Order 1987.	In article 2— (a) in paragraph (2), the definitions of "mark" and "trade mark"; (b) paragraph (3).
1988 c. 1.	Income and Corporation Taxes Act 1988.	In section 83, the words from "References in this section" to the end.
1988 c. 48.	Copyright, Designs and Patents Act 1988.	Sections 282 to 284. In section 286, the definition of "registered trade mark agent". Section 300.
1992 c. 12.	Taxation of Chargeable Gains Act 1992.	In section 275(h), the words "service marks" and "service mark".

(2)   The Trade Marks Rules 1994

(S.I. 1994 No. 2583)

Made –	*5th October 1994*
Laid before Parliament – – – – – – – – – – – – – – –	*7th October 1994*
Coming into force – – – – – – – – – – – – – – – – –	*31st October 1994*

ARRANGEMENT OF RULES

Collective and certification marks

22. Filing of regulations for collective and certification marks; Schs. 1 & 2.
23. Amendment of regulations of collective and certification marks; Sch. 1, para. 10 & Sch. 2, para. 11.

Disclaimers, limitations and alteration or surrender of registered trade mark

24. Registration subject to disclaimer or limitation; s.13.
25. Alteration of registered trade mark; s.44.
26. Surrender of registered trade mark; s.45.

Renewal and restoration

27. Reminder of renewal of registration; s.43.
28. Renewal of registration; s.43.
29. Delayed renewal and removal of registration; s.43.
30. Restoration of registration; s.43.

Revocation, invalidation and rectification

31. Procedure on application for revocation, declaration of invalidity and rectification of the register; ss.46, 47 & 64.

The register

32. Form of register; s.63(1).
33. Entry in register of particulars of registered trade marks; s.63(2).
34. Entry in register of particulars of registrable transactions; s.25.
35. Application to register or give notice of transaction; ss.25 & 27(3).
36. Public inspection of register; s.63(3).
37. Supply of certified copies, etc; s.63(3).
38. Request for change of name and address in register; s.64(4).
39. Removal of matter from register; s.64(5).

Change of classification

40. Change of classification; ss.65(2) & 76(1).
41. Opposition to proposals; ss.65(3) & 76(1).

Request for information, inspection of documents and confidentiality

42. Request for information; s.67(1).
43. Information available before publication; s.67(2).
44. Inspection of documents; ss.67 & 76(1).
45. Confidential documents.

Agents

46. Proof of authorisation of agent may be required; s.82.
47. Registrar may refuse to deal with certain agents; s.88.

Decision of registrar, evidence and costs

48. Decisions of registrar to be taken after hearing.
49. Evidence in proceedings before registrar; s.69.

The Secretary of State, in exercise of the powers conferred upon him by sections 4(4), 13(2), 25(1), (5) and (6), 34(1), 35(5), 38(1) and (2), 39(3), 40(4), 41(1) and (3), 43(2), (3), (5) and (6), 44(3), 45(2), 63(2) and (3), 64(4), 65, 66(2), 67(1) and (2), 68(1) and (3), 69, 76(1), 78, 80(3), 81, 82 and 88 of, paragraph 6(2) of Schedule 1 to, paragraph 7(2) of Schedule 2 to, and paragraphs 10(2), 11(2), 12 and 14(5) of Schedule 3 to, the Trade Marks Act 1994 (c. 26), after consultation with the Council on Tribunals pursuant to section 8(1) of the Tribunals and Inquiries Act 1992 (c.53), hereby makes the following Rules:

Preliminary

Citation and commencement

1.—These rules may be cited as the Trade Marks Rules 1994 and shall come into force on 31st October 1994.

Interpretation

2.—(1) In these Rules, unless the context otherwise requires—

"the Act" means the Trade Marks Act 1994;
"the Journal" means the Trade Marks Journal published in accordance with rule 65 below;
"the Office" means the Patent Office;
"old law" means the Trade Marks Act 1938 (c.22) (as amended) and any rules made thereunder existing immediately before the commencement of the Act;
"proprietor" means the person registered as the proprietor of the trade mark;
"publish" means publish in the Journal;
"send" includes give;
"specification" means the statement of goods or services in respect of which a trade mark is registered or proposed to be registered;
"United Kingdom" includes the Isle of Man.

(2) In these Rules, except where otherwise indicated, a reference to a section is a reference to that section in the Act, a reference to a rule is a reference to that rule in these Rules, a reference to a Schedule is a reference to that Schedule to these Rules and a reference to a form is a reference to that form as published by the registrar under rule 3 below.

(3) In these Rules references to the filing of any application, notice or other document are to be construed as references to its being sent or delivered to the registrar at the Office.

Forms and directions of the registrar under s.66

3.—(1) Any forms required by the registrar to be used for the purpose of registration of a trade mark or any other proceedings before him under the Act pursuant to section 66 and any directions with respect to their use shall be published and any amendment or modification of a form or of the directions with respect to its use shall be published (the forms required to be used are published in the special edition of the Trade Marks Journal dated 31st October 1994).

(2) A requirement under this rule to use a form as published is satisfied by the use either of a replica of that form or of a form which is acceptable to the registrar and contains the information required by the form as published and complies with any directions as to the use of such a form.

Requirement as to fees

4.—(1) The fees to be paid in respect of any application, registration or any other matter under the Act and these Rules shall be those (if any) prescribed in relation to such matter by rules under section 79 (fees) (see the Trade Marks (Fees) Rules 1994, S.I. 2584/1994).

(2) Any form required to be filed with the registrar in respect of any specified matter shall be subject to the payment of the fee (if any) prescribed in respect of that matter by those rules.

Application for registration

Application for registration; s.32

5. An application for the registration of a trade mark shall be filed on Form TM3 and shall be subject to the payment of the application fee and such class fees as may be appropriate.

Claim to priority; ss.35 & 36

6.—(1) Where a right to priority is claimed by reason of an application for protection of a trade mark duly filed in a Convention country under section 35 or in another country or territory in respect of which provision corresponding to that made by section 35 is made under section 36, particulars of that claim shall be included in the application for registration under rule 5 above and, where no certificate as is referred to in paragraph (2) below is filed with the application, such particulars shall include the country or countries and the date or dates of filing.

(2) Unless it has been filed at the time of the filing of the application for registration, there shall be filed, within three months of the filing of the application under rule 5, a certificate by the registering or other competent authority of that country certifying, or verifying to the satisfaction of the registrar, the date of the filing of the application, the country or registering or competent authority, the representation of the mark, and the goods or services covered by the application.

Classification of goods and services; s.34

7.—(1) For the purposes of trade mark registrations in respect of goods dated before 27th July 1938, goods are classified in accordance with Schedule 3 to these Rules, except where a specification has been converted, whether under the old law or under rule 40 below, to Schedule 4.

(2) For the purposes of trade mark registrations in respect of goods dated on or after 27th July 1938 and for the purposes of any registrations dated before that date in respect of which the specifications were converted under the old law, and for the purposes of trade mark registrations in respect of services, goods and services are classified in accordance with Schedule 4, which sets out the current version of the classes of the International Classification of Goods and Services (the International Classification is drawn up under the Nice Agreement concerning the International Classification of Goods and Services for the purposes of the Registration of marks of 15th June 1957 (as last revised on 13th May 1977) (Cmnd 6898). The current version of the International Classification is the Sixth Edition, which entered into force on 1st January 1992).

Application may relate to more than one class and shall specify the class

8.—(1) An application may be made for registration in more than one class of Schedule 4.

(2) Every application shall specify the class in Schedule 4 to which it relates; and if the application relates to more than one class in that Schedule the specification contained in it shall set out the classes in consecutive numerical order and list under each class the goods or services appropriate to that class.

(3) If the specification contained in the application lists items by reference to a class in Schedule 4 in which they do not fall, the applicant may request, by filing Form TM3A, that his application be amended to include the appropriate class for those items, and upon the payment of such class fee as may be appropriate the registrar shall amend his application accordingly.

Prohibition on registration of mark consisting of arms; s.4

9. Where a representation of any arms or insignia as is referred to in section 4(4) appears on a mark, the registrar shall refuse to accept an application for the registration of the mark unless satisfied that the consent of the person entitled to the arms has been obtained.

Address for service

10.—(1) For the purposes of any proceedings before the registrar under these Rules or any appeal from a decision of the registrar under the Act or these Rules, an address for service in the United Kingdom shall be filed by—
  (a) every applicant for the registration of a trade mark;
  (b) every person opposing an application for registration of a trade mark;
  (c) every applicant applying to the registrar under section 46 for the revocation of the registration of a trade mark, under section 47 for the invalidation of the registration of a trade mark, or under section 64 for the rectification of the register;
  (d) every person granted leave to intervene under rule 31(5) (the intervener); and
  (e) every proprietor of a registered trade mark which is the subject of an application to the registrar for the revocation, invalidation or rectification of the registration of the mark.

(2) The address for service of an applicant for registration of a trade mark shall upon registration of the mark be deemed to be the address for service of the registered proprietor, subject to any filing to the contrary under paragraph (1) above or rule 38(2) below.

(3) In any case in which an address for service is filed at the same time as the filing of a form required by the registrar under rule 3 which requires the furnishing of an address for service, the address shall be filed on that form and in any other case it shall be filed on Form TM33.

(4) Anything sent to any applicant, opponent, intervener or registered proprietor at his address for service shall be deemed to be properly sent; and the registrar may, where no address for service is filed, treat as the address for service of the person concerned his trade or business address in the United Kingdom, if any.

(5) An address for service in the United Kingdom may be filed at any time by the proprietor of a registered trade mark and by any person having an interest in or charge on a registered trade mark which has been registered under rule 34.

(6) Where an address for service is not filed as required by paragraph (1) above, the registrar shall send the person concerned notice to file an address for service within two months of the date of the notice and if that person fails to do so—

  (a) in the case of an applicant as is referred to in sub-paragraph (a) or (c), the application shall be treated as abandoned;

  (b) in the case of a person as is referred to in sub-paragraph (b) or (d), he shall be deemed to have withdrawn from the proceedings; and

  (c) in the case of the proprietor referred to in sub-paragraph (e), he shall not be permitted to take part in any proceedings.

Deficiencies in application; s.32

11. Where an application for registration of a trade mark does not satisfy the requirements of section 32(2), (3) or (4) or rule 5 or 8(2), the registrar shall send notice thereof to the applicant to remedy the deficiencies or, in the case of section 32(4), the default of payment and if within two months of the date of notice the applicant—

  (a) fails to remedy any deficiency notified to him in respect of section 32(2), the application shall be deemed never to have been made; or

  (b) fails to remedy any deficiency notified to him in respect of section 32(3) or rule 5 or 8(2) or fails to make payment as required by section 32(4), the application shall be treated as abandoned.

Publication, observations, oppositions and registration

Publication of application for registration; s.38(1)

12. An application which has been accepted for registration shall be published.

Opposition proceedings; s.38(2)

13.—(1) Notice of opposition to the registration of a trade mark shall be sent to the registrar on Form TM7 within three months of the date on which the application was published under rule 12, and shall include a statement of the grounds of opposition; the registrar shall send a copy of the notice and the statement to the applicant.

(2) Within three months of the date on which a copy of the statement is sent by the registrar to the applicant the applicant may file, in conjunction with notice of the same on Form TM8, a counter-statement; the registrar shall send a copy of the Form TM8 and the counter-statement to the person opposing the application.

(3) Within three months of the date on which a copy of the counter-statement is sent by the registrar to the person opposing the registration, that person shall file such evidence by way of statutory declaration or affidavit as he may consider necessary to adduce in support of his opposition and shall send a copy thereof to the applicant.

(4) If the person opposing the registration files no evidence under paragraph (3) above, he shall, unless the registrar otherwise directs, be deemed to have abandoned his opposition.

(5) If the person opposing the registration files evidence under paragraph (3) above or the registrar otherwise directs under paragraph (4) above, the applicant shall, within three months of the

date on which either a copy of the evidence or a copy of the direction is sent to the applicant, file such evidence by way of statutory declaration or affidavit as he may consider necessary to adduce in support of his application, and shall send a copy thereof to the person opposing the application.

(6) Within three months of the date on which a copy of the applicant's evidence is sent to him, the person opposing the application may file evidence in reply by statutory declaration or affidavit which shall be confined to matters strictly in reply to the applicant's evidence, and shall send a copy thereof to the applicant.

(7) No further evidence may be filed, except that, in relation to any proceedings before him, the registrar may at any time if he thinks fit give leave to either party to file evidence upon such terms as he may think fit.

(8) Upon completion of the evidence the registrar shall, if a hearing is requested by any party to the proceedings, send to the parties notice of a date for the hearing.

Decision of registrar in opposition proceedings

14.—(1) When the registrar has made a decision on the acceptability of an application for registration following the procedure under rule 13, he shall send the applicant and the person opposing the application written notice of it, stating the reasons for his decision.

(2) For the purpose of any appeal against the registrar's decision the date of the decision shall be the date when notice of the decision is sent under paragraph (1) above.

Observations on application to be sent to applicant; s.38(3)

15. The registrar shall send to the applicant a copy of any documents containing observations made under section 38(3).

Publication of registration; s.40

16. On the registration of the trade mark the registrar shall publish the registration, specifying the date upon which the trade mark was entered in the register.

Amendment of application

Amendment of application; s.39

17. A request for an amendment of an application to correct an error or to change the name or address of the applicant or in respect of any amendment requested after publication of the application shall be made on Form TM21.

Amendment of application after publication; s.39

18.—(1) Where, pursuant to section 39, a request is made for amendment of an application which has been published and the amendment affects the representation of the trade mark or the goods or services covered by the application, the amendment or a statement of the effect to the amendment shall also be published.

(2) Notice of opposition to the amendment shall be sent to the registrar on Form TM7 within one month of the date on which the application as amended was published under paragraph (1) above, and shall include a statement of the grounds of objection and, in particular, how the amendments would be contrary to section 39(2).

(3) The provisions of rule 13 shall apply to proceedings relating to the opposition to the amendment of the application as they apply to proceedings relating to opposition to the registration of a trade mark.

Division, merger and series of marks

Division of application; s.41

19.—(1) At any time before registration an applicant may send to the registrar a request on Form TM12 for a division of his application for registration (the original application) into two or more separate applications (divisional applications), indicating for each division the specification of goods or services; each divisional application shall be treated as a separate application for registration with the same filing date as the original application.

(2) Where the request to divide an application is sent after publication of the application, any objections in respect of, or opposition to, the original application shall be taken to apply to each divisional application and shall be proceeded with accordingly.

(3) Upon division of an original application in respect of which notice has been given to the registrar of particulars relating to the grant of a licence, or a security interest or any right in or under it, the notice and the particulars shall be deemed to apply in relation to each of the applications into which the original application has been divided.

Merger of separate applications or registrations; s.41

20.—(1) An applicant who has made separate applications for registration of a mark may, at any time before preparations for the publication of any of the applications have been completed by the Office, request the registrar on Form TM17 to merge the separate applications into a single application.

(2) The registrar shall, if satisfied that all the applications which are the subject of the request for merger—

(a)   are in respect of the same trade mark,

(b)   bear the same date of application, and

(c)   are, at the time of the request, in the name of the same person,

merge them into a single application,

(3) The proprietor of two or more registrations of a trade mark may request the registrar on Form TM17 to merge them into a single registration; and the registrar shall, if satisfied that the registrations are in respect of the same trade mark, merge them into a single registration.

(4) Where any registration of a trade mark to be merged under paragraph (3) above is subject to a disclaimer or limitation, the merged registration shall also be restricted accordingly.

(5) Where any registration of a trade mark to be merged under paragraph (3) above has had registered in relation to it particulars relating to the grant of a licence or a security interest or any right in or under it, or of any memorandum or statement of the effect of a memorandum, the registrar shall enter in the register the same particulars in relation to the merged registration.

(6) The date of registration of the merged registration shall, where the separate registrations bear different dates, be the latest of those dates.

Registration of a series of trade marks; s.41

21.—(1) The proprietor of a series of trade marks may apply to the registrar on Form TM3 for their registration as a series in a single registration and there shall be included in such application a representation of each mark claimed to be in the series; and the registrar shall, if satisfied that the marks constitute a series, accept the application.

(2) At any time before preparations of publication of the application have been completed by the Office, the applicant under paragraph (1) above may request on Form TM12 the division of the application into separate applications in respect of one or more marks in that series and the registrar shall, if he is satisfied that the division requested conforms with section 41(2), divide the application accordingly.

(3) At any time the applicant for registration of a series of trade marks or the proprietor of a registered series of trade marks may request the deletion of a mark in that series, and the registrar shall delete the mark accordingly.

(4) The division of an application into one or more applications under paragraph (2) above shall be subject to the payment of a divisional fee and such application and class fees as are appropriate.

Collective and certification marks

Filing of regulations for collective and certification marks; Schs. 1 & 2

22. Within nine months of the date of the application for the registration of a collective or certification mark, the applicant shall file Form TM35 accompanied by a copy of the regulations governing the use of the mark.

Amendment of regulations of collective and certification marks; Sch. 1, para. 10 and Sch. 2, para. 11

23.—(1) An application for the amendment of the regulations governing the use of a registered collective or certification mark shall be filed on Form TM36.

(2) Where it appears expedient to the registrar that the amended regulations should be made available to the public he shall publish a notice indicating where copies of the amended regulations may be inspected.

(3) Any person may, within three months of the date of publication of the notice under paragraph (2) above, make observations to the registrar on the amendments relating to the matters referred to in paragraph 6(1) of Schedule 1 in relation to a collective mark, or, paragraph 7(1) of Schedule 2 in relation to a certification mark; the registrar shall send a copy thereof to the proprietor.

(4) Any person may, within three months of the date of publication of the notice, file notice on Form TM7 to the registrar of opposition to the amendment, accompanied by a statement of the grounds of opposition, indicating why the amended regulations do not comply with the requirements of paragraph 6(1) of Schedule 1 or, as the case may be, paragraph 7(1) of Schedule 2.

(5) The registrar shall send a copy of the notice and the statement to the proprietor and thereafter the procedure in rule 13(2)–(8) shall apply to the proceedings as they apply to proceedings relating to opposition to an application for registration.

Disclaimers, limitations and alteration or surrender of registered trade mark

Registration subject to disclaimer or limitation; s.13

24. Where the applicant for registration of a trade mark or the proprietor by notice in writing sent to the registrar—
  (a) disclaims any right to the exclusive use of any specified element of the trade mark, or
  (b) agrees that the rights conferred by the registration shall be subject to a specified territorial or other limitation,
the registrar shall make the appropriate entry in the register and publish such disclaimer or limitation.

Alteration of registered trade marks; s.44

25.—(1) The proprietor may request the registrar on Form TM25 for such alteration of his registered mark as is permitted under section 44; and the registrar may require such evidence by statutory declaration or otherwise as to the circumstances in which the application is made.

(2) Where, upon the request of the proprietor, the registrar proposes to allow such alteration, he shall publish the mark as altered.

(3) Any person claiming to be affected by the alteration may within three months of the date of publication of the alteration under paragraph (2) send a notice on Form TM7 to the registrar of opposition to the alteration and shall include a statement of the grounds of opposition; the registrar shall send a copy of the notice and the statement to the proprietor and thereafter the procedure in rule 13(2)–(8) shall apply to the proceedings as they apply to proceedings relating to opposition to an application for registration.

Surrender of registered trade mark; s.45

26.—(1) Subject to paragraph (2) below, the proprietor may surrender a registered trade mark, by sending notice to the registrar—
   (a) on form TM22 in respect of all the goods or services for which it is registered; or
   (b) on form TM23, in respect only of those goods or services specified by him in the notice.
   (2) A notice under paragraph (1) above shall be of no effect unless the proprietor in that notice—
   (a) gives the name and address of any person having a registered interest in the mark, and
   (b) certifies that any such person—
      (i) has been sent not less than three months' notice of the proprietor's intention to surrender the mark, or
     (ii) is not affected or if affected consents thereto.
   (3) The registrar shall, upon the surrender taking effect, make the appropriate entry in the register and publish the same.

Renewal and restoration

Reminder of renewal of registration; s.43

27. At any time not earlier than six months nor later than one month before the expiration of the last registration of a trade mark, the registrar shall (except where renewal has already been effected under rule 28 below) send to the registered proprietor notice of the approaching expiration and inform him at the same time that the registration may be renewed in the manner described in rule 28 below.

Renewal of registration; s.43

28. Renewal of registration shall be effected by filing a request for renewal on Form TM11 at any time within the period of six months ending on the date of the expiration of the registration.

Delayed renewal and removal of registration; s.43

29.—(1) If on the expiration of the last registration of a trade mark, the renewal fee has not been paid, the registrar shall publish that fact; and if, within six months from the date of the expiration of the last registration, the request for renewal is filed on Form TM11 accompanied by the appropriate renewal fee and additional renewal fee, the registrar shall renew the registration without removing the mark from the register.
   (2) Where no request for renewal is filed as aforesaid, the registrar shall, subject to rule 30 below, remove the mark from the register.
   (3) Where, in the case of a mark the registration of which (by reference to the date of application for registration) becomes due for renewal, the mark is registered at any time within six months before the date on which renewal is due, the registration may be renewed by the payment of—
   (a) the renewal fee within six months after the actual date of registration; or
   (b) the renewal fee and additional renewal fee within the period commencing on the date six months after the actual date of registration (that is to say, at the end of the period referred to in paragraph (a)) and ending on the date six months after the due date of renewal;
and, where the fees referred to in paragraph (b) are not paid within the period specified in that paragraph the registrar shall, subject to rule 30 below, remove the mark from the register.
   (4) Where, in the case of a mark the registration of which (by reference to the date of application for registration) becomes due for renewal, the mark is registered after the date of renewal, the registration may be renewed by the payment of the renewal fee within six months of the actual date of registration; and where the renewal fee is not paid within that period the registrar shall, subject to rule 30 below, remove the mark from the register.

(5) The removal of the registration of a trade mark shall be published.

Restoration of registration; s.43

30.—(1) Where the registrar has removed the mark from the register for failure to renew its registration in accordance with rule 29 above, he may, upon a request filed on Form TM13 within six months of the date of the removal of the mark accompanied by the appropriate renewal fee and appropriate restoration fee, restore the mark to the register and renew its registration if, having regard to the circumstances of the failure to renew, he is satisfied that it is just to do so.
(2) The restoration of the registration shall be published, with the date of restoration shown.

Revocation, invalidation and rectification

Procedure on application for revocation, declaration of invalidity and rectification of the register; ss.46, 47 & 64

31.—(1) An application to the registrar for revocation under section 46 or declaration of invalidity under section 47 of the registration of a trade mark or for the rectification of an error or omission in the register under section 64 shall be made on Form TM26 together with a statement of the grounds on which the application is made.
(2) Where any application is made under paragraph (1) by a person other than the proprietor of the registered trade mark, the registrar shall send a copy of the application and its statement to the proprietor.
(3) Within three months of the date on which the registrar sends a copy of the application and the statement to the proprietor, the proprietor may file a counter-statement together with Form TM8 and the registrar shall send a copy thereof to the applicant:
Provided that where an application for revocation is based on the ground of non-use under section 46(1)(a) or (b), the proprietor shall file (within the period allowed for the filing of any counter-statement) evidence of the use by him of the mark; and if he fails so to file evidence the registrar may treat his opposition to the application as having been withdrawn.
(4) Subject to paragraph (2) above and paragraphs (6) and (7) below, the provisions of rule 13 shall apply to proceedings relating to the application as they apply to opposition proceedings for the registration of a trade mark, save that, in the case of an application for revocation on the grounds of non-use under section 46(1)(a) or (b), the application shall be granted where no counter-statement is filed.
(5) Any person, other than the registered proprietor, claiming to have an interest in proceedings on an application under this rule may file an application to the registrar on Form TM27 for leave to intervene, stating the nature of his interest and the registrar may, after hearing the parties concerned if so required, refuse such leave or grant leave upon such terms or conditions (including any undertaking as to costs) as he thinks fit.
(6) Any person granted leave to intervene (the intervener) shall, subject to the terms and conditions imposed in respect of the intervention, be treated as a party for the purposes of the application of the provisions of rule 13 to the proceedings on an application under this rule.
(7) When the registrar has made a decision on the application following any opposition, intervention or proceedings held in accordance with this rule, he shall send the applicant, the person opposing the application and the intervener (if any) written notice of it, stating the reasons for his decision; and for the purposes of any appeal against the registrar's decision the date when the notice of the decision is sent shall be taken to be the date of the decision.

The register

Form of register; s.63(1)

32. The register required to be maintained by the registrar under section 63(1) need not be kept in documentary form.

Entry in register of particulars of registered trade marks; s.63(2)

33. In addition to the entries in the register of registered trade marks required to be made by section 63(2)(a), there shall be entered in the register in respect of each trade mark registered therein the following particulars—

- (a) the date of registration as determined in accordance with section 40(3) (that is to say, the date of the filing of the application for registration);
- (b) the actual date of registration (that is to say, the date of the entry in the register);
- (c) the priority date (if any) to be accorded pursuant to a claim to a right to priority made under section 35 or 36;
- (d) the name and address of the proprietor;
- (e) the address for service (if any) as furnished pursuant to rule 10 above;
- (f) any disclaimer or limitation of rights under section 13(1)(a) or (b);
- (g) any memorandum or statement of the effect of any memorandum relating to a trade mark of which the registrar has been notified on Form TM24;
- (h) the goods or services in respect of which the mark is registered;
- (i) where the mark is a collective or certification mark, that fact; and
- (j) where the mark is registered pursuant to section 5(5) with the consent of the proprietor of an earlier trade mark or other earlier right, that fact.

Entry in register of particulars of registrable transactions; s.25

34. Upon application made to the registrar by such person as is mentioned in section 25(1)(a) or (b) there shall be entered in the register the following particulars of registrable transactions, that is to say—

- (a) in the case of an assignment of a registered trade mark or any right in it—
    - (i) the name and address of the assignee,
    - (ii) the date of the assignment, and
    - (iii) where the assignment is in respect of any right in the mark, a description of the right assigned;
- (b) in the case of the grant of a licence under a registered trade mark—
    - (i) the name and address of the licensee,
    - (ii) where the licence is an exclusive licence, that fact,
    - (iii) where the licence is limited, a description of the limitation, and
    - (iv) the duration of the licence if the same is or is ascertainable as a definite period;
- (c) in the case of the grant of any security interest over a registered trade mark or any right in or under it—
    - (i) the name and address of the grantee,
    - (ii) the nature of the interest (whether fixed of floating), and
    - (iii) the extent of the security and the right in or under the mark secured;
- (d) in the case of the making by personal representatives of an assent in relation to a registered trade mark or any right in or under it—
    - (i) the name and address of the person in whom the mark or any right in or under it vests by virtue of the assent, and
    - (ii) the date of the assent; and
- (e) in the case of a court or other competent authority transferring a registered trade mark or any right in or under it—
    - (i) the name and address of the transferee
    - (ii) the date of the order, and
    - (iii) where the transfer is in respect of a right in the mark, a description of the right transferred;

and, in each case, there shall be entered the date on which the entry is made.

Application to register or give notice of transactions; ss.25 & 27(3)

35.—(1) An application to register particulars of a transaction to which section 25 applies or to give notice to the registrar of particulars of a transaction to which section 27(3) applies shall be made, subject to paragraph (2) below,

(a) relating to an assignment or transaction other than a transaction referred to in sub-paragraphs (b) to (d) below, on Form TM16;

(b) relating to a grant of a licence, on Form TM50;

(c) relating to an amendment to, or termination of a licence, on Form TM51;

(d) relating to the grant, amendment or termination of any security interest, on Form TM24; and

(e) relating to the making by personal representatives of an assent or to an order of a court or other competent authority, on Form TM24.

(2) An application under paragraph (1) above shall—

(a) where the transaction is an assignment, be signed by or on behalf of the parties to the assignment;

(b) where the transaction falls within sub-paragraphs (b), (c) or (d) or paragraph (1) above, be signed by or on behalf of the grantor of the licence or security interest;

or be accompanied by such documentary evidence as suffices to establish the transaction.

(3) Where the transaction is effected by an instrument chargeable with duty, the application shall be subject to the registrar being satisfied that the instrument has been duly stamped.

(4) Where an application to give notice to the registrar has been made of particulars relating to an application for registration of a trade mark, upon registration of the trade mark, the registrar shall enter those particulars in the register.

Public inspection of register; s.63(3)

36.—(1) The register shall be open for public inspection at the Office during the hours of business of the Office as published in accordance with rule 64 below.

(2) Where any portion of the register is kept otherwise than in documentary form, the right of inspection is a right to inspect the material on the register.

Supply of certified copies etc; s.63(3)

37. The registrar shall supply a certified copy or extract or uncertified copy or extract, as requested on Form TM31R, of any entry in the register.

Request for change of name or address in register; s.64(4)

38.—(1) The registrar shall, on a request made on Form TM21 by the proprietor of a registered trade mark or a licensee or any person having an interest in or charge on a registered trade mark which has been registered under rule 34, enter any change in his name or address as recorded in the register.

(2) The registrar may at any time, on a request made on Form TM33 by any person who has furnished an address for service under rule 10 above, if the address is recorded in the register, change it.

Removal of matter from register: s.64(5)

39.—(1) Where it appears to the registrar that any matter in the register has ceased to have effect, before removing it from the register—

(a) he may, where he considers it appropriate, publish his intention to remove that matter, and

(b) where any person appears to him to be affected by the removal, he shall send notice of his intention to that person.

(2) Within three months of the date on which his intention to remove the matter is published, or notice of his intention is sent, as the case may be—

(a) any person may file notice of opposition to the removal on form TM7; and
(b) the person to whom a notice is sent under paragraph (1)(b) above may file, in writing—
    (i)   his objections, if any, to the removal, or
    (ii) a request to have his objections heard orally;

and where such opposition or objections are made, rule 47 shall apply.

(3) If the registrar is satisfied after considering any objections or oppositions to the removal that the matter has not ceased to have effect, he shall not remove it.

(4) Where there has been no response to the registrar's notice he may remove the matter; where representations objecting to the removal of the entry have been made((whether in writing or orally) the registrar may, if he is of the view after considering the objections that the entry or any part thereof has ceased to have effect, remove it or, as appropriate, the part thereof.

Change of classification

Change of classification; ss.65(2) & 76(1)

40.—(1) Subject to section 65(3), the registrar may—
(a) in order to reclassify the specification of a registered trade mark founded on Schedule 3 to one founded on Schedule 4, or
(b) consequent upon an amendment of the International Classification of Goods and Services referred to in rule 7(2) above,
make such amendments to entries on the register as he considers necessary for the purposes of reclassifying the specification of the registered trade mark.

(2) Before making any amendment to the register under paragraph (1) above the registrar shall give the proprietor of the mark written notice of his proposals for amendment and shall at the same time advise him that—
(a) he may make written objections to the proposals, within three months of the date of the notice, stating the grounds of his objections, and
(b) if no written objections are received within the period specified the registrar will publish the proposals and he will not be entitled to make any objections thereto upon such publication.

(3) If the proprietor makes no written objections within the period specified in paragraph (2)(a) above or at any time before the expiration of that period gives the registrar written notice of his intention not to make any objections, the registrar shall as soon as practicable after the expiration of that period or upon receipt of the notice publish the proposals.

(4) Where the proprietor makes written objections within the period specified in paragraph (2)(a) above, the registrar shall, as soon as practicable after he has considered the objections, publish the proposals or, where he has amended the proposals, publish the proposals as amended; and his decision shall be final and not subject to appeal.

Opposition to proposals; ss.65(3) & 76(1)

41.—(1) Notice of any opposition shall be filed on Form TM7 within three months of the date of publication of the proposals under rule 40 above and there shall be stated in the notice the grounds of opposition and, in particular, how the proposed amendments would be contrary to section 65(3).

(2) The registrar may require or admit evidence directed to the questions in issue and if so requested by any person opposing the proposal give that person the opportunity to be heard thereon before deciding the matter.

(3) If no notice of opposition under paragraph (1) above is filed within the time specified, or where any opposition has been determined, the registrar shall make the amendments as proposed and shall enter in the register the date when they were made; and his decision shall be final and not subject to appeal.

Request for information, inspection of documents and confidentiality

Request for information; s.67(1)

42. A request for information relating to an application for registration or to a registered trade mark shall be made on Form TM31C.

Information available before publication; s.67(2)

43. Before publication of an application for registration the registrar shall make available for inspection by the public the application and any amendments made to it and any particulars contained in a notice given to the registrar under rule 35.

Inspection of documents; ss.67 & 76(1)

44.—(1) Subject to paragraphs (2) and (3) below, the registrar shall permit all documents filed or kept at the Office in relation to a registered mark or, where an application for the registration of a trade mark has been published, in relation to that application, to be inspected.

(2) The registrar shall not be obliged to permit the inspection of any such document as is mentioned in paragraph (1) above until he has completed any procedure, or the stage in the procedure which is relevant to the document in question, which he is required or permitted to carry out under the Act or these Rules.

(3) The right of inspection under paragraph (1) does not apply to—

(a) any document until fourteen days after it has been filed at the Office;

(b) any document prepared in the Office solely for use therein;

(c) any document sent to the Office, whether at its request or otherwise, for inspection and subsequent return to the sender;

(d) any request for information under rule 42 above;

(e) any document issued by the Office which the registrar considers should be treated as confidential;

(f) any document in respect of which the registrar issues directions under rule 45 below that it be treated as confidential.

(4) Nothing in paragraph (1) shall be construed as imposing on the registrar any duty of making available for public inspection—

(a) any document or part of a document which in his opinion disparages any person in a way likely to damage him; or

(b) any document filed with or sent to the Office before 31st October 1994.

(5) No appeal shall lie from a decision of the registrar under paragraph (4) above not to make any document or part of a document available for public inspection.

Confidential documents

45.—(1) Where a document other than a form required by the registrar and published in accordance with rule 3 above is filed at the Office and the person filing it requests, at the time of filing or within fourteen days of the filing, that it or a specified part of it be treated as confidential, giving his reasons, the registrar may direct that it or part of it, as the case may be, be treated as confidential, and the document shall not be open to public inspection while the matter is being determined by the registrar.

(2) Where such direction has been given and not withdrawn, nothing in this rule shall be taken to authorise or require any person to be allowed to inspect the document or part of it to which the direction relates except by leave of the registrar.

(3) The registrar shall not withdraw any direction given under this rule without prior consultation with the person at whose request the direction was given, unless the registrar is satisfied that such prior consultation is not reasonably practical.

(4) The registrar may where he considers that any document issued by the Office should be treated as confidential so direct, and upon such direction that document shall not be open to public inspection except by leave of the registrar.

(5) Where a direction is given under this rule for a document to be treated as confidential a record of the fact shall be filed with the document.

Agents

Proof of authorisation of agent may be required; s.82

46.—(1) Where an agent has been authorised under section 82, the registrar may in any particular case require the personal signature or presence of the agent or the person authorising him to act as agent.

(2) Where after a person has become a party to proceedings before the registrar, he appoints an agent for the first time or appoints one agent in substitution for another, the newly appointed agent shall file Form TM33, and any act required or authorised by the Act in connection with the registration of a trade mark or any procedure relating to a trade mark may not be done by or to the newly appointed agent until on or after the date on which he files that form.

(3) The registrar may by notice in writing sent to an agent require him to produce evidence of his authority.

Registrar may refuse to deal with certain agents; s.88

47. The registrar may refuse to recognise as agent in respect of any business under the Act—
   (a) a person who has been convicted of an offence under section 84;
   (b) an individual whose name has been erased from and not restored to, or who is suspended from, the register of trade mark agents on the ground of misconduct;
   (c) a person who is found by the Secretary of State to have been guilty of such conduct as would, in the case of an individual registered in that register, render him liable to have his name erased from it on the ground of misconduct;
   (d) a partnership or body corporate of which one of the partners or directors is a person whom the registrar could refuse to recognise under paragraph (a), (b) or (c) above.

Decision of registrar, evidence and costs

Decisions of registrar to be taken after hearing

48.—(1) Without prejudice to any provisions of the Act or these Rules requiring the registrar to hear any party to proceedings under the Act or these Rules, or to give such party an opportunity to be heard, the registrar shall, before taking any decision on any matter under the Act or these Rules which is or may be adverse to any party to any proceedings before him, give that party an opportunity to be heard.

(2) The registrar shall give that party at least fourteen days' notice of the time when he may be heard unless that party consents to shorter notice.

Evidence in proceedings before registrar; s.69

49.—(1) Where under these Rules evidence may be admitted by the registrar in any proceedings before him, it shall be by the filing of a statutory declaration or affidavit.

(2) The registrar may in any particular case take oral evidence in lieu of or in addition to such evidence and shall, unless he otherwise directs, allow any witness to be cross-examined on his statutory declaration, affidavit or oral evidence.

Making and subscription of statutory declaration or affidavit

50.—(1) Any statutory declaration or affidavit filed under the Act or these Rules shall be made and subscribed as follows—
   (a) in the United Kingdom, before any justice of the peace or any commissioner or other officer authorised by law in any part of the United Kingdom to administer an oath for the purpose of any legal proceedings;

(b) in any other part of Her Majesty's dominions or in the Republic of Ireland, before any court, judge, justice of the peace or any officer authorised by law to administer an oath there for the purpose of any legal proceedings; and

(c) elsewhere, before a commissioner of oaths, notary public, judge or magistrate.

(2) Any document purporting to have affixed, impressed or subscribed thereto or thereon the seal or signature of any person authorised by paragraph (1) above to take a declaration may be admitted by the registrar without proof of the genuineness of the seal or signature, or of the official character of the person or his authority to take the declaration.

Registrar's power to require documents, information or evidence

51. At any stage of any proceedings before the registrar, he may direct that such documents, information or evidence as he may reasonably require shall be filed within such period as he may specify.

Registrar to have power of an official referee; s.69

52.—(1) The registrar shall in relation to the examination of witnesses on oath and the discovery and production of documents have all the powers of an official referee of the Supreme Court.

(2) The rules applicable to the attendance of witnesses before such a referee shall apply in relation to the attendance of witnesses in proceedings before the registrar.

Hearings before registrar to be in public

53.—(1) The hearing before the registrar of any dispute between two or more parties relating to any matter in connection with an application for the registration of a mark or a registered mark shall be in public unless the registrar, after consultation with those parties who appear in person or are represented at the hearing, otherwise directs.

(2) Nothing in this rule shall prevent a member of the Council on Tribunals or of its Scottish Committee from attending a hearing in his capacity as such.

Costs of proceedings; s.68

54. The registrar may, in any proceedings before him under the Act or these Rules, by order award to any party such costs as he may consider reasonable, and direct how and by what parties they are to be paid.

Security for costs; s.68

55.—(1) The registrar may require any person who is a party in any proceedings before him under the Act or these Rules to give security for costs in relation to those proceedings; and he may require security for the costs of any appeal from his decision.

(2) In default of such security being given, the registrar, in the case of the proceedings before him, or, in the case of an appeal, the person appointed under section 76 may treat the party in default as having withdrawn his application, opposition, objection or intervention, as the case may be.

Decision of registrar

56.—(1) When, in any proceedings before him, the registrar has made a decision following a hearing or, if a hearing has not been requested, after considering any submission in writing, he shall send notice of his decision in writing to each party to the proceedings, and for the purpose of any appeal against the registrar's decision, subject to paragraph (2) below, the date of the decision shall be the date when the notice is sent.

(2) Where a statement of the reasons for the decision is not included in the notice sent under paragraph (1) above, any party may, within one month of the date on which the notice was sent to

him, request the registrar on Form TM5 to send him a statement of the reasons for the decision and upon such request the registrar shall send such a statement; and the date on which that statement is sent shall be deemed to be the date of the registrar's decision for the purpose of any appeal against it.

Appeals

Appeal to person appointed; s.76

57.—(1) Notice of appeal to the person appointed under section 76 shall be sent to the registrar within one month of the date of the registrar's decision which is the subject of the appeal accompanied by a statement in writing of the appellant's grounds of appeal and of his case in support of the appeal.

(2) The registrar shall send the notice and the statement to the person appointed.

(3) Where any person other than the appellant was a party to the proceedings before the registrar in which the decision appealed against was made, the registrar shall send to that person a copy of the notice and the statement.

Determination whether appeal should be referred to court; s.76(3)

58.—(1) Within one month of the date on which the notice of appeal is sent by the registrar under rule 57(3) above;

(a) the registrar, or

(b) any person who was a party to the proceedings in which the decision appealed against was made,

may request that the person appointed refer the appeal to the court.

(2) Where the registrar requests that the appeal be referred to the court, he shall send a copy of the request to each party to the proceedings.

(3) A request under paragraph (1)(b) above shall be sent to the registrar; the registrar shall send it to the person appointed and shall send a copy of the request to any other party to the proceedings.

(4) Within one month of the date on which a copy of a request is sent by the registrar under paragraph (2) or (3) above, the person to whom it is sent may make representations as to whether the appeal should be referred to the court.

(5) In any case where, it appears to the person appointed that a point of general legal importance is involved in the appeal, he shall send to the registrar and to every party to the proceedings in which the decision appealed against was made, notice thereof.

(6) Within one month of the date on which a notice is sent under paragraph (5) above, the person to whom it was sent may make representations as to whether the appeal should be referred to the court.

Hearing of appeal; s.76(4)

59.—(1)Where the person appointed does not refer the appeal to the court, he shall send notice of the time and place appointed for the hearing of the appeal—

(a) where no person other than the appellant was a party to the proceedings in which the decision appealed against was made, to the registrar and to the appellant, and

(b) in any other case, to the registrar and to each person who was a party to those proceedings.

(2) The provisions of rule 48(2) and rules 49 to 55 shall apply to the person appointed and to proceedings before the person appointed as they apply to the registrar and to proceedings before the registrar.

(3) The person appointed shall send a copy of his decision, with a statement of his reasons therefor, to the registrar and to each person who was a party to the proceedings before him.

Correction of irregularities, calculation and extension of time

Correction of irregularities of procedure

60.—(1) Any irregularities in procedure in or before the Office or the registrar may be rectified, subject to paragraph (2) below, on such terms as he may direct.

(2) In the case of an irregularity or prospective irregularity—

(a) which consists of a failure to comply with any limitation as to times or periods specified in the Act, these Rules or the old law as that law continues to apply and which has occurred or appears to the registrar as likely to occur in the absence of a direction under this rule, and

(b) which is attributable wholly or in part to an error, default or omission on the part of the Office or the registrar and which it appears to him should be rectified.

he may direct that the time or period in question shall be altered in such manner as he may specify.

(3) Paragraph (2) is without prejudice to the registrar's power to extend any time or periods under rule 62 below.

Calculation of times and periods

61.—(1) Where, on any day, there is—

(a) a general interruption or subsequent dislocation in the postal services of the United Kingdom, or

(b) an event or circumstances causing an interruption in the normal operation of the Office,

the registrar may certify the day as being one on which there is an "interruption" and, where any period of time specified in the Act or these Rules for the giving, making or filing of any notice, application or other document expires on a day so certified the period shall be extended to the first day next following (not being an excluded day) which is not so certified.

(2) Any certificate of the registrar given pursuant to this rule shall be posted in the Office.

(3) If in any particular case the registrar is satisfied that the failure to give, make or file any notice, application or other document within any period of time specified in the Act or these Rules for such giving, making or filing was wholly or mainly attributable to a failure or undue delay in the postal services in the United Kingdom, the registrar may, if he thinks fit, extend the period so that it ends on the day of the receipt by the addressee of the notice, application or other document (or, if the day of such receipt is an excluded day, on the first following day which is not an excluded day), upon such notice to other parties and upon such terms as he may direct.

(4) In this rule "excluded day" means a day which is not a business day of the Office under the registrar's direction pursuant to section 80, as published in accordance with rule 64 below.

Alteration of time limits

62.—(1) The time or periods—

(a) prescribed by these Rules, other than the times or periods prescribed by the rules mentioned in paragraph (3) below, or

(b) specified by the registrar for doing any act or taking any proceedings,

may, at the request of the person or party concerned, be extended by the registrar as he thinks fit, upon such notice to any other person or party affected and upon such terms as he may direct.

(2) A request for the extension of a period prescribed by these Rules which is filed after the application has been published under rule 12 above shall be on Form TM9 and shall in any other case be on that form if the registrar so directs.

(3) The rules excepted from paragraph (1) above are rule 10(6) (failure to file address for service), rule 11 (deficiencies in application), rule 13(1) (time for filing opposition), rule 13(2) (time for filing counter-statement), rule 29 (delayed renewal) and rule 30 (restoration of registration).

(4) Subject to paragraph (5) below, a request for extension under paragraph (1) above shall be made before the time or period in question has expired.

(5) Where the request for extension is made after the time or period has expired, the registrar may, at his discretion, extend the period or time if he is satisfied with the explanation for the delay

in requesting the extension and it appears to him that any extension would not disadvantage any other person or party affected by it.

(6) Where the period within which any party to any proceedings before the registrar may file evidence under these Rules is to begin upon the expiry of any period in which any other party may file evidence and that other party notifies the registrar that he does not wish to file any, or any further, evidence the registrar may direct that the period within which the first mentioned party may file evidence shall begin on such date as may be specified in the direction and shall notify all parties to the dispute of that date.

Filing of documents, hours of business, Trade Marks Journal and translations

Filing of documents by electronic means

63. The registrar may, at his discretion, permit as an alternative to the sending by post or delivery of the application, notice or other document in legible form the filing of the application, notice or other document by electronic means subject to such terms or conditions as he may specify either generally by published notice or in any particular case by written notice to the person desiring to file any such documents by such means.

Directions on hours of business; s.80

64. Any direction given by the registrar under section 80 specifying the hours of business of the Office and business days of the Office shall be published (see the special edition of the Trade Marks Journal dated 31st October 1994) and posted in the Office.

Trade Marks Journal; s.81

65. The registrar shall publish a journal, entitled "The Trade Marks Journal", containing particulars of any application for the registration of a trade mark (including a representation of the mark), such information as is required to be published under these Rules and such other information as the registrar thinks fit.

Translations

66.—(1)Where any document or part thereof which is in a language other than English is filed or sent to the registrar in pursuance of the Act or these Rules, the registrar may require that there be furnished a translation into English of the document or that part verified to the satisfaction of the registrar as corresponding to the original text.

(2) The registrar may refuse to accept any translation which is in his opinion inaccurate and thereupon another translation of the document in question verified as aforesaid shall be furnished.

Transitional provisions and revocations

Pending applications for registration; Sch. 3, para. 10(2)

67. Where an application for registration of a mark made under the old law is advertised on or after 31st October 1994, the period within which notice of opposition may be filed shall be three months from the date of advertisement, and such period shall not be extendible.

Form for conversions of pending application; Sch. 3, para. 11(2)

68. A notice to the registrar under paragraph 11(2) of Schedule 3 to the Act, claiming to have the registrability of the mark determined in accordance with the provisions of the Act, shall be in the form set out in Schedule 2 to these Rules.

Revocation of previous Rules

69.—(1) The rules specified in Schedule 1 are hereby revoked.

(2) Except as provided by rule 67 above, where—

(a) immediately before these Rules come into force, any time or period prescribed by the Rules hereby revoked has effect in relation to any act or proceeding and has not expired, and

(b) the corresponding time or period prescribed by these Rules would have expired or would expire earlier,

the time or period prescribed by those Rules and not by these Rules shall apply to that act or proceeding.

Ian Taylor
Parliamentary Under Secretary of State for Trade and Technology
Department of Trade and Industry

5th October 1994

Rule 69

SCHEDULE I
REVOCATIONS

Rules revoked	Reference
The Trade Marks and Service Marks Rules 1986	S.I. 1986/1319
The Trade Marks and Service Marks (Amendment) Rules 1988	S.I. 1988/1112
The Trade Marks and Service Marks (Amendment) Rules 1989	S.I. 1989/1117
The Trade Marks and Service Marks (Amendment) Rules 1990	S.I. 1990/1459
The Trade Marks and Service Marks (Amendment) (No. 2) Rules 1990	S.I. 1990/1799
The Trade Marks and Service Marks (Amendment) Rules 1991	S.I. 1991/1431
The Trade Marks and Service Marks (Amendment) Rules 1994	S.I. 1994/2549

Rule 68

[Schedule 2 provided for exercise of the option under Sched. 3 para. 11 of the Act]

Rule 7(1)

SCHEDULE 3
CLASSIFICATION OF GOODS (PRE-1938)

Class 1 Chemical substances used in manufactures, photography, or philosophical research, and anti-corrosives.

Class 2 Chemical substances used for agricultural, horticultural, veterinary and sanitary purposes.

Class 3 Chemical substances prepared for use in medicine and pharmacy.

Class 4 Raw, or partly prepared, vegetable, animal, and mineral substances used in manufactures, not included in other Classes.

Class 5 Unwrought and partly wrought metals used in manufacture.

Class 6 Machinery of all kinds, and parts of machinery, except agricultural and horticultural machines and their parts included in Class 7.

Class 7 Agricultural and horticultural machinery, and parts of such machinery.

Class 8 Philosophical instruments, scientific instruments, and apparatus for useful purposes; instruments and apparatus for teaching.

Class 9 Musical instruments.

Class 10 Horological instruments.

Class 11 Instruments, apparatus, and contrivances, not medicated, for surgical or curative purposes, or in relation to the health of men or animals.

Class 12 Cutlery and edge tools.

Class 13 Metal goods, not included in other Classes.

Class 14 Goods of precious metals and jewellery, and imitations of such goods and jewellery.

Class 15 Glass.

Class 16 Porcelain and earthenware.

Class 17 Manufactures from mineral and other substances for building or decoration.

Class 18 Engineering, architectural, and building contrivances.

Class 19 Arms, ammunition, and stores, not included in Class 20.

Class 20 Explosive substances.

Class 21 Naval architectural contrivances and naval equipments not included in other Classes.

Class 22 Carriages.

Class 23 (a) Cotton yarn; (b) Sewing cotton.

Class 24 Cotton piece goods.

Class 25 Cotton goods not included in other Classes.

Class 26 Linen and hemp yarn and thread.

Class 27 Linen and hemp piece goods.

Class 28 Linen and hemp goods not included in other Classes.

Class 29 Jute yarns and tissues, and other articles made of jute, not included in other Classes.

Class 30 Silk, spun, thrown, or sewing.

Class 31 Silk piece goods.

Class 32 Silk goods not included in other Classes.

Class 33 Yarns of wool, worsted, or hair.

Class 34 Cloths and stuffs of wool, worsted, or hair.

Class 35 Woollen and worsted and hair goods, not included in other Classes.

Class 36 Carpets, floor-cloth, and oil-cloth.

Class 37 Leather, skins unwrought and wrought, and articles made of leather not included in other Classes.

Class 38 Articles of clothing.

Class 39 Paper (except paper hangings), stationery, and bookbinding.

Class 40 Goods manufactured from india-rubber and gutta-percha not included in other Classes.

Class 41 Furniture and upholstery.

Class 42 Substances used as food or as ingredients in food.

Class 43 Fermented liquors and spirits.

Class 44 Mineral and aerated waters, natural and artificial, including ginger beer.

Class 45 Tobacco, whether manufactured or unmanufactured.

Class 46 Seeds for agricultural and horticultural purposes.

Class 47 Candles, common soap, detergents; illuminating, heating, or lubricating oils; matches; and starch, blue, and other preparations for laundry purposes.

Class 48 Perfumery (including toilet articles, preparations for the teeth and hair, and perfumed soap).

Class 49 Games of all kinds and sporting articles not included in other Classes.

Class 50 Miscellaneous:—

(1) Goods manufactured from ivory, bone or wood, not included in other Classes.

(2) Goods manufactured from straw or grass not included in other Classes.

(3) Goods manufactured from animal and vegetable substances, not included in other Classes.

(4) Tobacco pipes.

(5) Umbrellas, walking sticks, brushes and combs for the hair.

(6) Furniture cream, plate powder.

(7) Tarpaulins, tents, rick-cloths, rope (jute or hemp), twine.

(8) Buttons of all kinds other than of precious metal or imitations thereof.

(9) Packing and hose.

(10) Other goods not included in the foregoing Classes.

Rule 7(2)

SCHEDULE 4
CLASSIFICATION OF GOODS AND SERVICES

Goods

Class 1 Chemicals used in industry, science and photography, as well as in agriculture, horticulture and forestry; unprocessed artificial resins, unprocessed plastics; manures; fire extinguishing compositions, tempering and soldering preparations; chemical substances for preserving foodstuffs; tanning substances; adhesives used in industry.

Class 2 Paints, varnishes, lacquers; preservatives against rust and against deterioration of wood; colorants; mordants; raw natural resins; metals in foil and powder form for painters, decorators, printers and artists.

Class 3 Bleaching preparations and other substances for laundry use; cleaning, polishing, scouring and abrasive preparations; soaps; perfumery, essential oils, cosmetics, hair lotions; dentifrices.

Class 4 Industrial oils and greases; lubricants; dust absorbing, wetting and binding compositions; fuels (including motor spirit) and illuminants; candles, wicks.

Class 5 Pharmaceutical, veterinary and sanitary preparations; dietetic substances adapted for medical use, food for babies; plasters, materials for dressings; material for stopping teeth, dental wax; disinfectants; preparations for destroying vermin; fungicides, herbicides.

Class 6 Common metals and their alloys; metal building materials; transportable buildings of metal; materials of metal for railway tracks; non-electric cables and wires of common metal; ironmongery, small items of metal hardware; pipes and tubes of metal; safes; goods of common metal not included in other classes; ores.

Class 7 Machines and machine tools; motors and engines (except for land vehicles); machine coupling and transmission components (except for land vehicles); agricultural implements; incubators for eggs.

Class 8 Hand tools and implements (hand operated); cutlery; side arms; razors.

Class 9 Scientific, nautical, surveying, electric, photographic, cinematographic, optical, weighing, measuring, signalling, checking (supervision), life-saving and teaching apparatus and instruments; apparatus for recording, transmission or reproduction of sound or images; magnetic data carriers, recording discs; automatic vending machines and mechanisms for coin-operated apparatus; cash registers, calculating machines, data processing equipment and computers; fire-extinguishing apparatus.

Class 10 Surgical, medical, dental and veterinary apparatus and instruments, artificial limbs, eyes and teeth; orthopaedic articles; suture materials.

Class 11 Apparatus for lighting, heating, steam generating, cooking, refrigerating, drying, ventilating, water supply and sanitary purposes.

Class 12 Vehicles; apparatus for locomotion by land, air or water.

Class 13 Firearms; ammunition and projectiles ; explosives; fireworks.

Class 14 Precious metals and their alloys and goods in precious metals or coated therewith, not included in other classes; jewellery, precious stones; horological and chronometric instruments.

Class 15 Musical instruments.

Class 16 Paper, cardboard and goods made from these materials, not included in other classes; printed matter; bookbinding material; photographs; stationery; adhesives for stationery or household purposes; artists' materials; paint brushes; typewriters and office requisites (except furniture); instructional and teaching material (except apparatus); plastic materials for packaging (not included in other classes); playing cards; printers' type; printing blocks.

Class 17 Rubber, gutta-percha, gum, asbestos, mica and goods made from these materials and not included in other classes; plastics in extruded form for use in manufacture; packing, stopping and insulating materials, flexible pipes, not of metal.

Class 18 Leather and imitations of leather, and goods made of these materials and not included in other classes; animal skins, hides; trunks and travelling bags; umbrellas, parasols and walking sticks; whips, harness and saddlery.

Class 19 Building materials (non-metallic); non-metallic rigid pipes for building; asphalt, pitch and bitumen, non-metallic transportable buildings; monuments, not of metal.

Class 20 Furniture, mirrors, picture frames; goods (not included in other classes) of wood, cork, reed, cane wicker, horn, bone, ivory, whalebone, shell, amber, mother-of-pearl, meerschaum and substitutes for all these materials, or of plastics.

Class 21 Household or kitchen utensils and containers (not of precious metal or coated therewith); combs and sponges; brushes (except paint brushes); brush-making materials; articles for cleaning purposes; steelwool; unworked or semi-worked glass (except glass used in building); (glassware, porcelain and earthenware not included in other classes.

Class 22 Ropes, string, nets, tents, awnings, tarpaulins, sails, sacks and bags (not included in other classes); padding and stuffing materials (except of rubber or plastics); raw fibrous textile materials.

Class 23 Yarns and threads, for textile use.

Class 24 Textiles and textile goods, not included in other classes; bed and table covers.

Class 25 Clothing, footwear, headgear.

Class 26 Lace and embroidery, ribbons and braid; buttons, hooks and eyes, pins and needles; artificial flowers.

Class 27 Carpets, rugs, mats and matting, linoleum and other materials for covering existing floors; wall hangings (non-textile).

Class 28 Games and playthings; gymnastic and sporting articles not included in other classes; decorations for Christmas trees.

Class 29 Meat, fish, poultry and game; meat extracts; preserved, dried and cooked fruits and vegetables; jellies, jams, fruit sauces; eggs, milk and milk products; edible oils and fats.

Class 30 Coffee, tea, cocoa, sugar, rice, tapioca, sago, artifical coffee; flour and preparations made from cereals, bread, pastry and confectionery, ices; honey, treacle; yeast, baking-powder; salt, mustard; vinegar, sauces (condiments); spices; ice.

Class 31 Agricultural, horticultural and forestry products and grains not included in other classes; live animals; fresh fruits and vegetables; seeds, natural plants and flowers; foodstuffs for animals, malt.

Class 32 Beers; mineral and aerated waters and other non-alcoholic drinks; fruit drinks and fruit juices; syrups and other preparations for making beverages.

Class 33 Alcoholic beverages (except beers).

Class 34 Tobacco; smokers' articles; matches.

Services

Class 35 Advertising; business management; business administration; office functions.

Class 36 Insurance; financial affairs; monetary affairs; real estate affairs.

Class 37 Building construction; repair; installation services.

Class 38 Telecommunications.

Class 39 Transport; packaging and storage of goods; travel arrangement.

Class 40 Treatment of materials.

Class 41 Education; providing of training; entertainment; sporting and cultural activities.

Class 42 Providing of food and drink; temporary accommodation; medical, hygienic and beauty care; veterinary and agricultural services; legal services; scientific and industrial research; computer programming; services that cannot be placed in other classes.

EXPLANATORY NOTE

This note is not part of the rules

These Rules revoke and replace the Trade Marks and Service Marks Rules 1986 (S.I. 1986/1319, as amended). They re-enact, with modifications and amendments of a drafting nature, several provisions of the 1986 Rules and make several changes of substance in order to give effect to the provisions of the Trade Marks Act 1994 ("the Act").

The changes of substance are as follows—

    (a) forms that are required by the registrar to be used for the purposes of registration and of any proceedings before him are not prescribed under these Rules; they are, however, required to be published in the Trade Marks Journal and user may, as before, satisfy the requirement to file on a form by filing either a replica of the form or a form acceptable to the registrar (rule 3);

    (b) a single application may relate to goods and services classified in more than one class of the classification (rule 8);

    (c) the requirements for providing an address for service have been simplified so that it is clear that such an address is only required for the purposes of any proceedings before the registrar (rule 10);

    (d) the time limits for correcting deficiencies in any application are clearly set out in a single rule (rule 11);

    (e) provision has been made for the filing of observations by third parties on the acceptability of marks, as is to be the case of the Community trade mark system to be introduced under

Council Regulation (EC) No. 40/94 of 20th December 1993; copies of such observations are to be sent to the applicant (rule 15);

(f) amendment of an application is restricted to corrections of errors or changes in the name and address of the applicant (where these appear in the mark) (rule 17);

(g) provision has been made for the division of applications (rule 19);

(h) provision has been made for the merging of applications providing this takes place before their publication for opposition purposes (rule 20);

(i) following the introduction of registration of collective marks in section 49 of the Act, provision is made for the filing of regulations concerning their use, and for their amendment and opposition to such amendment (rules 22 and 23);

(j) provision is made for the publication of voluntary disclaimers (rule 24);

(k) provision is made for the entry onto the register of details concerning registration in addition to those prescribed by section 63(2) of the Act (rule 33);

(l) provision is made for the entry of details of registered transactions covered by section 25 of the Act (rule 34);

(m) provision is made for the amendment of entries in the register consequent upon changes in the system of classification which have been agreed internationally (rule 40) and for opposition to such changes (rule 44);

(n) the provisions concerning the confidentiality of documents and the public's right to inspect documents filed at the Patent Office have been clarified (rules 43, 44 and 45);

(o) provision has been made for the acceptance of affidavits in addition to statutory declarations, and the manner of subscription has been simplified to make it easier for overseas applicants to meet the Patents Office's requirements (rule 50);

(p) provision is made for appeals to the person appointed by the Lord Chancellor under section 76 and for the procedure relating to the hearing of appeals by that person (rules 57 and 59);

(q) the procedures to be followed when correcting an error or an irregularity in procedure have been clarified (rule 60);

(r) provision is made for the extension of times or periods prescribed by these Rules or specified by the registrar (rule 62);

(s) the provisions governing the filing of documents cover filing by electronic means, thus making further rule changes (to cater for future developments) unnecessary (rule 63);

(t) the hours of business of the Office and business days of the Office as specified by the registrar are to be published in the Trade Marks Journal and posted in the Office (rule 64);

(u) formal provision is made for the publication of the Trade Marks Journal (rule 65);

(v) rule 67 provides that in the case of a pending application (i.e. one made under the old law) which is advertised on or after 31st October 1994, the period within which notice of opposition may be filed shall be three months from the date of advertisement and that such period shall not be extendible;

(w) rule 68 prescribes the form of the notice to the registrar claiming to have the registrability of a pending mark which has not been advertised before 31st October 1994 determined in accordance with the Act; and

(x) rule 69 provides that any unexpired time or period prescribed by the Rules revoked by these Rules shall continue to apply to any act or proceedings to which they applied before their revocation.

The addresses for the filing of documents at the Patent Office are prescribed in the Patent Office (Address) Rules 1991 (S.I. 1991/675), namely—

(i) Cardiff Road, Newport, Gwent NP9 1RH; and

(ii) 25 Southampton Buildings, London WC2A 1AY.

A compliance cost assessment is available, copies of which have been placed in the libraries of both Houses of Parliament. Copies of the assessment are also available from the Intellectual Property Policy Directorate of the Patent Office, Room 3/13, Hazlitt House, 45 Southampton Buildings, London WC2A 1AR.

(3)   Trade Marks Registry Forms*

FORM NUMBER	TITLE
TM3	Application to register a trade mark, (including certification mark & collective marks).
TM3A	Application for additional classes.
TM5	Request to the Registrar for a statement of grounds of decision.
TM7	Notice of opposition.
TM8	Form for counterstatement.
TM9	Request for extension of time on an application.
TM11	Renewal of registration.
TM12	Request to divide an application.
TM13	Request for the restoration and renewal of a registration removed from the Register because of non-payment of the renewal fee.
TM15	Notice under Schedule 3, paragraph 11 of the Act: Claim to have registrability of a mark applied for before 31st October 1994 determined under the Act. (Conversion of application).
TM16	Application to register a change of proprietor.
TM17	Request to merge either applications or registrations.
TM21	Request to change the details of an applications or a registration.
TM22	Notice to surrender a registration.
TM23	Notice of a partial surrender of the specification of goods or services for which the mark is registered.
TM24	Application to record/cancel a registrable transaction or memoranda relating to a trade mark but not an assignment or licence.
TM25	Request for alteration of a registered mark.
TM26	Application for the revocation or rectification of a registration or for it to be declared invalid.
TM27	Application to intervene in proceedings for revocation or rectification of a registration.
TM31C	Request for information about applications and registered marks.
TM31R	Request for Registrar's general certificate
TM33	Request to appoint an agent or to enter or change an address for service.
TM35	Filing of regulations governing the use of a certification or collective mark.
TM36	Application to amend the regulations governing the use of a certification or collective mark.
TM50	Application for the registration of a licensee for a registered trade mark.
TM51	Application to remove or amend a licence.

*These forms are reproduced in a special supplement of the Trade Marks Journal published by the Patent Office on October 31, 1994.

(4)   First Council Directive

of 21 December 1988
to approximate the laws of the Members States relating to trade marks
(89/104/EEC)

The Council of the European Communities,

Having regard to the Treaty establishing the European Economic Community, and in particular Article 100a thereof,

Having regard to the proposal from the Commission ([1]),

In cooperation with the European Parliament ([2]),

Having regard to the opinion of the Economic and Social Committee ([3]),

Whereas the trade mark laws at present applicable in the Member States contain disparities which may impede the free movement of goods and freedom to provide services and may distort competition within the common market; whereas it is therefore necessary, in view of the establishment and functioning of the internal market, to approximate the laws of Member States;

Whereas it is important not to disregard the solutions and advantages which the Community trade mark system may afford to undertakings wishing to acquire trade marks;

Whereas it does not appear to be necessary at present to undertake full-scale approximation of the trade mark laws of the Member States and it will be sufficient if approximation is limited to those national provisions of law which most directly affect the functioning of the internal market;

Whereas the Directive does not deprive the Member States of the right to continue to protect trade marks acquired through use but takes them into account only in regard to the relationship between them and trade marks acquired by registration;

Whereas Member States also remain free to fix the provisions of procedure concerning the registration, the revocation and the invalidity of trade marks acquired by registration; whereas they can, for example, determine the form of trade mark registration and invalidity procedures, decide whether earlier rights should be invoked either in the registration procedure or in the invalidity procedure or in both and, if they allow earlier rights to be invoked in the registration procedure, have an opposition procedure or an *ex officio* examination procedure or both; whereas Member States remain free to determine the effects of revocation or invalidity of trade marks;

Whereas this Directive does not exclude the application to trade marks of provisions of law of the Member States other than trade mark law, such as the provisions relating to unfair competition, civil liability or consumer protection;

Whereas attainment of the objectives at which this approximation of laws is aiming requires that the conditions for obtaining and continuing to hold a registered trade mark are, in general, identical in all Member States; whereas, to this end, it is necessary to list examples of signs which may constitute a trade mark, provided that such signs are capable of distinguishing the goods or services of one undertaking from those of other undertakings; whereas the grounds for refusal or invalidity concerning the trade mark itself, for example, the absence of any distinctive character, or concerning conflicts between the trade mark and earlier rights, are to be listed in an exhaustive manner, even if some of these grounds are listed as an option for the Member States which will therefore be able to

[1]   OJ No C 351, 31. 12. 1980, p. 1 and OJ No C 351, 31. 12. 1985, p. 4.
[2]   OJ No C 307, 14. 11. 1983, p. 66 and OJ No C 309, 5. 12. 1988.
[3]   OJ No C 310, 30. 11. 1981, p. 22.

maintain or introduce those grounds in their legislation; whereas Member States will be able to maintain or introduce into their legislation grounds of refusal or invalidity linked to conditions for obtaining and continuing to hold a trade mark for which there is no provision of approximation, concerning, for example, the eligibility for the grant of a trade mark, the renewal of the trade mark or rules on fees, or related to the non-compliance with procedural rules;

Whereas in order to reduce the total number of trade marks registered and protected in the Community and, consequently, the number of conflicts which arise between them, it is essential to require that registered trade marks must actually be used or, if not used, be subject to revocation; whereas it is necessary to provide that a trade mark cannot be invalidated on the basis of the existence of a non-used earlier trade mark, while the Member States remain free to apply the same principle in respect of the registration of a trade mark or to provide that a trade mark may not be successfully invoked in infringement proceedings if it is established as a result of a plea that the trade mark could be revoked; whereas in all these cases it is up to the Member States to establish the applicable rules of procedure;

Whereas it is fundamental, in order to facilitate the free circulation of goods and services, to ensure that henceforth registered trade marks enjoy the same protection under the legal systems of all the Member States; whereas this should however not prevent the Member States from granting at their option extensive protection to those trade marks which have a reputation;

Whereas the protection afforded by the registered trade mark, the function of which is in particular to guarantee the trade mark as an indication of origin, is absolute in the case of identity between the mark and the sign and goods or services; whereas the protection applies also in case of similarity between the mark and the sign and the goods or services; whereas it is indispensable to give an interpretation of the concept of similarity in relation to the likelihood of confusion; whereas the likelihood of confusion, the appreciation of which depends on numerous elements and, in particular, on the recognition of the trade mark on the market, of the association which can be made with the used or registered sign, of the degree of similarity between the trade mark and the sign and between the goods or services identified, constitutes the specific condition for such protection; whereas the ways in which likelihood of confusion may be established, and in particular the onus of proof, are a matter for national procedural rules which are not prejudiced by the Directive;

Whereas it is important, for reasons of legal certainty and without inequitably prejudicing the interests of a proprietor of an earlier trade mark, to provide that the latter may no longer request a declaration of invalidity nor may he oppose the use of a trade mark subsequent to his own of which he has knowingly tolerated the use for a substantial length of time, unless the application for the subsequent trade mark was made in bad faith;

Whereas all Member States of the Community are bound by the Paris Convention for the Protection of Industrial Property; whereas it is necessary that the provisions of this Directive are entirely consistent with those of the Paris Convention; whereas the obligations of the Member States resulting from this Convention are not affected by this Directive; whereas, where appropriate, the second subparagraph of Article 234 of the Treaty is applicable,

Has Adopted This Directive:

Article 1

Scope

This Directive shall apply to every trade mark in respect of goods or services which is the subject of registration or of an application in a Member State for registration as an individual trade mark, a collective mark or a guarantee or certification mark, or which is the subject of a registration or an application for registration in the Benelux Trade Mark Office or of an international registration having effect in a Member State.

Article 2

Signs of which a trade mark may consist

A trade mark may consist of any sign capable of being represented graphically, particularly words, including personal names, designs, letters, numerals, the shape of goods or of their packaging, provided that such signs are capable of distinguishing the goods or services of one undertaking from those of other undertakings.

Article 3

Grounds for refusal or invalidity

1. The following shall not be registered or if registered shall be liable to be declared invalid:
(a) signs which cannot constitute a trade mark;
(b) trade marks which are devoid of any distinctive character;
(c) trade marks which consist exclusively of signs or indications which may serve, in trade, to designate the kind, quality, quantity, intended purpose, value, geographical origin, or the time of production of the goods or of rendering of the service, or other characteristics of the goods or service;
(d) trade marks which consist exclusively of signs or indications which have become customary in the current language or in the *bona fide* and established practices of the trade;
(e) signs which consist exclusively of:
   (i) the shape which results from the nature of the goods themselves, or
   (ii) the shape of goods which is necessary to obtain a technical result, or
   (iii) the shape which gives substantial value to the goods;
(f) trade marks which are contrary to public policy or to accepted principles of morality;
(g) trade marks which are of such a nature as to deceive the public, for instance as to the nature, quality or geographical origin of the goods or service;
(h) trade marks which have not been authorized by the competent authorities and are to be refused or invalidated pursuant to Article 6*ter* of the Paris Convention for the Protection of Industrial Property, hereinafter referred to as the 'Paris Convention'.

2. Any Member State may provide that a trade mark shall not be registered or, if registered, shall be liable to be declared invalid where and to the extent that:
(a) the use of that trade mark may be prohibited pursuant to provisions of law other than trade mark law of the Member State concerned or of the Community;
(b) the trade mark covers a sign of high symbolic value, in particular a religious symbol;
(c) the trade mark includes badges, emblems and escutcheons other than those covered by Article 6*ter* of the Paris Convention and which are of public interest, unless the consent of the appropriate authorities to its registration has been given in conformity with the legislation of the Member State;
(d) the application for registration of the trade mark was made in bad faith by the applicant.
3. A trade mark shall not be refused registration or be declared invalid in accordance with paragraph 1(b), (c) or (d) if, before the date of application for registration and following the use which has been made of it, it has acquired a distinctive character. Any Member State may in addition provide that this provision shall also apply where the distinctive character was acquired after the date of application for registration or after the date of registration.
4. Any Member State may provide that, by derogation from the preceding paragraphs, the grounds of refusal of registration or invalidity in force in that State prior to the date on which the provisions necessary to comply with this Directive enter into force, shall apply to trade marks for which application has been made prior to that date.

Article 4

Further grounds for refusal or invalidity concerning conflicts with earlier rights

1. A trade mark shall not be registered or, if registered, shall be liable to be declared invalid:

(a) if it is identical with an earlier trade mark, and the goods or services for which the trade mark is applied for or is registered are identical with the goods or services for which the earlier trade mark is protected;

(b) if because of its identity with, or similarity to, the earlier trade mark and the identity or similarity of the goods or services covered by the trade marks, there exists a likelihood of confusion on the part of the public, which includes the likelihood of association with the earlier trade mark.

2. 'Earlier trade marks' within the meaning of paragraph 1 means:

(a) trade marks of the following kinds with a date of application for registration which is earlier than the date of application for registration of the trade mark, taking account, where appropriate, of the priorities claimed in respect of those trade marks:

(i)   Community trade marks;

(ii)   trade marks registered in the Member State or, in the case of Belgium, Luxembourg or the Netherlands, at the Benelux Trade Mark Office;

(iii) trade marks registered under international arrangements which have effect in the Member State;

(b) Community trade marks which validly claim seniority, in accordance with the Regulation on the Community trade mark, from a trade mark referred to in (a)(ii) and (iii), even when the latter trade mark has been surrendered or allowed to lapse;

(c) applications for the trade marks referred to in (a) and (b), subject to their registration;

(d) trade marks which, on the date of application for registration of the trade mark, or, where appropriate, of the priority claimed in respect of the application for registration of the trade mark, are well known in a Member State, in the sense in which the words 'well known' are used in Article 6 *bis* of the Paris Convention.

3. A trade mark shall furthermore not be registered or, if registered, shall be liable to be declared invalid if it is identical with, or similar to, an earlier Community trade mark within the meaning of paragraph 2 and is to be, or has been, registered for goods or services which are not similar to those for which the earlier Community trade mark is registered, where the earlier Community trade mark has a reputation in the Community and where the use of the later trade mark without due cause would take unfair advantage of, or be detrimental to, the distinctive character or the repute of the earlier Community trade mark.

4. Any Member State may furthermore provide that a trade mark shall not be registered or, if registered, shall be liable to be declared invalid where, and to the extent that:

(a) the trade mark is identical with, or similar to, an earlier national trade mark within the meaning of paragraph 2 and is to be, or has been, registered for goods or services which are not similar to those for which the earlier trade mark is registered, where the earlier trade mark has a reputation in the Member State concerned and where the use of the later trade mark without due cause would take unfair advantage of, or be detrimental to, the distinctive character or the repute of the earlier trade mark;

(b) rights to a non-registered trade mark or to another sign used in the course of trade were acquired prior to the date of application for registration of the subsequent trade mark, or the date of the priority claimed for the application for registration of the subsequent trade mark and that non-registered trade mark or other sign confers on its proprietor the right to prohibit the use of a subsequent trade mark;

(c) the use of the trade mark may be prohibited by virtue of an earlier right other than the rights referred to in paragraphs 2 and 4(b) and in particular:

(i)   a right to a name;

(ii)   a right of personal portrayal;

(iii) a copyright;

(iv) an industrial property right;

(d) the trade mark is identical with, or similar to, an earlier collective trade mark conferring a right which expired within a period of a maximum of three years preceding application;

(e) the trade mark is identical with, or similar to, an earlier guarantee or certification mark conferring a right which expired within a period preceding application the length of which is fixed by the Member State;

(f) the trade mark is identical with, or similar to, an earlier trade mark which was registered for identical or similar goods or services and conferred on them a right which has expired for failure to renew within a period of a maximum of two years preceding application, unless the proprietor of the earlier trade mark gave his agreement for the registration of the later mark or did not use his trade mark;

(g) the trade mark is liable to be confused with a mark which was in use abroad on the filing date of the application and which is still in use there, provided that at the date of the application the applicant was acting in bad faith.

5. The Member States may permit that in appropriate circumstances registration need not be refused or the trade mark need not be declared invalid where the proprietor of the earlier trade mark or other earlier right consents to the registration of the later trade mark.

6. Any Member State may provide that, by derogationfrom paragraphs 1 to 5, the grounds for refusal of registration or invalidity in force in that State prior to the date on which the provisions necessary to comply with this Directive enter into force, shall apply to trade marks for which application has been made prior to that date.

Article 5

Rights conferred by a trade mark

1. The registered trade mark shall confer on the proprietor exclusive rights therein. The proprietor shall be entitled to prevent all third parties not having his consent from using in the course of trade:

(a) any sign which is identical with the trade mark in relation to goods or services which are identical with those for which the trade mark is registered;

(b) any sign where, because of its identity with, or similarity to, the trade mark and the identity or similarity of the goods or services covered by the trade mark and the sign, there exists a likelihood of confusion on the part of the public, which includes the likelihood of association between the sign and the trade mark.

2. Any Member State may also provide that the proprietor shall be entitled to prevent all third parties not having his consent from using in the course of trade any sign which is identical with, or similar to, the trade mark in relation to goods or services which are not similar to those for which the trade mark is registered, where the latter has a reputation in the Member State and where use of that sign without due cause takes unfair advantage of, or is detrimental to, the distinctive character or the repute of the trade mark.

3. The following, *inter alia*, may be prohibited under paragraphs 1 and 2:

(a) affixing the sign to the goods or to the packaging thereof;

(b) offering the goods, or putting them on the market or stocking them for these purposes under that sign, or offering or supplying services thereunder;

(c) importing or exporting the goods under the sign;

(d) using the sign on business papers and in advertising.

4. Where, under the law of the Member State, the use of a sign under the conditions referred to in 1(b) or 2 could not be prohibited before the date on which the provisions necessary to comply with this Directive entered into force in the Member State concerned, the rights conferred by the trade mark may not be relied on to prevent the continued use of the sign.

5. Paragraphs 1 to 4 shall not affect provisions in any Member State relating to the protection against the use of a sign other than for the purposes of distinguishing goods or services, where use of that sign without due cause takes unfair advantage of, or is detrimental to, the distinctive character or the repute of the trade mark.

Article 6

Limitation of the effects of a trade mark

1. The trade mark shall not entitle the proprietor to prohibit a third party from using, in the course of trade,
    (a) his own name or address;
    (b) indications concerning the kind, quality, quantity, intended purpose, value, geographical origin, the time of production of goods or of rendering of the service, or other characteristics of goods or services;
    (c) the trade mark where it is necessary to indicate the intended purpose of a product or service, in particular as accessories or spare parts;
provided he uses them in accordance with honest practices in industrial or commercial matters.

2. The trade mark shall not entitle the proprietor to prohibit a third party from using, in the course of trade, an earlier right which only applies in a particular locality if that right is recognized by the laws of the Member State in question and within the limits of the territory in which it is recognized.

Article 7

Exhaustion of the rights conferred by a trade mark

1. The trade mark shall not entitle the proprietor to prohibit its use in relation to goods which have been put on the market in the Community under that trade mark by the proprietor or with his consent.

2. Paragraph 1 shall not apply where there exist legitimate reasons for the proprietor to oppose further commercialization of the goods, especially where the condition of the goods is changed or impaired after they have been put on the market.

Article 8

Licensing

1. A trade mark may be licensed for some or all of the goods or services for which it is registered and for the whole or part of the Member State concerned. A licence may be exclusive or non-exclusive.

2. The proprietor of a trade mark may invoke the rights conferred by that trade mark against a licensee who contravenes any provision in his licensing contract with regard to its duration, the form covered by the registration in which the trade mark may be used, the scope of the goods or services for which the licence is granted, the territory in which the trade mark may be affixed, or the quality of the goods manufactured or of the services provided by the licensee.

Article 9

Limitation in consequence of acquiescence

1. Where, in a Member State, the proprietor of an earlier trade mark as referred to in Article 4(2) has acquiesced, for a period of five successive years, in the use of a later trade mark registered in that Member State while being aware of such use, he shall no longer be entitled on the basis of the earlier trade mark either to apply for a declaration that the later trade mark is invalid or to oppose the use of the later trade mark in respect of the goods or services for which the later trade mark has been used, unless registration of the later trade mark was applied for in bad faith.

2. Any Member State may provide that paragraph 1 shall apply *mutatis mutandis* to the proprietor of an earlier trade mark referred to in Article 4(4)(a) or an other earlier right referred to in Article 4(4)(b) or (c).

3. In the cases referred to in paragraphs 1 and 2, the proprietor of a later registered trade mark shall not be entitled to oppose the use of the earlier right, even though that right may no longer be invoked against the later trade mark.

Article 10

Use of trade marks

1. If, within a period of five years following the date of the completion of the registration procedure, the proprietor has not put the trade mark to genuine use in the Member State in connection with the goods or services in respect of which it is registered, or if such use has been suspended during an uninterrupted period of five years, the trade mark shall be subject to the sanctions provided for in this Directive, unless there are proper reasons for non-use.

2. The following shall also constitute use within the meaning of paragraph 1:

  (a) use of the trade mark in a form differing in elements which do not alter the distinctive character of the mark in the form in which it was registered;

  (b) affixing of the trade mark to goods or to the packaging thereof in the Member State concerned solely for export purposes.

3. Use of the trade mark with the consent of the proprietor or by any person who has authority to use a collective mark or a guarantee or certification mark shall be deemed to constitute use by the proprietor.

4. In relation to trade marks registered before the date on which the provisions necessary to comply with this Directive enter into force in the Member State concerned:

  (a) where a provision in force prior to that date attaches sanctions to non-use of a trade mark during an uninterrupted period, the relevant period of five years mentioned in paragraph 1 shall be deemed to have begun to run at the same time as any period of non-use which is already running at that date;

  (b) where there is no use provision in force prior to that date, the periods of five years mentioned in paragraph 1 shall be deemed to run from that date at the earliest.

Article 11

Sanctions for non use of a trade mark in legal or administrative proceedings

1. A trade mark may not be declared invalid on the ground that there is an earlier conflicting trade mark if the latter does not fulfil the requirements of use set out in Article 10(1), (2) and (3) or in Article 10(4), as the case may be.

2. Any Member State may provide that registration of a trade mark may not be refused on the ground that there is an earlier conflicting trade mark if the latter does not fulfil the requirements of use set out in Article 10(1), (2) and (3) or in Article 10(4), as the case may be.

3. Without prejudice to the application of Article 12, where a counter-claim for revocation is made, any Member State may provide that a trade mark may not be successfully invoked in infringement proceedings if it is established as a result of a plea that the trade mark could be revoked pursuant to Article 12(1).

4. If the earlier trade mark has been used in relation to part only of the goods or services for which it is registered, it shall, for purposes of applying paragraphs 1, 2 and 3, be deemed to be registered in respect only of that part of the goods or services.

Article 12

Grounds for revocation

1. A trade mark shall be liable to revocation if, within a continuous period of five years, it has not been put to genuine use in the Member State in connection with the goods or services in respect of which it is registered, and there are no proper reasons for non-use; however, no person may claim that the proprietor's rights in a trade mark should be revoked where, during the interval between expiry of the five-year period and filing of the application for revocation, genuine use of the trade mark has been started or resumed; the commencement or resumption of use within a period of three months preceding the filing of the application for revocation which began at the earliest on expiry of the continuous period of five years of non-use, shall, however, be disregarded where preparations for the commencement or resumption occur only after the proprietor becomes aware that the application for revocation may be filed.

   2. A trade mark shall also be liable to revocation if, after the date on which it was registered,
   (a) in consequence of acts or inactivity of the proprietor, it has become the common name in the trade for a product or service in respect of which it is registered;
   (b) in consequence of the use made of it by the proprietor of the trade mark or with his consent in respect of the goods or services for which it is registered, it is liable to mislead the public, particularly as to the nature, quality or geographical origin of those goods or services.

Article 13

Grounds for refusal or revocation or invalidity relating to only some of the goods or services

   Where grounds for refusal of registration or for revocation or invalidity of a trade mark exist in respect of only some of the goods or services for which that trade mark has been applied for or registered, refusal of registration or revocation or invalidity shall cover those goods or services only.

Article 14

Establishment a posteriori *of invalidity or revocation of a trade mark*

   Where the seniority of an earlier trade mark which has been surrendered or allowed to lapse, is claimed for a Community trade mark, the invalidity or revocation of the earlier trade mark may be established *a posteriori*.

Article 15

Special provisions in respect of collective marks, guarantee marks and certification marks

   1. Without prejudice to Article 4, Member States whose laws authorize the registration of collective marks or of guarantee or certification marks may provide that such marks shall not be registered, or shall be revoked or declared invalid, on grounds additional to those specified in Articles 3 and 12 where the function of those marks so requires.

   2. By way of derogation from Article 3(1)(c), Member States may provide that signs or indications which may serve, in trade, to designate the geographical origin of the goods or services may constitute collective, guarantee or certification marks. Such a mark does not entitle the proprietor to prohibit a third party from using in the course of trade such signs or indications, provided he uses them in accordance with honest practices in industrial or commercial matters; in particular, such a mark may not be invoked against a third party who is entitled to use a geographical name.

Article 16

National provisions to be adopted pursuant to this Directive

   1. The Member States shall bring into force the laws, regulations and administrative provisions necessary to comply with this Directive not later than 28 December 1991. They shall immediately inform the Commission thereof.

   2. Acting on a proposal from the Commission, the Council, acting by qualified majority, may defer the date referred to in paragraph 1 until 31 December 1992 at the latest.

3. Member States shall communicate to the Commission the text of the main provision of national law which they adopt in the field governed by this Directive.

Article 17

Addresses

This Directive is addressed to the Member States.
Done at Brussels, 21 December 1988.

For the Council
The President
V. PAPANDREOU

(5)   Trade Marks Act 1938

This Appendix includes selected sections from the Trade Marks Act 1938 (as amended). The Trade Marks (Amendment) Act 1984 altered the 1938 Act to provide for the registration of marks for services. In doing so, it not only provided that a reference to goods should also be read as a reference to services, but also made some substantive changes to a number of sections in their application to service marks. In a work of this kind it is unnecessary to set out both versions (see how this has been done in *Kerly*, 12th ed.), so the sections set out below are the "goods" version of the Act, printed as amended. Where it is necessary to refer to the 1938 Act in relation to a service mark, reference should be made to the 1984 Act itself or to *Kerly*.

Sections Reproduced

REGISTRATION, INFRINGEMENT AND OTHER SUBSTANTIVE PROVISIONS

SECTION

Effect of registration and the action for infringement

No action for infringement of unregistered trade mark

2. No person shall be entitled to institute any proceedings to prevent, or to recover damages for, the infringement of an unregistered trade mark, but nothing in this Act shall be deemed to affect rights of action against any person for passing-off or the remedies in respect thereof.
Amended by 1984 Act, s.1(5)(a).

Registration to be in respect of particular goods

3. A trade mark must be registered in respect of particular goods or classes of goods, and any question arising as to the class within which any goods fall shall be determined by the Registrar, whose decision shall be final.

Right given by registration in Part A, and infringement thereof

4.—(1) Subject to the provisions of this section, and of sections seven and eight of this Act, the registration (whether before or after the commencement of this Act) of a person in Part A of the register as proprietor of a trade mark (other than a certification trade mark) in respect of any goods shall, if valid, give or be deemed to have given to that person the exclusive right to the use of the trade mark in relation to those goods and, without prejudice to the generality of the foregoing words, that right shall be deemed to be infringed by any person who, not being the proprietor of the trade mark or a registered user thereof using by way of the permitted use, uses in the course of trade a mark identical with or nearly resembling it in relation to any goods in respect of which it is registered, and in such manner as to render the use of the mark likely to be taken either—
   (a) as being used as a trade mark; or
   (b) in a case in which the use is use upon goods or in physical relation thereto or in an advertising circular or other advertisement issued to the public, as importing a reference to some person

having the right either as proprietor or as registered user to use the trade mark or to goods with which such a person as aforesaid is connected in the course of trade.

(2) The right to the use of a trade mark given by registration as aforesaid shall be subject to any conditions or limitations entered on the register, and shall not be deemed to be infringed by the use of any such mark as aforesaid in any mode, in relation to goods to be sold or otherwise traded in any place, in relation to goods to be exported to any market, or in any other circumstances, to which having regard to any such limitations, the registration does not extend.

(3) The right to the use of a trade mark given by registration as aforesaid shall not be deemed to be infringed by the use of any such mark as aforesaid by any person—

    (a) in relation to goods connected in the course of trade with the proprietor or a registered user of the trade mark if, as to those goods or a bulk of which they form part, the proprietor or the registered user conforming to the permitted use had applied the trade mark and has not subsequently removed or obliterated it, or has at any time expressly or impliedly consented to the use of the trade mark; or

    (b) in relation to goods adapted to form part of, or to be accessory to, other goods in relation to which the trade mark has been used without infringement of the right given as aforesaid or might for the time being be so used, if the use of the mark is reasonably necessary in order to indicate that the goods are so adapted and neither the purpose nor the effect of the use of the mark is to indicate otherwise than in accordance with the fact a connection in the course of trade between any person and the goods.

(4) The use of a registered trade mark, being one of two or more registered trade marks that are identical or nearly resemble each other, in exercise of the right to the use of that trade mark given by registration as aforesaid, shall not be deemed to be an infringement of the right so given to the use of any other of those trade marks.

.   .   .

Right given by registration in Part B, and infringement thereof

5.—(1) Except as provided by subsection (2) of this section, the registration (whether before or after the commencement of this Act) of a person in Part B of the register as proprietor of a trade mark in respect of any goods shall, if valid, give or be deemed to have given to that person the like right in relation to those goods as if the registration had been in Part A of the register, and the provisions of the last foregoing section shall have effect in like manner in relation to a trade mark registered in Part B of the register as they have effect in relation to a trade mark registered in Part A of the register.

(2) In any action for infringement of the right to the use of a trade mark given by registration as aforesaid in Part B of the register, otherwise than by an act that is deemed to be an infringement by virtue of the next succeeding section, no injunction or other relief shall be granted to the plaintiff if the defendant establishes to the satisfaction of the court that the use of which the plaintiff complains is not likely to deceive or cause confusion or to be taken as indicating a connection in the course of trade between the goods and some person having the right either as proprietor or as registered user to use the trade mark.

Saving for vested rights

7. Nothing in this Act shall entitle the proprietor or a registered user of a registered trade mark to interfere with or restrain the use by any person of a trade mark identical with or nearly resembling it in relation to goods in relation to which that person or a predecessor in title of his has continuously used that trade mark from a date anterior—

    (a) to the use of the first-mentioned trade mark in relation to those goods by the proprietor or a predecessor in title of his; or

    (b) to the registration of the first-mentioned trade mark in respect of those goods in the name of the proprietor or a predecessor in title of his;

whichever is the earlier, or to object (on such use being proved) to that person being put on the register for that identical or nearly resembling trade mark in respect of those goods under subsection (2) of section twelve of this Act.

Saving for use of name, address, or description of goods

8. No registration of a trade mark shall interfere with—
  (a) any bona fide use by a person of his own name or of the name of his place of business, or of the name, or of the name of the place of business, of any of his predecessors in business; or
  (b) the use by any person of any bona fide description of the character or quality of his goods, not being a description that would be likely to be taken as importing any such reference as is mentioned in paragraph (*b*) of subsection (1) of section four or in paragraph (*b*) of subsection (3) of section thirty-seven, of this Act.

Registrability and validity of registration

Distinctiveness requisite for registration in Part A

9.—(1) In order for a trade mark (other than a certification trade mark) to be registrable in Part A of the register, it must contain or consist of at least one of the following essential particulars:
  (a) the name of a company, individual, or firm, represented in a special or particular manner;
  (b) the signature of the applicant for registration or some predecessor in his business;
  (c) an invented word or invented words;
  (d) a word or words having no direct reference to the character or quality of the goods, and not being according to its ordinary signification a geographical name or a surname;
  (e) any other distinctive mark, but a name, signature, or word or words, other than such as fall within the descriptions in the foregoing paragraphs (a), (b), (c) and (d), shall not be registrable under the provisions of this paragraph except upon evidence of its distinctiveness.

(2) For the purposes of this section "distinctive" means adapted, in relation to the goods in respect of which a trade mark is registered or proposed to be registered, to distinguish goods with which the proprietor of the trade mark is or may be connected in the course of trade from goods in the case of which no such connection subsists, either generally or, where the trade mark is registered or proposed to be registered subject to limitations, in relation to use within the extent of the registration.

(3) In determining whether a trade mark is adapted to distinguish as aforesaid the tribunal may have regard to the extent to which—
  (a) the trade mark is inherently adapted to distinguish as aforesaid; and
  (b) by reason of the use of the trade mark or of any other circumstances, the trade mark is in fact adapted to distinguish as aforesaid.

Capability of distinguishing requisite for registration in Part B

10.—(1) In order for a trade mark to be registrable in Part B of the register it must be capable, in relation to the goods in respect of which it is registered or proposed to be registered, of distinguishing goods with which the proprietor of the trade mark is or may be connected in the course of trade from goods in the case of which no such connection subsists, either generally or, where the trade mark is registered or proposed to be registered subject to limitations, in relation to use within the extent of the registration.

(2) In determining whether a trade mark is capable of distinguishing as aforesaid the tribunal may have regard to the extent to which—
  (a) the trade mark is inherently capable of distinguishing as aforesaid; and

(b) by reason of the use of the trade mark or of any other circumstances, the trade mark is in fact capable of distinguishing as aforesaid.

(3) A trade mark may be registered in Part B notwithstanding any registration in Part A in the name of the same proprietor of the same trade mark or any part or parts thereof.

Prohibition of registration of deceptive, etc., matter

11. It shall not be lawful to register as a trade mark or part of a trade mark any matter the use of which would, by reason of its being likely to deceive or cause confusion or otherwise, be disentitled to protection in a court of justice, or would be contrary to law or morality, or any scandalous design.

Prohibition of registration of identical and resembling trade marks

12.—(1) Subject to the provisions of subsection (2) of this section, no trade mark shall be registered in respect of any goods or description of goods that is identical with or nearly resembles a mark belonging to a different proprietor and already on the register in respect of—
(a) the same goods,
(b) the same description of goods, or
(c) services or a description of services which are associated with those goods or goods of that description.

(2) In case of honest concurrent use, or of other special circumstances which in the opinion of the Court or the Registrar make it proper so to do, the Court or the Registrar may permit the registration by more than one proprietor in respect of—
(a) the same goods,
(b) the same description of goods, or
(c) goods and services or descriptions of goods and services which are associated with each other of marks that are identical, or nearly resemble each other.
subject to such conditions and limitations, if any, as the Court or Registrar, as the case may be, may think it right to impose.

(3) Where separate applications are made by different persons to be registered as proprietors respectively of marks that are identical or nearly resemble each other, in respect of—
(a) the same goods,
(b) the same description of goods, or
(c) goods and services or descriptions of goods and services which are associated with each other,
the Registrar may refuse to register any of them until their rights have been determined by the Court, or have been settled by agreement in a manner approved by him or on an appeal (which may be brought either to the Board of Trade or to the Court at the option of the appellant) by the Board or the Court, as the case may be.

Registration in Part A to be conclusive as to validity after seven years

13.—(1) In all legal proceedings relating to a trade mark registered in Part A of the register (including applications under section thirty-two of this Act) the original registration in Part A of the register of the trade mark shall, after the expiration of seven years from the date of that registration, be taken to be valid in all respects, unless—
(a) that registration was obtained by fraud, or
(b) the trade mark offends against the provisions of section eleven of this Act.

(2) Nothing in subsection (1) of section five of this Act shall be construed as making applicable to a trade mark, as being a trade mark registered in Part B of the register, the foregoing provisions of this section relating to a trade mark registered in Part A of the register.

Registration subject to disclaimer

14. If a trade mark–
  (a) contains any part not separately registered by the proprietor as a trade mark; or
  (b) contains matter common to the trade or otherwise of a non-distinctive character;
the Registrar or the Board of Trade or the Court, in deciding whether the trade mark shall be entered or shall remain on the register, may require, as a condition of its being on the register,—
      (i) that the proprietor shall disclaim any right to the exclusive use of any part of the trade mark, or to the exclusive use of all or any portion of any such matter as aforesaid, to the exclusive use of which the tribunal holds him not to be entitled; or
      (ii) that the proprietor shall make such other disclaimer as the tribunal may consider necessary for the purpose of defining his rights under the registration:
    Provided that no disclaimer on the register shall affect any rights of the proprietor of a trade mark except such as arise out of the registration of the trade mark in respect of which the disclaimer is made.

Words used as name or description of an article or substance

15.–(1) The registration of a trade mark shall not be deemed to have become invalid by reason only of any use, after the date of registration, of a word or words which the trade mark contains, or of which it consists, as the name or description of an article or substance:
    Provided that, if it is proved either—
  (a) that there is a well-known and established use of the word or words as the name or description of the article or substance by a person or persons carrying on a trade therein, not being use in relation to goods connected in the course of trade with the proprietor or a registered user of the trade mark or (in the case of a certification trade mark) goods certified by the proprietor; or
  (b) that the article or substance was formerly manufactured under a patent (being a patent in force on, or granted after, the twenty-third day of December nineteen hundred and nineteen), that a period of two years or more after the cesser of the patent has elapsed, and that the word or words is or are the only practicable name or description of the article or substance;
the provisions of the next succeeding subsection shall have effect.
    (2) Where the facts mentioned in paragraph (a) or (b) of the proviso to the foregoing subsection are proved with respect to any word or words, then—
  (a) if the trade mark consists solely of that word or those words, the registration of the trade mark, so far as regards registration in respect of the article or substance in question or of any goods of the same description, shall be deemed for the purposes of section thirty-two of this Act to be an entry wrongly remaining on the register;
  (b) if the trade mark contains that word or those words and other matter, the Court or the Registrar, in deciding whether the trade mark shall remain on the register, so far as regards registration in respect of the article or substance in question and of any goods of the same description, may in case of a decision in favour of its remaining on the register require as a condition thereof that the proprietor shall disclaim any right to the exclusive use in relation to that article or substance and any goods of the same description of that word or those words, so, however, that no disclaimer on the register shall affect any rights of the proprietor of a trade mark except such as arise out of the registration of the trade mark in respect of which the disclaimer is made; and
  (c) for the purposes of any other legal proceedings relating to the trade mark,—
      (i)   if the trade mark consists solely of that word or those words, all rights of the proprietor, whether under the common law or by registration, to the exclusive use of the trade mark in relation to the article or substance in question or to any goods of the same description, or
      (ii) if the trade mark contains that word or those words and other matter, all such rights of the proprietor to the exclusive use of that word or those words in such relation as

aforesaid, shall be deemed to have ceased on the date at which the use mentioned in paragraph (a) of the proviso to the foregoing subsection first became well known of the proviso to the foregoing subsection first became well known and established, or at the expiration of the period of two years mentioned in paragraph (b) of that proviso.

(3)No word which is the commonly used and accepted name of any single chemical element or single chemical compound, as distinguished from a mixture, shall be registered as a trade mark in respect of a chemical substance or preparation, and any such registration in force at the commencement of this Act or thereafter shall, notwithstanding anything in section thirteen of this Act, be deemed for the purposes of section thirty-two of this Act to be an entry made in the register without sufficient cause, or an entry wrongly remaining on the register, as the circumstances may require:

Provided that the foregoing provisions of this subsection shall not have effect in relation to a word which is used to denote only a brand or make of the element or compound as made by the proprietor or a registered user of the trade mark, as distinguished from the element or compound as made by others, and in association with a suitable name or description open to the public use.

Effect of limitation as to colour, and of absence thereof

16. A trade mark may be limited in whole or in part to one or more specified colours, and in any such case the fact that it is so limited shall be taken into consideration by any tribunal having to decide on the distinctive character of the trade mark.

If and so far as a trade mark is registered without limitation of colour, it shall be deemed to be registered for all colours.

Procedure for, and duration of, registration

Application for registration

17.—(1) Any person claiming to be the proprietor of a trade mark used or proposed to be used by him who is desirous of registering it must apply in writing to the Registrar in the prescribed manner for registration either in Part A or in Part B of the register.

(2) Subject to the provisions of this Act, the Registrar may refuse the application, or may accept it absolutely or subject to such amendments, conditions or limitations, if any, as he may think right.

(3) In the case of an application for registration of a trade mark (other than a certification trade mark) in Part A of the register, the Registrar may, if the applicant is willing, instead of refusing the application, treat it as an application for registration in Part B and deal with the application accordingly.

(4) In the case of a refusal or conditional acceptance, the Registrar shall, if required by the applicant, state in writing the grounds of his decision and the materials used by him in arriving thereat, and the decision shall be subject to appeal to the Board of Trade or to the Court at the option of the applicant.

(5) An appeal under this section shall be made in the prescribed manner, and on the appeal the tribunal shall, if required, hear the applicant and the Registrar, and shall make an order determining whether, and subject to what amendments, modifications, conditions or limitations, if any, the application is to be accepted.

(6) Appeals under this section shall be heard on the materials stated as aforesaid by the Registrar, and no further grounds of objection to the acceptance of the application shall be allowed to be taken by the Registrar, other than those so stated as aforesaid by him, except by leave of the tribunal hearing the appeal. Where any further grounds of objection are taken, the applicant shall be entitled to withdraw his application without payment of costs on giving notice as prescribed.

(7) The Registrar or the Board of Trade or the Court, as the case may be, may at any time, whether before or after acceptance, correct any error in or in connection with the application, or may permit the applicant to amend his application upon such terms as the Registrar or the Board of Trade or the Court, as the case may be, may think fit.

Assignment and transmission

Powers of, and restrictions on, assignment and transmission

22.—(1) Notwithstanding any rule of law or equity to the contrary, a registered trade mark shall be, and shall be deemed always to have been, assignable and transmissible either in connection with the goodwill of a business or not.

(2) A registered trade mark shall be, and shall be deemed always to have been, assignable and transmissible in respect either of all the goods in respect of which it is registered, or was registered, as the case may be, or of some (but not all) of those goods.

(3) The provisions of the two foregoing subsections shall have effect in the case of an unregistered trade mark used in relation to any goods as they have effect in the case of a registered trade mark registered in respect of any goods, if at the time of the assignment or transmission of the unregistered trade mark it is or was used in the same business as a registered trade mark, and if it is or was assigned or transmitted at the same time and to the same person as that registered trade mark and in respect of goods all of which are goods in relation to which the unregistered trade mark is or was used in that business and in respect of which that registered trade mark is or was assigned or transmitted.

(4) Notwithstanding anything in the foregoing subsections, a trade mark shall not be, or be deemed to have been, assignable or transmissible in a case in which as a result of an assignment or transmission there would in the circumstances subsist, or have subsisted, whether under the common law or by registration, exclusive rights in more than one of the persons concerned to the use in relation to,

(a) the same goods,
(b) the same description of goods, or
(c) goods and services or descriptions of goods and services which are associated with each other,

of trade marks nearly resembling each other or of identical trade marks, if, having regard to the similarity of the goods or the association of the goods and services or description of goods and services and to the similarity of the trade marks, the use of trade marks in exercise of those rights would be, or have been, likely to deceive or cause confusion:

Provided that, where a trade mark is, or has been, assigned or transmitted in such a case as aforesaid, the assignment or transmission shall not be deemed to be, or to have been, invalid under this subsection if the exclusive rights subsisting as a result thereof in the persons concerned respectively are, or were, having regard to limitations imposed thereon, such as not to be exercisable by two or more of those persons in relation to goods to be sold, or otherwise traded in, within the United Kingdom (otherwise than for export therefrom) or in relation to goods to be exported to the same market outside the United Kingdom.

(5) The proprietor of a registered trade mark who proposes to assign it in respect of any goods in respect of which it is registered may submit to the Registrar in the prescribed manner a statement of case setting out the circumstances, and the Registrar may issue to him a certificate stating whether, having regard to the similarity of the goods or the association of the goods and services or descriptions of goods and services and to the similarity of the trade marks referred to in the case, the proposed assignment of the first-mentioned trade mark would or would not be invalid under the last foregoing subsection, and a certificate so issued shall, subject to the provisions of this section as to appeal and unless it is shown that the certificate was obtained by fraud or misrepresentation, be conclusive as to the validity or invalidity under the last foregoing subsection of the assignment in so far as such validity or invalidity depends upon the facts set out in the case, but, as regards a certificate in favour of validity, only, if application for registration under section twenty-five of this Act of the title of the person becoming entitled is made within six months from the date on which the certificate is issued.

(6) Notwithstanding anything in subsection (1) to (3) of this section, a trade mark shall not, on or after the appointed day, be assignable or transmissible in a case in which as a result of an assignment or transmission thereof there would in the circumstances subsist, whether under the common law or by registration:

(a) an exclusive right in one of the persons concerned to the use of the mark limited to use in relation to goods to be sold, or otherwise traded in, in a place or places in the United Kingdom; and

(b) an exclusive right in another of the persons concerned to the use of a mark identical with or nearly resembling the mark referred to in paragraph (a) above in relation to—

(i) the same goods,

(ii) the same description of goods, or

(iii) services which are associated with those goods or goods of that description

limited to use in relation to goods to be sold, or otherwise traded in, or services for use, or available for acceptance, in another place or places in the United Kingdom:

Provided that, on application in the prescribed manner by the proprietor of a trade mark who proposed to assign it, or of a person who claims that a trade mark has been transmitted to him or to a predecessor in title of his on or after the appointed day, in any such case, the Registrar, if he is satisfied that in all the circumstances the use of the trade marks in exercise of the said rights would not be contrary to the public interest, may approve the assignment or transmission and an assignment or transmission so approved shall not be deemed to be, or to have been, invalid under this subsection or under subsection (4) of this section, so, however, that in the case of a registered trade mark this provision shall not have effect unless application for the registration under section twenty-five of this Act of the title of the person becoming entitled is made within six months from the date on which the approval is given or, in the case of a transmission, was made before that date.

(7) Where an assignment in respect of any goods of a trade mark that is at the time of the assignment used in a business in those goods is made, on or after the appointed day, otherwise than in connection with the goodwill of that business, the assignment shall not take effect until the following requirements have been satisfied, that is to say, the assignee must, not later than the expiration of six months from the date on which the assignment is made or within such extended months from the date on which the assignment is made or within such extended period, if any, as the Registrar may allow, apply to him for directions with respect to the advertisement of the assignment, and must advertise it in such form and manner and within such period as the Registrar may direct.

(8) Any decision of the Registrar under this section shall be subject to appeal to the Court.

·   ·   ·

Use and non-use

Removal from register and imposition of limitations on ground of non-use

26.–(1) Subject to the provisions of the next succeeding section, a registered trade mark may be taken off the register in respect of any of the goods in respect of which it is registered on application by any person aggrieved to the Court or, at the option of the applicant and subject to the provisions of section fifty-four of this Act, to the Registrar, on the ground either—

(a) that the trade mark was registered without any bona fide intention on the part of the applicant for registration that it should be used in relation to those goods by him, and that there has in fact been no bona fide use of the trade mark in relation to those goods by any proprietor thereof for the time being up to the date one month before the date of the application; or

(b) that up to the date one month before the date of the application a continuous period of five years or longer elapsed during which the trade mark was a registered trade mark and during which there was no bona fide use thereof in relation to those goods by any proprietor thereof for the time being:

Provided that (except where the applicant has been permitted under subsection (2) of section twelve of this Act to register an identical or nearly resembling trade mark in respect of the goods in question or where the tribunal is of opinion that he might properly be permitted so to register such a trade mark) the tribunal may refuse an application made under paragraph (a) or (b) of this subsection in relation to any goods, if it is shown that there has been before the relevant date or during the relevant period, as the case may be, bona fide use of the mark by the proprietor thereof for the time being in relation to—

(i) goods of the same description, or

(ii) services associated with those goods or goods of that description,

being goods or, as the case may be, services in respect of which the mark is registered.

(2) Where in relation to any goods in respect of which a trade mark is registered—

(a) the matters referred to in paragraph (b) of the foregoing subsection are shown so far as regards non-use of the trade mark in relation to goods to be sold, or otherwise traded in, in a particular place in the United Kingdom (otherwise than for export from the United Kingdom), or in relation to goods to be exported to a particular market outside the United Kingdom; and

(b) a person has been permitted under subsection (2) of section twelve of this Act to register an identical or nearly resembling trade mark in respect of those goods under a registration extending to use in relation to goods to be sold, or otherwise traded in, in that place (otherwise than for export from the United Kingdom), or in relation to goods to be exported to that market, or the tribunal is of opinion that he might properly be permitted so to register such a trade mark;

on application by that person to the Court or, at the option of the applicant and subject to the provisions of section fifty-four of this Act, to the Registrar, the tribunal may impose on the registration of the first-mentioned trade mark such limitations as the tribunal thinks proper for securing that the registration shall cease to extend to such use as last aforesaid.

(3) An applicant shall not be entitled to rely for the purposes of paragraph (b) of subsection (1), or for the purposes of subsection (2), of this section on any non-use of a trade mark that is shown to have been due to special circumstances in the trade and not to any intention not to use or abandon the trade mark in relation to the goods to which the application relates.

Registered users

28.—(1) Subject to the provisions of this section, a person other than the proprietor of a trade mark may be registered as a registered user thereof in respect of all or any of the goods in respect of which it is registered (otherwise than as a defensive trade mark) and either with or without conditions or restrictions.

The use of a trade mark by a registered user thereof in relation to goods with which he is connected in the course of trade and in respect of which for the time being the trade mark remains registered and he is registered as a registered user, being use such as to comply with any conditions or restrictions to which his registration is subject, is in this Act referred to as the " permitted use" thereof.

(2) The permitted use of a trade mark shall be deemed to be use by the proprietor thereof, and shall be deemed not to be use by a person other than the proprietor, for the purposes of section twenty-six of this Act and for any other purpose for which such use is material under this Act or at common law.

(3) Subject to any agreement subsisting between the parties, a registered user of a trade mark shall be entitled to call upon the proprietor thereof to take proceedings to prevent infringement thereof, and, if the proprietor refuses or neglects to do so within two months after being so called upon, the registered user may institute proceedings for infringement in his own name as if he were the proprietor, making the proprietor a defendant.

A proprietor so added as defendant shall not be liable for any costs unless he enters an appearance and takes part in the proceedings.

(4) Where it is proposed that a person should be registered as a registered user of a trade mark, the proprietor and the proposed registered user must apply in writing to the Registrar in the prescribed manner and must furnish him with a statutory declaration made by the proprietor, or by some person authorised to act on his behalf and approved by the Registrar—

(a) giving particulars of the relationship, existing or proposed, between the proprietor and the proposed registered user, including particulars showing the degree of control by the proprietor over the permitted use which their relationship will confer and whether it is a term of their relationship that the proposed registered user shall be the sole registered user or that there shall be any other restriction as to persons for whose registration as registered users application may be made;

(b) stating the goods in respect of which registration is proposed;

(c) stating any conditions or restrictions proposed with respect to the characteristics of the goods, to the mode or place of permitted use, or to any other matter; and

(d) stating whether the permitted use is to be for a period or without limit of period, and, if for a period, the duration thereof;

and with such further documents, information or evidence as may be required under the rules or by the Registrar.

(5) When the requirements of the last foregoing subsection have been complied with, if the Registrar, after considering the information furnished to him under that subsection, is satisfied that in all the circumstances the use of the trade mark in relation to the proposed goods or any of them by the proposed registered user subject to any conditions or restrictions which the Registrar thinks proper would not be contrary to the public interest, the Registrar may register the proposed registered user as a registered user in respect of the goods as to which he is so satisfied subject as aforesaid.

(6) The Registrar shall refuse an application under the foregoing provisions of this section if it appears to him that the grant thereof would tend to facilitate trafficking in a trade mark.

(7) The Registrar shall, if so required by an applicant, take steps for securing that information given for the purposes of an application under the foregoing provisions of this section (other than matter entered in the register) is not disclosed to rivals in trade.

(8) Without prejudice to the provisions of section thirty-two of this Act, the registration of a person as a registered user—

(a) may be varied by the Registrar as regards the goods in respect of which, or any conditions or restrictions subject to which, it has effect, on the application in writing in the prescribed manner of the registered proprietor of the trade mark to which the registration relates;

(b) may be cancelled by the Registrar on the application in writing in the prescribed manner of the registered proprietor or of the registered user or of any other registered user of the trade mark; or

(c) may be cancelled by the Registrar on the application in writing in the prescribed manner of any person on any of the following grounds, that is to say—

(i) that the registered user has used the trade mark otherwise than by way of the permitted use, or in such a way as to cause, or to be likely to cause, deception or confusion;

(ii) that the proprietor or the registered user misrepresented, or failed to disclose, some fact material to the application for the registration, or that the circumstances have materially changed since the date of the registration;

(iii) that the registration ought not to have been effected having regard to rights vested in the applicant by virtue of a contract in the performance of which he is interested.

(9) Provision shall be made by the rules for the notification of the registration of a person as a registered user to any other registered user of the trade mark, and for the notification of an application under the last foregoing subsection to the registered proprietor and each registered user (not being the applicant) of the trade mark, and for giving to the applicant on such an application, and to all persons to whom such an application is notified and who intervene in the proceedings in accordance with the rules, an opportunity of being heard.

(10) The Registrar may at any time cancel the registration of a person as a registered user of a trade mark in respect of any goods in respect of which the trade mark is no longer registered.

(11) Any decision of the Registrar under the foregoing provisions of this section shall be subject to appeal to the Court.

(12) Nothing in this section shall confer on a registered user of a trade mark any assignable or transmissible right to the use thereof.

Use of one of associated or substantially identical trade marks equivalent to use of another

30.—(1) Where under the provisions of this Act use of a registered trade mark is required to be proved for any purpose, the tribunal may, if and so far as the tribunal thinks right, accept use of an associated registered trade mark, or of the trade mark with additions or alterations not substantially affecting its identity, as an equivalent for the use required to be proved.

(2) The use of the whole of a registered trade mark shall for the purposes of this Act be deemed to be also a use of any registered trade mark, being a part thereof, registered in the name of the same proprietor by virtue of subsection (1) of section twenty-one of this Act.

* * *

Rectification and correction of the register

General power to rectify entries in register

32.—(1) Any person aggrieved by the non-insertion in or omission from the register of any entry, or by any entry made in the register without sufficient cause, or by any entry wrongly remaining on the register, or by any error or defect in any entry in the register, may apply in the prescribed manner to the Court or, at the option of the applicant and subject to the provisions of section fifty-four of this Act, to the Registrar, and the tribunal may make such order for making, expunging or varying the entry as the tribunal may think fit.

(2) The tribunal may in any proceeding under this section decide any question that it may be necessary or expedient to decide in connection with the rectification of the register.

(3) In case of fraud in the registration, assignment or transmission of a registered trade mark, the Registrar may himself apply to the Court under the provisions of this section.

(4) Any order of the Court rectifying the register shall direct that notice of the rectification shall be served in the prescribed manner on the Registrar, and the Registrar shall on receipt of the notice rectify the register accordingly.

(5) The power to rectify the register conferred by this section shall include power to remove a registration in Part A of the register to Part B.

* * *

GENERAL AND MISCELLANEOUS

*Offences and restraint of use of Royal Arms**

Fraudulent application or use of trade mark an offence

58A.—(1) It is an offence, subject to subsection (3) below, for a person–
  (a) to apply a mark identical to or nearly resembling a registered trade mark to goods, or to material used or intended to be used for labelling, packaging or advertising goods, or
  (b) to sell, let for hire, or offer or expose for sale or hire, or distribute–
      (i)   goods bearing such a mark, or
      (ii) material bearing such a mark which is used or intended to be used for labelling, packaging or advertising goods, or
  (c) to use material bearing such a mark in the course of a business for labelling, packaging or advertising goods, or
  (d) to possess in the course of a business goods or material bearing such a mark with a view to doing any of the things mentioned in paragraphs (a) to (c),
when he is not entitled to use the mark in relation to the goods in question and the goods are not connected in the course of trade with a person who is so entitled.

(2) It is also an offence, subject to subsection (3) below, for a person to possess in the course of a business goods or material bearing a mark identical to or nearly resembling a registered trade mark

---

* Sections 58A and 58B were inserted by the Copyright, Designs and Patents Act 1988.

with a view to enabling or assisting another person to do any of the things mentioned in subsection (1)(a)to (c), knowing or having reason to believe that the other person is not entitled to use the mark in relation to the goods in question and that the goods are not connected in the course of trade with a person who is so entitled.

(3) A person commits an offence under subsection (1) or (2) only if–
  (a) he acts with a view to gain for himself or another, or with intent to cause loss to another, and
  (b) he intends that the goods in question should be accepted as connected in the course of trade with a person entitled to use the mark in question;

and it is a defence for a person charged with an offence under subsection (1) to show that he believed on reasonable grounds that he was entitled to use the mark in relation to the goods in question.

(4) A person guilty of an offence under this section is liable–
  (a) on summary conviction to imprisonment for a term not exceeding six months or a fine not exceeding the statutory maximum,or both;
  (b) on conviction on indictment to a fine or imprisonment for a term not exceeding ten years, or both.

(5) Where an offence under this section committed by a body corporate is proved to have been committed with the consent or connivance of a director, manager, secretary or other similar officer of the body, or a person purporting to act in any such capacity, he as well as the body corporate is guilty of the offence and liable to be proceeded against and punished accordingly.

In relation to a body corporate whose affairs are managed by its members "director" means a member of the body corporate.

(6) In this section "business" includes a trade or profession.

Delivery of offending goods and material

58B.—(1) The court by which a person is convicted of an offence under section 58A may, if satisfied that at the time of his arrest or charge he had in his possession, custody or control–
  (a) goods or material in respect of which the offence was committed, or
  (b) goods of the same description as those in respect of which the offence was committed, or material similar to that in respect of which the offence was committed, bearing a mark identical to or nearly resembling that in relation to which the offence was committed,

order that the goods or material be delivered up to such person as the court may direct.

(2) For this purpose a person shall be treated as charged with an offence–
  (a) in England, Wales and Northern Ireland, when he is orally charged or is served with a summons or indictment;
  (b) in Scotland, when he is cautioned, charged or served with a complaint or indictment.

(3) An order may be made by the court of its own motion or on the application of the prosecutor (or, in Scotland, the Lord Advocate or procurator-fiscal), but shall not be made if it appears to the court unlikely that any order will be made under section 58C (order as to disposal of offending goods or material).

(4) An appeal lies from an order made under this section by a magistrates' court–
  (a) in England and Wales, to the Crown Court, and
  (b) in Northern Ireland, to the county court;

and in Scotland, where an order has been made under this section, the person from whose possession, custody or control the goods or material have been removed may, without prejudice to any other form of appeal under any rule of law, appeal against that order in the same manner as against sentence.

(5) A person to whom goods or material are delivered up in pursuance of an order under this section shall retain it pending the making of an order under section 58C.

(6) Nothing in this section affects the powers of the court under section 43 of the Powers of Criminal Courts Act 1973, section 223 or 436 of the Criminal Procedure (Scotland) Act 1975 or Article 7 of the Criminal Justice (Northern Ireland) Order 1980 (general provisions as to forfeiture in criminal proceedings).

Supplemental

Interpretation

68.—(1) In this Act, unless the context otherwise requires, the following expressions have the meanings hereby assigned to them respectively, that is to say–

"the appointed day" has the meaning assigned to it by section seventy-one of this Act;

"assignment" means assignment by act of the parties concerned;

"the Court" means (subject to provisions relating to Scotland, Northern Ireland or the Isle of Man) Her Majesty's High Court of Justice in England;

"limitations" means any limitations of the exclusive right to the use of a trade mark given by the registration of a person as proprietor thereof, including limitations of that right as to mode of use, as to use in relation to goods to be sold, or otherwise traded in, in any place within the United Kingdom, or as to use in relation to goods to be exported to any market outside the United Kingdom;

"mark" includes a device, brand, heading, label, ticket, name, signature, word, letter, numeral, or any combination thereof;

"permitted use" has the meaning assigned to it by subsection (1) of section twenty-eight of this Act;

"prescribed" means [subject to provisions relating to Northern Ireland] in relation to proceedings before the Court, prescribed by rules of court, and, in other cases, prescribed by this Act or the rules;

"the register" means the register of trade marks kept under this Act;

"registered trade mark" means a trade mark that is actually on the register;

"registered user" means a person who is for the time being registered as such under section twenty-eight of this Act;

"the Registrar" means the Comptroller-General of Patents, Designs and Trade Marks;

"the rules" means rules made by the Board of Trade under section thirty-six or section forty of this Act;

"trade mark" means, except in relation to a certification trade mark, a mark used or proposed to be used in relation to goods for the purpose of indicating, or so as to indicate, a connection in the course of trade between the goods and some person having the right either as proprietor or as registered user to use the mark, whether with or without any indication of the identity of that person, and means, in relation to a certification trade mark, a mark registered or deemed to have been registered under section thirty-seven of this Act;

"transmission" means transmission by operation of law, devolution on the personal representative of a deceased person, and any other mode of transfer not being assignment;

"United Kingdom" includes the Isle of Man.

(2) References in this Act to the use of a mark shall be construed as references to the use of a printed or other visual representation of the mark, and references therein to the use of a mark in relation to goods shall be construed as references to the use thereof upon, or in physical or other relation to, goods.

(2A) For the purposes of this Act goods and services are associated with each other if it is likely that those goods might be sold or otherwise traded in and those services might be provided by the same business, and so with descriptions of goods and descriptions of services.

(2B) References in this Act to a near resemblance of marks are references to a resemblance so near as to be likely to deceive or cause confusion.

(3) In the application of this Act to Scotland, the expressions "injunction," "plaintiff" and "defendant" mean respectively "interdict," "pursuer" and "defender."

INDEX

References are to the paragraph numbers of the main text, except for those prefixed 'A', which are references to Appendix A.